17 -

AL-ANON INFORMATION SERVICE
1 (916) 334-2970
1 (888) 482-4240

How AL-ANON WORKS

for Families & Friends of Alcoholics

▲ Al-Anon Family Groups
Hope for families & friends of alcoholics

For information and catalog of literature write World Service Office for Al-Anon and Alateen:

Al-Anon Family Group Headquarters, Inc.
1600 Corporate Landing Parkway
Virginia Beach, Virginia 23454-5617
Phone: (757) 563-1600   Fax: (757) 563-1655
www.al-anon.alateen.org/members   wso@al-anon.org

This book is also available in: French, Portuguese, and Spanish.

Al-Anon/Alateen is supported by members' voluntary contributions and from the sale of our Conference Approved Literature.

Library of Congress Catalog Card No. 95-75626
ISBN-978-0-910034-26-5

Publisher's Cataloging in Publication

How Al-Anon works for families and friends of alcoholics/Al-Anon Family Groups.

p. cm.
includes index
ISBN-978-0-910034-26-5

1. Alcoholics—Family relationships. 2. Children of Alcoholics. 3. Al-Anon Family Group Headquarters, Inc. I. Al-Anon Family Group Headquarters, Inc.
HV5132.H69 1995   362.292'3
QB195-20009

Approved by
World Service Conference
Al-Anon Family Group

Preamble

The Al-Anon Family Groups are a fellowship of relatives and friends of alcoholics who share their experience, strength, and hope, in order to solve their common problems. We believe alcoholism is a family illness and that changed attitudes can aid recovery.

Al-Anon is not allied with any sect, denomination, political entity, organization, or institution; does not engage in any controversy; neither endorses nor opposes any cause. There are no dues for membership. Al-Anon is self-supporting through its own voluntary contributions.

Al-Anon has but one purpose: to help families of alcoholics. We do this by practicing the Twelve Steps, by welcoming and giving comfort to families of alcoholics, and by giving understanding and encouragement to the alcoholic.

Suggested Preamble to the Twelve Steps

Al-Anon Books that may be helpful:

Alateen—Hope for Children of Alcoholics (B-3)

The Dilemma of the Alcoholic Marriage (B-4)

The Al-Anon Family Groups—Classic Edition (B-5)

One Day at a Time in Al-Anon (B-6), Large Print (B-14)

Lois Remembers (B-7)

Alateen—a day at a time (B-10)

As We Understood... (B-11)

...In All Our Affairs: Making Crises Work for You (B-15)

Courage to Change—One Day at a Time in Al-Anon II (B-16),
  Large Print (B-17)

From Survival to Recovery: Growing Up in an Alcoholic Home (B-21)

Courage to Be Me—Living with Alcoholism (B-23)

Paths to Recovery—Al-Anon's Steps, Traditions, and Concepts (B-24)

Living Today in Alateen (B-26)

Hope for Today (B-27), Large Print (B-28)

Opening Our Hearts, Transforming Our Losses (B-29)

Contents

PART TWO: AL-ANON EXPERIENCES

Preface

How Al-Anon Works for Families & Friends of Alcoholics
opens wide the door to a remarkable fellowship of courageous
men and women who have experienced the sometimes subtle,
but nonetheless devastating effects of another's alcoholism. It
invites us in to see how Al-Anon helps families of alcoholics to
overcome even the most negative aspects of their lives and, in
turn, extend hope and help to others.

This is the essential book on Al-Anon Family Groups. It
answers every question we might think to ask including, "Can
Al-Anon help me?"

Even the casual reader is captivated by pages filled with
refreshing, down-to-earth wisdom drawn from thousands of
Al-Anon members sharing their very personal experience,
strength, and hope.

Sparks of recognition and understanding flash again and
again as we begin to grasp the enormous impact the alcoholism
of someone close has had on our physical, emotional, and spiritual well-being.

To the millions of men, women, and children who have been
affected by the alcoholism of another, this book extends the
most precious of all gifts—hope.

A Special Word to Anyone Confronted with Violence

Al-Anon's gentle process unfolds gradually, over time. But those of us facing violent, potentially life-threatening situations may have to make immediate choices to ensure safety for ourselves and our children. This may mean arranging for a safe house with a neighbor or friend, calling for police protection, or leaving money and an extra set of car keys where they can be collected at any time in case of emergency.

It is not necessary to decide how to resolve the situation once and for all—only how to get out of harm's way until this process of awareness, acceptance, and action can free us to make choices for ourselves that we can live with.

Anyone who has been physically or sexually abused or even threatened may be terrified of taking action at all. It can require every ounce of courage and faith to act decisively. But no one has to accept violence. No matter what seems to trigger the attack, we all deserve to be safe.

TAPPING OTHER RESOURCES

Al-Anon's purpose is to help families and friends of alcoholics. We come together to find help and support in dealing with the effects of alcoholism. In time we discover that the principles of our program can be practiced "in all our affairs." But there are times when, in order to work through especially challenging circumstances, we may need more specialized support from mental, spiritual, physical, or legal advisors. Many of us have benefited from taking care of these needs in addition to coming to Al-Anon.

...In All Our Affairs: Making Crises Work for You, © Al-Anon Family Group Headquarters, Inc., 1990, 2005.

PART ONE

THE

AL-ANON

PROGRAM

1

The Many Faces of Al-Anon

I can remember feeling ambitious, waking up excited about my day, having loads of energy. I don't know when all that slipped away. Now it's all I can do to pull myself out of bed. I barely keep myself or my children washed and fed, and then only out of a sense of guilt or embarrassment. I didn't see it coming. I just slowly lost touch with the part of me that was able to care, and I don't have a clue how to find it again...

Everyone thought we were the perfect family. We always looked so good and behaved so beautifully in public. My friends used to say they wished that they could have my life instead of their own. I had so much to be grateful for. But something about my life just wasn't right. I couldn't put my finger on it. I just knew I wasn't happy...

It almost broke my heart to see my son spending his 21st birthday in jail, but there was nothing I could do about it. He's really a good guy, but he's had such bad luck. He gets in trouble all the time, and it's usually not all his fault. I let him live at home and try to give him everything he could want, but trouble just seems to find him. I would do anything for that boy, stay home with him, get him an apartment of his own, find him a job, take care of him, anything, if only it would help. I'm sick with worry...

My mom drinks too much. When she gets drunk, she calls me names and sometimes she hits my sister and gives her a black eye. But she's really great when she's not drinking, you know, and I love her a lot. If I got better grades and kept my room cleaner, she wouldn't be so miserable and have to drink. I tried staying out of the house more often so that she wouldn't have to see me and be disappointed, but that made her drink even more. She even came to the basketball game at school and dragged me out by the back of the neck in front of everybody because she thought I was trying to shame her. She said I was out doing bad things with boys and now I can't go out at all. I didn't want to go back to school, but she said she'd kill me if I didn't. So I go. Everybody makes fun of me or feels sorry for me. So I come home right after school. I don't mind so much if it will help my mom not to drink. But sometimes I just want to crawl into the closet and never come out...

I feel like there must be some secret to happiness, something that everybody else knows and that I am supposed to know as well, and if I could just figure it out, I would feel great about my life. But no matter how hard I try, I just can't find the answer. I've tried everything—church groups, social groups, therapy, biofeedback, psychics—and I think I've read every self-help book ever written... you name it, I've looked for answers there. Sometimes I've found a little comfort, but nothing that ever lasted, nothing that ever really changed my life. I feel like something is missing, like something is wrong with me...

I'm so tired of everybody always being so angry. My parents argued all the time I was growing up, now my wife is on my back, and nothing I do is ever good enough for my kids. If only I had different people in my life, maybe I wouldn't feel so lousy all the time. But I can't seem to leave. I had an affair for a while, thinking that I had finally found someone who would treat me right, but once I got to know her better, I realized that she was just as angry and bitter as all the rest of them...

I don't get it. My husband claims he's an alcoholic. I don't know what he's up to, but I'm sure he's no alcoholic. He doesn't drink any more than anybody else. Everybody we know drinks. And he still has a good job. He's clean, well-dressed, successful, the life of every party. I think he's doing this to make me look bad. If he loved me, he wouldn't humiliate me like this. That's the real problem. He doesn't love me anymore...

None of us comes to Al-Anon because our lives resemble the "happily-ever-after" of fairy tales. We come to Al-Anon because we are grappling with an assortment of problems. We hope to find some answers, but doubt that there is any hope to be found anywhere. Other people's stories seem so different from ours that we may not recognize that we have anything in common with one another. But whether we realize it or not, there is a common thread. Each of us has been affected by someone else's drinking problem.

At first, for a variety of reasons, we may not be aware of any drinking problem. We may come to Al-Anon at the urging of a counselor, judge, treatment center, or friend, certain that we are in the wrong place. Many of us believe that we know the real problem with our friend or relative—and that it has nothing to do with alcohol. We identify the problem as a bad temper, immaturity, too much or too little religion, lack of will power, bad luck, the wrong boss or the wrong friends or the wrong city, the children, the in-laws, physical illness or disability, financial irresponsibility, or any number of other things. When it is suggested that the underlying problem may be alcoholism, we balk. After all, alcoholics are dirty, smelly, deranged bums who live on the street and have lost everything they once cherished. Or at least this may be what we've always believed.

In reality, many alcoholics have jobs, homes, families, and untarnished images of respectability. Their drinking may not be readily apparent, or it may seem barely noticeable compared to the problems that often result from or go hand-in-hand with the drinking—the violence, financial and legal problems, insults and excuses, unreliable and irresponsible behavior. Besides, if everyone in our lives drinks to excess, alcoholic drinking may seem perfectly normal.

For those of us who never even knew the drinker, recognizing the true nature of the problem can be even more difficult. We may have been affected by the alcoholism of a grandparent or distant relative whom we barely knew, or by relatives or friends who have been sober as long as we've known them. Yet the effects of this disease are no less profound and far-reaching. Often, our relatives never recognized the effects of alcoholism and inadvertently passed on those effects to us. We may, for instance, have picked up the struggle in the form of daily bouts with anxiety, or we may have difficulty trusting anyone or anything, always waiting for chaos or disaster to strike, even when all seems well.

Even if we have no idea whether or not anyone around us has had a drinking problem, we can see the effects of alcoholism in our own lives if we know what to look for. We who have been affected by someone else's drinking find ourselves inexplicably haunted by insecurity, fear, guilt, obsession with others, or an overwhelming need to control every person and situation we encounter. And although our loved ones appear to be the ones with the problems, we secretly blame ourselves, feeling that somehow we are the cause of the trouble, or that we should have been able to overcome it with love, prayer, hard work, intelligence, or perseverance.

We know something is very wrong but we can't figure out what it is, or we think we have identified the problem but can never seem to solve it. We may suspect that drinking has something to do with our situation, but we don't really want to think about it; after all, alcoholism can be embarrassing. Or we may be acutely aware of the drinking and its destructive consequences and feel responsible for doing something about it. We look for our answers in other people— "if only she'd change, I'd be fine"—yet can never quite convince anyone else to go along with our plans. As a result, we feel victimized by these "insensitive" people who, we believe, could make our lives better if they cared about us enough to make a few changes. At the same time, many of us blame ourselves—"If only I were more _____, he wouldn't do these terrible things." We continue to struggle and we continue to lose. Worst of all, we lose hope.

Few of us come to Al-Anon hoping to change ourselves. More often we come because everything we have done to solve our problems has failed, and we have run out of ideas. We come to comply with the suggestion of the alcoholic's treatment center or the court, or to help a newly sober friend or relative. An unexpected loss, such as a request for divorce or the illness or death of a loved one, may lead us to Al-Anon. We may try our first Al-Anon meeting only to support a friend who needs help in dealing with an alcoholic situation, but recognize similar problems in our own lives as the meeting progresses.

Even those of us who can identify the problem as active alcoholism probably have no idea what to do about it. We only know that we've tried lots of things that didn't work. We may have poured out liquor, hidden it, hidden money that might pay for it, even taken a few drinks ourselves in order to leave less for the alcoholic or to feel more a part of their lives. Most of us have argued, pleaded, bargained, threatened, walked out, come back, given ultimatums, failed to carry them out, or carried them out and felt guilty. We've tried to reason with the drinkers, scheduled their free time, monitored their behavior. We've complained; we've prayed. We've tried to avoid doing anything that might cause the alcoholic to drink. We've searched for opportunities to make the drinker see how destructive their drinking can be. Mostly, we've hurt and we've worried. Now we turn to Al-Anon as a last resort, hoping to find a way to put an end to the drinking once and for all, or to convince a loved one to get help.

Those of us who are no longer around active alcoholism can be even more stymied. Obviously, we don't have the option of trying to change the alcoholic. So we've changed our circumstances, our jobs, clothes, friendships, locations, religions, practically everything about ourselves, but nothing seems to have a lasting impact on our suffering. We, too, turn to Al-Anon in hope of finding some kind of relief.

We come to Al-Anon for many different reasons but we stay for only one—we want our lives to get better.

2

Help and Hope

When we come to Al-Anon, we are greeted by others whose lives have taken turns similar to ours. As the meeting begins, we hear the following words of welcome and somehow sense that these words are spoken from the heart.

SUGGESTED AL-ANON/ALATEEN WELCOME
Chairperson: We welcome you to the _____ Al-Anon/Alateen Family Group and hope you will find in this fellowship the help and friendship we have been privileged to enjoy.

We who live or have lived with the problem of alcoholism understand as perhaps few others can. We, too, were lonely and frustrated, but in Al-Anon/Alateen we discover that no situation is really hopeless and that it is possible for us to find contentment, and even happiness, whether the alcoholic is still drinking or not.

We urge you to try our program. It has helped many of us find solutions that lead to serenity. So much depends on our own attitudes, and as we learn to place our problem in its true perspective, we find it loses its power to dominate our thoughts and our lives.

The family situation is bound to improve as we apply the Al-Anon/Alateen ideas. Without such spiritual help, living with an alcoholic is too much for most of us. Our thinking becomes distorted by trying to force solutions, and we become irritable and unreasonable without knowing it.

The Al-Anon/Alateen program is based on the Twelve Steps (adapted from Alcoholics Anonymous), which we try, little by little, one day at a time, to apply to our lives, along with our slogans and the Serenity Prayer. The loving interchange of help among members and daily reading of Al-Anon/Alateen literature thus make us ready to receive the priceless gift of serenity.

Anonymity is an important principle of the Al-Anon/Alateen program. Everything that is said here, in the group meeting and member-to-member, must be held in confidence. Only in this way can we feel free to say what is in our minds and hearts, for this is how we help one another in Al-Anon/Alateen.

3

Finding Help

It takes great courage to take the risk and go to that first Al-Anon meeting. It isn't easy to go against old beliefs and fears and reach out to other people for strength, guidance, and support. Finding the willingness to admit that we need help can be one of the greatest challenges we ever face, but it can also be one of the most rewarding. When we finally realize that we are sick and tired of being sick and tired, we open a door to unlimited possibilities for change, for hope, and for a happier and richer life.

REACHING OUT TO OTHERS

Yet, at first, reaching out for help may actually seem more dangerous than continuing to struggle alone. Before coming to Al-Anon, the surest way to survive was to handle everything by ourselves, to keep quiet about our problems, and to trust no one so that no one could disappoint us. Without the support of people who understood the disease of alcoholism, we learned to tough it out alone. We became experts at keeping secrets and creating the appearance of normalcy in the midst of crisis. We avoided people because it was easier to be alone than to pretend all the time. We hid our shame, our fear, our rage.

Those of us who had tried turning to others for help were often disappointed. Well-meaning friends and family members may have offered plenty of advice, but few were truly able to understand our circumstances or offer useful suggestions. In fact, some of the advice we blindly followed did far more harm than good. Our efforts left us feeling more alone and ashamed than ever. Without a helpful place to turn to or an understanding shoulder to cry on, we held our secrets inside, where they festered. We became increasingly frightened, insecure, and unable to cope. Each day was little more than a struggle to survive, and after a while, we began to question whether it was worth the bother. We lost all hope of finding any way out of our difficulty.

With this background, it can be difficult to believe that sharing our experiences with other people could do anything but add to our pain and isolation. Yet reaching out to others is the key to recovering from the effects of alcoholism. The difference is that we must choose these people with great care, to ensure that they really can help. We find the encouragement, help, and support we've been seeking in Al-Anon. What a miraculous feeling to discover that many, many others do understand what we are going through. As incredible as it may sound, in these meetings we encounter people who have known the same fear and suffering, the confusion and the despair that we have, yet by coming together and sharing their experience, strength, and hope, they are able to move beyond their pain and begin to build better, happier lives. That's why attending Al-Anon meetings is so important. After having suffered alone with the effects of this brutal disease, the Al-Anon fellowship is an unexpectedly rich and nourishing source of compassion and support.

HOW DO I FIND AN AL-ANON MEETING?

Al-Anon is listed in the phone books in many cities. Sometimes this telephone number connects the caller with an Al-Anon Information Service that can answer questions and provide local meeting times and locations. Sometimes recorded information is offered about where to find a nearby Al-Anon meeting. Similar information can often be found in local newspapers, especially in towns too small to maintain an Al-Anon Information office. But because anonymity is such a critical factor, Al-Anon meetings can occasionally be difficult to find. Sometimes the simplest and most straight-forward way to connect with an Al-Anon group is to contact the Al-Anon World Service Office by calling 1-888-4AL-ANON (888-425-2666), U.S. They have information regarding every registered Al-Anon group around the world and are always happy to aid us in finding the help we need.

WHAT KIND OF PEOPLE WILL I FIND IN AL-ANON?

Some of us know from the moment we walk into an Al-Anon meeting that we are exactly where we belong. Others come to our first Al-Anon meeting, look around, and see a roomful of people who look, dress, and even act differently than we do, and we wonder whether people who seem so different could possibly have anything to offer us. As we keep coming back, we discover that, although the differences among us may be great, we have much in common.

We come to Al-Anon from all walks of life. We live in small towns and big cities, from Bangladesh to Paris to Dubuque. We are barely educated, and we have post-graduate degrees. We are deeply religious, and we subscribe to no religion at all. We represent all races, political affiliations, sexual orientations, professions, and economic and social realms. We are young and not so young, wealthy and impoverished, men and women. We are as different as night and day. On the surface it may seem that we have nothing in common, but if you look deeper, it's easy to see that each of us has been affected by the ravages of another's alcoholism. Whether we are the parents, lovers, adult children, spouses, siblings, co-workers, or friends of alcoholics, and whether the alcoholics in our lives are living or dead, actively drinking, or sober for years, when we join together to share our experience, strength, and hope, we find that we have a great deal to offer one another.

As we keep coming back, we learn from each other that alcoholism is a disease that affects not only the drinker but those around the drinker as well. We find that there are simple tools that can change the way we feel about ourselves and our circumstances, tools that can help us to get more out of living and to find excitement and opportunity where once we found only a struggle to survive. As we watch those around us in our meetings begin to find greater freedom and greater joy in their lives, most of us realize that, no matter what situation we face or how desperate we feel, there is good reason for hope.

Alcoholism doesn't discriminate. It strikes the most socially prominent of families as frequently as it afflicts the downtrodden. In Al-Anon, we learn that if we set aside our differences, keep an open mind, and try to learn from one another, we can find a powerful force for healing. Together, we can accomplish what is nearly impossible alone—we can overcome the devastating effects of this terrible disease and learn to live again.

4

Understanding Ourselves and Alcoholism

Alcoholism is a confusing disease, and much about it seems to defy logic. As a result, most of us come to Al-Anon with a great many unanswered questions.

I swore I'd never, ever associate with anyone like my alcoholic parents. Now I find myself surrounded by, employed by, even married to people just like them. How could this happen?

He's finally sober in A.A., and everything is going well for him. Why am I still so miserable?

Doctors at the treatment center insist that my child is an alcoholic, but I don't believe them. She's only 12, and I've never seen her falling-down drunk—the way alcoholics get. Couldn't the doctors be mistaken?

Just when we finally seem to be getting ahead, there is always some sort of setback or crisis. The person I live with never seems to get very upset. She just pours herself a drink. I'm the one who gets hysterical. Why am I always the one who cares so much? Why do I always have to solve all the problems?

Of course, people in my family drank, but I wouldn't call them alcoholics. Besides, what does that have to do with me?

My problem is picking the wrong people to fall in love with. I can't seem to have an intimate relationship that doesn't blow up in my face. Do you think there is a connection?

I don't really mind the drinking. What I mind are the bills piling up, the insults, violence, trouble with the law, sexual problems, and all the rest. How can I stop all this from happening?

Why do the problems of alcoholic relatives who have been dead for years continue to affect my life?

I think I'm losing my mind. I seem to be remembering terrible things about my past, but my family denies that any of these things ever happened. Yet I can't shake the feeling that what I am remembering is the truth. Who do I believe?

To the best of my knowledge, no one in my family ever drank. But in every other respect, they behaved exactly like alcoholics. How could that be?

She promises that she'll never drink again, and two days later she's on another bender. What can I do to get her to stop drinking once and for all?

I never knew the alcoholic until he had been sober for many years. Yet I find myself obsessed with his behavior, affected by his every mood, and increasingly unable to act on my own behalf. Could this have anything to do with alcoholism?

How can I cope with the pain of watching her drink? I loved her so much, but I'm beginning to hate her. I can't seem to stop myself.

I thought that sobriety would bring us closer together, but it has actually driven us farther apart. Now the alcoholic insists that I need help as well. I don't understand it. I'm not the one with the problem. Why should I go to any meetings?

I was miserable for so long because all I felt was pain. But that was "normal." What do I do now that I don't feel anything at all?

SEARCHING FOR ANSWERS

Although most of us come to Al-Anon impatient for answers to these and many other questions, there aren't always quick or simple solutions to such complicated matters. Reaching out for help in Al-Anon is unlike asking for help in most other places. In Al-Anon, we do not give advice. Nobody tells anyone else what to do about their own private situation. For example, we neither advocate nor oppose staying married or getting divorced, confronting the alcoholics in our lives or keeping quiet, allowing our children to live at home or asking them to move out, breaking contact with our families or continuing to develop our relationships. These and countless other difficult decisions are uniquely personal and can only be made by the individuals involved. In fact, we suggest that newcomers to Al-Anon make no major decisions for quite some time after coming to Al-Anon, because we find that our perspective on our circumstances undergoes a dramatic change during that time. By waiting, we often find options we had not considered previously and discover that, over time, we become better able to make decisions we can live with. Thus, it would be absurd for any of our members to advocate one course of action or another. We don't know what is best for another person.

Instead, we offer our own experience, strength, and hope. We talk about the problems we ourselves have encountered and how we have used the principles and practices of the Al-Anon program to help work through our problems. We share our feelings, our growth, and our pain. We listen and we learn, identifying with the stories others tell and discovering new ways to approach our particular circumstances by hearing how others have dealt with similar issues. We suggest that you take what you like and leave the rest. Some of what we say may be helpful; some may not. Each of us is free to pick and choose, to use whatever seems useful, and to disregard the rest.

CHANGING OUR FOCUS

What we *don't* do is spend a lot of time talking about the alcoholic. Instead, we learn to put the focus on ourselves. At first this approach may not seem to make much sense. After all, it is often much easier to recognize the alcoholic's problems than our own. Most of us feel certain that if only he or she would stop drinking, or work a better program of recovery, or change in this attitude or that behavior, everything would be fine. What we fail to realize or accept is that alcoholism is a disease. An uncontrollable desire to drink is only one symptom of that disease. So many of us have longed for the day when the alcoholic in our lives would find sobriety, only to be dismayed when sobriety ushered in a whole new set of difficulties. Taking care of one symptom, even a major symptom, does not cure the whole disease. Many alcoholics are fortunate enough to find sobriety—and through programs such as Alcoholics Anonymous are able to make a long-term commitment to recovery. There is great hope for those who are able to choose this path, but sobriety does not put an end to alcoholism. Although it can be arrested, alcoholism has no known cure.

"But surely," we argue, "sobriety is desirable, and there must be something we can do to help! There has to be something we can say that will make a difference, or some sort of help or support or information we can provide that will convince our alcoholic loved ones to get the help they need or to make sure they continue on the path to recovery!"

Again, as the American Medical Association will attest, alcoholism is a disease. Would the right word stop the spread of cancer or make chemotherapy more effective? Would our help, good looks, higher income, or cleaner house overcome the progression of Alzheimer's Disease? Our compassion and support might make a loved one's struggle with illness easier to bear, but it is simply not within our power to cure someone else's disease. We are powerless over another's alcoholism. We didn't cause the disease. We can't control it. And we can't cure it.

So if we can't stop the drinking or guarantee sobriety, why should we come to Al-Anon? As Al-Anon's first public service announcement used to say, "You can see what the drinking is doing to the alcoholic. But can you see what it is doing to you?"

LEARNING ABOUT ALCOHOLISM

Al-Anon's pamphlet, *Understanding Ourselves and Alcoholism,* explains it this way:

"Alcoholism is a family disease. Compulsive drinking affects the drinker and it affects the drinker's relationships. Friendships, employment, childhood, parenthood, love affairs, and marriages all suffer from the effects of alcoholism. Those special relationships in which a person is really close to an alcoholic are affected most, and we who *care* are the most caught up in the behavior of another person. We react to an alcoholic's behavior. Seeing that the drinking is out of hand, we try to control it. We are ashamed of the public scenes but try to handle it in private. It isn't long before we feel we are to blame and take on the hurts, the fears, and the guilt of an alcoholic. We, too, can become ill.

"Even well-meaning people often begin to count the number of drinks another person is having. We may pour expensive liquor down drains, search the house for hidden bottles, or listen for the sound of opening cans. All our thinking becomes directed at what the alcoholic is doing or not doing and how to get the drinker to stop drinking. This is our *obsession.*

"Watching fellow human beings slowly kill themselves with alcohol is painful. While alcoholics don't seem to worry about the bills, the job, the children, or the condition of their health, the people around them usually begin to worry. We often make the mistake of covering up. We try to fix everything, make excuses, tell little lies to mend damaged relationships, and worry some more. This is our *anxiety.*

"Sooner or later the alcoholic's behavior makes other people angry. As we realize that the alcoholic is telling lies, using us, and not taking care of responsibilities, we may begin to feel that the alcoholic doesn't love us. We often want to strike back, punish, and make the alcoholic pay for the hurt and frustration caused by uncontrolled drinking. This is our *anger.*

"Sometimes those who are close to the alcoholic begin to pretend. We accept promises and trust the alcoholic. Each time there is a sober period, however brief, we want to believe the problem has gone away forever. When good sense tells us there is something wrong with the alcoholic's drinking and thinking, we still hide how we feel and what we know. This is our *denial*.

"Perhaps the most severe damage to those of us who have shared some part of life with an alcoholic comes in the form of the nagging belief that we are somehow at fault. We may feel it was something we did or did not do—that we were not good enough, not attractive enough, or not clever enough to have solved this problem for the one we love. These are our *feelings of guilt*."

LIVING WITH SOBRIETY

Those of us whose loved ones are recovering in A.A. are also affected by this family disease. We, too, react to alcoholism. We monitor the progress of sobriety, counting the number of meetings attended just as we once counted drinks, and we scan for inconsistencies or signs of slips. We walk on eggshells, careful to do nothing that might upset the newly recovering alcoholic, or we view sobriety with skepticism, unwilling to trust the changes we see. We expect a great transformation from the alcoholic—and worry when our expectations are not met. After years of waiting for a more intimate, nurturing, or amiable relationship, or of hoping that the burden of household responsibilities will finally be shared, many of us are frustrated to discover that our hopes remain unfulfilled and we feel more alone than ever.

Living with a sober alcoholic can seem like living with an entirely different person. Although we may be incredibly grateful for our loved one's sobriety, many of us resent the new, more active role the alcoholic now wishes to play in making family decisions, or the independence they suddenly display. We feel uncomfortable with all the changes over which we have no control. Although we fervently wanted change during the drinking days, this may not be what we had in mind. Some of us grow jealous of the time the alcoholic spends going to meetings or talking and socializing with other A.A. members. And suddenly, after demanding so many changes from the alcoholic, we find him or her making similar demands of us!

SEEKING SOLUTIONS FOR OURSELVES

Clearly, a loved one's sobriety does not solve all our problems. Nor does physical separation, or even death. Even those of us who have not been involved with any alcoholics for many years find that we continue to be affected by the family disease. In short, the effects of alcoholism—obsession, anxiety, anger, denial, and feelings of guilt—tend to persist until we seek recovery *for ourselves.*

The drama of other people's problems can be very distracting, especially when those people are alcoholics. But in Al-Anon we discover that the problem does not lie solely within another person; the problem is also within us. The behavior of an alcoholic friend, spouse, child, sibling, employer, or parent may have led us to Al-Anon, but we soon realize that our own thinking has become distorted. Al-Anon helps us to stop wasting time trying to change the things over which we have no control and to put our efforts to work where we do have some power—over our own lives.

5

Becoming Aware

We come to Al-Anon seeking change. We want to end our pain, and we turn to Al-Anon in the hope of finding out what to do. But we aren't yet ready to take action, no matter how eager we are or how impatient we feel. Change is a process, and we in Al-Anon recognize that becoming aware is the first stage of this process. This involves taking an honest look at ourselves and our circumstances. Although it sounds simple, after years of hiding the unpleasant aspects of reality from ourselves as well as others, most of us find an honest appraisal to be a struggle.

RECOGNIZING ALCOHOLISM

Sometimes we don't recognize alcoholism even when it is staring us in the face. Having lived with drinking for many years, we may have accepted it as normal and never felt overly concerned. Perhaps we envisioned alcoholics as filthy, rag-clad derelicts and never considered that our well-kempt, successful friend or relative might be an alcoholic, even if his or her drinking obviously is excessive. It never occurred to us that reactions to a long-forgotten alcoholic relative could have an affect on our everyday lives years later, or that we could be adversely affected by a relationship with a sober alcoholic. Illusions about alcoholism abound, and most of us simply were not aware of the nature of the disease or of its impact on us, the families and friends of alcoholics. Ignorance is neither a sin nor a crime, but it is an obstacle to seeing our situation realistically.

Then, too, we may see the problems in our lives and yet fail to recognize alcoholism as the source. Perhaps we attribute these problems to finances or employment, or blame lack of time, education, or opportunity for our troubles. We may consider them merely the vicissitudes of life, struggles that everyone has to deal with. Because we have already attributed our problems to one source or another, we fail to notice that each one fits neatly into the grand scheme of alcoholism, the family disease.

There are other obstacles, as well. Few of us managed to survive the chaos, confusion, and pain of an alcoholic environment without developing coping mechanisms that enabled us to protect ourselves emotionally from situations we didn't feel capable of handling. When our circumstances or our feelings seemed too painful or frightening to bear, we may have distorted, suppressed, rationalized, or ignored them altogether.

Perhaps we were aware of an alcoholic's denial, but never realized that it could be a characteristic of everyone who is affected by the disease. Just as many alcoholics insist that they don't have a problem and refuse to talk about their drinking, many friends and family members do not acknowledge that any problems exist. We truly *cannot* see, hear, feel, or otherwise perceive what may be readily apparent to others. Ironically, because our entire lives are wrapped up in the disease of alcoholism, we can fail to notice its presence.

Emotional survival skills also can alter the way we see past events and relationships. When memories of horrors from the past are too shocking or painful, we may unconsciously block them out. We simply don't remember. Even if we fervently wish we could remember, these memories remain locked away, continuing to control our lives by limiting or altering our behavior. Without being aware of it, we continue to react to the traumatic events of our past rather than to the reality of our lives today.

When life went from loving and peaceful one minute to chaotic and dangerous the next, so that we never knew what to expect, many of us coped with the resulting sense of helplessness and confusion simply by choosing to believe only one of these realities. For example, those of us who dealt with sporadic, alcoholic bouts of verbal abuse at home might have wanted to believe that we lived in a wonderful family environment because it seemed true some of the time. By choosing to acknowledge only one portion of reality, we explained away the random verbal attacks by treating them as exceptions, mistakes, or one-time occurrences. Each such episode devastated us as if it were the first, yet we soon reverted to the reality we chose to see, once again painting a picture of bliss and harmony that was bound to let us down.

Or we may have latched on to the opposite reality, perceiving that life was chaotic and that moments of peace or good humor were not to be trusted. In this case, we denied ourselves the enjoyment of kindness, love, pleasure, and good will. We remained perpetually on guard.

Living with alcoholism caused us to suppress or ignore our emotions, our desires, our hopes. We hid our real feelings in order to survive, and in time we forgot we ever *had* feelings. We succeeded in insulating ourselves so well that we no longer participated enthusiastically in life. In attempting to protect ourselves, we let our personalities slip away until we were emotionally numb.

STRUGGLING WITH REALITY

Few of us intentionally refused to see the reality of our lives or the circumstances in which we find ourselves. But the truth is that most of us have indeed done so. In Al-Anon, we eventually come to see the many ways we had unknowingly blocked out whole segments of our past and present. We recognize situations in which we had unconsciously convinced ourselves that what we saw happening simply wasn't so. At the same time, we understand that we were doing the best we could at the time, trying to survive, to adapt to the way our lives were affected by alcoholism before we found the help of Al-Anon.

With the help and support of our program and our fellowship, we come to see how much energy was previously spent on escaping, ignoring, fleeing, and denying. We recognize that, today, our energy can be put to more constructive use in healing ourselves and our relationships.

All too often in the past, reality interfered with our plans. Crisis shattered the fantasy. Our perceptions proved unreliable, and we were increasingly less able to cope. We couldn't evaluate our options. We couldn't even trust our own memories.

When circumstances first forced us to become aware of our distressing situation, we were often unwilling or unable to accept the reality we had been forced to see. With renewed vigor, we adopted new coping mechanisms in order to survive. Perhaps we made a conscious decision to ignore the problems, hoping they would vanish on their own. Or we rationalized. We told ourselves and others that almost everyone drinks too much from time to time; we insisted that the situation wasn't as bad as it seemed. Or we recognized the alcoholic's drinking problem but denied that we had been affected. We distracted ourselves, blaming our boss, or destiny, or the government for the problems we encountered. We put great energy into looking good in public, making sure that everyone thought we were doing just fine, never letting anyone know when we were vulnerable and hurting, never letting on what happened behind closed doors. In an effort to be loyal, we lied, made excuses, and laughed off the alcoholic's behavior as well as our own.

Some of us created fantasy lives so that we didn't have to think about the pain in which we actually lived. These fantasies could be extremely pleasant, too good to be true, where everyone was kind and loving, all our needs and desires were satisfied, and we felt happy all the time. Some of the fantasies created a darker world in which we imagined the pain, guilt, or death of the alcoholics in our lives in the misguided belief that their absence would free us from our torment. Others had vengeful fantasies, visualizing the alcoholics (or others) suffering for the suffering we believed they had inflicted upon us, and imagining a kind of power over our circumstances that we lacked in real life.

Until we were able to face reality, we honestly could not see that we played a crucial role in creating our own misery. Nor did we recognize that we had been so severely affected by the disease that we ourselves became ill.

SEEING MORE REALISTICALLY

Coming to Al-Anon, we begin to look realistically at our situations. Some of us are forced to face facts when circumstances demand our attention, as when a loved one is arrested or files for divorce. Having our world shattered can leave us feeling disoriented and panicky. At such times, Al-Anon can be a lifesaver. When our sense of reality proves unreliable, we need help to regain our footing. Al-Anon provides a simple Step-by-Step approach to rebuilding our lives and our self-confidence in an atmosphere of unconditional love.

Others are free to come to terms with reality more gradually. Many of us discover that we no longer need the same survival tactics now that we have the support of a fellowship that truly understands and the tools of the program that help us to deal with problems that once overwhelmed us. Our old defenses become not only unnecessary but clearly undesirable.

Developing an ability to see things as they really are and to find healthier, more appropriate ways of dealing with the people and circumstances we encounter is not always easy or comfortable. Most of us have had good reasons for hiding certain information from ourselves—it hurt! It probably still does. It isn't easy to see the suffering of a loved one, to admit—even to ourselves—that a close relative has sexually or physically abused us, to come to grips with the fact that the people we have turned to for love and acknowledgement are incapable of giving it, or to recognize that we ourselves have become narrow-minded, vindictive, pessimistic, submissive, fearful, despondent, petty, shrewish, nagging, controlling, or overbearing. We may be dismayed to find that the negative thinking and behavior that we developed to protect us from the painful experiences of our lives have in fact seeped into every corner of our world. It's as if we've allowed our defense mechanisms to protect us from all of life rather than risking adventuresome participation in it. And in trying to avoid the unpleasant aspects of our lives, we have also missed out on many of the joys.

It isn't easy to accept the ways in which we have been affected by another's alcoholism. But the fact is, we have. Somewhere inside, many of us know this instinctively. Until we take the time to look at ourselves honestly, we may never be free of the bondage in which alcoholism holds us captive.

No matter what we must face about ourselves and those we love, there is more to see than just the devastation of alcoholism. As we learn to separate ourselves from the effects of this illness, we find that we have some splendid personality traits that have nothing to do with alcoholism. We are loving, lovable people with a great deal to give and a great capacity for joy. It often takes time to locate this positive part of ourselves and bring it to the surface. Years of stuffing our feelings and our sense of self may have shoved it down so deep that we forget it even exists, but with patience, that brightness will eventually re-emerge. That's one reason why it is worthwhile for many of us to go through the often difficult, frustrating, and scary process of becoming aware—there are wonderful and unexpected gifts and treasures waiting on the other side.

As long as we continue to hide the truth from ourselves, it will continue to fester inside. In the past, we may have needed to tough things out alone, but we are no longer struggling alone against the effects of alcoholism. Today we have a program to help us. The support that we receive in Al-Anon makes it possible to let the truth come to the surface where we can work with it.

We have a right to expect more from life than mere survival. We are here because we are ready to heal. We are ready to look at ourselves and our lives with new eyes. We are ready to become aware.

6

The *Family* Disease
of Alcoholism

THE PART WE PLAY

Awareness begins by learning about the family disease of alcoholism. Everyone in an alcoholic relationship—friends, co-workers, family members, as well as the alcoholic—plays a part in the dynamics of this disease. In order to make any changes in our circumstances, we must try to discover the part we play.

In general, alcoholics act, and we, who are involved with them, react. The active alcoholic gets drunk, behaves irrationally or irresponsibly, and becomes the center of attention. Those around him or her react to the drinking and its consequences. In a state of intoxication, alcoholics aren't worried about the problems their actions are creating; instead, those around the alcoholics worry for them. We believe we must take on the responsibility of doing for the alcoholics what they seem unable or unwilling to do for themselves.

In the beginning, many of us are genuinely concerned and merely want to help a relative or friend who is obviously not well. But as time passes and the situation worsens, we cease to recognize that we have a choice in the matter. In fact, the choices available to some of us in the past were quite limited. Those who grew up around alcoholism or dealt with abuse may have felt forced to take certain actions on the alcoholic's behalf for the sake of our own safety. Eventually, even when no real danger exists, most of us have come to believe that our help is imperative, whether we want to offer it or not. The alcoholic becomes more and more dependent. After a while, we can't imagine allowing the alcoholic to sleep through another day of work without calling in sick, or allowing another bounced check to be ignored. It becomes more desirable to stay home than to risk another public humiliation. And many of us can't stand the tension of waiting for the consequences of drinking to manifest; we feel compelled to intervene.

Alcoholics act and we react. No one can tell the drinker any-thing—he or she calls all the shots. Alcohol fosters an exaggerated sense of confidence and well-being, prompting the drinker to act like a little god with all the answers. At the same time the drinker becomes increasingly irrational. In response, we argue, trying to get him or her to see more realistically. It becomes essential to prove we are right. As time passes, we continue to justify our own positions, yet in the face of the alcoholic's vehemence, we begin to doubt ourselves and our perceptions. If the alcoholic has told us that the drinking is our fault because we are so noisy or so disobe-dient, we become compulsively quiet or strive for perfect obedience night and day, regardless of the cost to ourselves. In time, the more confident the alcoholic seems, the more insecure we become. We begin to agree even when we know that what is being said is wrong. We do whatever is demanded of us to avoid conflict, knowing that we never seem to win any arguments or convince the alcoholic that we are right. We lose the ability to say "no."

The same pattern holds true when the alcoholics in our lives make promises they can't keep. For example, they promise not to miss another little league game, business meeting, or dinner date. They swear that next time they won't drink, or stay out all night, or get violent. Or they promise to exercise will power. They switch to beer, thinking that beer will have less power over them than hard liquor. Or they throw out all the liquor in the house, only to be so driven by the disease that they are compelled to find some form of alcohol and settle for mouthwash or cough syrup. And again, we react. Forgetting about hundreds of broken promises in the past, we believe that the alcoholics can indeed control their drinking. We decide that everything is going to be different now—better! Denying what our past experience has taught us, we count on these promises with all our hearts. We set ourselves up for almost inevitable disap-pointment. And then, when the alcoholics fail to control alcoholism, a disease which is quite beyond their control, we are devastated, resentful, and enraged. We see ourselves as helpless victims and fail to recognize that we have volunteered for that role by choosing to believe wholeheartedly in what we knew from experience would probably not happen.

Those of us who haven't been associated with an alcoholic in many years can continue to react to alcoholic patterns of behavior as well. The low self-esteem that evolved as a result of past failures and episodes of abuse or neglect persists. For the love and attention we never received in the past, we look to people who are unavailable to us. We avoid conflict, but now we do so with employers, other relatives, or authority figures rather than with the alcoholic. Or we seek out conflict, believing that the best defense is a good offense. If we sense that a confrontation is coming, we create a diversion and pick a fight over some other issue. Many of us become so accustomed to living in chaos and crisis that we feel completely lost in its absence. Consequently, when everything is going well, we sabotage ourselves, creating a crisis. This may make us miserable, but at least we know how to function in such a situation. We may also perpetuate a variety of compulsive behaviors without having any idea what prompts us to do so. The survival techniques we developed while living with the active disease have become a way of life. It may never have occurred to us that there is any other way to live.

This pattern also persists in sobriety. Many of us have seen our sober loved ones go through "dry drunks," periods during which the alcoholic's behavior in sobriety seems identical to the active drinking days. Naturally, most of us fall right back into our old behavior as well. Even if our loved one is a model of sobriety, fear that the alcoholic might drink, the desire to manage his or her sobriety, unresolved resentments from the drinking days, and personality or lifestyle changes that take place during recovery can also trigger unhealthy reactions from those of us who care about a recovering alcoholic. The disease and its effects persist into sobriety. Unless we friends and relatives choose recovery for ourselves, the dynamics of the disease will continue to dominate our relationships.

RECOGNIZING OUR OPTIONS

Alcoholics act and family members and friends react. Most of the time, we react because we don't realize we have a choice. It's automatic. In Al-Anon, we are reminded that we have choices. Just because the alcoholic gets drunk, acts out, fails to meet an obligation, declares that the sky is orange, or makes or breaks a promise, does not mean that those who care about him or her must do what we have always done before. We are not trapped. We have choices.

It's as if we were holding one end of a rope and an alcoholic grabbed the other end and started to tug. Most of us would react automatically. We would tug back. It never occurs to us that we don't have to play. If we knew we had options, we might choose to drop the rope. There is no tug-of-war unless both players hang on to their ends. By taking note of what we do in reaction to alcoholic behavior, we can begin to see the choices we are already unconsciously making. Further examination, discussion with other Al-Anon members, and use of the slogans and Steps can help us to discover options we never knew we had. Perhaps we will even decide to drop the rope.

For example, some alcoholics feel guilty about their need to drink and find it much easier to blame the drinking on someone else. Such alcoholics often provoke those around them, trying to start an argument or create a crisis. We who live or work with them tend to react to this provocation, arguing back, defending ourselves against unjust accusations, making accusations of our own. In the end, the alcoholic gets exactly what he or she was looking for—an excuse to drink. Dry or sober alcoholics sometimes use the same tactics to create a diversion so that everyone's attention will be drawn away from a topic or situation with which they are uncomfortable. Dropping the rope means recognizing the pattern and choosing not to play the same part any more. We notice the provocative behavior, and we notice exactly what we do in response.

Perhaps the alcoholic provokes by accusing us of being lazy, and we react by playing martyr and listing all the things we do for him or her. In response, the alcoholic resents our self-righteous attitude, and we feel unappreciated and sorry for ourselves. The discussion quickly escalates into an argument that almost always ends the same way—with the alcoholic storming out the door to escape at the nearest bar. Once we are clear about the part we play, we can choose to try a different response. For instance, the next time we are accused of laziness, we might decide not to react. Perhaps we will keep quiet or simply change the subject. We might leave the room or busy ourselves with some task. We may take a moment to acknowledge *to ourselves* that the accusation is not true, and that it is the disease of alcoholism, and not our loved one, that is speaking. Or, knowing that at times we can be lazy, we might even smile pleasantly and agree. There are no right or wrong responses. Many of us find that it doesn't much matter how we break the pattern, only that we do so.

The alcoholic may not take too kindly to this change, especially at first. The alcoholic needs a drink, and the only way he or she can take one comfortably is by picking a fight. If the drinker's first efforts fail because we refuse to play our customary role, he or she is likely to try again. If we become condescending or self-righteous about the new role we are choosing to play, or smug about the alcoholic's failure to provoke us, we defeat ourselves. Not only will our poor attitudes provide just the excuse the alcoholic is looking for, but they will continue to pit us against a disease we simply cannot defeat. We are powerless over another's alcoholism. If we continue to engage in a losing battle, there will be no end to the frustration and despair that led us to try this new tack in the first place. We seek real change. It is not our goal to be "right." It is not our goal to "win." Our goal is to do everything we can to heal ourselves and our relationships. This takes diligence, patience, and above all, practice.

As we become increasingly aware of the dynamics of the family disease, many of us discover that we have performed a particular function in our family or group. Friends and family members play a wide variety of supporting roles in the family disease, all of which attempt to control the uncontrollable disease of alcoholism and to bring order into the unpredictable and often explosive living or working environment. We don't realize that, by playing our part, we actually contribute to sustaining the disease of alcoholism. We may serve as the enabler, rescuing the alcoholic from unpleasant consequences of his or her own making. Or we may play the victim, unwillingly stepping in and covering for the alcoholic who is too drunk or hung over to fulfill job or family responsibilities. Perhaps we find that our role has been to take the blame whenever anything goes wrong, even when we weren't remotely involved. Others provide comic relief, serving to create a light-hearted distraction from the sorrow of life in an alcoholic home. And some of us provoke, venting our pent-up frustration and resentment, providing the alcoholic with an excuse to drink, and poisoning ourselves with our growing bitterness.

All of these supporting roles work together to maintain a balance in which the alcoholic can continue to play his or her role with as little discomfort as possible. Thus, when any member of this alcoholic circle stops playing his or her part, the entire group is affected.

CHANGING THE PART WE PLAY IN THE FAMILY DISEASE

This is why the most helpful and most loving action any family member can take is to get help for ourselves. By recovering from the effects of this disease, we become able to stop playing our part in the family disease. The balance is disrupted. Suddenly it is no longer so comfortable for the alcoholic. While he or she may continue to receive the loving support of the recovering family member, the disease is left unsupported. It is as if a group of four stood in a river, getting drenched while holding the alcoholic over their heads to keep him or her dry, and eventually one member of the group refused to continue to hold up his or her end. The entire system would collapse and, as a result, the alcoholic would get wet. Without others to remove the painful consequences of his or her actions, the alcoholic may become so uncomfortable that he or she chooses to pursue recovery. Likewise, other family members and friends may recognize how much they have been affected by the family disease and seek help for themselves. But there are no guarantees. While health in one person frequently inspires health in those around him or her, it doesn't always work that way. Sometimes the alcoholic simply finds a way to adapt, creating a new system to support the disease.

Most of us want the very best for those we love, and the best we can offer may be our refusal to contribute any further to their path of destruction. We cannot make choices for other people, even for those most important to us. We are not gods, and we can't truly know what is best for anyone else, no matter how obvious a particular course of action may seem to us at the time. Most of us had to hit a "bottom," a point of personal agony, before we were ready to make real changes in our lives. Alcoholics and others suffering from the effects of this family disease deserve the same chance to hit a "bottom" of their own. Along the way, there may be many awful, painful lessons for them to learn, and it can be excruciating to have to stand by and watch a loved one suffer through those experiences. Some never learn at all. But we are powerless over alcoholism. We cannot hasten the process, nor can we spare a loved one from it. All we can do is to serve as an example of the joy and serenity that recovery can provide, and respect the rights of our loved ones to make the choices they need to make, even if we despise the nature of those choices.

LEARNING MORE ABOUT ALCOHOLISM

The more we know about alcoholism, the better able we are to cope with it. That's why Al-Anon encourages us to learn as much as possible about the disease. Reading Al-Anon literature every day has given many of us a profound insight into this family disease and how to deal with it successfully. Some of us also attend open A.A. meetings to learn about the alcoholic's experience. Hearing the stories of recovering alcoholics can be very eye-opening. Few of us realize that the alcoholics in our lives often suffer terribly, sometimes even more than we do. By listening, we can learn to distinguish the person from the disease, to have compassion for their efforts and their pain, and to recognize that they, too, are powerless over alcohol. We also learn about characteristics of the disease that we may have misinterpreted. For instance, most alcoholics experience blackouts, periods during which everything they say and do vanishes from their memory. After a night of outrageous drunken behavior, it can be hard to believe that the alcoholic cannot remember some of the appalling actions that seem so indelibly etched in our minds. In such situations, many of us have accused our loved ones of lying. But blackouts are actual symptoms of the disease of alcoholism, randomly erasing even the most memorable events. The more we know about the disease, the more likely we are to respond to alcoholic behavior with compassion, understanding that we are dealing with a person who is sick rather than someone who is bad, weak, stupid, or cruel.

Al-Anon literature and open A.A. meetings can also teach us about the way the disease can persist in sobriety. For example, it takes some alcoholics several tries before achieving sobriety. Others drink again after many years of recovery in A.A. A recovering alcoholic who takes a drink is said to have had a "slip." A single slip may be enough to convince the alcoholic to make a deeper commitment to recovery, or it can be the beginning of a whole new chapter of drinking.

Alcoholism is a progressive disease that can be arrested but not cured. Therefore, we who are affected by another's alcoholism can best ensure our own continuing serenity if we learn to depend on ourselves for our well-being, rather than on another person's sobriety. As we become increasingly aware of our behavior, our choices, and the part we play or have played in the alcoholic situation, we become much better able to make changes that allow us to create a life we can be proud to live.

7

Breaking Our Isolation

NO OBLIGATIONS

When it becomes clear that the best thing we can do for ourselves and our loved ones is to get help for ourselves, many of us decide to go to an Al-Anon meeting. Because we may be reluctant to open up to strangers, we are relieved to learn that we can attend Al-Anon meetings without being obligated to say a word to anyone. We don't have to justify why we have come or explain our concerns to anyone. We are always welcome to participate in the meetings and to open up only as much or as little as we feel comfortable doing, but no one will ever force anyone else to share. We can simply show up and listen until we feel comfortable getting more actively involved.

OPENING UP

In time, however, most of us find it important to begin to talk about the things that trouble us. In Al-Anon, it is often said that we are only as sick as our secrets. A key to breaking the stranglehold that alcoholism has on our lives is to begin to open up and let those secrets out. Part of the isolation of this disease is the belief that we are *unique*, that no one has done or said or felt the terrible things that we have done, said, and felt, and that no one could possibly understand. Therefore, we hide the truth at all costs. Until we challenge this sense of uniqueness by sharing our thoughts with other people who have known the shame and isolation of alcoholism, we may never find out that it is not real. As the Suggested Closing for our meetings reminds us, "Whatever your problems, there are those among us who have had them too." We are not alone, and we need to unlearn the thinking that tells us that no one understands—this simply isn't true. Not everyone has been where we have been or felt what we have felt, but turning to those in Al-Anon who have also suffered the effects of alcoholism is different from turning to uninformed friends and neighbors. Although our stories may differ, we who live or have lived with alcoholism have a rare understanding of one another. Reaching out to other members is essential because a vital part of recovering from alcoholism's effects is breaking our isolation. To do so we have to muster the courage to share.

SHARING

Sharing involves revealing something about ourselves to others. Perhaps we mention something new that has happened in our lives or discuss feelings of depression or happiness. We may reveal a long-guarded secret or express confusion about a present situation. In the beginning, some of us merely share that we are glad to be at a meeting. What matters is that we begin to open up.

But not everyone feels comfortable opening up to a roomful of strangers, especially at their first Al-Anon meeting. And some subjects are too personal, too detailed, or too embarrassing for such a public discussion. That's why sponsorship is so important.

SPONSORSHIP

Sponsorship is one of the chief resources we use to help us to cope with and recover from the effects of alcoholism. A Sponsor is someone with whom we can share about ourselves and our circumstances in detail. Most of us choose a Sponsor who has been involved with Al-Anon for some time, someone who is familiar enough with the program to help us learn to apply it to our own lives. Although most of Al-Anon's principles and techniques involve simple, easy-to-grasp ideas, slogans, or actions, knowing when and how to put them to work in our lives can be very confusing, and a Sponsor can be a great help.

Between Al-Anon meetings, we can call our Sponsor when we face a difficult situation, achieve a goal, feel confused, or just want to talk. It's wonderful to have someone to turn to who already knows our story, someone who has made a commitment to be there to listen and to share with us, someone who can offer a different perspective on our situations, someone who respects our privacy and will keep what we say absolutely confidential. A Sponsor is a friend, a confidant who has experienced alcoholism's devastating effects and yet has learned through Al-Anon to find serenity and hope. He or she listens, shares experience, strength, and hope, and offers support and encouragement.

But a Sponsor does not have all the answers. He or she is just another human being who is recovering from the effects of alcoholism. None of us is finished with our personal growth, no matter how long we have been in Al-Anon. As Sponsors, we must be especially careful to avoid giving specific advice about what to do or not to do in a particular situation. The idea is to help our fellow members find their own answers in their own time.

When looking for a Sponsor, it sometimes helps to attend several different Al-Anon meetings in order to come into contact with a variety of members, although it is not always possible to do so. Most of us look for someone who is actively trying to apply the Al-Anon program to his or her life. This means that we look for Sponsors who try to take the various principles and practices the program offers and apply them to their own lives. For example, many of us seek a Sponsor who works the Twelve Steps, observes the Twelve Traditions, is active in service work, reads Al-Anon literature, uses the slogans, and seems to share from the heart. It is also suggested, in most instances, that we choose a Sponsor of the same sex to avoid complications and romantic or physical involvements that might make the relationship less beneficial. But this is not an inflexible rule. The most important thing is to be willing to reach out and ask for the help we need, human to human. If we hear someone with whom we identify, we can speak with them after the meeting or ask for their phone number. If we feel comfortable with them and feel we could develop a rapport, perhaps we will ask them to sponsor us.

At first, many of us feel reluctant to ask anyone to make such a big commitment to us. Alcoholism has often taken a heavy toll on our self-esteem, and we feel unworthy to ask for so much attention. We don't want to impose or be a burden to anyone. It can take a while to discover that such a request is not a burden but a privilege and an honor. Sponsorship is a mutually beneficial relationship. It allows Sponsors to focus on the Al-Anon principles in a new way, and provides them an opportunity to practice the Twelfth Step. No one works the program harder than a willing newcomer, and many longtime members are inspired by those we sponsor to renew our commitment to our own recovery by the efforts and the progress of others. We often see a reflection of ourselves in those we sponsor. We may recognize areas in which we need to work harder and places where we are overly hard on ourselves. We see how far we've come and how much farther we have to go. And we hear in what is shared with us and in our responses exactly what we ourselves most need to hear. Sponsorship is a tool our Higher Power can use to help both of us to grow.

Most of us are flattered to be asked to sponsor another member, but sometimes, for any of a variety of reasons, the person being asked may be unable to say "yes." If our first choice is unavailable, then we are encouraged to ask someone else. For many of us, there is no greater resource for building trust and learning to communicate honestly and with dignity than sponsorship. The sooner we avail ourselves of this opportunity, the sooner we can start to grow in these areas. Nonetheless, each of us works this program at our own pace. There is no right or wrong time to find a Sponsor. Some of us are ready right away, some of us wait quite a while before we feel moved to take this step, and some of us never choose it at all. It is never too late to get a Sponsor, and we are free to change Sponsors at any time.

Sponsors cannot make the Al-Anon program work for others. Each of us, Sponsor and sponsored alike, must apply the Al-Anon Steps, principles, and practices ourselves. And even the most dedicated Sponsor cannot be available all the time. It is important to remember that a Sponsor is only one of many voices in Al-Anon. If help is not available in the first place we look, it is our responsibility to reach out to other members. Our needs are important. It is up to us to make sure that they are met.

KEEPING IN TOUCH

Between meetings, sharing with other Al-Anon members by telephone is one way to meet these needs. It not only helps us to get through a crisis, it allows us to practice looking at our everyday lives from a new point of view, an Al-Anon point of view. Recovery from the effects of another's alcoholism involves our changing old attitudes that don't work for us and replacing them with attitudes that do work, replacing attitudes that encourage us to feel badly about ourselves and others with those that allow us to view the world more positively. We learn to see several options where we once saw none at all, and we begin to look at our lives in a new and exciting way. Such a major transformation cannot happen overnight, and none of us, even the most dedicated, can do it alone. We need help, guidance, and a fresh perspective. Most of all, we need to practice what we learn. Before trying a new approach to a problem, we may want to talk it over with another Al-Anon member. Before sending an important letter or facing a confrontation or resolving an argument, we might want to do a trial run during a telephone conversation with someone who will support our efforts. This can be a wonderful way to clarify our thinking and boost our confidence. Many of us insist that those we sponsor collect and use several other phone numbers on a regular basis. No one person represents the entire wisdom of Al-Anon. Keeping in touch with several members while maintaining a close relationship with a Sponsor can offer the best of both worlds.

Some Al-Anon groups offer newcomers the names and telephone numbers of members who are willing to receive Al-Anon phone calls, even from total strangers. At other Al-Anon meetings, members are encouraged to listen as others share, and whenever they hear someone with whom they identify—someone whose story, experience, or feelings seem similar to their own, or is particularly inspiring—to speak with them during a break or after the meeting and ask if they might exchange phone numbers and stay in touch between meetings. Most members are quite willing to talk with another member. Some of us are early risers and some are night owls, so it makes sense to ask when it is appropriate to call. Loneliness can strike at any time, and crisis knows no schedule. Most of us feel much more secure knowing that there are people we can talk with whenever the need arises.

Whenever we do call, it is very important to respect the anonymity of all members. If someone else answers the phone or if we get an answering machine, unless we're told otherwise, we should avoid references to Al-Anon. Not everyone in the household or workplace may know about this person's Al-Anon membership, and our carelessness could put them in an awkward or even a dangerous position. Anonymity can be a life and death matter to someone who lives with a violent alcoholic. So when we call, it is best to avoid mentioning the program. Some of us say, "This is Susan. I spoke with you on Thursday night. My number is____...." Others just leave a name and number, knowing that they can identify themselves later when they actually speak with the person.

LITERATURE

Sometimes we need to connect with Al-Anon at inconvenient moments, such as the middle of the night. We may be reluctant to awaken an Al-Anon friend over a minor matter, even though our need for contact is real. Between meetings and when other people are not available, Al-Anon literature can offer us the comfort of knowing that our problems are not unique and we are not alone. Our pamphlets and books provide valuable information about the disease of alcoholism and how to cope with its effects. The single page leaflet entitled *Detachment* contains wonderfully straightforward suggestions about how to cope with another person's alcoholism. Some of our literature addresses specific areas of concern. In *Living with Sobriety*, Al-Anon members speak of some of the frustrations and joys that occur when a family member finds sobriety. *From Survival to Recovery: Growing Up in an Alcoholic Home* is an inspiring book that offers help to all who have experienced another's alcoholism, especially adult children of alcoholics. *The Dilemma of the Alcoholic Marriage* examines the ways in which relationships are affected by alcoholism. *...In All Our Affairs: Making Crises Work for You* presents concrete examples of how members deal with difficult situations that often go hand in hand with alcoholism, such as infidelity, violence, verbal and sexual abuse, money and employment problems, disease, jail, separation, and divorce.

Courage to Change, a collection of daily meditations, offers a nugget of Al-Anon wisdom for each day of the year. And *Al-Anon's Twelve Steps & Twelve Traditions* provides a detailed discussion of the crucial guidelines that form the basis of the Al-Anon program.

All of these and many other books and pamphlets remind us that countless thousands of others have been through the same struggles and have found their way through them.

One informal Al-Anon resource that has helped so many of us begin to feel that we belong is getting together with other Al-Anon members for coffee. Some of us make plans over the phone, but often it happens much more spontaneously. After a meeting, when people are standing around talking, someone will suggest going out for a bite to eat. At first, many of us, feeling out of place, hesitate to join in, but the discussions after meetings can be even more enlightening and nurturing than the meetings themselves. Great healing can be found in this kind of fellowship for those who are willing to join in.

LONE MEMBER SERVICE

We are a worldwide fellowship. Al-Anon meetings can be found in some of the most remote places on earth. There are, however, quite a few locations in which no Al-Anon groups exist at this time. Even where meetings are available, some of our members may be unable to attend as a result of illness, disability, or other lifestyle restrictions. Breaking alcoholism's isolating impact is no less crucial for those who do not have access to meetings than for the rest of us. To serve the needs of these people, Al-Anon has created the Lone Member Service, which puts them in touch with other Al-Anon members. These may be other lone members, but more often they are members who regularly attend Al-Anon meetings and are eager to correspond by mail about what they've learned and experienced in the program. Anyone who is interested should contact the Lone Member Service at the World Service Office.

THE BENEFITS OF FELLOWSHIP

Clearly, Al-Anon offers many ways to reach out for the loving support and comfort each of us needs and deserves. By coming together, we gain strength and confidence. We learn that we are not really so unique, and we find hope for ourselves in the progress we see all around us. But fellowship is just one part of our story of healing and change.

8

Twelve Steps

After trying just about everything to put an end to the terrible frustration and suffering that goes hand in hand with alcoholism, most of us were reluctant to turn our hope or our energy toward yet another attempt at improving our lot in life. But out of desperation, or blind luck, or the grace of God, we came to Al-Anon and found comfort and support as we heard parts of our story told again and again by others who had been through similar experiences. So we returned to the meetings and tentatively tried out the suggestions we heard there. As these suggestions proved helpful and we began to find solutions that led to serenity, we decided to embrace the Al-Anon program and do whatever is necessary to heal. We took a leap of faith, knowing that we would have to work hard and probably would change in ways that we might not be able to predict. Clearly, it was worth the effort.

PRACTICAL TOOLS FOR CHANGE

But where did we go from there? What could we do to move our lives forward in a dramatically healthier direction? The single most productive way to grab hold of all that the Al-Anon program has to offer is to take the Twelve Steps. They are the essence of our program, the underlying principles upon which all recovery in Al-Anon is based.

In a way, the Steps are a "How-to" guide that helps us find answers to our most pressing questions, answers that previously eluded us. In the process, we get to know ourselves. By showing us how to make peace with the past, the Steps help us learn to live in the reality of the present. We begin to take care of ourselves, even to challenge ourselves. We come to forgive ourselves as well as others—and ultimately to love more profoundly than ever before. But unlike other "How-to" approaches, the Steps do not presume to hand out pat answers to complicated, personal questions. Instead, they offer a process that enables us to find those answers for ourselves.

Taking the Steps is an ongoing learning experience in which every action brings us a new awareness of ourselves. Even our mistakes offer great riches because they can lead to meaningful insights. In this sense, every attempt we make to follow this spiritual path is a positive one and we can't make a wrong move. This is fortunate, since taking the Steps is neither a simple nor straightforward process. In fact, much of the time, we simply muddle through.

Although there is no single way to approach the Steps, many of us have found it most beneficial to take them one at a time, in order. Each Step builds upon the previous one. Many newcomers, impatient for change, try to take all of the Steps at once or attempt to skip directly to what they consider the "action" Steps. But all of the Steps are "action" Steps, and each one has a crucial role to play in the process of recovery. It may be helpful at first to learn about the Steps in general, and then to concentrate specifically on the first three Steps, beginning with Step One, and applying them to our lives as best we can. With a solid grasp of these early Steps, we establish a firm foundation on which to build a new and more satisfying way to live.

After a while, we try to understand the Steps in greater depth. Hoping to grasp their wisdom, we read about them, think about them, write about them, talk about them, and listen to what others have learned from their explorations. We ponder the individual words as well as whole phrases and try to discover how they might apply to our particular circumstances. And then we plunge in again, doing what we think the particular Steps suggest.

We may take a Step quickly, only to return to it again and again, or we may spend years meditating and exploring a single Step. Whether we embrace these concepts wholeheartedly or resist them with vehemence, any honest response helps us to grow. As time passes, we find that our understanding of the Steps changes—and may even contradict earlier interpretations—for we continue to grow and to change. Gradually, we discover a richness and a depth within their words that we had never suspected. We come to realize that we have experienced a spiritual awakening, and we know we will never again be the same.

We have embarked upon an extraordinary, potentially life-changing spiritual journey, the journey of recovery from the effects of alcoholism. Every step we take on this journey moves us toward becoming more fully the men and women we are capable of being. But we needn't wander aimlessly, struggling on our own without direction to find our way. Al-Anon's Twelve Steps show us the way. Through the Steps we can fill that empty place within us where loneliness and pain reside. We come alive in a way we never experienced before. We realize that we belong and that we are loved. The following is a brief overview of this remarkable path of spiritual development and personal growth.

TWELVE STEPS

1. We admitted we were powerless over alcohol—that our lives had become unmanageable.
2. Came to believe that a Power greater than ourselves could restore us to sanity.
3. Made a decision to turn our will and our lives over to the care of God *as we understood Him.*
4. Made a searching and fearless moral inventory of ourselves.
5. Admitted to God, to ourselves, and to another human being the exact nature of our wrongs.
6. Were entirely ready to have God remove all these defects of character.
7. Humbly asked Him to remove our shortcomings.
8. Made a list of all persons we had harmed, and became willing to make amends to them all.
9. Made direct amends to such people wherever possible, except when to do so would injure them or others.
10. Continued to take personal inventory and when we were wrong promptly admitted it.

11. Sought through prayer and meditation to improve our conscious contact with God *as we understood Him*, praying only for knowledge of His will for us and the power to carry that out.
12. Having had a spiritual awakening as the result of these steps, we tried to carry this message to others, and to practice these principles in all our affairs.

STEP ONE

We admitted we were powerless over alcohol—that our lives had become unmanageable.

Each of our lives has been devastated by someone else's drinking. We cannot change that fact. We have been profoundly affected by the disease of alcoholism. Its effects continue to permeate our lives. Nor can we change the behavior or the attitudes of those around us. We can't even put a stop to the drinking. We are powerless over alcohol. As long as we persist in the delusion that we can control or cure alcoholism, its symptoms, or its effects, we continue to fight a battle that we cannot win. Our self-esteem suffers, our relationships suffer, and our ability to enjoy life suffers. All of our energy is wasted on a hopeless endeavor until there is nothing left over for attending to our own needs. Our lives have become unmanageable.

Whether or not we live with active drinking, life is unmanageable whenever we lose perspective about what is and is not our responsibility. We take offense at actions that have nothing to do with us. Or we intervene where it is inappropriate and neglect our legitimate obligations to ourselves and others. Our misplaced concern for others becomes intrusive, meddling, resented, and doomed to failure. Instead of helping those we care about, we demonstrate a lack of respect for them and create discord in our relationships.

When our preoccupation with others distracts us from our responsibilities to attend to our own physical, emotional, and spiritual health, we suffer. Our health and self-esteem decline. We become incapable of accepting reality, coping with change, or finding happiness. Our lives fly out of control.

With this First Step, we admit that we did not cause, cannot control, and cannot cure the alcoholic, the disease of alcoholism, or the fact that we have been affected by this disease. We are powerless over alcohol—and its effects on us. By ourselves, we can do nothing to overcome the effects of this disease. In fact, our attempts to exert power over alcohol have made our lives unmanageable.

Taking the First Step allows a great weight to fall from our shoulders. We let go of the losing battle we have been waging. We recognize that there is no point in continuing the fight. We surrender completely.

This is no small achievement. The battle against alcoholism has become the basis for many of our relationships. Putting an end to this battle requires completely redefining what we believe about ourselves, others, and our relationships. For example, many of us have confused love with interference. We don't know how to show affection or support without giving advice, seeking to sway another's decisions, or trying to get those we love to do what *we* think will bring them happiness. We confuse caring with controlling because we don't know how to allow others the dignity of being themselves. Those of us who learned to control whatever we could in order to survive in an alcoholic environment now continue to try to control everything and everybody without realizing what we are doing. From past experience, we are terrified to let others do as they wish. But we only harm ourselves and others when we insist upon approaching every interaction in this way. Our relationships are damaged, and our lives become even more unmanageable. Thus, even when there are no alcoholics directly involved, the effects of alcoholism continue to dominate. So we take the First Step. We admit we are powerless over alcohol and that our lives have become unmanageable.

Al-Anon does not promise that every alcoholic will get sober, or that sobriety will solve our problems or fix our relationships. We may never have the family of our dreams or win the love of those who have no love to give. But our program does offer us hope, because it is all about change. By being honest and admitting that the power we tried to wield over alcoholism was never readily available to us, we let go of the illusion that kept us imprisoned in an endless cycle of repetitious, self-defeating behavior and inevitable disappointment.

It's as if we are lost in a desert. Not far away is a freshwater stream, but until now we have failed to notice it because we have been chasing a mirage, an imaginary oasis that recedes whenever we approach. Only when we finally stop, take stock of what our efforts have produced, and admit that we have been pursuing an illusion, can we turn in a direction that will actually meet our needs. Likewise, when we let go of the illusion of power over alcohol and over other people, we move in a more positive, productive, and rewarding direction. We move toward hope.

STEP TWO
Came to believe that a Power greater than ourselves could restore us to sanity.

One definition of insanity is performing the same action again and again, each time expecting to achieve a different result. Any of us who have been affected by the family disease of alcoholism have experienced this and other forms of insanity. Living with the effects of another's alcoholism has given us a lopsided view of life. Yet, no matter how distorted our outlook or how out of control our lives seem, and regardless of the impact of the alcoholic's behavior, help is available to us.

The alcoholic cannot heal our wounds; neither can our willpower, quick-wittedness, or perseverance. Turning to these sources again and again is no more useful—or sane—than going to a car lot to buy groceries. Having continually failed to resolve our difficulties ourselves, most of us finally realize we must look for help in a more promising place. What we seek is something greater, beyond our own abilities, a source of help, comfort, guidance, and strength unrestricted by our human limitations. Our need for such assistance has become obvious, but so many of our needs have gone unsatisfied in the past that we hardly dare to hope that we might find the help we need. In the process of taking Step Two, we open our hearts and minds to the possibility that such a power *could* actually exist in our lives.

Some of us get an inkling that there might be a power that can do what we, by ourselves, cannot, when we first attend an Al-Anon meeting and actually experience a moment of relief from our suffering. Having walked through the door feeling anxious and confused, unsure about what we were looking for, we are often surprised to find ourselves feeling better and more at peace by the time we leave. Even if we were furious, shame-filled, or guilt-ridden, there is something amazing, something transforming, that happens at an Al-Anon meeting. We can't quite put our finger on what that "something" is or why we come away with a greater sense of peace than we walked in with. But it feels too good to ignore. So we go to another meeting and discover that that "something" is still there. Maybe, just maybe, we have found some sort of power that could do for us what we haven't been able to do for ourselves. We come to believe that there could be a Power greater than ourselves, a power greater than alcoholism.

In Step Two, what has been impossible for us on our own becomes possible because we have placed ourselves in the presence of something that surpasses our individual human capacity. Just by attending a meeting or opening up to a Sponsor or seeking solace in Al-Anon literature, we have reached out for the help of a Power greater than ourselves and have tapped into the collective wisdom of our fellowship.

In time, we come to believe that only a Power greater than ourselves has the power to restore us to sanity. To take Step Two, we don't have to believe that this will happen, only that it *could*. Step Two is about possibility, and that is why it is about hope.

STEP THREE

Made a decision to turn our will and our lives over to the care of God as we understood Him.

In Step Two, we came to believe that there was hope for a saner and more serene way of life. In Step Three, we decide to choose that way of life by turning to a God of our understanding for help.

Some of us already have a comfortable relationship with a Power greater than ourselves. But the concept of a God or a Higher Power can be a difficult one to accept for those of us who have no particular spiritual beliefs, and for those who have had negative experiences with religious organizations in the past. Al-Anon is not a religious program, but it is a spiritual one. Our Twelve Steps speak of a Power greater than ourselves and a God of our understanding. We do not impose a particular image or definition of that God or Higher Power. Instead, we leave it up to individual members to define these terms for themselves, and to find a personal, spiritual relationship that allows them to benefit from what our program has to offer.

Some of us have a very clear and specific sense of a God or Higher Power. Others have no idea who or what this Power may be, but try to keep our minds open to the possibility that more information will be revealed in time. For some, a Higher Power is the God of our religious upbringing. Others prefer to identify a very different God, one who is more personal, loving, gentle, and beneficent than the God we knew in the past. We may find a Power greater than ourselves in natural law, universal love, beauty, a mountain or a thunderstorm or the many wonders of nature, creativity, and any number of other sources. Some of us continue to use the collective wisdom of our Al-Anon group as a Higher Power, noting that wonderful insights and changes take place when we avail ourselves of that wisdom. The God of our understanding may be male or female, an inanimate object, disembodied spirit, or force of nature.

But regardless of the God we come to understand, we are careful to avoid imposing our personal beliefs on one another. Rather, we respect that each of us has a right to choose any Higher Power that seems best suited to us, one to whom we will be willing to turn over our will and our lives. Now we must make the decision to do just that.

Deciding to turn to a Power greater than ourselves for help may seem like a tremendous gamble, but really, what do we have to lose? We know that our old self-reliance and determination have let us down again and again. It only makes sense to try another way.

So we choose differently. We make a decision, a commitment to take all of our concerns and feelings, worries, fears, resentments, loves, dreams, wishes, thoughts, choices, and relationships—in short, our will and our lives—and place them in the care of the God of our understanding. We don't have to figure anything out, know what the results will be, or even feel comfortable letting go of our efforts to control. All we need do is make a decision. By making such a commitment, we stop setting ourselves up for the failure we have known in the past when we've tried to manipulate people and events that were beyond our control. Instead, we make the decision to "turn it over."

It is much easier to "turn over" a problem that is relatively unimportant. Many of us find it easy to surrender the results of a trip to the gas station or what to eat for breakfast. It can be much harder to let go of the things that really matter. When trying to make a major decision, take an action that will have long-term consequences, or trust that we will be cared for in the midst of a crisis, it is tempting to revert to our old habits of self-reliance, worry, and force of will. Such matters seem too important to risk. Likewise, if we have struggled for years to prevent the alcoholic in our lives from drinking, it is no simple task to let go of our efforts and worries. We may have to remind ourselves again and again that we have never been able to control the drinking, to know the future in advance, to figure out the "right" decision, or to worry our way to serenity. So we must go somewhere else for help. The only consistent source of help for matters that are beyond our control is a Power greater than ourselves, and that is where we decide to turn when we take Step Three.

Whether we have a well-defined relationship with God or a vague sense of some intangible force, choosing to turn our will and our lives over to God's care doesn't automatically make all of our problems disappear. We have simply made a decision. But by doing so, we have opened a door for help and stepped out of the way. We can only deepen our commitment every time we surrender anew.

When we take the Third Step and make this decision, we place ourselves in a position in which, no matter what happens in our lives, we can trust that we will be guided and cared for. We are no longer in charge. By placing ourselves in the care of the God of our understanding, we put ourselves in much more capable hands.

STEP FOUR
Made a searching and fearless moral inventory of ourselves.

Many of us can readily provide an impressive list of the admirable qualities of our friends and loved ones, but when called upon to list our own positive qualities, we may find it difficult to name even a few. One of alcoholism's effects is to lower our self-esteem, creating the illusion that others are valuable and praiseworthy while we are deficient. One of the most important functions of Step Four is to allow us the opportunity to discover that we ourselves possess those same fine qualities we so admire in others.

Step Four is an inventory, a list of characteristics, thought and behavior patterns, relationships, and events that make us who we are today. We wouldn't hesitate to take inventory if we owned a toy store. It would be essential to know that we had too many dolls, not enough frisbees, or just the right number of board games. Such information would allow us to make adjustments and bring our business into balance.

A personal inventory does the same thing. It helps us to take stock of ourselves. This Step makes it possible to learn about ourselves, our strengths and weaknesses, our unconscious habits and unrecognized talents, our unspoken shame, secret delights, and hidden passions. The key to Step Four is that it be taken fearlessly, free from judgment. It makes no more sense to berate ourselves for being short on patience than it does to berate ourselves because teddy bears are in short supply in our toy store. By looking at and accepting ourselves as we truly are, we can make decisions about who we choose to become.

It is often suggested that we begin our inventory by concentrating exclusively on our character assets, our positive traits. Most of us are accustomed to finding fault with ourselves, and we overlook or negate the fact that we really are terrific, caring people at heart.

That's why it is imperative to take the time to search out and identify all that is commendable about ourselves. By acknowledging our strengths, we can use them as the basis for the new life we are creating for ourselves. And once we have acknowledged our positive attributes, laudable characteristics, and special talents, we can better maintain some objectivity as we delve into the not-so-desirable areas of our behavior and attitudes.

Steps One, Two, and Three lay the groundwork for this Step. Without the spiritual basis formed in the first three Steps, a searching moral inventory can quickly become a weapon of self-abuse. If we are not ready to use this Step fearlessly, we may still be confused about the purpose of taking inventory, and probably have unfinished business with the previous three Steps.

All of these Steps, including the Fourth, are means of positive change. They are not intended to create guilt or diminish an already damaged self-image. To the contrary, they allow us to observe ourselves as we are, see through our illusions, take care of unresolved issues from the past, make conscious choices here and now, and recognize where to turn for strength, support, and guidance. The Steps are here for our growth and betterment. Each one in turn has something important to offer, and each plays a crucial role in restoring us to physical, emotional, and spiritual wholeness.

The Fourth Step should not be rushed into, but it should not be skipped either; it is too valuable a tool to ignore. Although it can be daunting to sit still and look carefully at ourselves, Step Four can create fantastic opportunities to move our lives in a more positive direction. Until we know exactly where we are, we cannot know where we are headed.

STEP FIVE

Admitted to God, to ourselves, and to another human being the exact nature of our wrongs.

Step Four helped us to learn about ourselves, our strengths and our shortcomings. In taking Step Five, we acknowledge what our inventory has helped us to discover, revealing these insights not only to ourselves and our Higher Power, but to another person as well.

The thought of admitting our darkest secrets to someone else can be frightening at first. We fear that our wrongs are worse than anyone else's, and that we would be humiliated if we ever admitted them to another human being. Perhaps the alcoholic in our lives has led us to believe that we are horrible people; perhaps we created this damaging illusion ourselves. But if we can summon the courage to challenge these fears, and can go ahead and take Step Five in spite of them, we take a huge stride toward personal freedom.

Not only does Step Five help us to learn that what we have done isn't so terrible or so irredeemable, but also that there are people who will love us unconditionally, even if they know the very worst about us. Most of us are astonished to discover that we are the only ones who judge ourselves and our wrongs harshly. This Step can dramatically change the way we look at ourselves and others, and most of us find it well worth the effort.

First, we admit what we have learned to the God of our understanding. The purpose of this admission is to "come clean" before God, to allow ourselves to be exactly who we are within this vitally important spiritual relationship.

Then we admit to ourselves what our inventory has revealed. In other words, we take responsibility for ourselves. We avoid the temptation to justify our behaviors and attitudes, blame others, or excuse our past wrongs. We also avoid giving in to the urge to dismiss our talents and invalidate our character assets. We simply say, "This is who I am."

Finally, we admit this information to another human being. It's important to choose someone who understands this Step, someone who is supportive, loving, and compassionate and who will listen without judging or condemning. Although our most beloved and trusted friend may be the alcoholic in our lives, most of us find it unwise to work this Step with him or her. There is too much potential for conflict and emotional complications. Instead, because it can be very helpful to share this experience with someone who has already worked Step Five, many of us work this Step with our Sponsor or another trusted Al-Anon friend. Others choose a therapist or member of the clergy with whom they feel comfortable. We share in detail, not only listing our wrongs but discussing them in depth, and when we are finished, we try to keep an open mind to hear what the other person may choose to offer in response. Many of us find that our Higher Power can speak to us through others, and this is a prime opportunity for such communication.

We often pay particular attention to our limitations when we take Step Five because these are the things that hold us back and interfere with our ability to live happier, healthier lives. We try to identify "the exact nature of our wrongs," the motives or patterns behind these shortcomings, recognizing that many of our past errors were merely symptoms of an underlying problem or weakness of character. For example, our inventory might have unearthed occasions when we stole cookies from our local market. Upon closer examination, we may realize that the underlying problem was a fear that we wouldn't have enough to eat. Fear is often thought to be a lack of faith—we are afraid because we do not trust that our Higher Power will take care of our needs. Thus, we might determine that a lack of faith, rather than a propensity for theft, is the exact nature of our wrong in this case.

But we also acknowledge our talents, our strengths, our positive actions and attributes. Perhaps it has become clear through our inventory that the driving force in our life today is a tremendous willingness to do whatever it takes to heal. Although we have made a concerted effort to attend Al-Anon meetings, reach out to others, read Al-Anon literature, and take the Twelve Steps, we may have overlooked the fact that we are doing something wonderful for ourselves. No longer are we pursuing a path of self-destruction. Instead, we are committed to changing our lives. This is something worth celebrating, something in which we can take pride. This and other positive changes deserve acknowledgment. Describing these changes, traits, and talents to someone else makes it much more difficult to casually dismiss them.

We are building a new life. Some of the building process involves tearing down materials that stand in the way of our plans. But the process also involves taking the best of what we already have and expanding upon it. Our character assets can form the basis of a life centered around self-love and self-caring if we recognize and admit their importance.

STEP SIX
Were entirely ready to have God remove all these defects of character.

In Steps Four and Five, we uncovered aspects of our lives and our personalities that needed change. Most of us are uncomfortable with these aspects of ourselves and want to get rid of them as quickly as possible. But Step Six says nothing about changing ourselves or making our own defects of character go away. In fact, this Step points out that we are powerless to remove our defects of character by ourselves. Instead, we are reminded that we are in a partnership with a Power greater than ourselves. Our role in this partnership is to accept ourselves as we are, flaws and all, and to become willing to let go of all that stands in the way of our health and growth. No other action is required. The rest is up to a Power greater than ourselves.

In other words, in Step Six we learn to "Let Go and Let God." This means that we must once again learn to trust the God of our understanding to do for us what we cannot do for ourselves. It isn't always easy, because we know too much to remain comfortable with our defects. As we catch ourselves acting them out, we don't like what we see. We want to be proud of ourselves and feel at peace with our behavior, yet we are increasingly embarrassed at what we find ourselves saying and doing. These actions, attitudes, and habits do not reflect the person we are striving to become.

At this point, many of us try once more to change ourselves. For instance, if we have always been too busy focusing on everyone else's problems while ignoring our own, we might try to force ourselves to mind our own business. We are often dismayed at how quickly our efforts fail. Although enormous energy goes into focusing on ourselves, many of us find that we continue to be preoccupied with other people's lives.

Sometimes we have to try to make these changes on our own—and fail—before we can honestly say we are *entirely* ready for God's help. After a lifetime of self-sufficiency, most of us need to be reminded that there are limits to what we can achieve without help. Paradoxically, by accepting our limitations, we can avail ourselves of unlimited possibilities. With God's help, we can overcome seemingly impossible obstacles. Miracles can grace our lives, and serenity can take the place of despair. Our defects of character can be blessings in disguise, because in order to be free of them, we must deepen our faith, and that spiritual depth will bless our lives.

Our strength lies in accepting our role in our relationship with God, and trusting that a Higher Power will play a significant role as well. No longer must we struggle alone, attempting the impossible. We need only "Let Go and Let God."

STEP SEVEN
Humbly asked Him to remove our shortcomings.

Many people confuse humility with humiliation. But humiliation is a form of abuse and has no place in our spiritual growth. When we speak of humility, we speak about self-acceptance. In Step Six, we learned to accept our part in our relationship with our Higher Power. We recognized that we are not all-powerful and that there are limits to what we can achieve by ourselves. We can no longer go back to the oblivion of denial, yet we're not capable of effectively eliminating those aspects of our personalities that cause us embarrassment or make our lives unmanageable. We have little choice but to accept ourselves as we are, with all our limitations. And chief among those limitations is the fact that we cannot cure ourselves. By accepting that God can do for us what we cannot do for ourselves, we begin to achieve the humility that is necessary for change to take place. In Step Seven, we put that acceptance to work. We take action.

Nonetheless, even after we accept the fact that we need the assistance of a Higher Power, many of us try to figure out exactly what we need and hand our Higher Power a list of tasks to fulfill on our behalf. This is not humility; this is self-will. True humility is based upon letting go of self-will and relying instead upon the will of our Higher Power. Again, we admit that our own resources have let us down and we need help. To ask for such help is to take a huge leap of faith—to truly place ourselves, our futures, and our actions in the care of God.

Then, for the first time in the Twelve Steps, we *ask* God directly for help. We neither grovel, regarding our needs as shameful, nor do we demand, treating our needs as all-important. There are a variety of ways to ask. We may pray, meditate, visualize, write, speak aloud, or sing our requests, but whatever form we choose, we communicate our desire to be free of excess baggage. We simply speak from the heart.

STEP EIGHT
Made a list of all persons we had harmed, and became willing to make amends to them all.

Most of us come to Al-Anon with a distorted sense of responsibility. At first, some of us are unable to name a single person we have harmed, feeling that we have been the victims of other people's cruel or insensitive behavior rather than the perpetrators. We are so focused on others that we miss the fact that our own behavior has not always been so wonderful. No matter how pure our intentions, our actions have consequences, and sometimes, intentionally or unintentionally, we hurt those around us. At the time, we may have rationalized our poor treatment of others, feeling that we were only reacting to the way we had been treated or that we had no choice. But if we set all self-justification aside and keep the focus strictly on ourselves, we must admit that we were responsible for causing harm.

Others of us carry an unwarranted burden of responsibility, believing ourselves to be the source of most of the pain and suffering in our lives and in the lives of those around us. We feel that we have harmed everyone with whom we have come in contact. This is just as much a distortion of reality as thinking we have done no harm. Sometimes people's suffering is of their own making. Sometimes pain is just a part of life. And sometimes we contribute to the problem. Step Eight provides an opportunity to learn the difference between what is and is not our responsibility and to take a more realistic look at the effects of our actions.

Nowhere does this Step say that we listed the harm others have done to us. Although we do not have to accept unacceptable behavior, it is not our job to pass judgment upon what others do or to punish anyone for their wrongs. Our job is to concentrate on *our* part in our conflicts with others and what *we* have done to cause harm.

Usually there is one person upon whom we have inflicted the greatest damage—*ourselves*. Most of us have been crueler and more negligent to ourselves than to anyone else. By our reactions to the disease of alcoholism and our desperate efforts to survive in difficult situations, we have harmed ourselves mentally, physically, and spiritually. So before any other names are added to our Eighth Step list, most of us need to write our own name.

Once our list is made, we face the task of becoming willing to make amends. It is not enough to simply admit to ourselves that we have been at fault. Taking responsibility for our actions means making amends for the harm we have done. We needn't concern ourselves with the form our amends will take at this point—that comes in Step Nine. For now, our only concern is finding the willingness to do what is necessary to right past wrongs. This willingness may not arrive all at once. In fact, some of us find it helpful at first to divide our list into three columns: those amends we are willing to make, those we may possibly make, and those we cannot imagine ourselves ever making. As time and healing progress, most of us find ourselves gradually becoming willing to make even those inconceivable amends, because we learn that we owe it to ourselves to do so. As with the rest of recovery, becoming willing to make amends is a process that takes time.

In considering the Eighth Step, it is important to remember that, until we can take this Step in a spirit of self-love and healing, we may not be ready for it. Step Eight, like the other Steps, is a step toward healing. It is not about humiliating ourselves or making others feel better at our expense. It is about owning up to what we have done and becoming willing to free ourselves from the guilt and shame our actions have caused us.

STEP NINE

*Made direct amends to such people wherever possible,
except when to do so would injure them or others.*

Having listed those we have harmed, we are now faced with the task of making amends. We cannot undo what has been done in the past. We can express our regrets and make a commitment to try not to repeat past mistakes, but what's done is done. By taking Step Nine, we rid ourselves of the guilt that has weighed us down for so long. By facing the harm we have done and finding the most suitable form of amends for the situation, we can clean up whatever mess we have created and leave the past in the past.

There are many ways to make direct amends, from simple, straightforward apologies to changed attitudes and altered behavior. Sometimes amends must be made in person; at other times, a letter, phone call, or monetary form of restitution is more suitable. It often helps to review the situation with an Al-Anon friend or Sponsor in order to determine what would be most helpful to us and most appropriate to the circumstances. Prayer and self-honesty are also illuminating.

Occasionally, bringing up the past would only re-open old wounds and make matters worse. Direct amends are not appropriate if they will cause further harm. In such a case, amends might be made by avoiding the harmful behavior so that we will not hurt anyone else in the same way. For example, if we have harmed an elderly relative who has asked us to refrain from any further communication, and therefore cannot make direct amends, we might vow never to repeat the same mistake with anyone else we encounter. Or perhaps we will choose to write a heartfelt letter of amends to that person and to read it to our Sponsor instead of mailing it. Or we might devote some time to helping out in a retirement center as a way of demonstrating to ourselves that we really want to do things differently.

But this must not become a convenient excuse to avoid the important spiritual work that this Step suggests. Step Nine speaks of making *direct* amends wherever possible. The emphasis of this Step is on facing those we have harmed and setting the record straight. We wouldn't want embarrassment or resentment to tempt us to avoid an apology that we need to make or the repayment of a debt we owe. Nobody is standing watch over us to make sure we take this Step with sincerity. We are the only ones who will ever truly know. If we wish to be free from the terrible, suffocating weight of guilt, we must take whatever action is necessary to make amends for the harm we have caused. Only then will we find real relief.

With this Step, we have an opportunity to choose the kind of person we would like to become and the kinds of relationships in which we would like to be involved. By making amends, we admit that we are human like everyone else and cease to set ourselves apart from others. We do not beat ourselves up for having made mistakes, we merely admit that we made them and do what we can to correct them. Our actions show that we have enough respect for ourselves and others to own up to the harm we have done. We commit ourselves to justice. We demonstrate that we wish to be fair, honest, and mature. Step Nine is not about relieving our guilt at the expense of others, nor is it about setting ourselves up for abuse. The purpose of Step Nine is to do what we can to heal ourselves and our relationships, and to set ourselves free.

STEP TEN

Continued to take personal inventory and when we were wrong promptly admitted it.

In the Fourth Step, we began a process of self-examination by taking inventory of ourselves. With the help of our Higher Power, we continued this process in subsequent Steps as we tried to act upon what we learned about ourselves, building upon our strengths and striving to be free from our shortcomings. We learned to take responsibility for ourselves and to turn the rest over to our Higher Power. For most of us, this is a cleansing and empowering experience. But it is only the beginning of a lifelong process of spiritual renewal and growth.

Step Ten is a daily commitment to continue this healing, life-affirming process. We continue to examine ourselves and our lives, focusing not only on our errors and shortcomings, but also on our successes, our improvements, and our gifts. We acknowledge the areas in which we are changing and make adjustments as we grow. This process allows us to connect, to bring ourselves more fully to our relationships. It serves as an ongoing reminder that we are not really so different from one another. As we treat ourselves with honesty and compassion, we become capable of extending such treatment to others. We recognize that change doesn't happen overnight and that, in recovery as in much of life, we often take one step back for every two steps forward.

This Step must be taken with sincere self-honesty but also with great compassion. We are doing our best. We are human, and we will fall short of perfection. Instead of justifying our mistakes and creating new sources of guilt, we can simply admit to ourselves that we were wrong as soon as we realize it, making amends whenever appropriate. It's as if we have cleaned up a badly corroded automobile. Now we are faced with the choice of maintaining it and responding immediately when we see signs of new corrosion, or ignoring the problem until it becomes as unbearable as it was before. Step Ten allows us to maintain ourselves in good working condition, free of unnecessary burdens.

STEP ELEVEN
Sought through prayer and meditation to improve
our conscious contact with God as we understood Him,
praying only for knowledge of His will for us and the
power to carry that out.

By the time we have taken the previous ten Steps, our own experience is all the proof we need that some Power greater than ourselves is working in our lives. We have learned that we need never be alone or at a loss for what to do, because this Power is always available to comfort and guide us. So it is only natural that we would want to take whatever actions we can to consciously improve our relationship with the God of our understanding.

Prayer and meditation are the vehicles we use for spiritual communication. But the terms "prayer" and "meditation" mean different things to different people, and we are encouraged to interpret them in any way that works for us. Perhaps we repeat the prayers of a particular religion, write letters to God in our own words, or simply ask a Higher Power for help. We might set aside a half hour of quiet time and listen to our thoughts, or concentrate on a pleasant image, or clear our minds and focus on deep breathing. Prayer and meditation take many different forms, but they all have a common goal—to put us in better and more conscious touch with the God of our understanding, the proven source of strength, love, and hope in our lives. Many of us find it important to set aside time every day to tap into this source.

In the past, most of us said frantic prayers in the hope that God would do *our* will and give us what we wanted. But our experience has shown us that our will often gets us into trouble and generally leads to disappointment in the end. Most of us have learned the hard way that the only will worth pursuing, the only guidance worth praying for, is knowledge of the will of God. Only God knows what is best for all concerned. So our efforts to strengthen our spiritual lives focus on seeking only God's will—and the power to carry it out. For no matter how weak or uncertain we may feel, tremendous power is available to us when we turn to the source of unlimited Power. With such spiritual help, we can accomplish previously unimaginable goals, even the goal of living happy and gratifying lives.

STEP TWELVE

*Having had a spiritual awakening as the result of these
steps, we tried to carry this message to others, and to practice
these principles in all our affairs.*

This Step implies that by working all of the Steps, we will
undergo a spiritual awakening. Although a spiritual awakening is a
highly personal experience, many of us define it as a kind of transformation, a radical change in perception that occurs as a result
of our taking the Steps. Sometimes a spiritual awakening happens
abruptly—in a flash of insight or the instantaneous removal of an
obsession—and the whole world suddenly looks new. More com-
monly, though, we experience a gradual awakening of the spirit,
a gentle metamorphosis in the way we see ourselves and others,
a slow and subtle unfolding of our own inner beauty. Some of us
actually feel reborn, hopeful, free of the fears and burdens that had
previously prevented us from truly living. Thus, although our circumstances may not have changed, our lives improve dramatically
because we perceive them in a new and clearer way.

Before coming to Al-Anon, few of us would have believed that
such a transformation was possible. Having been affected by a disease that robbed us of our dreams and paralyzed us with fear and
rage or numbed our emotions, we doubted that there was any reason
to hope for a better life. Nonetheless, as a result of the Al-Anon
program and its Twelve Steps, we have become living proof that
miracles happen. Naturally, we want to share our personal message of hope with any friends or family members of alcoholics who
still suffer the effects of another's drinking. Some of us would never
have found this wonderful way of life had it not been for the generous sharing and encouragement of other Al-Anon members, and we
are more than grateful for any opportunity to pass this gift on to others who may need it.

It is important, however, to remember that the message we carry
is the result of working *all* the Steps and applying them to every
aspect of our lives. When we first came to Al-Anon, many of us
wanted to carry the message to others before taking even the First

Step ourselves. Others used this part of the Twelfth Step to justify their efforts to push the alcoholic into a treatment program. But in time, as we work the Steps, we realize that we cannot carry a message we have not learned for ourselves. In the meantime, we carry our message of experience, strength, and hope every time we share at an Al-Anon meeting, make or accept a program telephone call, or perform a service for our group. Each of us has a great deal to offer to others, and that will only grow as we grow.

Most of us came to Al-Anon to cope with a specific, alcohol-related problem. When we first learned a new Al-Anon principle or practice, we immediately applied it to that most troubling area of our lives. But as we recover, as alcoholism and its effects no longer dominate our thoughts, we find that these spiritual principles apply not only to alcoholic situations, but to all aspects of our lives. An Al-Anon slogan can help to resolve a conflict with a co-worker; a Step may clarify what actions we need to take in a legal dispute or may identify a long-buried desire and make it possible to achieve; a Tradition can guide us in establishing household rules or running a business meeting. In Al-Anon's book, ...*In All Our Affairs,* members from all over the world speak of the many difficult situations that often accompany alcoholic relationships—infidelity, financial problems, physical and sexual abuse, divorce, and other challenges—and the Al-Anon principles that helped them to cope.

Al-Anon offers us so much more than a handful of problem-solving techniques for dealing with alcoholic relationships. In time, we also discover principles that can guide us through uncertainty and open doors to opportunities we never dreamed of. Our futures are unwritten books. With the help of the Twelve Steps and the other Al-Anon principles, we will fill those pages with a life that is rich in love, constructive action, and spiritual well-being.

9

The Al-Anon Slogans

Unlike some of Al-Anon's practices and principles that take a while to learn and apply, the Al-Anon slogans are easy to learn and remember. You may have heard some of these slogans hundreds of times before without ever taking them seriously or trying to put them to work. After all, they are clichés, and easy to disregard. But it is their very simplicity that makes them so powerful.

When confronted with a confusing or upsetting situation, a slogan can be a lifesaver. If we are at a loss for what to do, these simple yet profound sayings can clarify our thinking. For example, when fears about the future cloud our ability to make a pressing decision, we can apply the slogan "One Day at a Time" and focus on this day only, remembering that our fears may not reflect reality because the future has yet to be written. When suddenly faced with a complex, seemingly overwhelming problem, we can put "First Things First," knowing that some actions are more important than others and that we cannot do everything at once.

Slogans serve as gentle, calming reminders that our circumstances might not be as impossible or as desperate as they at first appear. These concise expressions of wisdom offer quick reassurance that we really are able to cope with whatever life brings, prompting us to take constructive action and to treat ourselves and others with compassion and respect. Even when we are too new to Al-Anon or too overwhelmed by our circumstances to recall one of the many Al-Anon principles that may apply, a simple slogan can put the entire situation into perspective.

"Keep It Simple"

When coping with the baffling and often overwhelming effects of alcoholism, the simpler and more straightforward the approach, the better. The slogan, "Keep It Simple," makes just that point. When life seems unmanageable or confusing, many of us unknowingly complicate matters even further by trying to anticipate everything that could go wrong, so that we will be prepared to respond. This slogan reminds us that we can't control every possible outcome to every situation and that trying to do so makes our lives more difficult and more stressful than they already are. When we "Keep It Simple," we try to take things at face value, looking at what is actually happening rather than the 50 things that might or might not follow. Perhaps we can approach large projects and challenges slowly, step by step, in manageable stages rather than all at once. Sometimes we must act with haste, but not every new task or unexpected event is a crisis. Our initial, fearful responses may arise more from habit rather than necessity. In time, we learn that if we are feeling paralyzed and overwhelmed, we may be complicating matters or taking on more than we can handle for this moment or this day, and that we may have better luck by simplifying what we are trying to accomplish. We can relax and try to be more gentle with ourselves, trusting that by putting one foot in front of the other, we will eventually get where we are going.

"But for the Grace of God"

This slogan, an abbreviated version of "There, but for the grace of God, go I," is a reminder to approach other people with compassion. Many of us have long since become impatient, critical, and resentful of those around us, especially the alcoholics in our lives. But when other people's attitudes and actions bother us, we can remember that, were it not for the grace of our Higher Power, we could easily be in their shoes. We cannot truly know what others are struggling with, nor is it our job to punish them for any suffering we feel they might have caused. Vindictiveness, vengeance, resentment, blame, and hard-heartedness do us far more harm than anyone else. Is this what we want to put our energy into cultivating? Perhaps we might find a more positive use for our time, finding gratitude for the blessings we have received and recognizing that every single human being, even those suffering from alcoholism, is doing the best they can.

"Easy Does It"

Al-Anon's Suggested Welcome explains that without the spiritual help of our program, many of us try to "force solutions." When our efforts to overcome another's alcoholism get us nowhere, we resolve to try even harder. When we are impatient for an answer and no answer comes to us, we take an action at random just to feel we are doing *something*. When the square peg fails to fit into the round hole, we refuse to give up and try to force it into place. As a result, our frustration mounts, our anxiety increases, we feel like failures, and we vow to try even harder. In short, our thinking becomes distorted. With the slogan, "Easy Does It," Al-Anon suggests a simple alternative to this destructive and frustrating pattern. Sometimes even doing *nothing* can be far more productive!

We have tried doing things the hard way. This slogan reminds us that, while "hard" doesn't do it, "easy" often does. We may not have all the answers today. This is not a failure, only a reality. It is not always our job to solve every problem. Perhaps we are expecting too much of ourselves or others. In fact, we may know everything we need to know for this day. If and when the time is right, more will be revealed. "Easy Does It" reminds us that a gentler approach might make a tough situation much more bearable.

Or maybe we are trying to take on something that is not our responsibility. Struggling harder will only make things more difficult. But if we adopt a kinder, more relaxed attitude, we may be able to see the situation more clearly and act more appropriately.

"First Things First"

When life becomes chaotic, it is easy to lose track of what needs immediate attention and what does not. Small obstacles can seem like crises, and major problems can be overlooked. An alcoholic's rage over a paper cut can take precedence over a medical emergency because the rage is so loud and so demanding—and because we have become accustomed to reacting to whatever the alcoholic demands. As a result, not only do we overlook critical situations, but we often neglect those quiet but important needs of our own that might make our lives more enjoyable. We neglect our health, find little time to give our children loving attention, and set aside any urge we may feel to have fun.

"First Things First" encourages us to take a moment to set priorities. Before we react, we can ask ourselves what is of primary importance right now. When planning our morning, we can consider which of our more quiet needs might deserve attention. In the midst of a heated discussion, we can stick with the topic that concerns us and set aside other matters that are not so pressing. When there doesn't seem to be enough hours in the day, we can accept our limitations and make choices about what has to be done at once and what can be postponed. We are not superhuman; we cannot do it all. "First Things First" helps us to make more workable choices and to live with the choices we make.

"Just for Today"

This slogan is a commitment to set aside the past and the future and live in this one day only. When we deal with today only, seemingly impossible projects become manageable. Conflicts that would have consumed all of our attention can be addressed for a reasonable amount of time if we recognize that they may not have to be resolved completely and at once. And "Just for Today," we can make small changes in our actions and attitudes, explore new possibilities and take a few tiny risks, all of which can help us to move forward in a positive direction.

Many Al-Anon members begin by trying to adopt one or two of the suggestions contained in the leaflet entitled *Just for Today*. It doesn't matter which ones we choose; they can all help us put this one day to use and learn that managing a single day can be the beginning of a new and better life:

"Just for today I will try to live through this day only, and not tackle all my problems at once. I can do something for 12 hours that would appall me if I felt that I had to keep it up for a lifetime.

"Just for today I will be happy. This assumes to be true what Abraham Lincoln said, that 'Most folks are as happy as they make up their minds to be.'

"Just for today I will adjust myself to what is, and not try to adjust everything to my own desires. I will take my 'luck' as it comes, and fit myself to it...

"Just for today I will have a program. I may not follow it exactly, but I will have it. I will save myself from two pests: hurry and indecision...

"Just for today I will be unafraid. Especially I will not be afraid to enjoy what is beautiful, and to believe that as I give to the world, so the world will give to me."

"Let It Begin with Me"

The Al-Anon program helps us to stop focusing so intently on what those around us say, do, and feel, and instead to put the focus on ourselves. When we are tempted to blame others for our problems or to justify our own poor behavior by pointing to the poor behavior of others, this slogan reminds us where our focus rightfully belongs. We are responsible for our actions, regardless of how others behave. When we feel the need to change a situation, we can apply this slogan, and start with what we can improve. Would a change of attitude on our part make things work more smoothly? Are we making a positive contribution to what is happening, or merely standing by and criticizing, waiting for others to take care of the situation for us? "Let It Begin with Me" is a way to change the things we can—especially our own attitudes—instead of waiting for everyone else to change to suit us.

Often, a very legitimate need or desire goes unrecognized

because we expect that need to be met by someone else. We may be yearning for more honesty in a relationship, or for more pleasurable weekends, yet taking no responsibility for our own part in addressing these needs. This is like going hungry while waiting for someone who doesn't cook to make dinner. "Let It Begin with Me" might suggest that we go ahead and cook for ourselves, go out for dinner, or make plans with someone who cooks. In short, we take responsibility for getting our own needs met.

Thus, if we have a mental wish list of the things we want a parent, child, spouse, friend, or employer to do for us or bring to our relationship, we might consider ways to satisfy those wishes in another manner or with other people. If we have often been disappointed by an undependable friend, instead of waiting for that person to change, we might try to stop depending on him or her. Perhaps someone else in our life would be more reliable when we really need to count on someone. We might also ask ourselves if we have been consistently reliable in all of our relationships. Sometimes the things that bother us most about others are the very things we do ourselves without realizing it. Similarly, what we most admire in others can be the very traits we are capable of cultivating in ourselves.

"How Important Is It?"

This slogan helps us gain perspective. If we take the time to think about what really matters to us, we may include such concerns as health, serenity, adequate food and shelter, and loving support from others. Each of us is free to determine for ourselves what is truly of value, but most of us agree that we often get upset about matters of little consequence. Compared to whether or not we will have enough to eat today, how important is it if we overcook the chicken for dinner? Is forgetting to pick up a newspaper worth the cost of our serenity? What price are we willing to pay to win an argument or prove to other people that we are right? How important is it if a call we have been expecting doesn't come through, or if a loved one makes a choice we do not like? Does a partner's unkind words in the morning merit a whole day of misery, obsession, and hostility? Does it merit even five minutes of unhappiness? Does it really matter? Must we take it personally? Is it worth the price of self-recrimination, resentment of others, or hours of worry? Just "How Important Is It?"

Even if we decide that the situation is important, we can ask ourselves whether it is important *today*. Are we living in the unknown future, worrying about things that may never come to pass? Today is all we have. Why waste this precious gift of time on trivial concerns when we could be appreciating the fact that we have everything that we truly need? The perspective we gain when we apply this slogan makes it possible to set aside petty worries, minor irritations, and baseless judgments so that we might celebrate the extraordinary richness and wonder that life offers.

"Think"

One of the effects of alcoholism is that most of us tend to *react* to everything we encounter, often perceiving minor incidents as major crises. Rather than choosing to act on our own behalf, we allow other people's actions and demands to dictate what we do and thus show little regard for our own interests. As a result, we often feel victimized, at the mercy of whatever difficulty life puts in our path. This slogan reminds us that instead of automatically reacting to every provocation, request, or demand that comes along, we can "Think" before we act, making choices that are in our best interest.

Some of us are surprised to discover that "Think" is a slogan. After all, some of our most concerted thinking has gotten us into deep trouble. The difference today is that our thinking has changed—we try not to waste our time scheming about how to get others to change or worrying about matters over which we have no control. Instead, we learn to put our minds to work where they can do us the most good. We "Think" about the part we play in creating our own joy or sorrow and what we can do to enhance our lives and improve our interactions with others. We "Think" about the Twelve Steps and try to apply them to our own particular circumstances. We "Think" about how to include our Higher Power in our everyday lives. We are no longer trapped by the distorted, self-destructive thinking of the past. With Al-Anon's help, we are learning to put our thoughts to more productive use.

"One Day at a Time"

There are many ways to solve a problem, approach a new undertaking, cope with a fear, and prepare for a change. Many of us have tried tackling such projects by peering into the future and trying to anticipate and resolve every glitch we think we might encounter, making decisions based upon information we do not really possess because the future has not yet happened. Rarely is this a satisfying approach. In most cases, we cannot anticipate every possible turn of events, so no matter how diligently we have prepared, we are eventually caught off guard. Meanwhile, we have expended so much time and energy trying to predict future events, soothe future hurts, and prevent future consequences, that we have missed out on today's opportunities. And the magnitude of the task we have set for ourselves has left us drained, overwhelmed, and distraught.

For most of us, a much more practical approach to our challenges and fears is to take them "One Day at a Time." We can't do anything about the future because the future is not within our grasp today. Worrying about it, trying to manipulate it, anticipating it—all these activities simply remove us from this moment. We can't change the future, but by making the most of this day, we prepare ourselves to be able to handle whatever comes tomorrow. We may wonder whether or not to trust a loved one's renewed commitment to sobriety, but there is no way to predict what will happen in the long run. We can only choose how we will respond today.

We can respond to the changes we see before us, confronting the new challenges and enjoying the gifts that a loved one's sobriety can bring, or we can allow ourselves to become obsessed with the possibility of yet another slip. We cannot know what will happen, and we needn't deny any possibility, desirable or undesirable. But wasting today worrying about tomorrow will not make us any better prepared for difficulties that may present themselves. If they do manifest, those painful problems will not hurt any less tomorrow, whether we have stewed about them or set them aside today. All of our preparation will not have spared us a single ounce of pain. In fact, it will have lengthened our suffering, since we'll have added all that extra worrying time. So if there is no advantage to trying to live in the future, it only makes sense to stay here in the present and make the very best of every precious moment we are given.

Another advantage in living "One Day at a Time" is that we break huge, overwhelming tasks into smaller, more attainable goals. We may not be able to resolve a dispute with a boss or a loved one for all time, but perhaps we can come to an agreement for this one day. We may not be able to pay off an entire debt right now, but perhaps we can pay a small portion of it, knowing that small portions eventually add up to large sums. We cannot do what we cannot do. Worrying about going hungry tomorrow won't put more food on the table, it will only make us forget to appreciate the food we have today. This day is ripe with opportunities for joy, for sorrow, for experiencing the full range of human emotion and experience. Isn't it time we took advantage of it?

"Keep an Open Mind"

Guidance can take many forms, and it often comes when least expected. Words of wisdom may fall from the mouth of a small child or from the ramblings of someone we dislike. We never know where we will find inspiration or help. If we "Keep an Open Mind," we make ourselves available to receive that help, no matter where it comes from. By limiting where we expect to find our answers, we may miss out on important opportunities to improve our lives. Thus, it is best to remember that a newcomer to Al-Anon is as likely as a longtime member to say just the "right" words to spark a new awareness, and sometimes dinner with friends or an evening at a movie may enlighten us about a problem as readily as an hour of concentrated effort to resolve the problem directly.

When we turn our will and our lives over to the care of a Higher Power, we affirm that we need guidance. Our job now is to keep our minds open, knowing that life-changing help can take any avenue, any form, any voice. Our teachers are all around us. Let's make room for every single one.

"Live and Let Live"

This is a two-part slogan. In dealing with alcoholism, many of us focus most intently upon the latter part of the slogan, the "let live" part. Having felt so overly responsible for other people's choices and actions, it can be a great struggle to grant others the dignity to make decisions for themselves and allow them to deal with the results. We use this slogan as a reminder to get off their backs and "let" them live. In this way, everyone benefits. The people in our lives benefit because they are finally receiving the respect that is every person's due. Now they are free to enjoy the fruits of their positive efforts and to reap the consequences of their more destructive behavior. Regardless of what they choose to do about it, by minding our own business and getting out of the way, we allow others to be themselves. Meanwhile, we free ourselves from all kinds of burdens that were never ours to carry. Thus, we, too, have the opportunity to face ourselves.

That's where the other part of this slogan comes in—the "Live" part. Many of us have suffered a great deal of neglect as a result of the family disease of alcoholism, much of it from ourselves. Distracted or consumed by the problems of others, we have neglected our own bodies, minds, and spirits. Sponsors and other Al-Anon friends can help us to find ways to address needs that have gone unrecognized or unaddressed in the past. This slogan encourages us to make a special effort to treat ourselves well. It reminds us that making a life for ourselves, regardless of what others are doing or not doing, must be a top priority. Other people are not the only ones who merit our respect. We, too, deserve to treat ourselves with dignity. We have a right to really "Live," and indeed it is our responsibility to do so.

"Let Go and Let God"

This slogan can be an antidote to the desire many of us have to control the uncontrollable. Instead of relying upon our ego or self-will to direct our lives and the lives of others, we draw upon the strength, wisdom, and compassion of a Power greater than ourselves. Instead of hanging on for dear life, we "Let Go and Let God."

We have often been our own greatest enemies, standing in the way of the help we need. When we put this slogan to work, we get out of the way. We let go of the problem, the need to know what will happen and when, the obsession with other people's choices, the thoughts and concerns that waste our time and energy because we cannot resolve them by ourselves. And we let God take care of them.

When we feel we have run out of options and nothing is going the way we expected, when we don't know what to do or can't figure out what there is to do, we can "Let Go and Let God." When life is going smoothly and we are trying out new and exciting ideas and actions, we can remember Who is in charge of the results, and "Let Go and Let God." When an Al-Anon friend goes through a difficult time and we don't know how to show our support, all we need do is to let them know we are available and to "Let Go and Let God." This slogan gives us permission to replace stress, worry, and suffering with serenity and faith. It's okay to relax and let life happen. We can rest assured that the answers, choices, actions, and thoughts we need will come to us when the time is right because we have placed them in the hands of our Higher Power.

10

Changed Attitudes

How often have we seen a particular event or even an entire week as either all good or all bad? If the alcoholic drank, or if a friend was depressed, our day was ruined. Likewise, if it rained on the day we had looked forward to a picnic, we were miserable. Now that we are in Al-Anon and learning to focus on ourselves, we find that our world is neither all black nor all white. Now, the difference between a good day or a bad day has little to do with what happens or with what other people do or feel. We can have a good day in sunny or stormy weather, when everything goes according to our plans or when dinner is burnt and we run out of milk and the cash machine eats our bank card. We can even have a good day while the alcoholic in our lives is still drinking, because today we know that the kind of day we have depends on our own attitudes.

THE POWER OF ATTITUDE

As Shakespeare suggested, "There is nothing either good or bad but thinking makes it so." Consciously or otherwise, our attitudes affect the way we perceive everything that happens in our lives, so that the life we experience often has more to do with the way *we interpret* what happens than with the events themselves. Nobody wants to get sick; illness can be uncomfortable, sometimes excruciatingly so. But if we wind up in bed with a bad cold or with something more serious, we nonetheless have choices about how we will view the experience. We can once again perceive ourselves as victims, dwell on all of the things we are unable to do, and feel terribly sorry for ourselves—or we can treat the situation as a blessing in disguise. Being unexpectedly incapacitated may actually leave us feeling unexpectedly relieved, temporarily free from everyday pressures. We can take advantage of the opportunity to rest, to take stock, to catch up on some of the quieter activities we may have neglected, or simply to be good to ourselves. Realizing that we often take for granted both our health and the precious time we have been given in this life, we may develop a fresh appreciation for both, making each day that much more fulfilling.

In other words, as the cliché goes, we can perceive the glass as half-empty or half-full. Our choice will determine the world we experience and will color the way we feel about ourselves and others.

This is especially true for those of us who know first hand the effects of another's alcoholism. Many of us tend to have a habit of negative thinking that causes us to see only the grim side of our situations. When looking toward the future, we imagine the worst, becoming so busy worrying or trying to protect ourselves that we neglect to enjoy ourselves along the way. Rather than turning to others, we brace ourselves for disappointment and withdraw from the joyful opportunities of life. When our expectations are not met or when our plans are disrupted, we feel sorry for ourselves and angry with those we think are responsible, often using these reverses to justify our own unfinished work, broken promises, or neglected responsibilities.

Changing such self-defeating attitudes is essential to recovery, but we have to be honest with ourselves. There is no value in pretending to have a sunny outlook when we really perceive a situation to be painful or frightening, or when we feel the world is a gloomy place. We are seeking genuine change, not denial. And the first step in changing our negative attitudes is becoming *aware* of them, a process that rarely happens overnight.

Even after we recognize a self-defeating attitude, we may be dismayed to find it popping up unexpectedly again and again. The attitude seems to stand out. We wonder how we ever could have missed it and whether others have been aware of how destructive it is. But before we can take effective action, before we can actually change a negative outlook to a positive one or change self-pity into gratitude, we have to accept ourselves precisely the way we are. We need to admit that the disturbing habit or attitude is a part of us. We need to acknowledge our feelings and perceptions as they are, and we also need to cultivate the willingness to change. Because we cannot do this alone, we ask our Higher Power for help. As we become willing, we search for positive aspects in every situation and find gifts hidden in even the most trying times. Gradually, and at first imperceptibly, our outlook shifts until the world actually appears brighter and more inviting. In time, situations that would have given rise to any number of negative attitudes pass almost unnoticed. We may even find something in these situations for which we can be grateful.

GRATITUDE

Actively practicing gratitude is one way we can promote attitude adjustment. Instead of taking for granted the many blessings in our lives, we make a point to mentally acknowledge them until doing so becomes a habit. Writing them down in a "gratitude list" and then reading the list to our Sponsor or sharing it with other Al-Anon members helps us realize that there are many things in our lives for which we are truly grateful.

In times of distress, we may see little for which to be thankful, but if we make the effort, we are certain to find a few and thereby shed some light on an otherwise dreary view. Sometimes it helps to start with our most basic or immediate needs—food on the table, a roof over our heads, and clothing. We may then find that we are grateful for more modest incidents and gestures—kind words, Al-Anon friends, a bit of humor in an otherwise serious situation, a moment of serenity, or an indication that we are beginning to heal.

Gratitude enables us to savor the unrecognized good that surrounds us, no matter what the circumstances. As we become accustomed to noticing the positive aspects of our lives, we begin to recognize small, subtle gifts and cloaked opportunities when they appear in our day-to-day experience. Eventually, as we continue to practice, we actually do find something to be grateful for, even in painful or difficult situations. We replace our victim mentality with an attitude of gratitude. Instead of feeling drained, overwhelmed, and stressed by the circumstances we encounter, we begin to feel empowered and capable of coping, even flourishing, because we have learned that our Higher Power can use every situation, every relationship, every experience, to enhance our lives and foster strength, faith, and personal growth. Thus, *everyone* and *everything* has a special gift to offer us. We need only open our eyes to see it.

SERENITY PRAYER

New attitudes often evolve from a new way of seeing. One way Al-Anon suggests to gain perspective is to think about the words of the Serenity Prayer as we say them:

God grant me the serenity
To accept the things I cannot change,
Courage to change the things I can,
And wisdom to know the difference.

This prayer can be extremely helpful because it encourages us to turn to a Power greater than ourselves in sorting out what we can and cannot do.

Often our greatest source of discomfort is our continuing attempt to change people and events over which we are powerless. The Serenity Prayer reminds us that we cannot achieve the impossible. Instead, we can stop trying to play God and accept the very real possibility that the people and events in our lives are part of the greater vision of a Higher Power. In doing so, it becomes easier to accept the things we cannot change.

Yet there are plenty of situations in which we *can* act effectively to improve our circumstances—changing what we can. It takes courage to see ourselves as we really are and to attempt to make positive, lasting changes, especially when we are reluctant to change at all. We ask the God of our understanding to provide us with the impetus to act, acknowledging that what we can most readily change is ourselves.

The gift of wisdom enables us to know when to act and when to let go. In the Serenity Prayer, we turn to the God of our understanding for the attributes necessary to live life more fully: serenity, courage, and wisdom.

EXPECTATIONS

One obstacle over which many of us stumble as we attempt to battle this disease of attitudes is our own expectations. There is no better way to make ourselves feel victimized and helpless than by harboring unrealistic expectations of ourselves and others, or by confusing expectations with needs and insisting that they be met. Attaching our well-being to a particular action or outcome is very risky. In essence, we make that situation a kind of higher power— we give our power over to other people and circumstances. At any moment, a turn of events could dash the dreams and plans upon which we've built our lives.

Life is far too uncertain for such misplaced faith. So it is in our best interest to examine our expectations. Are they realistic, or based in fantasy? Do we hold them loosely, with the flexibility to let them go or to make adjustments as further information comes along, or do we cling tightly to these flimsy ideas and invest our self-worth, our entire well-being in them? If we allow our expectations to dominate, we set ourselves up to be victims or martyrs again and again.

But here, too, we have the ability to change our attitudes. We can adjust our expectations so that they are more realistic. We can also detach from them, anchoring our well-being and peace of mind in our Higher Power rather than any external situation. By seeking only the knowledge of God's will for us and the power to carry that out (Step Eleven), we make great strides toward developing an unshakeable inner peace and a sense of security that cannot be threatened by mere circumstances.

SERENITY

This is what some of us mean when we speak of serenity. With serenity, we are no longer limited by fears or illusions. We can be fully ourselves and trust that, with the help of a Higher Power, we will be able to handle anything that happens. We replace the daily dread and insecurity that have dominated us in the past with a new-found confidence and a profound sense of well-being. This is one of the goals we seek for ourselves in Al-Anon. Although we may have come to Al-Anon with very different intentions in mind, by practicing the principles of our program, we can achieve inner peace and become capable of realizing far more than we ever imagined. Many of our hopes and dreams become attainable. Others cease to matter so much. Serenity may be the most precious gift we receive because it allows us to know that our lives are in the care of a Power greater than ourselves and therefore, even in the midst of chaos, there is hope.

11

Detachment, Love, and Forgiveness

PERSONAL BOUNDARIES

Al-Anon recovery is about reclaiming our own lives. We do this by learning to focus on ourselves, build on our strengths, and ask for and accept help with our limitations. But many of us find it difficult even to begin this self-focused process because we have lost track of the separation between ourselves and others, especially the alcoholic. Having interceded for so long on the alcoholic's behalf, constantly reacting, worrying, pleasing, covering up, smoothing over, or bailing him or her out of trouble, we have often taken upon our shoulders responsibilities that don't rightfully belong to us. The result is that we lose the sense of where we leave off and the alcoholic begins. We have become so enmeshed with another person's life and problems that we have lost the knowledge that we are separate individuals. When asked about ourselves, we often respond by talking about the alcoholic. We perceive ourselves to be so connected that, if something happens to the alcoholic, it seems only right, only natural, for us to respond.

Many of us even confuse this absence of personal boundaries with love and caring. For example, from the moment the alcoholic goes out the door, we sit, immobilized, unable to do anything but think obsessively about him or her. We lose the ability to distinguish between the alcoholic and ourselves until the alcoholic's past, current, and potential actions become our sole focus. This is not love; it's obsession. When we cease to live our own lives because we are so preoccupied with the lives of others, our behavior is motivated by fear. Not only is it harmful to a relationship to hover anxiously or suspiciously over a loved one night and day, it is also extremely self-destructive.

Likewise, when we cancel our own plans and stay home because we fear that the alcoholic will drink if left alone, we may protest that we act out of loving self-sacrifice for the sake of the alcoholic. More likely, it is an effort to feel that we have some power over the drinking. The choice to abandon our own plans for such a purpose is an act of fear, not an act of love. Canceling plans and staying home to avoid the consequences of "defying" the alcoholic is another form of self-abandonment and has nothing to do with love.

Genuine, healthy love isn't self-destructive. It doesn't diminish us or strip us of our identities, nor does it in any way diminish those we love. Love is nourishing; it allows each of us to be more fully ourselves. The enmeshment that characterizes an alcoholic relationship does just the opposite.

DETACHMENT

Detachment is one of the most valuable techniques Al-Anon offers those of us who seek to reclaim ourselves. Simply put, detachment means to separate ourselves emotionally and spiritually from other people.

If someone we love had the flu and cancelled plans with us, most of us would understand. We wouldn't take it personally or blame the person for being inconsiderate or weak. Instead, in our minds, we would probably separate the person from the illness, knowing that it was the illness, rather than our loved one, that caused the change of plans. This is detachment. And we can use it to see alcoholism in the same compassionate yet impersonal way. When alcoholism causes a change in plans, or sends harsh words or other unacceptable behavior in our direction, we needn't take it any more personally than we would take the flu symptoms. It is the disease rather than the individual that is responsible. By seeing the person as separate from the disease, by detaching, we can stop being hurt by groundless insults or angered by outrageous lies. If we can learn to step back from alcoholism's symptoms and effects just as we would from the sneezing of a person with a cold, we will no longer have to take those effects to heart.

Learning to detach often begins by learning to take a moment before reacting to alcoholic behavior. In that moment we can ask ourselves, "Is this behavior coming from the person or the disease?" Although at first the answer may not be clear to us, in time it becomes easier to discern whether alcoholism or our friend or relative has prompted the disturbing behavior. This distinction makes us better able to emotionally distance ourselves from the behavior. We can remember that although alcoholics often surround themselves with crisis, chaos, fear, and pain, we need not play a part in the turmoil. Blaming others for the consequences of their own choices and acting out verbally or physically are some of the smokescreens that alcoholics use to conceal the real source of the trouble—alcoholism. Everyone's attention goes to the harsh word, the broken glass, or the bounced check rather than to the disease. It becomes automatic to defend against the insult, weep or rage at the thrown glass, scramble to cover the bounced check. But by naming the disease, we see through the alcoholic's smokescreen and therefore needn't be distracted by it at all. Instead of taking the behavior personally, in time we can learn to say to ourselves, "That's just alcoholism," and let it go.

Simply knowing that alcoholism is the source of the unacceptable behavior is not sufficient, however. We may have to take action to help us achieve greater emotional distance. We might change the subject, leave the room or even the house, or involve ourselves in some physically demanding activity. We may need the support or perspective that only a Sponsor or fellow Al-Anon member can provide. An Al-Anon call or meeting could be just what we need to help us separate ourselves from the symptoms and effects of the disease without separating ourselves from the human being.

At first, we might not detach very gracefully. Many of us have done so with resentment, bitter silence, or loud and angry condescension. It takes time and practice to master detachment. Beginning the process is important, even if we do it badly at first and must later make amends. But it is even more important to remember that establishing personal boundaries is not the same as building walls. Our goal is to heal ourselves and our relationships with other human beings, not to coldly distance ourselves, especially from the people who matter most to us. In fact, detachment is far more compassionate and respectful than the unfeeling distancing or the compulsive involvement many of us have practiced in the past, for when we detach with love, we accept others exactly as they are.

Detachment with love allows us to hate the disease of alcoholism, yet step back from that disease in order to find love for the alcoholic. For some of us, this love was apparent all along. For others, love may be the last emotion we would associate with the alcoholic. Those of us who grew up in an abusive alcoholic environment may be hard pressed to summon any love for the alcoholics we have known.

FORGIVENESS

Resentment will do nothing except tear us apart inside. No one ever found serenity through hatred. No one ever truly recovered from the effects of alcoholism by harboring anger or fear, or by holding on to grudges. Hostility keeps us tied to the abuses of the past. Even if the alcoholic is long gone from our lives or has refrained from drinking for many years, we, too, need to learn to detach. We need to step back from the memories of alcoholic behavior that continue to haunt us. We begin to detach when we identify the disease of alcoholism as the cause of the behavior and recognize that our ongoing struggle with unpleasant memories is an effect of that disease. We, too, must find within us compassion for the alcoholic who suffered from this terrible illness.

Each of us is worthy of love, and each of us is doubly blessed when we are able to dig down past our grievances and resentments, no matter how justified we may feel in harboring them, and find within ourselves the recognition of that part of the other person that is and always will be lovable. How better could we learn that we ourselves are eternally and irrevocably lovable than by recognizing that same quality in everyone around us?

Yet some of us balk at the idea of adopting such an attitude toward people who, in the past, may have caused us great physical, emotional, financial, or spiritual harm. If we find their behavior totally reprehensible, why should we bother to look for a place within ourselves that can relate to them with love? Aren't some things simply unforgivable?

To answer these questions, we must ask another: What is the purpose of our recovery? If we are truly in pursuit of serenity, of healing, of a sense of inner peace that will help us to deal with and possibly even enjoy whatever life brings, we must improve the way we interact with others. This doesn't mean that we close our eyes to the unacceptable or tolerate the intolerable. It has no bearing on what behavior we will accept, nor on whether or not we continue our present relationships. It simply means that we cultivate the ability to look beneath the surface. By shifting our focus away from the objectionable behavior and looking more deeply, we recognize a part of every human being that remains untouched by disease, the part of each of us that deserves unconditional love and respect regardless of the circumstances. It is equally possible to appreciate this quality in those whom we do not know as it is in someone with whom we hope to spend a lifetime. This is what forgiveness is all about. We don't forgive the actions another person has chosen, because it was never our job to judge the person for those actions in the first place. Instead, we forgive when we acknowledge our common humanity with everyone, even the person we feel the most entitled to condemn. In this spirit, we can even forgive ourselves, no matter what we've done or how guilty or shame-filled we may feel. We, too, deserve love.

Forgiveness is no favor. We do it for no one but ourselves. We simply pay too high a price when we refuse to forgive. Lingering resentments are like acid eating away at us. Rehearsing and re-rehearsing old injuries robs us of all that is precious. Shame never liberated a single spirit. And self-righteousness never softened a heart. Can we afford to perpetuate such self-destructiveness? Surely we can make better use of our time and energy. Although we may despise what others have done, if we keep in mind that everything we are now trying to do has the goal of healing us, we are bound to decide that the best thing we can do for ourselves is to forgive.

12

Taking Care of Ourselves

Alcoholism is a threefold disease—physical, mental, and spiritual. Many of us have neglected our health on all three of these fronts, so our recovery from the effects of alcoholism must be threefold as well.

TREATING OURSELVES WELL

It takes a firm commitment to make our own well-being a priority. In the past, some of us neglected to care for ourselves because we were waiting for someone else to take care of us. And some of us were so concerned with another person's well-being that we failed to attend to our own. But in Al-Anon we are learning to take responsibility for tending to our needs.

At first, few of us felt comfortable giving ourselves such attention. It seemed selfish to make these efforts on our own behalf. We may even have been taught as children that other people's needs rightfully come first.

But how can we take care of others if we are falling apart through lack of the most basic care? In Al-Anon we learn to put "First Things First." Just as airline passengers are instructed to put on their own oxygen masks before helping their children or fellow passengers with theirs, we must learn to attend to our own well-being first. We owe it to ourselves to give ourselves the love, care, and attention we need and deserve, even if the needs of others sometimes have to wait.

For some, the easiest way to learn how to nurture ourselves is to do for ourselves what we would normally do or wish to do for a loved one. We might have a habit of skipping meals or eating poorly and quickly when alone but preparing sumptuous and nourishing feasts when our loved ones are present. By putting ourselves in our loved ones' position, we can see that we deserve much better treatment.

OUR PHYSICAL HEALTH

We might consider what we can do to improve and maintain good health. Our physical bodies require rest, exercise, a nutritious diet, and appropriate medical care, and all of these are areas that merit conscientious planning. Something as simple as a daily walk can make a tremendous difference in the way we feel. Perhaps we will get an occasional massage, or take a few minutes for a nap when we are tired. If we often skip meals because we can't seem to squeeze them into our busy schedules, we can make an effort to block out mealtimes in advance and treat those time commitments with the same respect we would give to any other appointment. When we are ill, we can learn to take proper care of ourselves, cutting down on our activities, drinking extra fluids, getting the rest we need, and seeing a doctor when necessary, even if illness strikes at an inconvenient time. By attending to our physical needs, we go a long way toward making our lives more manageable.

OUR MENTAL AND EMOTIONAL HEALTH

Mentally and emotionally, we can find ways to stimulate our minds and validate our feelings. We can read books we enjoy or put our thoughts on paper in an essay or a letter. We might begin a new course of study or learn a new skill and open ourselves to some different interests. We can strive to become more honest with ourselves about what we think and feel; we can find appropriate ways to express ourselves. We might examine our emotions, whether alone, with a Sponsor, or with professional help.

Because recovery involves tremendous inner change and upheaval in addition to whatever outside changes are occurring, many of us need to take extra care of ourselves emotionally. The feelings aroused when denial is challenged, new projects are tackled, and a whole new way of life is adopted can be overpowering. We may experience tremendous fear, rage, guilt, or depression. Change, even wonderful, positive change, almost always involves some grief for the old way of life we are letting go, even if that way of life kept us miserable.

For those of us who have been emotionally shut down for years, the sudden flood of emotion can be frightening. If we keep in mind that this intense emotional turmoil is usually a temporary and natural part of the process of recovery, we may more easily accept the experience and take steps to make ourselves as comfortable as possible under the circumstances. It is especially important to provide ourselves with a place to express these feelings where we will receive the support and encouragement we need, such as a regular Al-Anon meeting at which we feel comfortable sharing. It is also important to be reminded that feelings aren't facts. No matter how intense the feelings may be, they are only feelings. They are *reactions* to, rather than reflections of, reality. Therefore, they are not necessarily the best basis for decision-making. Other people can help us to value the experience of our emotions without acting on them in ways that we might regret once the feelings have passed.

Some of us begin to remember long-suppressed traumatic events from the past that are emotionally devastating to relive. Suddenly, explosive feelings erupt that we were not capable of handling at the time of the trauma. They seem uncontrollable and terrifying, and we may fear they will never stop. Of course, this experience *will* eventually pass and the feelings *will* depart, but in the meantime we need to treat ourselves with extra tenderness. Emotional trauma can be even more disturbing than physical trauma. Just as we would need time to heal after major surgery, we need to recover from the emotional effects of past abuse, abandonment, or violation.

But not all of our emotional experiences are unpleasant. We may also discover new joy, passion, creativity, excitement, and a sense of wonder. It is essential to make room in our lives and in our psyches for all of these new, positive feelings that can energize the pursuit of further growth and make life so much more enjoyable.

OUR SPIRITUAL HEALTH

The third important aspect of self-care is spiritual. Many of us find it crucial to take time every single day to improve our conscious contact with the God of our understanding. This may be a half-hour of meditation, the repetition of a special prayer, a quiet, thoughtful walk in the woods, or a searching letter to our innermost selves. Many of us find spiritual inspiration and solace that is especially suited to those affected by another's alcoholism in *One Day at a Time in Al-Anon* (*ODAT*) or *Courage to Change*, Al-Anon's daily meditation books. Artistic expression fosters spiritual growth in some, while organized religion works best for others.

As important as it is to set time aside for spiritual "exercise," it is even more important to recognize that our spiritual selves require ongoing attention. Morning prayers may not provide all of the spiritual sustenance we need for the entire day any more than a mid-morning snack will satisfy all of our nutritional needs. We seek to make our Higher Power a constant companion, turning to the God of our understanding for guidance and spiritual nourishment throughout the day and night. We actively pursue this goal when we say a prayer before answering the phone or take a moment to listen for that still small voice inside us before making a decision, even a minor decision. And when we notice opportunities and gifts, even in difficult situations, we are strengthened by keeping our gratitude for our Higher Power's loving assistance in the forefront of our minds.

SETTING PRIORITIES AND LIMITS

One easy-to-remember acronym for self-care is HALT, borrowed from our A.A. friends. It reminds us that when we are *H*ungry, *A*ngry, *L*onely, or *T*ired, we have needs that require our attention, needs that may be preventing us from acting in a positive, affirming way. We are encouraged to "Halt!" and to tend to these needs as soon as possible. This simple, loving reminder can prevent our saying or doing things we might regret and can help us to avoid rash decisions.

Another way we learn to take care of ourselves is to define our personal limits. This involves determining for ourselves what we will and will not do or accept. It can be as simple as setting our bedtime at 10:00 P.M. or as difficult as deciding not to tolerate any more verbal abuse. Such limits help us to know in advance what our options are and how we feel about them so that, when faced with a stressful situation where we may not be thinking clearly, we will have some idea of what is in our best interest.

It is entirely up to us to determine what is acceptable to us and what is not. The same behavior that is intolerable to one person won't bother another person at all.

Our personal limits, however, do not dictate a code of behavior for others. Limits are not threats or methods of manipulation. They are merely facts. They state, "I will leave the party if I feel uncomfortable around other people's drinking," rather than, "I'd better not catch you drinking at this party," or "Promise me you won't drink this time." Certainly, there are times when it is highly appropriate to communicate our limits to those who might be affected by them, but we should consider our motives first. Are we informing them of factual information they deserve to have, or are we using limits as a way of trying to force change? We might also pause before voicing these limits to be sure we are prepared to follow through. Otherwise, we risk seriously diminishing our credibility and diminishing our own self-esteem.

BUILDING SELF-ESTEEM

At some point in our recovery, most of us must confront our low self-esteem. Years of abuse and neglect, not only by others but by ourselves, have often left us with a poor self-image. We feel inconsequential, hopelessly flawed, doomed to failure, and unworthy of the kind of care and attention we would give to those we love. We certainly don't love ourselves. In order to overcome these feelings of inadequacy and self-hatred, many of us must force ourselves mechanically to go through the motions of taking care of ourselves. We learn to *act as if* we love ourselves and behave accordingly. We don't have to feel worthy to see the dentist, we merely have to show up for the appointment. Our teeth get just as clean, and perhaps that will lift our spirits just a bit. We may be uncomfortable about taking the time for a massage or a bubble bath when we could be worrying on behalf of someone else, but improving our lives may not always feel comfortable at first. When in doubt, we can try to choose the action most likely to enhance self-esteem. Even if we are only going through the motions, our loving behavior will help us to feel better about ourselves. In time, our actions will become more comfortable, and we will begin to feel more deserving until our self-esteem gradually reaches a healthier level.

Other Al-Anon members can also help us to learn to build self-esteem. Sometimes we have to surround ourselves with those who accept and love us before we can learn to love ourselves. Those of us who have been told or have told ourselves for so long that we are awful, pathetic creatures may not be able to recognize how magnificent we really are, how courageous, warm, lovable, fascinating, and loving we are at heart, until we see those qualities reflected in those who can see us more clearly than we see ourselves. When those we admire treat us as worthwhile human beings, we tend to be more open to the possibility that they *could be right*. We learn by their example. We may never have had role models who cared for themselves properly, or we may have forgotten how it was done. But we do have the right to learn these skills just as we would any other, and one of the best ways to learn is to observe others who have mastered the art and are willing to share with us what they know.

COPING WITH PHYSICAL ABUSE

One of the most dangerous consequences of low self-esteem is that it allows us to tolerate abusive behavior because we feel we deserve no better treatment. This is wholly untrue. No one deserves abuse. Each of us is doing the absolute best we can all the time, and that is enough. We must make an effort to alter our self-image and combat self-loathing so that we will no longer feel at all inclined to accept the unacceptable.

But such an undertaking won't happen overnight. In the meantime, it is critically important that any of us dealing with physical abuse take steps to insure our safety and the safety of our children. Again, we may have to act as if we felt we deserved better treatment, and we owe it to ourselves to make that effort. We need time to recover, time to heal enough to be capable of making rational decisions, and we must do what we can to allow ourselves that time. For example, we might choose to remain in a potentially violent or abusive environment but provide ourselves with an escape route by hiding car keys, money, and other essentials where they can be retrieved at a moment's notice. We could arrange with a friend to have access to a shelter at any hour if the need arises. Or perhaps we prefer to remove ourselves from harm's way altogether, at least temporarily. We might seek a restraining order, request police assistance, or seek therapeutic or legal help. Al-Anon doesn't advocate any particular course of action. We are not urged either to stay or to go. Our concern is that each of our members has the opportunity to gain enough recovery to make clear, well-thought-out decisions about our lives. Some behavior, such as physical abuse, is never acceptable. All of us deserve to remain safe long enough to discover this for ourselves.

13

Communication

Once we are able to take care of ourselves, we have much more to bring to our relationships with others. The way we relate to others depends in large part upon the way we communicate, so it is useful, when examining our relationships, to consider what we say and how we say it.

For instance, do we say what we mean and mean what we say? Do we state our needs and desires or sit back and wait for others to read our minds? Do we agree to do things that we really don't want to do, saying "yes" when we mean "no"? Do we express our feelings and communicate our appreciation for those in our lives, or do we keep silent or deny what we feel out of fear or habit?

RECOGNIZING OLD PATTERNS

Many of us have formed patterns of communication that linger even though they may have outlived their usefulness. For example, before recovery, many of us kept quiet or agreed to unreasonable requests in order to avoid conflict. At the time, we lacked the ability to take a stand or act on our own behalf. Today, we might perpetuate that behavior out of habit even though we have other alternatives.

Now that we are working to improve our lives, we may want to stop making promises and threats we will not carry out. For example, swearing that the alcoholic will have to leave if he or she ever takes another drink undermines our credibility if it is merely an idle threat. Before uttering such vows, we would be wise to ask ourselves whether or not we mean what we say. We may also have to learn to say "no" some of the time, even if it means disappointing others, when the request is important to them. Such honesty is not only good for us, it's much more respectful of other people than grudgingly offered favors laced with resentments.

Some of us keep our wants, needs, thoughts, and feelings to ourselves, expecting that anyone who truly loved us would somehow figure them out, or at least ask the right questions at the right time. But people, even those who love us a great deal, cannot always guess what is in our hearts and minds, nor is it their job to do so. Part of our obligation to ourselves is to stop putting life on hold while waiting for others to allow us to live it. Communicating what we want others to know about us is strictly our responsibility.

Sometimes we may hesitate to speak out because we fear the consequences of doing so, yet we overlook the consequences we pay by keeping quiet. Such silence can perpetuate our frustration, reinforce our fear of conflict, and cause us to believe that what we have to say really is unimportant. In this way, we demonstrate a lack of respect for ourselves and for other people. All we have to offer to anyone is ourselves. If we hold back and timidly refuse to risk being ourselves, we diminish our relationships.

It is worth noting, however, that if we are dealing with someone who is drunk or violent, this kind of honesty may be ill-advised. Real communication requires at least some participation by both parties, and if one of those parties is not in his or her right mind, the effort is likely to be wasted. It may even be dangerous. In such a case, talking things over with a Sponsor can help us determine an appropriate course of action.

Then there are those of us who never hesitate to say what is on our minds. We don't stop to think about what we wish to convey, or how best to say it, we just automatically spit out the words. Not everyone needs to know everything that comes into our minds, and some circumstances are not always suitable for personal discussions. Honesty is a great gift to give to any relationship, but diplomacy and consideration for the feelings of others and the appropriateness of the situation are also important. Many of us benefit from learning the value of silence.

This is especially true of those of us prone to dispensing unwanted advice or criticism. Since we can't truly know what is best for other people, our opinion about what they should or shouldn't do is likely to do more harm than good. We can be supportive without trying to influence other people's choices. If asked, we can share our own experiences without insisting on appearing to have all the answers.

We can communicate our faith in the ability of other people to solve their own problems rather than trying to do it for them. We can learn that sometimes it is best to keep our mouths shut.

Likewise, those of us who rarely have anything constructive or positive to say may have to be quiet until we can find a more balanced way to talk to others. If the only attention we have ever received was critical or negative, we may know no other way to relate to others. But such negativity is destructive. Gossip is equally destructive. Not only do we avoid focusing on ourselves when we gossip, but our disrespect for others reinforces self-defeating attitudes about relationships. When we gossip, we create a judgmental and competitive atmosphere in which no one can feel comfortable about being themselves or expressing feelings. Because gossip undermines Al-Anon's healing nature, it is considered one of three obstacles to success in Al-Anon. The other obstacles—dominance and discussion of inappropriate topics such as specific religious tenets at Al-Anon meetings—are also communication problems that we need to take seriously if we hope to grow and heal in Al-Anon. Pausing before we speak and thinking about what we are really trying to say can be the beginning of healthier interactions.

On the other hand, cold, angry silence can be more biting than vicious words. Are we silent because it is in our best interest to say nothing or because we have nothing to say, or are we using silence as a weapon? Here, too, care must be taken to be clear about our motives.

We are also wise to examine our motives when we find ourselves repeatedly airing the same thoughts. It is marvelous to be able to express ourselves, but do we have a hidden agenda? When we state our feelings about the actions of another person for the fourth time, it's likely we are trying to make that person change those actions rather than simply trying to share openly. Or perhaps we are attempting to influence other people's reactions to someone we love. Do we reiterate the same point hoping to find just the right words or just the right moment to get a particular response? This is not self-expression. This is manipulation. By examining our motives, we can better stop ourselves from sabotaging the healthy interchange of ideas we are trying to cultivate.

HOW WE SAY WHAT WE SAY

But not all of our communication is determined by what we do or do not say. It also depends upon how we say it. Not only our choice of words, but also our attitudes, facial expressions, and tone of voice can either open a channel or slam a door, regardless of the subject being discussed. All people, from the cashier at the drug store to our children, deserve our courtesy. Any message can be conveyed with courtesy, even one of outrage. If we treat people well when we speak what is in our minds and hearts, they are much more likely to hear what we have to say.

This takes courage. It is much easier to let our words convey compliance while our tone of voice expresses contempt. This is a way of communicating anger without taking responsibility for it. Instead, we have the option to say exactly how we feel with as much respect as we can muster. We are apt to get better results this way, but even if we don't, we will know that we have behaved with integrity. As we become the kind of people we can admire, we learn more appropriate ways to express our thoughts and feelings.

LISTENING

Of course, communication is a two-way street. Not only is it important to improve the way we express ourselves, we must also examine the way we allow others to express themselves. We needn't always respond to what is said nor accept everything we hear as truth, but we do hope to develop relationships in which all concerned can be themselves and say what is on their minds and in their hearts. Are we good listeners? Do we grant other people the time to say what they need to say, to clarify their thoughts, even to say things we don't like to hear? Or do we interrupt, finish other people's sentences for them, or stop listening altogether while we prepare our response? Are we open-minded about what others have to say, or do we quickly become defensive? Most of us find that if we want others to hear what we have to say with courtesy, we must extend the same consideration to them.

But being a good listener is more than a matter of courtesy. Al-Anon's slogan, "Listen and Learn," reminds us that if we have the self-discipline to be quiet and pay attention to others' words, we can learn a tremendous amount about ourselves and our world.

FOCUSING ON OURSELVES

Our goal is to build healthy, respectful relationships. By applying the Al-Anon slogan, "Let It Begin with Me," we can see that it is not good enough to wait for others to treat us well before we are considerate of them. Most of us find that after a while we begin to attract what we give out. If we are consistently warm and respectful, we tend to attract respect and warmth from others. It may not take the form we expect or come from everyone we encounter, but if we focus on ourselves, choose behavior we feel is appropriate, and let go of the results, our communication as a whole is bound to improve.

DEALING WITH CONFLICT

Does this mean that we never engage in arguments? Of course not. Conflict is part of every relationship. In fact, the more we recover, the more likely we may be to encounter conflict. We are bound to have increasingly strong opinions and to stand up for them because we believe in ourselves. Arguments can be constructive experiences that help to clear the air or they can be brutal attacks that undermine the connection between two people. The choice is ours to make. We can argue in order to win, to exert power, to prove the other person wrong and to mete out punishment for any slight we might have perceived, or we can argue for the purpose of making peace.

Few of us look forward to a disagreement, much less an argument, but when faced with conflict we have the option to embrace it, realizing that we are each doing the best we can. And we can accept our differences. We can even accept that not all conflicts can or should be resolved, and allow ourselves and others the right to do, think, and say whatever each believes without demanding agreement or resolution. Keeping in mind the fact that arguments are not the only option available when a conflict arises, we can engage in discussions that permit both parties to air their views and learn from one another. As we learn to exchange and build upon ideas, we develop the ability to work together toward common goals and to interact with others in a more intimate, more meaningful way. We can treat one another with respect, especially when we disagree.

14

Service

PUTTING LOVE INTO ACTION

We hear a lot in Al-Anon about unconditional love. Such love makes no demands, exacts no payment, has no expectations. We are free to give it without anticipating or even wanting anything in return because the experience of loving in this way is so rewarding in and of itself that we are grateful for the opportunity. Often without being aware of it, we receive love of this kind without any sense of obligation to pay it back and without fear that the bill will come tomorrow. There is no "If you really loved me, you would _____," no "After all I've done for you...." Unconditional love asks for nothing except expression. It blesses both the giver and the receiver.

Love with no strings attached is a foreign concept for many of us. Some of us experience it for the first time when we come to Al-Anon. As the Suggested Closing to our meetings states, "After a while, you'll discover that though you may not like all of us, you'll love us in a very special way—the same way we already love you." Our survival as a fellowship depends on unconditional love. We are brought together through a common problem and united by a common goal. We need each other. Each member is important, yet nothing is required of any member except what he or she freely wishes to give. There are no strings. And we respond to this freely given love by feeling that it is safe and desirable to keep coming back. Surrounded by this unqualified support, we who are so vulnerable and so wounded begin to heal.

It takes practice to learn to love unconditionally. An exceptional opportunity to put this new way of relating into effect is by volunteering to help an Al-Anon group through service work. Every contribution has value for the group and enables us to grow as individuals. From putting away chairs after a meeting to representing the group at the local, district, or Area level, Al-Anon provides a wide range of opportunities to practice giving unconditionally. Perhaps we will speak at a meeting or become the group's Secretary. We can make the coffee, set out the Al-Anon literature, or read the Suggested Welcome at the start of the meeting. We can serve by reaching out to welcome a newcomer. Another form of service is to submit our thoughts and experiences to the Literature Service at the Al-Anon World Service Office. Such contributions are essential to the creation of new, up-to-date, relevant literature. Sponsorship is another superb and rewarding form of service.

All of these and many other activities help Al-Anon as a whole, our group in particular, and ourselves. It might seem that we, who have received so much from this wonderful program, have an obligation to do just that, to help Al-Anon, to repay what we have been given. But this is not the case. Again, service is the practice of unconditional love. There are no "shoulds," no obligations. We are welcome to contribute to the well-being of our individual groups and our fellowship as a whole, but it is not required, no matter how far we have come or how much we have received. This frees us to give only what we wish, knowing that we do so for our own growth.

Service in Al-Anon allows us to stretch ourselves and to practice the Al-Anon principles while we connect with others with whom we can be ourselves. It is an opportunity to attempt something we actually can achieve and to gain self-esteem by doing something of value. At a time when many of us find ourselves easily preoccupied, service provides a way to keep busy without getting ourselves into trouble, adding structure to an otherwise scattered or disorganized schedule and providing an anonymous and nurturing environment in which to explore and to grow.

We discover that when we reach out to others, our own pain diminishes and our recovery begins to soar. Although there was a time when many of us shied away from such activities, fearing that we had so little we could hold on to without giving part of ourselves away, this is no longer a concern. Today, as we continue to practice all we have learned, we care for ourselves physically, mentally, and spiritually far better than we had ever thought possible. Part of that self-caring involves understanding that love is not lessened when given away. In fact, the more love we offer, the more love we will find within ourselves. Thus, whenever we truly give of ourselves, almost magically we find that there is more of our *selves* to give.

Ironically, the only real way to keep the riches we receive is to give them away. By taking advantage of these opportunities to practice unconditional love, we make love an ongoing part of our lives and we learn that by giving, we always receive.

Al-Anon's booklet, *When I Got Busy, I Got Better* offers invaluable information about this crucial area of recovery. And nowhere is the spirit of Al-Anon service more clearly articulated than in the prayer on the back of the *Just for Today* bookmark:

"Lord, make me an instrument of Thy peace. Where there is hatred, let me sow love; where there is injury, pardon; where there is doubt, faith; where there is despair, hope; where there is darkness, light; and where there is sadness, joy.

"O, Divine Master, grant that I may not so much seek to be consoled, as to console; to be understood, as to understand; to be loved, as to love; for it is in giving that we receive, it is in pardoning that we are pardoned, and it is in dying that we are born to eternal life."

15

Keep Coming Back

WHY WE KEEP COMING TO AL-ANON

Newcomers to Al-Anon are often surprised to meet so many long-time members. Many of us continue to attend meetings years after the problems that first brought us to Al-Anon have passed, because the program continues to enrich our lives. We continue to change and we are changed by circumstances we encounter, but because we have practiced the Al-Anon principles in all our affairs, our lives have improved beyond imagining. We can't afford to take these changes for granted. What was once learned is quickly forgotten without continued renewal, practice, and support.

So we keep coming back. For some, Al-Anon becomes a spiritual home. Others of us simply love the way we feel when we are with people who speak so openly and so sincerely about what really matters to them. The friendships we make in Al-Anon are often extremely close and enduring. But most of us keep coming back because Al-Anon helps to keep us sane and serene, even in the midst of difficult challenges, as long as we continue to use the Twelve Steps to work on ourselves.

We change with every new moment of every day. Most of us come to meetings to make the most of all these changes in our lives, to experience them with the love and support of our friends in Al-Anon, and to grow in a positive, healthy direction.

We know that Al-Anon is not a magic shop that makes all our problems vanish so that we can live happily ever after. Rather, it is a program through which we learn to better cope with our problems, celebrate our joys and our triumphs, feel all of our feelings, and know that everything that happens—the happy and the sad alike—will eventually pass. Again and again in life, we will pass through periods of great difficulty and periods of serenity and confidence. Change can be just as painful after 20 years of recovery as it is for a newcomer.

The difference is that after 20 years, we know from our own experience that "this too shall pass." The pain will eventually ease.

Since there is no "arrival," no magical day on which we suddenly achieve serenity and live on forever free from stress or strain, most of us eventually learn to be patient. We find that we can trust the process of recovery to move us ever forward, even if it sometimes feels as if we're moving backwards. We learn from each experience, and over time we build quite a storehouse of wisdom as a result. Pain may hurt as much as ever, but as time passes, we can put that pain in context so that suffering no longer dominates our whole life. We can separate ourselves from our pain, so that pain—as well as happiness and every other emotion—becomes merely another vehicle for growth.

WHERE DOES THE AL-ANON JOURNEY BEGIN?

So where do we begin this monumental task of changing our lives? For most of us, it has already begun. By seeking out and reading this book, for example, we have demonstrated a willingness to change. Similarly, by attending Al-Anon meetings and talking to other members, we have put ourselves in a position in which change can happen, even if we doubt that change is possible.

In the beginning, and at each subsequent stage of recovery, our job is to do only what we *can* do. Sometimes that means bringing the body to a meeting and hoping the mind will follow. By acting on our willingness, we make room for a Power greater than ourselves to do for us what we cannot do for ourselves. We need only open the door to let the healing begin.

16

Twelve Traditions

GUIDELINES FOR WORKING, LIVING, AND GROWING TOGETHER

In an alcoholic environment, it is difficult to know what is expected. Rules are often unspoken but rigidly enforced. And those rules are likely to change at any moment, without warning, at the whim of the alcoholic. The result is an atmosphere of anxious confusion. We struggle to follow these impossible rules in order to please the alcoholic or at least to keep the peace, but when we can't keep pace with the sudden, unannounced changes, we fail. Thus, no matter how hard we try, we are always in the wrong, always subject to criticism.

That's why many of us are relieved to learn that no one in Al-Anon is standing over us, rule book in hand, waiting for errors. No one will tell us to leave if we don't work the program "correctly," if we say the "wrong" thing, or make the "wrong" decision. Al-Anon doesn't work that way.

The big surprise for most of us is that this nonjudgmental approach creates a peaceful, consistent organization. Nobody takes over and tells everyone else what to do. Yet the Al-Anon message continues to be conveyed, undiluted, in meeting after meeting, year after year, all over the world. The Twelve Traditions make this possible.

The Traditions are a set of guidelines that hold our program together. They advise us about how to avoid involving ourselves in anything that might interfere with our common interests, and they help us to remain focused on our purpose. They suggest ways to make group decisions that are in the best interest of all concerned and provide a structure that is based on spiritual principles. They keep the Al-Anon message consistent, unaltered by the latest trend in self-help books, therapies, talk shows, or philosophies.

Many of us have never learned how to get along harmoniously with others. We don't know how healthy families operate. We are surprised but grateful to find that these spiritual guidelines can also help in our personal lives. Just as they can provide unity within our meetings, they can help us have healthier, more positive relationships.

The Traditions work so well that the Al-Anon program has been there consistently to ease the suffering of families and friends of alcoholics since our beginning in 1951. The Traditions are suggestions, not rules. We, who have found serenity and a better way of life through recovery in Al-Anon, turn to the Traditions for guidance because we want that opportunity for recovery to continue to be available to us and to those who come after us. We observe the Traditions because they work. We refer to this as "obedience to the unenforceable," and our survival as an organization depends on it. Therefore, our individual recovery is as intimately bound to the guidance of the Twelve Traditions as it is to the Twelve Steps, and it is in our best interest to make them an important part of our lives.

It is as if we were shipwrecked on an uninhabited island and lacked the skills we needed to provide ourselves with food and shelter. If a set of instructions that guaranteed our survival descended from the sky, we would make it a high priority to follow those instructions. Likewise, for those of us whose lives have been torn apart by alcoholism, ensuring our survival as a fellowship by adhering to the Traditions is just as crucial.

TWELVE TRADITIONS

1. Our common welfare should come first; personal progress for the greatest number depends upon unity.
2. For our group purpose there is but one authority—a loving God as He may express Himself in our group conscience. Our leaders are but trusted servants—they do not govern.
3. The relatives of alcoholics, when gathered together for mutual aid, may call themselves an Al-Anon Family Group, provided that, as a group, they have no other affiliation. The only requirement for membership is that there be a problem of alcoholism in a relative or friend.

4. Each group should be autonomous, except in matters affecting another group or Al-Anon or AA as a whole.

5. Each Al-Anon Family Group has but one purpose: to help families of alcoholics. We do this by practicing the Twelve Steps of AA *ourselves*, by encouraging and understanding our alcoholic relatives, and by welcoming and giving comfort to families of alcoholics.

6. Our Family Groups ought never endorse, finance or lend our name to any outside enterprise, lest problems of money, property and prestige divert us from our primary spiritual aim. Although a separate entity, we should always co-operate with Alcoholics Anonymous.

7. Every group ought to be fully self-supporting, declining outside contributions.

8. Al-Anon Twelfth Step work should remain forever non-professional, but our service centers may employ special workers.

9. Our groups, as such, ought never be organized; but we may create service boards or committees directly responsible to those they serve.

10. The Al-Anon Family Groups have no opinion on outside issues; hence our name ought never be drawn into public controversy.

11. Our public relations policy is based on attraction rather than promotion; we need always maintain personal anonymity at the level of press, radio, films, and TV. We need guard with special care the anonymity of all AA members.

12. Anonymity is the spiritual foundation of all our Traditions, ever reminding us to place principles above personalities.

TRADITION ONE

Our common welfare should come first; personal progress for the greatest number depends upon unity.

For many of us, living with alcoholism was so disruptive and chaotic that it seemed to require ignoring our own needs or those of others. There was no middle ground or balance. There certainly was no unity.

When we first come to Al-Anon, no one else's problems seem as important or as pressing as our own. Our personal pain is all we are aware of, and our personal progress is all that matters. But as we keep coming back, we begin to gain some perspective on our troubles, and we find that in order to heal, we must concern ourselves with the needs of others.

This may seem a contradiction, since so much of our program is dedicated to learning how to focus on ourselves rather than on the alcoholics in our lives. But we do not exist in a vacuum, and in the long run we cannot heal by cutting ourselves off from others or by treating their needs as unimportant. Although our own well-being must be our top priority, there is nothing healthy or spiritual about complete self-absorption. In Al-Anon, we seek a balance. Because it is essential that we learn to interact with other people in a healthy way, the needs and concerns of others merit our attention. Our "common welfare" becomes a primary goal, assuring that we treat ourselves and those around us as equals. As we learn to treat others with respect and earn their respect, we begin to let go of an "us versus them" mentality and understand what unity means.

This becomes true in our personal lives as well as in our recovery program. In time, we see that our own recovery actually depends upon the well-being of our group and of Al-Anon as a whole. For our own sake, we must consider our common welfare.

Al-Anon's Declaration of Unity puts it this way: "Each member of the fellowship is a significant part of a great circle of hope. While respecting each other's individuality, our common welfare must come first. Our recovery depends on our mutual need and an atmosphere of trust." (Unanimous motion, 1984 World Service Conference)

This means that our personal agenda may have to take a back seat from time to time. For example, we may be going through a traumatic experience and have an urgent need to talk about it at length in a meeting. But because we are not the only ones who need to discuss what is on our minds, it may be best for all concerned if we limit the length of our sharing, at least until the meeting is over. At that point we are encouraged to find a more appropriate outlet—speaking at length with a Sponsor or fellow Al-Anon member—in order to express ourselves fully. This way, the well-being of the group is maintained and our personal needs are met.

When members are unified, meetings thrive. By learning to consider others, we remember that we are part of the human race. No longer alone, we gain the privileges and the responsibilities of belonging. Our personal problems, opinions, desires, plans, and feelings are very important, and we owe it to our group, as well as to ourselves, to express them when it is appropriate. But other people's interests are also important. We are part of a family, the Al-Anon family, and its vitality is in our hands.

TRADITION TWO

For our group purpose there is but one authority—a loving God as He may express Himself in our group conscience. Our leaders are but trusted servants—they do not govern.

Our enduring strength may lie in the fact that we are a fellowship of equals. No one member, regardless of education, political clout, or professional expertise, is any more valuable to the fellowship than any other member. We are all experts because of our experience, and we are all beginners because our lives are in a constant state of growth and change. Newcomers are as likely as longtime members to utter words that inspire and inform. So we have no reason to look to any one person or small group of people as authorities.

In fact, we recognize only one authority over our groups and our fellowship as a whole: a loving God of our understanding. We have seen that as individuals we cannot possibly contend with the effects of alcoholism without spiritual help. We turn to the same source of guidance in order to learn how best to work together toward our common goal of recovery. Just as many of us find a Power greater than ourselves in the collective wisdom of our Al-Anon group, we seek spiritual guidance for our groups in the same collective wisdom. We call this a "group conscience," the voice of the majority of members. We believe it represents the greatest good for the greatest number.

We reach this majority through discussion. In Al-Anon, each of us has an equally important voice. As members, we have an obligation to express that voice and to vote according to our convictions, even if we are the only ones who believe that idea. One dissenting person may point out something essential that no one else has considered. We are strengthened by our diversity, even when we disagree.

Ultimately, our leaders are subject to the will of the many—the will of the group. Their job is to serve, not to dominate; to carry out the decisions made by the group, not to make those decisions themselves.

When we use this Tradition in our personal lives, we learn to consider a loving God as the ultimate authority in all our interactions and in everything we do. We ask our Higher Power for willingness to seek what is best for everyone concerned, instead of for only one or two people. By actively listening with an open mind to everyone, and by withholding judgment until we have had an informed discussion, we learn reasonable ways to avoid or resolve conflict. We can look at any responsibilities we have in our lives as opportunities for serving others instead of trying to control them. We don't make decisions for others that are not our responsibility to make, trusting that their Higher Power is guiding each of them as we are guided.

TRADITION THREE

The relatives of alcoholics, when gathered together for mutual aid, may call themselves an Al-Anon Family Group, provided that, as a group, they have no other affiliation. The only requirement for membership is that there be a problem of alcoholism in a relative or friend.

Our goal as a fellowship is clear. We exist for the sole purpose of helping those affected by the family disease of alcoholism. Although we may find other common interests, develop a wonderful social life, and share philosophical views with other members, our only purpose as an organization is to come together for mutual aid—to help each other recover from the effects of another person's drinking. Even if everyone in our group feels strongly about a political cause, charitable function, religious philosophy, or another Twelve Step program, we cannot afford to affiliate ourselves with any outside cause. The Third Tradition assures us that the help we have found will continue to be available to anyone who seeks it, without its being diluted or altered by the latest trend or the views of a few members.

This Tradition refers to the "relatives of alcoholics." In this case, the word "relatives" designates not only those related by blood, but any of us who have had a relationship of some sort with an alcoholic. Regardless of personal creed, economic status, sexual orientation, or religious background, anyone who has been affected by another's drinking is welcome in our fellowship. There is no other requirement for membership.

Unlike most other organizations, membership in Al-Anon is strictly a personal matter. We are never asked to sign up, fill out forms, pay initiation fees, or meet another's qualifications for membership. We become members simply by choosing to attend.

It is not always easy for newcomers to know whether or not they belong. Many of us had to overcome years of denial before we even suspected that alcoholism existed in our families. All we knew at first was that we identified strongly with the feelings we heard expressed in meetings and that we felt at home. Without having been part of an Al-Anon group, we might never have realized that we had been affected by this disease. Had anyone demanded that we justify our participation in an Al-Anon group, we probably couldn't have done so. Fortunately, it is left to us to decide for ourselves in our own time whether or not we are qualified for membership. Thus, even if they feel uncertain about whether or not they are in the right place, newcomers are always welcome in Al-Anon.

Tradition Three can also help us in fulfilling our personal goals for recovery. Too often, many of us have felt directionless, easily distracted by the wants and needs of others. We tried to be all things to all people, and lost our own identity in the process. We focused so much on everyone else that when asked what activities we truly enjoyed, we were often left speechless. By applying this Tradition, we can gain a sense that we belong here, and that we deserve to control and guide our own lives.

TRADITION FOUR

Each group should be autonomous, except in matters affecting another group or Al-Anon or AA as a whole.

As newcomers, we are often encouraged to attend several different Al-Anon meetings because each meeting has its own atmosphere and its own personality. Meetings differ because each group is free to make many decisions for itself. Tradition Four grants freedom of choice to each individual group over when and where to meet and how to conduct its meetings.

One group may open the meeting by saying the Serenity Prayer, reading the Twelve Steps, and announcing the topic. Another group begins with introductions, reads various pieces of Al-Anon literature aloud, makes Al-Anon-related announcements, and proceeds with open sharing on any topic relating to alcoholism or its effects. A meeting may be held in early morning in a large auditorium or at night in a tiny church basement. Because each group is allowed such autonomy, the members themselves are free to create an atmosphere and a meeting agenda that will best suit the needs of the group.

The only restriction on this freedom is that the well-being of Al-Anon and A.A. must take precedence over the interests of any one group. As we saw in the First Tradition, our unity is essential to our survival as a fellowship. No group should make decisions that would detract from that unity.

Thus we refrain from discussing other Twelve Step groups, philosophies, or therapies in our meetings. Only Al-Anon materials are used at Al-Anon meetings. We do not impose this restriction to pass judgment on material produced by others, but because, by focusing exclusively on the Al-Anon philosophy in our meetings, we avoid a great deal of confusion. The Al-Anon principles form the basis of our recovery, and anything that undermines or confuses those principles can be detrimental to the program as a whole. As individuals, we are free to pursue anything and everything outside of the meeting that contributes to our health and well-being. We are encouraged to learn all we can about alcoholism. But as a group, we must remain clear about why we have come together and what we hope to accomplish.

On a personal level, Tradition Four reminds us that although we have a right to do what we believe is best for us, so do those around us. We need to be considerate of others and not infringe upon their freedom. With this understanding comes not only independence, but also mutual respect and dignity. It can be summarized by the slogan "Live and Let Live."

TRADITION FIVE

Each Al-Anon Family Group has but one purpose: to help families of alcoholics. We do this by practicing the Twelve Steps of AA ourselves, by encouraging and understanding our alcoholic relatives, and by welcoming and giving comfort to families of alcoholics.

The essence of all healing is love, and the Fifth Tradition demonstrates the loving nature of the Al-Anon program. In Al-Anon we learn to love ourselves as well as others. This often means changing both our attitudes and our behavior in all that we do everyday. It means putting an end to lingering hostilities and adopting an attitude of tolerance, courtesy, and appreciation in our daily interactions with family and friends.

This love is confirmed by our group's purpose—to help families and friends of alcoholics. We cannot accomplish this entirely at our meetings. While we learn about the Steps by listening to fellow members, we grow by practicing the Steps in our personal lives. We recover as we offer compassion to alcoholics and let others who need our program know what Al-Anon has to offer.

If we did not "practice these principles in all our affairs," we would notice the effect on our group. Wouldn't it be awful to attend an

Al-Anon meeting where everyone complained about the alcoholics, blaming them for all of our problems? Certainly, pent-up resentments need release, and Sponsors can be extremely helpful in working on those areas and putting them into perspective. But we don't come together to blame, criticize, and gossip. We come together to recover from the effects of alcoholism on ourselves. We learn that no one else is responsible for solving our problems or making us happy. That is our responsibility. The point is not what others can do to improve, but what we can do to improve. We take the Twelve Steps because we want to have rich, full, satisfying lives, and no one else can give that to us. Taking the Steps is an act of self-love.

Everyone deserves love—even those who have treated us badly. Holding on to blame and resentment hurts us far more than it hurts anyone else. Harboring ill feelings toward the alcoholics in our lives keeps us tied to an ongoing cycle of bitterness that can only make us feel miserable and victimized. Changed attitudes aid recovery. We can strive to understand the alcoholics, recognizing that they suffer from a disease that affects their thoughts and actions. Like any other human beings, they are doing their best with what they have, and they deserve our compassion and respect. Adopting this attitude may be the most generous gift we can give—to ourselves.

We also extend love to family, friends, and others who, like us, have been affected by another's drinking, carrying our message of hope and healing through the Twelve Steps. Our literature, public outreach materials, and public service announcements provide information to those who have been affected by another's alcoholism but are unaware that help is available. We also reach out to those families and friends of alcoholics who reside in hospitals and prisons, and we share our information with the medical and therapeutic community. We do not push our philosophy on those who are not interested. We simply and discreetly let it be known that there is help available to those who wish to pursue it.

There may be no better reminder of what we are attempting to achieve in Al-Anon than the painful struggle of someone who needs help with an alcoholic situation. Al-Anon exists for the sole purpose of helping such families and friends of alcoholics. Our groups carry out this purpose by giving a warm welcome to all newcomers and by giving love, comfort, and support to anyone who seeks it. We try to appreciate what a privilege it is to contribute to a fellow member's freedom from the desperation and despair that accompany alcoholism. When any one of us is healed, we all heal a little.

TRADITION SIX

Our Family Groups ought never endorse, finance or lend our name to any outside enterprise, lest problems of money, property and prestige divert us from our primary spiritual aim. Although a separate entity, we should always co-operate with Alcoholics Anonymous.

As private individuals, we are welcome to involve ourselves with any endeavor that interests us. There are many worthwhile causes that deserve our time and attention. Sometimes we are presented with opportunities for personal, material, political, or social gain that are too good to pass up. But as an Al-Anon group, we must avoid such involvement at all costs. Al-Anon's primary spiritual aim, helping families and friends of alcoholics, would be compromised should we affiliate ourselves in any way with even the most worthy outside causes, activities, or organizations.

This Tradition, however, should never be interpreted as an attempt to hold us back from providing the comfort and aid we exist to offer, or from carrying the Al-Anon message to those who need it. Activities such as sponsoring an Alateen function or making Al-Anon literature available to the public are appropriate because they support our primary purpose. Instead, the Sixth Tradition urges us to avoid activities or relationships that are potentially harmful— involvements that could interfere with our ability to help families and friends of alcoholics.

We do have a special relationship with one outside group: Alcoholics Anonymous. Although we are completely separate and unaffiliated with A.A., we owe a debt of gratitude to the program from which we adopted the Twelve Steps. We cooperate with A.A. in a variety of ways. For example, we might offer our Al-Anon experience, strength, and hope by serving as speakers at special A.A. meetings or conferences. Or we might share convention facilities or joint Al-Anon and A.A. information offices under certain conditions. The point is to graciously support the A.A. program when we can while maintaining our own distinct identity.

Tradition Six can also benefit us when applied personally. It reminds us to keep our serenity and spirituality as our first priorities. Rather than losing our focus with other distractions, we learn to put "First Things First." By taking an inventory of our motives, we can keep our lives balanced. We can share the benefits of Al-Anon by our own behavior toward family members, but we accept that not everyone will seek the help that we have found. This Tradition also reminds us that it is possible to cooperate with others while remaining true to our principles.

TRADITION SEVEN
Every group ought to be fully self-supporting, declining outside contributions.

Before Al-Anon, we often looked outside of ourselves for our peace of mind. If only the alcoholics in our lives would stop drinking, we would be okay. As we obsessed about them, we failed to look after ourselves.

In Al-Anon we learn to take responsibility for our own recovery rather than expecting others to do our work for us. With the help of our Higher Power and our fellow members, we realize we no longer need to look for inner contentment outside of ourselves. We begin to care for ourselves financially, emotionally, physically, and spiritually.

The idea of self-support found in Tradition Seven is essential to Al-Anon. It works within our personal lives and it works within our groups, Areas, and world service. Although there are no dues or fees for membership, Al-Anon is a self-supporting program.

Because we accept no outside funding, as members we are asked to participate in supporting our own groups as well as Al-Anon world services by contributing what we can. As we give, we gain a greater sense of belonging and responsibility for the health of our group.

Each group is urged to take responsibility for its own well-being. Basic to this is to be financially self-supporting. Even the most well-meaning offers of monetary support from outside Al-Anon can adversely affect our groups. By taking care of our own needs, we can remain free from outside influence. Our finances have no strings attached. This allows our groups to be independent, and we benefit by seeing that we are capable of meeting our own needs.

Each group is encouraged to designate a portion of its money to support Al-Anon at the local, Area, national, and international levels. Our contributions make it possible for local service offices and our World Service Office to provide information to anyone who wants to find an Al-Anon meeting in our area. The World Service Office also maintains an international meeting list so that wherever we travel, we are likely to be able to make contact with an Al-Anon group. Our monthly magazine, *The Forum,* could not exist without the support of our groups. Our donations enable Al-Anon's message to be carried to those in hospitals and prisons. They also make it possible for Al-Anon literature to be translated into more than 30 languages, allowing the comfort and wisdom of our program to be carried to millions of people all over the world. These are only a few of the many functions made possible by our contributions. Thus, when we support the service arms of our fellowship, we ensure that the Al-Anon message will continue to be available to anyone who needs it.

But financial support is only part of the story. As individual members, we support our groups through active participation. Al-Anon's literature and other materials are developed from the personal sharings of our members. These stories of experience, strength, and hope help to unify and sustain our fellowship, providing topics for discussion within meetings and food for thought between meetings.

Our groups are strengthened whenever we show up at meetings and share our experiences with one another. We offer support when we listen to a fellow Al-Anon member who needs to be heard and when we exchange ideas and encouragement. These are forms of Al-Anon service. Other forms of service, such as setting up chairs or serving as Group Secretary, are equally indispensable. Al-Anon survives and grows because of the involvement and commitment of its members at many levels—from the group to world service.

TRADITION EIGHT

Al-Anon Twelfth Step work should remain forever non-professional, but our service centers may employ special workers.

We do Twelfth Step work whenever we carry the Al-Anon message to others. As a fellowship of equals, we have a tremendous amount of experience, strength, and hope to share with one another, and with those outside our fellowship who still struggle with the effects of another's drinking. We, who know the loneliness and frustration of living with alcoholism, can provide an extraordinary form of help and support. As experts on living with alcoholism by virtue of our own experience, we help each other by sharing what we have felt and what we have learned rather than by giving advice. By sharing what we have learned with those who know little about our program but a great deal about the desperation of an alcoholic environment, we strengthen our own recovery while helping others. So, as a fellowship, we do not look to any professionals for our answers. We look to one another, under the guidance of a Power greater than ourselves.

But we are a huge, worldwide organization and we need the help of some full-time workers, experts in their own fields, in order to continue functioning efficiently. We are also subject to local and federal laws. Producing literature, maintaining communication with thousands of groups all over the world, keeping the books, and many other tasks require qualified workers. Paid employees are often necessary at the local or Area level as well, staffing the Literature Distribution Center (LDC) or operating an Al-Anon Information Service (AIS). These workers are guided by the Twelve Traditions and the

Twelve Concepts of Service explained in our *Service Manual*. Thus they, too, contribute to Al-Anon's unity and well-being.

Tradition Eight can also help us define clear boundaries between ourselves and the people in our personal lives. We no longer need to fix everyone else's problem by offering unsolicited advice. We help others by sharing who we are, not by acting as resident experts. As we follow Al-Anon principles, we do our best to set a good example, showing those around us that there is hope for a better life.

We also need to know when to draw the line in taking care of ourselves. We no longer expect to solve all our problems alone. We give ourselves permission to ask for help. Sometimes we can find this help from Al-Anon. We rely on professionals when it is necessary.

TRADITION NINE
Our groups, as such, ought never be organized; but we may create service boards or committees directly responsible to those they serve.

Our groups have a simple structure. We elect or appoint officers or ask for volunteers to chair meetings, make coffee, set out Al-Anon literature, and perform other activities essential to the smooth operation of the group. The informal, friendly atmosphere of our meetings allows our members to be themselves. Anyone and everyone in a group is welcome to give of themselves, reaching out to others in mutual aid, serving as an officer, or volunteering to help with special events.

For example, sometimes a group will undertake a project or celebration, such as a group's anniversary party or a special Al-Anon speakers' meeting, that requires planning and organization. Under such circumstances, members may form service boards or committees.

Our officers and committee members do not wield authority; they are here only to serve. Because of their generous contributions of time and energy, the group functions more smoothly. And those who serve the group also benefit, because every act of service is an act of love that shines upon the giver as well as the recipient.

Some branches of Al-Anon, such as the World Service Office and Al-Anon Information Services, function as Al-Anon's service arms. They tend to be structured in a more conventional, businesslike fashion in order to operate effectively. But their purpose is service; they have no power to direct or control the individual groups or members.

Tradition Nine encourages simplicity in the structure of our personal lives as well. We don't need to be overly rigid in defining rules to govern our behavior and the behavior of others. We attain order and balance in our lives more easily when we let others take responsibility for themselves, as we take responsibility for our own actions. Humility and gratitude will keep us from trying to control outcomes. While remaining sensitive to the needs of others, we can continue to focus on our own responsibility and "Let Go and Let God."

TRADITION TEN

The Al-Anon Family Groups have no opinion on outside issues; hence our name ought never be drawn into public controversy.

Arguments and conflicts are such a part of living with alcoholism that we often become embroiled in the middle of a fight without even knowing why. Frequent verbal (and even physical) attacks cause many of us to become very defensive.

In Al-Anon we learn not to overreact to the words and actions of others. While many of us discover for the first time that we actually have opinions of our own, we also realize that everyone else has just as much right to their opinions as we do to ours. We find there is a difference between a discussion and an argument. We need not convince anyone else that our opinion is right, and we avoid ridiculing or embarrassing others. When provoked, many of us have found that responding with "You may be right," "Thank you for your opinion—I'll consider that," or "I'll pray about that" have far more positive results than reacting with denial, defensiveness, or recrimination.

We often learn this personal application of Tradition Ten by first applying it at Al-Anon meetings, where people of widely different backgrounds, interests, and opinions join together for a single purpose. Our program is so universal in its appeal that members with diametrically opposed views can still find common ground. Tradition Ten suggests that, as a group, we focus on our common ground and avoid taking a stand on any other matters. Our attention belongs on what we can share rather than on what is bound to keep us apart.

It is essential that Al-Anon remain politically, socially, and philosophically neutral. Otherwise, we might alienate many of those we are here to help. There is room in our fellowship for members with every point of view. Taking sides would have to exclude somebody, and since every one of our members is important and worthy of our help and our respect, such an exclusion would be a great loss to us all.

Even if we come under criticism from those outside our program, we cannot afford to be lured into controversy. Just as we learn to stop reacting to an alcoholic's provocation, we need not react to anyone's opinions or prodding or be tempted to adopt a defensive or aggressive position. We must keep our focus on our primary purpose and not allow ourselves to become distracted.

TRADITION ELEVEN

Our public relations policy is based on attraction rather than promotion; we need always maintain personal anonymity at the level of press, radio, films, and TV. We need guard with special care the anonymity of all AA members.

It is important that those who need what Al-Anon offers have the opportunity to hear about us. Each of us has benefited from the accessibility of the Al-Anon program, and it is important that we remain visible and available to those who seek our help. So we carry Al-Anon's message of hope with the help of the press, through public service announcements on radio and television, and in our Al-Anon literature. On a personal level, we may share with others who have been affected by another's alcoholism how Al-Anon has helped us to rebuild our lives.

On the other hand, we are not here to sell ourselves to anyone; we are here to help one another to recover from the effects of alcoholism. So we allow our program to remain in the public eye, but instead of recruiting, preaching, or proselytizing, we apply the principle of attraction and let the success of this wonderful way of life speak for us.

Sometimes the best advertisement is a good example. By becoming more serene, we demonstrate that something marvelous is happening in our lives. When we handle problems with a new clarity and decisiveness, or when we lovingly detach from a situation that once would have filled us with despair, the change in us becomes apparent. When we find gratitude and even joy in small, everyday matters that previously would have escaped our attention, we serve as examples of the healing power of our program. Instead of preaching about what we feel Al-Anon could do for others, we let our actions speak for us, demonstrating how Al-Anon has helped us. As a result of our recovery, others may be attracted to Al-Anon because they want what we have. This is what we mean when we speak of attraction rather than promotion.

Naturally, many of us are excited about all that Al-Anon has done for us, and we may fervently wish to share this experience with others who have been affected by alcoholism. We have a great deal to share with those who wish to listen. At times we may even feel tempted to drag friends or relatives to our meetings because we think they need to hear what we are saying. But we can do more harm than good by trying to push others into coming to Al-Anon against their will. We must respect the rights of others to make choices for themselves.

We do try to let the public and the professional community know that we are here if needed, but we do so with care. We wouldn't want anyone to be discouraged from getting the help they need because they took a dislike to a particular personality who acted as a spokesperson. In a fellowship as diverse as ours, no one member could adequately represent us. So we maintain our anonymity when dealing with the media.

We are especially careful to preserve the anonymity of A.A. members. The stigma of alcoholism can ruin a reputation, even after the alcoholic has gotten sober. We wouldn't want to be responsible for anyone losing their job or their health insurance, for example, through our carelessness or gossiping. So when we speak of our Al-Anon experience, we make sure that it is *our* story, and not the alcoholic's, that we tell.

Applying the principles of this Tradition in our personal lives means that we do our best to model the Al-Anon way of life. When we are good examples to others, we present far more compelling reasons for them to respond positively than when we beg, coax, or nag. This approach is attraction, not promotion. We learn to speak for ourselves, but never presume to speak for anyone else. We respect the privacy of others and acknowledge their right to have their own ideas and grow at their own pace. Likewise, we acknowledge and fulfill our own right to do the same.

TRADITION TWELVE
Anonymity is the spiritual foundation of all our Traditions, ever reminding us to place principles above personalities.

Perhaps the single most important principle in Al-Anon is that concerning anonymity. Anonymity is our spiritual foundation because it is the basis of the trust that makes our program possible. We are able to attend Al-Anon meetings whenever and wherever we choose because we know that our privacy will be respected. No one will run to other members, friends, employers, or the press and report on intimate details of our personal lives. No one will tell an alcoholic spouse or loved one about our feelings or our plans. Unless each of us is free to share as openly as we like without fear that our words will be repeated, none of us can safely use the resources available to us in Al-Anon.

Although there are no enforcers in Al-Anon who will compel us to protect one another's anonymity, we have to trust that the information we disclose will be carefully guarded. We count on the "obedience to the unenforceable" on which all our Traditions depend. Otherwise we couldn't possibly attend.

By attending Al-Anon, some of us risk even more than hurt feelings or a bruised reputation. Those of us who deal with violent alcoholics put our physical safety on the line every time we walk into a meeting. Anonymity and confidentiality can sometimes be a matter of life and death.

We don't pick and choose whose anonymity we will respect and whose we will violate. Rather, we respect the privacy of every member. We refrain from mentioning the appearance of a celebrity in our home group, just as we keep quiet about an Al-Anon friend's latest problems or achievements if we learned about them in a meeting or in a confidential setting. Members expect that what they share with another member will be protected even if not disclosed within an actual meeting. This is one way in which we place principles above personalities.

There may always be certain Al-Anon members we dislike, and we may be tempted to judge their progress or discount their words. But a Power greater than ourselves can use anyone to communicate His or Her will for us, if we are willing to listen. If we let personalities interfere with our spiritual goals, we cheat ourselves out of important opportunities. If another member repeats information shared with them, we should remind them of this spiritual principle.

Personalities can also overcome Al-Anon principles when we place those we admire on a pedestal, relying on them instead of God for guidance. What would happen to our recovery if it depended completely upon one or two well-intentioned but fallible human beings—possibly a Sponsor or a member in a leadership role? It would fall apart the minute they disappointed us or violated our confidence in some way.

The spiritual principles underlying the Twelfth Tradition can be applied to any aspect of our lives and are not limited to what we do at our meetings. Anonymity teaches us humility. We are encouraged to act according to our own conscience rather than seeking the praise or attention of others. We do what we feel is right because it gives us a sense of satisfaction and self-esteem, not in order to gain applause. In fact, anonymous gestures can mark some of our greatest and most worthy accomplishments.

Even though done anonymously, these actions strengthen a positive self-image and identity.

Our recovery from the effects of alcoholism allows us to become more fully the men and women we are capable of being. As we grow, we learn to choose behavior that we can feel good about. When we commit ourselves to the spirit of anonymity, and to placing principles above personalities, we choose a path of personal integrity—we become people who keep confidences, refuse to gossip, and respect the privacy of all we encounter. We are living for a higher purpose, doing our best to follow the will of a Power greater than ourselves.

17

Twelve Concepts of Service

LEARNING AND GROWING AS WE CARRY THE MESSAGE

Early in our recovery we might jump at the chance to practice Step Twelve and try "to carry this message to others," even though we have only recently begun to work Step One. The pamphlets on the literature table at our meeting seem to have the names of family members and special friends written on the front pages. Wouldn't this be a perfect way to take Al-Anon home with us after the meeting? Putting the right pamphlet in the right place at the right time could solve all our problems. But even if we could convince our loved ones to read the material, it's another matter entirely for them to share our enthusiasm for recovery. Disappointed, we usually end up where we started—powerless and back at Step One.

Eventually, however, as we move through the Steps, we begin to change the way we conduct ourselves. As we focus on ourselves and change the things we can, we are no longer obsessed with what others are doing and how they react to us. We are surprised when friends and relatives begin to point out, "You seem so much more relaxed," and ask, "What's going on with you?" They respond positively to the way we are behaving and feeling. When we give them information to help answer their questions, they are often genuinely interested in what we tell them.

Although we might be compelled to try the Twelfth Step very early in our recovery, the urge to apply the Twelve Traditions to our lives usually takes longer. A few of us don't even like it when members read the Twelve Traditions during meetings. Principles such as "Our common welfare should come first" and "Personal progress for the greatest number depends upon unity" seem so far removed from the kind of interaction we are familiar with in our alcoholic families.

Kindness, patience, and trustworthiness on the part of dedicated Al-Anon members eventually lead us to take a closer look at how we can conduct ourselves differently in our relationships—within and outside of our meeting rooms. The trusted servants in our groups are those who volunteer to serve us in ways that earn our respect and appreciation. When we ask them in so many words how we can become more like them, they tell us it is easy. They say, "The secret is service," and let us know that if we volunteer, they will give us the help we need to become successful at whatever we need to do.

As we follow their suggestions and take on service positions, these trusted servants share that just as Al-Anon has guides for personal growth in the Twelve Steps and guides for group growth in the Twelve Traditions, it has guides for our growth through service in the Twelve Concepts of Service. These Concepts help us conduct the business of our worldwide fellowship using the same principles found in the Twelve Steps and Twelve Traditions. By using them, we can also enhance our personal recovery and our relationships with each other. Al-Anon's three Legacies, Recovery through the Steps, Unity through the Traditions, and Service through the Concepts, interconnect to create the foundation of our program.

Service work often involves making decisions that affect others. This is a challenge for many of us affected by alcoholism. Some of us leap to decisions without thinking things through. Others become paralyzed by fear and defer all actions to those around them, but complain loudly about their decisions. Some of us simply procrastinate until it is too late, thereby making decisions by not deciding.

Because the Concepts of Service show us healthy ways to work with others and make wise, constructive decisions, they can be very useful in situations at home and at work, as well as in Al-Anon service. Applying the Concepts to our personal lives helps us develop our leadership skills, take on responsibility with confidence, and find a better balance in our lives.

All of the Twelve Concepts connect to each other like the stories of a building. It is difficult to separate the Concepts without losing the basic strength and meaning they have as a unified structure. Just as reaching the 12th floor of a building requires that we climb up through the first 11 stories, so it is with the Concepts of Service.

The Twelve Concepts of Service make Al-Anon's continued existence possible by showing how Twelfth Step work can be carried throughout the world. By applying the Concepts, all members can learn to relate better to each other, to other groups, and to work with a greater sense of unity throughout the entire service structure to help carry Al-Anon's message to all those in need of it. These same Concepts can also help us relate better to our families, friends, coworkers, community, and people in general.

"The Steps show me how to love myself, the Traditions show me how to love others, and the Concepts show me how to love the world that I live in."—*Paths to Recovery*

TWELVE CONCEPTS OF SERVICE

1. The ultimate responsibility and authority for Al-Anon world services belongs to the Al-Anon groups.
2. The Al-Anon Family Groups have delegated complete administrative and operational authority to their Conference and its service arms.
3. The right of decision makes effective leadership possible.
4. Participation is the key to harmony.
5. The rights of appeal and petition protect minorities and insure that they be heard.
6. The Conference acknowledges the primary administrative responsibility of the Trustees.
7. The Trustees have legal rights while the rights of the Conference are traditional.
8. The Board of Trustees delegates full authority for routine management of Al-Anon Headquarters to its executive committees.
9. Good personal leadership at all service levels is a necessity. In the field of world service the Board of Trustees assumes the primary leadership.
10. Service responsibility is balanced by carefully defined service authority and double-headed management is avoided.

11. The World Service Office is composed of selected committees, executives and staff members.

12. The spiritual foundation for Al-Anon's world services is contained in the General Warranties of the Conference, Article 12 of the Charter.

GENERAL WARRANTIES OF THE CONFERENCE

In all proceedings the World Service Conference of Al-Anon shall observe the spirit of the Traditions:

1. that only sufficient operating funds, including an ample reserve, be its prudent financial principle;

2. that no Conference member shall be placed in unqualified authority over other members;

3. that all decisions be reached by discussion vote and whenever possible by unanimity;

4. that no Conference action ever be personally punitive or an incitement to public controversy;

5. that though the Conference serves Al-Anon it shall never perform any act of government; and that like the fellowship of Al-Anon Family Groups which it serves, it shall always remain democratic in thought and action.

CONCEPT ONE

The ultimate responsibility and authority for Al-Anon world services belongs to the Al-Anon groups.

When living with alcoholism, responsibility is often handled in extremes. We either take all the responsibility or we take none.

With the help of Al-Anon, we realize that we are ultimately responsible for our own serenity and our own happiness. We are responsible for taking care of ourselves physically, emotionally, and spiritually. We gradually learn to let go of our perception that we are ultimately responsible for other people, places, and things.

This same principle is also true for our worldwide fellowship. The Twelve Concepts, like the Twelve Steps and Twelve Traditions, give us permission to be responsible persons in our own lives. Furthermore, the Concepts guide us to apply spiritual principles in the service that sustains and nurtures our recovery program. The ultimate responsibility for its continued existence rests with our groups.

During its earliest days, the World Service Office (then known as the Clearing House) polled each group whenever a decision needed to be made. As Al-Anon grew, this process became unwieldy. Since 1961, the groups have exercised their ultimate responsibility and authority by selecting a Group Representative to help elect a Delegate to speak for all the groups in their Area (usually a state or province). Each group has equal responsibility and authority. If a group accepts responsibility by choosing and supporting a Group Representative, then it is in position to exercise its authority.

Because the groups are represented by their Area Delegates at the World Service Conference, the groups are no longer polled on every decision. However, they remain ultimately responsible for our fellowship. There are many decisions and actions for which groups are responsible. These include reaching out to the public and professionals within their communities, supporting their trusted servants, cooperating with other local Al-Anon groups, and communicating with the Al-Anon service arms that serve them.

As part of their responsibilities, groups cover expenses for their Group Representative to attend Area Assemblies. Likewise, groups contribute time and money to support the district and Area to ensure that by the attendance of these trusted servants, these voices can be heard at all levels of Al-Anon service, including the annual World Service Conference. Just as important, the groups provide the opportunities for their representatives to make announcements and to bring back information and reports to the meeting.

The idea behind Concept One, both in world service and in our personal lives, can be condensed as this: If something is important to us, we need to do our part—whatever we realistically can do—to make it happen.

CONCEPT TWO

The Al-Anon Family Groups have delegated complete administrative and operational authority to their Conference and its service arms.

Our wise founders were aware of our tendency to take on too much, too fast, and to hold on too tightly for too long. Therefore, just as Concept One reminds us we have responsibilities, Concept Two reiterates that we are not alone. We no longer have to try to do everything by ourselves. We learn that we can cooperate with others and delegate certain responsibilities, while still remaining ultimately responsible. As a broad example, it is our own responsibility that we do not starve to death. But that does not mean we have to prepare every bite of food ourselves.

One of the ways we learn healthy examples of delegating responsibility and authority is through what is known in Al-Anon as the "links of service." By a democratic process, the group selects a Group Representative. The Group Representatives in a district choose their District Representative, and the Group Representatives elect a Delegate who represents all of the groups in their Area at the annual World Service Conference. Each Delegate at the World Service Conference draws guidance from Tradition Two, "For our group purpose there is but one authority—a loving God as He may express Himself in our group conscience. Our leaders are but trusted servants; they do not govern."

When the World Service Conference convenes every spring, the attending Delegates represent the groups in all Areas throughout the United States, Canada, Bermuda, and Puerto Rico. The World Service Conference constitutes Al-Anon's largest group conscience. As individuals, all Conference members strive to apply the principles of Tradition One, "Our common welfare should come first; personal progress for the greatest number depends upon unity."

In a spirit of service to the groups they represent and out of a desire to maintain the unity of Al-Anon worldwide, the Delegates share responsibility with the Board of Trustees and administrative members of the World Service Office staff in order to direct Al-Anon's resources for the coming year. Without complete administrative and operational authority delegated by the groups, the World Service Conference would be unable to guide the business of Al-Anon.

CONCEPT THREE
The right of decision makes effective leadership possible.

Responsibility and authority go hand in hand. Realistically, there cannot be one without the other. If we delegate a task to someone, we also need to give them the authority to do their best without our constant interference. This requires trust that the other person is fully capable. When we give others the freedom to exercise judgment without criticism, we help them develop dignity, confidence, and trust in themselves.

We need to be as clear as possible when we delegate a task to someone, especially if we have specific expectations. If we send someone to the store for bread, and have in mind that we want whole wheat bread, it is important for us to communicate this. If we are not specific, we have no right to criticize if we receive pumpernickel instead.

A combination of trust and freedom is at the heart of Concept Three. Before Al-Anon's leaders prepare to deal with important issues at district meetings, Area Assemblies, and the World Service Conference, our groups often conduct group conscience meetings to provide input. The Group Representative, in turn, shares the results of these group discussions with the other Group Representatives and the District Representative for possible presentation at the next Area Assembly.

The groups trust their leaders and share their points of view with them. They also give their leaders the freedom to consider new information and to exercise their best judgment when the time comes to vote.

Trust is what empowers our leaders to do their work. It not only builds confidence at all levels of service, but it also inspires our leaders to treat their role as a privilege, not as permission to wield power just for the sake of power.

If leaders knowingly abuse the trust that their groups give them, the group conscience that advises and supports them can also remove them. Our leaders are always accountable to those they serve, but as long as our world services function reasonably well, our leaders deserve the trust that will continue to help them do a good job.

CONCEPT FOUR
Participation is the key to harmony.

For many of us, participation is not the key to harmony in an alcoholic home. Involving ourselves in actions or discussions usually leads to conflict and discord. As a result, some of us learn to pick fights, while others isolate and stuff our feelings.

Through Al-Anon, however, we discover new ways to participate and be a part of the world around us, rather than be apart from it. Just as Concept Three encourages mutual trust, Concept Four concerns mutual respect. When we honestly respect ourselves and those around us, we begin to look at everyone as equals—not as our inferiors or superiors. Without this respect, participation can be the key to chaos.

Participation is not the same as interference. It is not an excuse to meddle. We learn to offer our help rather than insist that we know best. If our time, energies, or opinions are not invited, we gracefully allow others the right to handle things in their own way. When we ask others to do a job, even in our homes, we learn to release our desire to either micromanage or take the job back if it isn't being done the way we would do it.

In the ongoing growth and development of the worldwide fellowship of Al-Anon Family Groups, all of us have a part to play. Participation usually begins when we regularly attend the meeting we come to think of as our home group and share our experience, strength, and hope.

We participate whenever we are asked to perform Al-Anon service work, help choose and support the Group Representative, make contributions, or share our opinions.

What Concept Four does not do is give us permission to intrude on another person's area of responsibility. Members who are already in positions to serve the group deserve our support, encouragement, and trust. We may offer our assistance beyond our own level of responsibility, but our participation depends on whether our offer to help has been accepted. Participation is essential, but it is helpful to remember that the goal is harmony, not dominance.

CONCEPT FIVE
The rights of appeal and petition protect minorities and insure that they be heard.

Whenever we have a decision to make, it is important to remain open-minded. Brilliant suggestions can come from the least likely of sources. If, in practicing the earlier Concepts, we have developed trust and respect toward those around us, we will want to hear them out before making up our mind on any issue. This does not mean we instantly change our minds in an effort to people-please, merely that we want to hear all sides of an issue.

Likewise, if we share a contrary opinion, we have learned in Al-Anon the difference between expressing ourselves and trying to control others. If we keep saying the same thing again and again, instead of saying it once and letting it go, we are probably attempting to control.

This remains as true when we take an informed group conscience in Al-Anon as much as it does when we make decisions in our personal or work lives. The majority isn't necessarily always right. What if a key piece of information is missing? A slight shift in perspective might help the majority find a solution that would be good for all concerned. We need to insure that the minority voice will always be heard, not just to protect individuals who have differing opinions, but also for the good of Al-Anon as a whole.

Minority opinions are not always strong or vocal. Often they can be timid and shy, lacking the confidence and sense of safety that comes when numbers of people agree on a position or point of view.

It is for everyone's benefit that we encourage anyone with a minority opinion to speak up.

Tyranny, however, is not an option whether by the majority or a minority. Once the minority has been respectfully heard, the body may or may not choose to reconsider the issue at hand. Having been heard, the group conscience is accepted and supported by all involved, regardless of the final decision.

The purpose of Concept Five is to ensure access to everyone's ideas so that all decisions are based on the best information available.

CONCEPT SIX
The Conference acknowledges the primary administrative responsibility of the Trustees.

Concept Six is about shared leadership. It can pertain to any relationship in which we cannot accomplish everything alone. Rather than become exhausted in futile attempts to do it all, as we might have done in the past, we learn to cooperate. We apply the principles of delegation, authority, and responsibility.

In working together, balancing leadership is a necessity. We also attain a balance of resources. Communication is also a priority, so that everyone is fully aware of the progress, or lack of it, that we are making. At home, if we give someone a job, we can expect to receive information about the progress made.

As we apply Concept Six to world services, the need for shared leadership between the World Service Conference and the Trustees becomes obvious. The primary responsibility of the Conference is to provide Al-Anon as a whole with guiding principles and a sense of direction. It would be impossible in a one week annual meeting for the Conference to involve itself in all of the administrative duties of the World Service Office or Al-Anon services worldwide. Therefore administrative oversight of the World Service Office is delegated to the Board of Trustees, which meets quarterly.

Trustees report back to the Conference, but that doesn't mean they have to ask permission before taking action. In keeping with the delegated responsibility found in this Concept, the Board will know when to consult and when to act. The same principle applies to every level of service, as well as in our personal lives, when we are clear in the delegation of responsibility as to what outcomes are to be realized.

CONCEPT SEVEN
The Trustees have legal rights while the rights of the Conference are traditional.

Concept Seven further defines the responsibilities, authorities, and delegation required for us to achieve all we want to in a realistic, reasonable manner. We all have needs, hopes, plans, and dreams, but living in a real world, we also have legal and financial responsibilities.

This Concept can be easily applied to the different members in a family. Everyone in the family has a role and a responsibility, and these are accepted and observed in our daily lives. While all family members are equally important, and all but the youngest of children have their own responsibilities, the parents or adult guardians are the ones who sign the mortgage papers and make sure the bills are paid. They are also held legally accountable for the actions of the family as a whole.

On a world service level, Concept Seven clearly describes the difference between the World Service Conference and the Board of Trustees. The Conference is Al-Anon's largest group conscience, guardians of our spiritual principles in the Twelve Traditions and the Twelve Concepts of Service. The Board, on the other hand, constitutes the legal entity of Al-Anon and is ultimately responsible for Al-Anon's funds, services, our adherence to the law, and the necessity to protect Al-Anon's resources by taking legal action if required.

Rarely does the Board of Trustees find itself in the position of countermanding the will of the Conference. This right is never invoked without serious consideration of the consequences for the Conference and the Al-Anon fellowship.

Our spiritual democracy is maintained by the shared relationship between the traditional rights of the Conference and the legal rights of the Board.

CONCEPT EIGHT

The Board of Trustees delegates full authority for routine
management of Al-Anon Headquarters
to its executive committees.

Due to problems with responsibility and trust, many of us learned in dealing with alcoholism that, "If you want a job done right, you have to do it yourself." Concept Eight gives us a further reminder that there is an easier way, but it requires us to let go of some of our control. When we match various responsibilities in our lives with people who have the skill and experience to carry them out, it becomes easier to pass on a job and not bear the entire load ourselves.

This is also the case in our efforts to do Twelfth Step work on a worldwide level. Just as the groups have done in Concept Two, and the Conference has done in Concept Six, in Concept Eight the Board acknowledges that it can't do everything, either. It delegates some things to an Executive Committee. This Committee meets to oversee the operations of the World Service Office, so that the Board can focus on the larger picture and not get lost in the details.

Concept Eight reflects the growth of Al-Anon as a fellowship and a corporation, as well as the practical need for delegation of authority over day-to-day operations. Early in Al-Anon's development, volunteers were used for a variety of duties. Their success and Al-Anon's expansion inevitably led to the current situation where it is no longer feasible for a volunteer group to do all of the work. Trustees continue to be volunteers, while paid employees work full-time to answer phones, provide information, produce and disseminate literature, and provide many other services that are needed.

The daily concerns, issues, and functions of the World Service Office require the hands-on leadership of an Executive Director. As a member of the Executive Committee, the Executive Director is instrumental in setting priorities for day-to-day operations. The Executive Director oversees the staff in carrying out the work that is necessary to accomplish the Conference's and Board's priorities with Executive Committee oversight. In turn, the Executive Committee reports to the Board of Trustees, which is ultimately responsible for the finances, services, and legal obligations of Al-Anon Family Group Headquarters, Inc. on behalf of the fellowship.

CONCEPT NINE

Good personal leadership at all service levels is a necessity. In the field of world service the Board of Trustees assumes the primary leadership.

Whether we consider ourselves leaders or not, we can all embody leadership qualities in our actions. These qualities include responsibility, tolerance, stability, flexibility, judgment, and vision. They reflect confidence, patience, dependability, and wisdom. These are qualities we all strive for as we practice the Al-Anon program. When we demonstrate these qualities, we inspire them in others.

At home or work, when we demonstrate good leadership skills, the family or the staff benefits. If we power drive a decision based on our self-will, no one benefits and we are once again isolated and alone.

Nevertheless, Al-Anon encourages "Progress Not Perfection." We don't have to be talented in all these areas at once. There are different talents for different jobs. As we grow in Al-Anon, we often find that we have cultivated leadership skills without even knowing it. We can apply them to our personal lives as well as to our service responsibilities.

All of us in Al-Anon have opportunities to be leaders. Good personal leadership might be just what it takes to lead a potential member to recovery—not by promotion or pressure, but by example. We might be the only example of Al-Anon that a nonmember ever sees. What we say and do to show respect for them and ourselves might inspire the relatives or friends of an alcoholic to try a new way of life.

The Board of Trustees represents Al-Anon to the world at large and sets the direction for our World Service Office. It is absolutely essential that Board members exemplify the finest leadership qualities to be found in our fellowship.

CONCEPT TEN
Service responsibility is balanced by carefully defined service authority and double-headed management is avoided.

Whether we are practicing Concept Ten in our service roles or in our daily lives, our actions are the same. We no longer presume that we are required to carry the full load by ourselves. We set clear goals for any project and trust everyone involved to accomplish them. Whether we assign or accept a task, if we intend the job to be successful, it is important that the one doing the work understands what is required in order to be responsible and accountable. It is also essential that everyone is clear about what our responsibilities include and don't include.

Carefully defined service authority can help to prevent us from taking over, which can erode the confidence and effectiveness of other people. When we designate both the responsibility and the authority required to perform a task, we make it possible for others to decide the best way to get the job done and to be successful. It also prevents the wasted resources and conflicts that will inevitably occur from double-headed management—when two people or groups of people are doing the same task without communicating with each other.

CONCEPT ELEVEN
The World Service Office is composed of selected committees, executives and staff members.

Concept Eleven is about partnership and collaboration. The spiritual principle it embodies is that we are not alone and that we do not need to work in isolation. It reflects our collective experience, which has shown us that with mutual trust, respect for each other, and dedication to a common goal, we can achieve amazing results.

At the World Service Office, partnerships and cooperation abound. Paid and unpaid workers share responsibilities and offer insights for extending the hand of Al-Anon and Alateen as effectively and efficiently as possible to families and friends of alcoholics throughout the world.

The mix of volunteers, committees, executives, and staff members embodies the diversity of the fellowship and exemplifies the equal voice that each Al-Anon member brings to their individual Al-Anon family group. The same spiritual principles that guide personal recovery from alcoholism also direct the business practices of Al-Anon. Whether applied to Al-Anon service or our personal lives, these principles help us work and live in harmony with each other.

There is no difference between good spiritual practice and good business practice. As our cofounder Lois W. said, "I don't think there is a spiritual part of the program. I think Al-Anon is a spiritual program. Every activity can have a spiritual motive."

CONCEPT TWELVE
The spiritual foundation for Al-Anon's world services is contained in the General Warranties of the Conference, Article 12 of the Charter.

GENERAL WARRANTIES OF THE CONFERENCE
In all proceedings the World Service Conference of Al-Anon shall observe the spirit of the Traditions:
1. that only sufficient operating funds, including an ample reserve, be its prudent financial principle;
2. that no Conference member shall be placed in unqualified authority over other members;
3. that all decisions be reached by discussion vote and whenever possible by unanimity;
4. that no Conference action ever be personally punitive or an incitement to public controversy;
5. that though the Conference serves Al-Anon it shall never perform any act of government; and that like the fellowship of

Al-Anon Family Groups which it serves, it shall always remain democratic in thought and action.

Wealth, prestige, and power can be obstacles to spiritual growth, so our founders created the General Warranties of the Conference to offset them. The Warranties reinforce the principles as developed in the Twelve Traditions and the Twelve Concepts of Service. They show how to apply Al-Anon's principles in matters of finance, personal authority, and decision-making, without resorting to personal punishment or public controversy. They call for Al-Anon members—and Al-Anon's world services—to operate in democratic ways that are compatible with our highest view of ourselves as members of Al-Anon.

The Warranties are about prudence. Prudence is not tightfistedness or fear. It is the ability to apply skill and good judgment in the use of resources. It requires balance. When we acquire balance in personal relations, money matters, and in our contact with the world, we are acting prudently.

Concept Twelve shows that there is no difference between who we are as Al-Anon members and what we do as an organization. There is no double standard. There are no special circumstances that call for a suspension of our ideals. We are not to act one way with the alcoholic and another way with the rest of the world. To the best of our abilities, we practice the Al-Anon principles in every aspect of our lives.

18

Al-Anon's History

The marvelous thing about Al-Anon is that it was founded by people just like us, people who struggled with the pain and isolation of involvement with an alcoholic, people who needed help. Certainly, Al-Anon's pioneers gave of themselves with great courage and generosity. Without their dedication and hard work, our program would not exist, and we remember them with a gratitude that extends beyond words. But when we acknowledge the contributions made by Al-Anon's founders, we look to the examples they themselves have set. What better legacy could we receive than the knowledge that ordinary men and women like ourselves can truly make a difference?

When Alcoholics Anonymous began in 1935, almost nothing was known about the effects of alcoholism on anyone other than the alcoholic. A.A.'s cofounders, Bill W. and Dr. Bob S., were not experts on alcoholism, they were men in the grip of the disease who came together to help one another stay sober. Like so many other family members, the wives of these men, Lois W. and Annie S., had done everything they could think of to get their husbands to stop drinking, but to no avail.

Lois, in fact, had been advised to give up. Her husband, she was told, was a hopeless alcoholic who would surely die or be institutionalized as a result of his drinking. But when Ebby T., a dear friend of Bill's who was also an alcoholic, miraculously found sobriety, both Bill and Lois had reason to hope. Bill's friend had found help through the Oxford Group, a Christian movement with which Bill and Lois soon became involved in New York. In Akron, a city southeast of Cleveland, Ohio, Annie S. persuaded her husband to join this same spiritual movement that had a reputation for helping alcoholics. Although neither Bill nor Dr. Bob embraced every aspect of the Oxford Group and although both eventually left the movement, many of the spiritual principles of A.A. and Al-Anon are based upon the tenets of the Oxford Group.

Lois attended these meetings with her husband but gave little thought to applying the spiritual principles to her own life. As far as she was concerned, her life would be fine if Bill could maintain sobriety. To her dismay, Bill's sobriety didn't bring Lois the happiness she expected. After playing a central role in his life during the drinking years, she felt that in sobriety he no longer needed her. Like so many of us, Lois became increasingly resentful and full of self-pity. Her house was filled with displaced alcoholics her husband brought home, and he spent more time with them than he spent with her! When she hurled a shoe at Bill in the heat of an argument, Lois realized that her own life was out of control. She needed help, the same kind of spiritual help that her husband had found, first in the Oxford Group, and subsequently in the Twelve Steps.

Lois wasn't alone in this discovery. Other wives of alcoholics were expressing frustration and confusion through their letters to A.A.'s magazine, *The A.A. Grapevine.* At the time, it was customary for wives to accompany their alcoholic husbands to A.A. meetings and take charge of refreshments. (In those days, most A.A. members were men.) All across the country, wives would congregate in kitchens or anterooms and talk about their common experiences and common problems.

We owe a tremendous debt of gratitude to Alcoholics Anonymous, from which much of our program was derived. When A.A.'s "Big Book," *Alcoholics Anonymous*, was published in 1939, many wives of recovering alcoholics read about A.A.'s spiritual principles and began discussing them with one another. As they witnessed the remarkable impact A.A.'s Twelve Steps were having on their spouses, these women wondered whether the same Steps might benefit them. Those who had tried to apply the Steps to their own lives by themselves had made only limited progress, since all they knew about the Steps came from alcoholics who were trying to stay sober. They didn't understand their own reactions to another's alcoholism, or how the disease could continue to affect their lives even after their spouses had found sobriety. So, in cities across the nation, women began to meet in their homes to study A.A.'s Twelve Steps. These informal gatherings were the forerunners of Al-Anon meetings.

The original Family Groups were linked together for the first time in 1950, when one enterprising wife created *The San Francisco Family Club Chronicle*. This magazine, which included editorials, correspondence from families of alcoholics, and inspirational quotations from a wide variety of philosophers, would later be known as *The Family Forum* and subsequently, *The Forum*. Within a year, its pumpkin-colored pages connected the Family Groups not only across the U.S., but as far away as Australia and South Africa.

The need was great to come together in fellowship and to discuss how A.A. principles might be adapted and applied to the lives of other family members. But it was still not clear whether these groups existed primarily to help the alcoholics or to seek recovery for their own members, and much debate ensued. A.A. encouraged family participation, and family members who were finding help in these groups began telling others about their experiences. Wives of actively drinking alcoholics began to learn about the family groups and as time passed, the membership grew to include men, adult children of alcoholics, parents, and others with various relationships to alcoholics. Soon, groups calling themselves "Non-Alcoholics Anonymous" or A.A. Auxiliaries were springing up at an astonishing rate.

During this time, Lois and Bill traveled all over the world to speak to A.A. groups and they found Family Groups forming everywhere they went. In 1950, Bill suggested to Lois that she open a service office through which all these groups could register, communicate with each other, receive literature, and become more unified. This office could also provide the public and the professional community with information about the effects of alcoholism. And it could be a source of comfort and strength to which confused and despairing relatives and friends of alcoholics could reach out for help. At first, Lois wasn't interested. A few years earlier, after 33 years of marriage, she and Bill had finally purchased their first home, "Stepping Stones," and Lois had more domestic plans in mind for her immediate future. But the need for such an office was great, and as time passed, the idea sounded more and more appealing. After speaking with the wives of A.A. Delegates to the 1951 A.A. General Service Conference, Lois decided to take on the project. The result was the formation of the Al-Anon Clearing House, later incorporated as Al-Anon Family Group Headquarters, Inc. and subsequently known to the fellowship as the World Service Office for Al-Anon and Alateen.

Leaning upon each other because there was no one else in the beginning, Lois and her friend, Anne B., the founder of Westchester County's first Family Group, began working together to respond to the correspondence that was pouring into A.A.'s Alcoholic Foundation. Anne, a painfully shy woman, began seeking recovery with other wives of alcoholics when she realized that fear dominated her life, fear that was intensified by living with an actively drinking alcoholic. Anne's involvement with this fledgling Family Group and her commitment to the Twelve Steps helped to release her from a lifetime of this nearly incapacitating fear and inspired her to become Lois's "Little Man Friday" in Al-Anon's early days.

Lois and Anne rented a post office box and worked in the second floor study at Stepping Stones. Contacting each of the 87 groups registered with A.A., they suggested coming together as a single fellowship. Their letter sought suggestions regarding a name for the organization and requested the groups' permission to adopt the Twelve Steps of A.A. The vast majority responded enthusiastically, and the name "Al-Anon," a contraction of "Alcoholics Anonymous," was soon chosen.

A.A.'s Twelve Steps were adopted, word for word, with the exception of the Twelfth Step. Since Al-Anon's purpose was to help friends and family members of alcoholics rather than to help alcoholics achieve sobriety, the Twelfth Step was altered so that it spoke of carrying the Al-Anon message to "others" rather than to "alcoholics." This single word change helped to give Al-Anon its own purpose and laid the groundwork for a later adaptation of the Twelve Traditions of A.A.

Al-Anon's founders knew from A.A.'s example that some guidelines would be essential to maintain unity and stability. Lois wrote asking for input from the groups and outlined Al-Anon's commitment to anonymity. The Traditions went through four drafts before being approved for adoption by the A.A. General Service Conference in 1955 and subsequently accepted by Al-Anon at its first trial World Service Conference in 1961.

There was an immediate need for literature that answered frequently-asked questions and clarified Al-Anon's principles. With guidance from Bill, Lois and Anne wrote *Purposes and Suggestions for Al-Anon Family Groups*, a pamphlet that emphasized the importance of focusing on oneself in meetings and cautioned against gossip and complaining about the alcoholic. Their first effort at a hardbound book, *Al-Anon Family Groups*, appeared in 1955.

Correspondence rapidly increased in volume. More help and more office space were needed to keep up with the demand. Unsolicited donations that trickled in from time to time helped Lois and Anne to open a tiny office. On January 9, 1952, the newly-named Al-Anon Family Groups moved into a second floor loft in the Old A.A. Clubhouse in New York City. It soon became affectionately known as "Lois's icebox" in the winter and "Lois's sweatshop" in the summer because of the conditions the early volunteers endured while trying to meet the needs of this young organization. Although short on money, furniture, and supplies, they were the proud owners of a two-drawer filing cabinet and a half share in a mimeograph machine.

A small group of dedicated volunteers made it possible for this tiny operation to grow and to flourish. Some of these men and women came to play a prominent role in Al-Anon's later history, such as Margaret D. who served as editor of *The Forum* for 20 years, and Henrietta S., Al-Anon's first General Secretary. Before holding that position, Henrietta became Al-Anon's first paid worker in 1953, receiving a scant $35 for three full days of work each week.

Lois and Anne had personally financed the initial expenses of the Clearing House, but they couldn't continue to do so indefinitely. Letters requesting financial support for the office received a mixed response. Some groups responded enthusiastically, while others, having established their own local area network upon which they relied for information and unity, declined. Money continued to be tight. Volunteers saved wrapping paper and string to cut down on mailing costs. One member "donated" typing paper from her employer's office. Lois saved the cardboard that came with Bill's shirts when they came back from the cleaners to use in packaging literature orders! Yet there was always enough money to keep going for another day.

More and more Family Groups were started as people noticed the changes in friends and family members who were finding serenity and sanity in Al-Anon and wondered how they could make such changes in their own lives. As membership grew, Al-Anon head-quarters adjusted accordingly, moving to larger and larger spaces and hiring paid professional staff to keep up with the ever-growing needs of the fellowship. Individual groups recognized the impor-tance of their individual contributions, and literature sales added to the organization's relative financial stability. But fiscal concerns have always been part of Al-Anon's history and continue to force cutbacks and changes, especially in the difficult economic times of the 1990's.

Committees were required to oversee Al-Anon's various special services, including literature, budget, policy, and publicity. Local Al-Anon Information Service offices were later established to dis-seminate local Al-Anon meeting information and to handle inqui-ries from friends and family members of alcoholics who reached out to Al-Anon for help. Anne and the volunteers compiled a *World Directory* so that Al-Anon's help could be found almost anywhere in the world. Today, the *World Directory* is accessed through a toll-free telephone number, further assisting all who need Al-Anon to find a meeting wherever they may travel. From 87 original groups, Al-Anon has grown to many thousands of groups meeting in over 130 countries around the world.

In the early years, Anne B. became chairman of the Prison Groups Committee, forerunner of the Institutions Committee. Even in those days, making information available to those who didn't know how to find help was a critical aspect of Al-Anon's existence. Like many of us, Anne was quite shy and had difficulty speaking in public. Yet because of this ordinary woman's extraordinary efforts, many thou-sands of relatives of alcoholics found help and personal growth in

Al-Anon and, when the whole family situation improved, many of the alcoholics found it possible to achieve and maintain sobriety.

The need for literature far exceeded Lois and Anne's ability to produce it in those early days, so they often recommended the writings of others, including Norman Vincent Peale and Dale Carnegie. A.A.'s "Big Book" was an important source of information to early Al-Anon groups. Some of the Al-Anon pamphlets still in use today were written by non-members. *So You Love an Alcoholic* was developed by the Texas Commission on Alcoholism. *Alcoholism, a Merry-Go-Round Named Denial* and *A Guide for the Family of the Alcoholic*, were written by a good friend and advocate of Al-Anon, the Reverend Joseph Kellermann, the former director of the Charlotte, North Carolina Council on Alcoholism. Local Al-Anon groups also developed their own literature. *Freedom from Despair*, for example, was created by the San Diego Family Group. But the vast majority of the literature was developed by Al-Anon's Literature Committee. *One Day at a Time in Al-Anon (ODAT)*, was written in the late 1960's by a self-taught writer, Alice B., the youthful, 72-year-old chairman of Al-Anon's Literature Committee. This extraordinary daily reader became a favorite of members worldwide and has been translated into 28 languages.

But some of the literature was inconsistent with Al-Anon's Traditions, approaching the family disease from a religious or political slant. The need for a unified literature policy became apparent and led, in 1963, to the adoption of a Conference Approval process by which literature that consistently reflects Al-Anon principles is developed.

Today, Al-Anon's body of literature continues to expand to meet the needs of a growing membership in a changing world. Our books and pamphlets, such as *From Survival to Recovery: Growing Up in an Alcoholic Home, Living with Sobriety, ...In All Our Affairs*, and *As We Understood...*, are compiled by Al-Anon's Literature Service from the personal thoughts and experiences of our members.

In 1957, a California teenager named Bob was the subject of an article in the *AA Grapevine*. Bob, whose father was in A.A. and whose mother was in Al-Anon, had struggled unsuccessfully with problems of his own until his parents urged him to apply the principles of their programs to his life. Alateen began when Bob joined with five other young people who had been affected by the alcoholism of a family member. Bob and Bill M., an A.A. member and prime mover in the establishment of Alateen, kept in close touch with Lois, who urged the newly forming groups to immediately adopt Al-Anon's Twelve Steps and Twelve Traditions. Typically, these groups were sponsored by an Al-Anon member who provided structure and support while allowing the Alateens to run their own meetings. The Alateen Committee, formed in 1959, sent a questionnaire to each Alateen group and published the results, outlining Alateen's policies on membership, the function of an Alateen group's Al-Anon Sponsor, funding, and other such matters. Like Al-Anon, Alateen grew rapidly, despite fluctuations in membership due to competing interests, summer vacations, and inconsistencies inherent in teenage lifestyles. Magazine articles brought national publicity and inquiries about help for youngsters. In time, Alateen began publishing its own literature, releasing the hardcover book, *Alateen—Hope for Children of Alcoholics* in 1973. Regional conventions continue to unify and spark the enthusiasm of Alateen members.

Although Al-Anon literature developed first in the U.S., it addressed a universal need. In the 1960's, members voluntarily began translating Al-Anon literature into the languages of other countries, and Al-Anon groups began to appear in all corners of the earth.

The forerunner of today's Lone Member Service was started by an Al-Anon member through a publication originally known as *World Hello*. This publication made it possible for Al-Anon members to have "Al-Anon meetings by mail" in communities where no meetings existed or where members were physically unable to attend meetings. A similar service for inmates was started in 1991 by the Institutions Service of the World Service Office.

In order to achieve a wider group conscience, a trial World Service Conference met in 1961. Representing Al-Anon membership as a whole, the Conference sought to focus on mainstream Al-Anon experience and to keep the program unified and on course. So successful was the experience that the Conference became a permanent institution, charged with guarding the Traditions and overseeing Al-Anon policies.

With an annual budget in the millions of dollars, Al-Anon's World Service Office supports a salaried staff, many of whom are Al-Anon members. These members oversee each activity, including reaching out to the public and professionals, development of Conference Approved Literature, archiving historic materials, connecting lone members, producing *The Forum*, providing support for groups and electronic meetings, planning the annual World Service Conference, coordinating with General Service Offices throughout the world, and providing Alateen services. Volunteers continue to play a vital role, serving as Trustees, committee members, and Delegates, answering phone calls, assembling literature packets, and generally keeping Al-Anon operating.

Al-Anon may not look the same as it did in 1951, but its purpose hasn't changed. We exist to offer help, comfort, strength, and information to those whose lives have been affected by the disease of alcoholism in a relative or friend. No matter how large our organization grows, we are committed to making sure that each person who comes in contact with Al-Anon receives the same individual, personal attention that they received when only a handful of Family Groups existed. When we look back to the dedicated pioneers who gave so generously of themselves, we see men and women just like us, the men and women who create Al-Anon's future.

PART TWO

AL-ANON

EXPERIENCES

Sharings of experience, strength, and hope

These sharings reflect the combined experiences of the men and women all over the world, from all walks of life, who have found help and hope in Al-Anon. We begin with the story of one of Al-Anon's founders, Lois W.

1

Lois's Story

Bill started drinking shortly before we were married, and although I didn't realize it then, he was an alcoholic from the very beginning. When he took one drink, he couldn't seem to stop until he was too drunk to lift another drink. I was greatly concerned, but I still had confidence that our life together would be so complete and rich that he would have no need for liquor. As time went on, his drinking grew worse.

Since we had no children, my one purpose in life was to help him get over this terrible habit. Aside from his drinking, we were very happy together. We liked the same things and were most companionable. Finally, when the drinking became practically constant, he, too, realized he must do something about it, and together we tried everything we could think of. He set up all kinds of plans for control. He read books on psychology and religion; he went to sanitariums. During two successive summers I gave up my job, and we escaped for three months to the country for renewal and rebuilding. Nothing worked. I had to assume family responsibilities and make all decisions.

By now Bill did nothing but drink. He was afraid to leave the house for fear the police would pick him up. We lived entirely to ourselves. We had dropped all our friends or been dropped by them and we saw as little of our families as possible. Our whole life had simmered down to one terrific fight against alcohol. It was tragic indeed to watch such a fine man become completely beaten and hopeless.

An old friend whom we considered a confirmed drunkard came to see Bill to tell of his "release" from alcoholism by spiritual means. Bill, encouraged by the picture of his friend's bright eyes and hopeful story, went to the hospital to clear his own thinking. Here the miracle happened and Bill became a changed man, almost overnight. We were awestruck by this amazing transformation. In our happiness and gratitude neither of us doubted that his sobriety would last. (As I bring this story up to date, his sobriety lasted until his death in 1971. His friend's sobriety, unfortunately, was of shorter duration, but he was sober a number of years before his death in 1966.)

Bill figured that since a miracle had happened to him and his friend it could happen to others, so he worked endlessly and tirelessly to help alcoholics. We had the house full of drunks in all stages of sobriety. It seemed to me he was trying to dry out all the drunks in the world.

We gratefully went to meetings of the fellowship to which our hopeful friend belonged, and Bill used their half-dozen spiritual principles in his work with alcoholics. Later, when he wrote the A.A. book, he expanded the number to Twelve Steps so as to be sure there were no loopholes through which a drunk could escape.

After a while I began to wonder why I was not as happy as I ought to be, since the one thing I had been yearning for all my married life had come to pass. Then one Sunday, Bill asked me if I was ready to go to the meeting with him. To my own astonishment as well as his, I burst forth with, "Damn your old meetings!" and threw a shoe as hard as I could.

This surprising display of temper over nothing pulled me up short and made me start to analyze my own attitudes. By degrees I saw that I had been wallowing in self-pity, that I resented the fact that Bill and I never spent any time together any more, and that I was left alone while he was off somewhere scouting up new drunks or working with old ones. I felt on the outside of a very tight little clique of alcoholics that no mere wife could enter. My pride was hurt by the fact that a friend, another alcoholic, had been able to do for Bill in a short time what I had tried and failed to do all our married years.

My life's purpose of sobering up Bill, which had made me feel desperately needed, had vanished. I sought something to fill the void. As I began to be honest with myself, I recognized how greatly Bill had developed spiritually and how necessary to his sobriety was his feverish activity with alcoholics. I decided to strive for my own spiritual growth. I used the same principles as he did to learn how to change my attitudes.

Several years later, Bill and I found that strained relations such as ours often developed in families after the first starry-eyed period of sobriety was over. We were heartsick and puzzled to discover that, though alcoholics were recovering through this wonderful new program, their home lives were often difficult. We began to learn how many adjustments had to be made and that the partner of the alcoholic also needed to live by a spiritual program.

Soon, small groups composed of the family members of alcoholics in A.A. sprang up all over the country. They had a threefold purpose: to grow spiritually through living by the Twelve Steps of Alcoholics Anonymous; to give encouragement and understanding to the alcoholic in the home; and to welcome and give comfort to the families of new or prospective A.A. members.

Today Al-Anon groups have spread over this country, Canada, and many other lands. Many agencies, too, recognize that alcoholism is a family problem and that recovery can be greatly hastened by family understanding.

A.A. and Al-Anon often speak of the Twelve Steps as tools. An extension of this idea came to me one day. There is a striking analogy between working on ourselves and cultivating a garden.

Our inheritance and early environment compose the soil out of which grow our thoughts and actions, both flowers and weeds. To raise flowers we must get rid of the weeds.

Our garden tools are these principles of A.A. and Al-Anon: knowledge of ourselves and our motives, honesty in facing ourselves as we really are, a desire to help others, and an awareness of God.

We must keep cultivating with these really effective implements lest our garden be overrun by weeds.

Soils vary; some are rocky, sandy, or swampy, while others are very fertile. But whatever the soil, there are appropriate flowers that can be grown. Even the desert blooms.

One gardener may find it difficult to uproot the weeds because his tools are constantly being dulled against many large rocks. But by repeated sharpening of his hoe and by careful selection of his plants, at last he may be able to grow a very charming rock garden.

Yet another, because he is too sure of the fertility of his plot and takes it for granted that he will have a beautiful garden because his soil is rich, does not bother to cultivate. This gardener may someday wake up to find his garden filled with insidious weeds, the weeds of smugness and self-righteousness that thrive in fertile ground.

In just this way the garden of many a martyred, self-pitying wife or husband of an alcoholic can become choked and unproductive.

The Al-Anon Family Groups point out the need to cultivate the gardens of our lives and show us how this can be done through the use of A.A.'s Twelve Steps.

My work on the Steps, over a period of years is the following:

STEP ONE
We admitted we were powerless over alcohol—that our lives had become unmanageable.

I was just as powerless over my husband's alcoholism as he was, since I had failed in every way I tried to control his drinking. My own life was indeed unmanageable, as I was forced into doing and being that which I did not want to do or be. I tried to manage Bill's life, although not even able to manage my own. I wanted to get inside his brain and turn the screws in what I thought was the right direction. I, too, was powerless over alcohol. It took me a long time to see this.

STEP TWO
Came to believe that a Power greater than ourselves could restore us to sanity.

Because my thinking was distorted and my nerves overwrought, I had fears and attitudes that certainly were not sane. Finally I realized that I, too, had to be restored to sanity and that only by having faith in God, in A.A. (and later in Al-Anon), in my husband, and myself, could this come about.

STEP THREE
Made a decision to turn our will and our lives over to the
care of God as we understood Him.

Self-sufficiency, caused by the habit of acting as mother, nurse, caretaker, and breadwinner, as well as always thinking myself on the credit side of the ledger with my alcoholic husband on the debit side, resulted in my having a smug feeling of rightness. At the same time, illogically, I felt a failure at my life's job of helping Bill to sobriety. All this made me blind for a long time to the fact that I needed to turn my will and my life over to the care of God. I believe smugness is the very worst sin of all. Only with great difficulty does a shaft of light pierce the armor of self-righteousness.

STEP FOUR
Made a searching and fearless moral inventory
of ourselves.

Here is where, when I tried to be really honest, I received a tremendous shock. Many of the things that I thought I did unselfishly were, when I tracked them down, pure rationalizations—rationalizations to get my own way about something. This disclosure doubled my urge to live by the Twelve Steps as thoroughly as I could.

STEP FIVE
Admitted to God, to ourselves, and to another human being
the exact nature of our wrongs.

I found this was just as necessary for me to do as it was for an alcoholic, even more so perhaps, because of my former "mother-and-bad-boy" attitude toward Bill. Admitting my wrongs helped to balance our relationship, to bring it closer to the ideal partnership in marriage.

At first I was deeply hurt because someone else had done in a

few moments what I had tried my whole married life to do. Now I
have learned that a wife can rarely, if ever, do this job. The alcoholic feels his wife's account has been written on the credit page
of life's ledger; and he believes his own has been on the debit
side. Therefore, she cannot possibly understand. Another alcoholic, with a similar debit entry, immediately identifies himself as
no non-alcoholic can.

I found no peace of mind until I recognized this important fact.

STEP SIX
*Were entirely ready to have God remove all these
defects of character.*

There were selfish attitudes that I had felt justified in keeping
because of what Bill or someone else had done to me. I had to try
very hard to want God to remove these. There was, for instance, my
self-pity at losing Bill's companionship, now that the house was full
of alcoholics and we had little time to visit alone with each other.
I didn't realize the importance of his working with others nor did
I know how deep and consuming an absorption in A.A. it takes to
banish the obsession with alcohol.

STEP SEVEN
Humbly asked Him to remove our shortcomings.

"Humbly" was a word I never fully understood. It used to seem
servile to me. Today it means seeing myself in true relation to my
fellow man and to God.

While striving for humility myself, it was inspiring to see my
husband's growth in the same direction. From an inferiority-ridden
person during his drinking days, Bill in A.A. at first bounced way
up to superiority, but then leveled off and gained very real humility.

Slowly and with difficulty I realized I, too, had been beset by
both inferiority and superiority, superiority over Bill in the old days

while he was drinking and then inferiority to him as he made rapid progress in A.A.

STEP EIGHT
Made a list of all persons we had harmed, and became willing to make amends to them all.

At first I couldn't think of anyone I had harmed. But when I broke through my own smugness even a little, I saw many relatives and friends whom I had resented and to whom I had given short, irritable answers, imperiling long-standing friendships. In fact, I remember one friend at whom I threw a book when, after a nerve-wracking day, he annoyed me. (Throwing seems to have been my pet temper outlet.)

I try to keep my list of persons harmed up-to-date, and I also try to shorten it.

STEP NINE
Made direct amends to such people wherever possible, except when to do so would injure them or others.

This is just as important for me as for the alcoholic. I found that when I cleaned away the debris of the past by making amends for each harm done, I had taken an important step towards building a bulwark against any hard knocks that might later come along, as well as gaining serenity and joy in living.

STEP TEN
Continued to take personal inventory and when we were wrong promptly admitted it.

It is astounding how each time I take an inventory I find some new rationalization, some new way I have been pulling the wool over my own eyes. It is easy to fool oneself about motives, and admitting it is hard—but very beneficial.

STEP ELEVEN
Sought through prayer and meditation to improve our conscious contact with God as we understood Him, *praying only for knowledge of His will for us and the power to carry that out.*

I am just beginning to understand how to pray. Bargaining with God is not real prayer, and asking Him for what I want, even good things, I've had to learn is not the highest form of prayer. I used to think I knew what was good for me. Therefore I, the captain, would give my instructions to my lieutenant, God, to carry out. That is very different from praying only for the knowledge of God's will for me and the power to carry it out.

Today's living is so involved that much time for meditation is hard to find. But I've set aside a small amount of time night and morning. I am so filled with thankfulness to God that gratitude is one of my principal subjects for meditation; gratitude for all the love and beauty and friends around me; gratitude even for the hard days of long ago that taught me so much. Thus, I have made a start toward improving my conscious contact with God.

STEP TWELVE

Having had a spiritual awakening as the result of these steps, we tried to carry this message to others, and to practice these principles in all our affairs.

I am like many Al-Anon members whose spiritual awakening was a slow developing experience. But all of us, whether our awakening was sudden or gradual, need to continue our efforts toward growth. One either moves forward or slips backward. I sincerely hope there has been a change for the better between my old and new self, and that tomorrow, next month, next year there will continue to be a better new self.

Nothing has done more to urge me forward than the need to carry the Al-Anon message to the families of alcoholics who are seeking a way out of their dilemma. The helping of others over the same thorny path that one has already trod strengthens both travelers, the helper and the one being helped.

2

A Grandmother Learns to "Live and Let Live"

I didn't come to Al-Anon when my son passed out on the front porch in the middle of winter. I worried. I cried. He could have frozen to death! So I tried to reason with him. I punished him. But I didn't try to get help for myself. It never occurred to me to do so.

Nor did I come to Al-Anon after my son failed to appear at his high school graduation because he was drunk, or when I discovered that he had taken my car and all the money in my wallet and disappeared for two weeks. I made excuses. I told myself and everyone else, "Boys will be boys."

I didn't come to Al-Anon when my son's lovely fiancée came to me in tears just before the wedding because she was worried about my son's drinking—terrified that she was making a grave mistake. I comforted her and told her that he'd grow out of it. I was in such a state of denial that I convinced myself that marriage would settle him down. Then I could stop worrying about him.

Likewise, when my son got drunk, blew up at his boss, and lost his job two days after the birth of my granddaughter, I tried to explain away the problem. It was the stress. I offered to help out with finances until he found employment. I told myself that being a father would help him to grow up, and that I owed it to all of them to do whatever I could to ease the transition. A year later, I was still paying the bills.

What finally drove me to distraction and forced me to stop denying my son's alcoholism was watching the effects of his illness on my granddaughters. I had been part of their lives since they were born. I gave one granddaughter her first bath and walked the floor with the other during her first night so that her parents could sleep. It broke my heart to see the emptiness and confusion in their eyes in the midst of the chaos in their home, or to hear my son scream at them when they were so tiny and so innocent. Soon he came home only sporadically.

I made visitation arrangements in order to see the girls. My daughter-in-law shut down completely. She rarely bathed them or washed their clothes. Often their hair was greasy and their little bodies had an odor. Their shoes were too small. Sometimes, when they came to spend the night or the weekend, their suitcase was full of moldy clothes. They seemed so withdrawn, so frightened, so much older than their years and at such a young age.

Many times I had thoughts of keeping them with me and refusing to return them to their mother, and after I dropped them off I cried, sometimes for days. I cried for all the innocent children being affected by this disease. At times my heart physically hurt.

For a time, the pain was so great that I tried to stay away, but I couldn't deny the pull I felt to rescue those sweet girls. I even tried contacting various social service agencies, but there was nothing anyone could do. Finally I went to Al-Anon. Fortunately for me, I found a wonderful meeting where I was able to learn from other grandparents.

When my denial began to break down and I discovered that I was powerless over everything that went on in my granddaughters' lives outside of my home, I was overcome with anger and sadness. Daily, they were being affected by alcoholism, and there was nothing I could do about that. I wished that life could have been easier for them and raged at God for letting them grow up so neglected.

But time passed, and more and more good Al-Anon seeped into me. I began to meditate on the Serenity Prayer, and it was a source of great solace. My Sponsor helped me to realize that, although I was powerless to change my granddaughters' situation, I could give them unconditional love and support when I was with them. This meant that I had to set aside my sense of the tragedy of their lives and stop viewing them with pity—or their parents with hostility. This was no easy task. I found it extremely hard to drop these attitudes because accepting their situation felt like condoning it, but I realized that I was hurting the girls even more by my attitudes. They deserved better.

And I was hurting myself. The blame and the anger were eating me alive. My stomach was always upset, and I felt so empty and tired at the end of the day. I didn't like the person I had become. There is nothing attractive about bitterness or hard-heartedness. It was time to stop focusing on everyone else, time to stop passing judgment, time to accept the things I could not change. So I let go of the drama and tried to live in the present, grateful that I was allowed to be a part of their lives at all. Many grandparents are not so fortunate.

I chose to take the high road, looking beyond the sorrow, loving them no matter what, and I began to change the things I could. I now keep clothes and hair ribbons, toys and dolls at my house. With their mother's consent, we shop for shoes and coats. I make sure to take them to interesting places and to spend lots of time outdoors in the sunshine. We read books and play in the garden. When we are apart, I write and send cards.

I also try to see the positive in their situation. Their mother is teaching them manners. They are loving, caring sisters who are there for each other. And they have a home and food and toys, and a lot of other things many children will never have, including a grandmother who loves them very much.

At one point, I had to relocate to another small town not too far from my grandchildren but quite a distance from my Al-Anon group. The only Al-Anon meeting in my new town wasn't to my liking. None of the members seemed to be working the Twelve Steps, and there was little attention paid to the Twelve Traditions. But I knew I needed a regular Al-Anon meeting, so I decided to start one myself. With the help of the World Service Office, which provided me with all the information I needed to start a meeting, I found a small, inexpensive room for rent in a local hospital and waited for others to join me. Only one or two people came to the meeting at first, but then, suddenly, around the winter holidays, the meeting became quite popular. We even had some longtime members from neighboring towns who appreciated having an Al-Anon meeting that emphasized the principles of the program. Soon, other meetings were begun in the area, and I had the option of filling up with good Al-Anon wisdom several nights each week. And I kept getting better.

I do not know why terrible things happen to good people, or why innocent children are subjected to the ravages of such a horrible disease as alcoholism. Obviously, it is not for me to know. In going through the Twelve Steps with my Sponsor and my group, I have had to resolve my frustration over this matter. It is fruitless to blame God for the workings of a world I cannot possibly understand. Things are the way they are. I can let such tragedy consume me as I throw temper tantrums and wallow in self-pity, but since I clearly cannot change other people's situations, such a choice seems like a waste of precious life.

The only alternative I can find is to accept that life isn't always fair or kind, even to those who seem most deserving of kindness, and choose to live a full and rich life anyway. Sacrificing my serenity will not bring a moment's peace to my granddaughters. But becoming a happier, more loving person may help them. I hope that they will benefit from having a relatively healthy role model in their lives, but even if they don't, I must make the most of the life I've been given. It is too precious a gift to squander merely because other people make decisions I do not like.

The slogan "Live and Let Live" has taken on a deeper meaning for me because my son chooses not to be a part of my life, and although I find his decision difficult to accept, I feel I must respect it. In the meantime, I am grateful to be allowed to be an active grandmother in the life of his two daughters.

I don't know what the future holds for these girls. I do know that the Al-Anon program makes it possible for me to maintain a growing relationship with them. As a mother to my son, I did not fare too well. Perhaps now I have been given the opportunity to be a *grand* mother! With the help of God and this program, anything is possible!

3

New Faith Helps a Wife Find Peace

I came to my alcoholic marriage with three character defects firmly in place. I didn't realize this at the time; I thought I was almost perfect—character defect #1. My parents, especially my mother, had always encouraged me and thought the world of me. Life was great, right?

Well, not quite. Early on, when I came home from school in tears because the other children had made fun of me, the usual parental response was, "They didn't mean it. They like you!" If I said I was angry, my mother replied, "No you're not! Nice girls like you don't get angry." And if I said I didn't like something or someone, I was told, "Yes, you do!" This set the stage for character defect #2—denial. If anything was unpleasant, I just refused to believe it existed, and everything was "fine."

So peace reigned in our home. I was never yelled at. In fact, the few times I was ever reprimanded at all I was taken into the dining room, which was big and dark and quiet, and my mother whispered about how much sadness I was causing the people who loved me. Then she would say, "What would people think if they saw you acting like that?" What other people saw, what other people thought, that was all that ever really mattered. Happiness came whenever people liked the way we looked or the way we did things, or praised our decisions. So character defect #3—people-pleasing—was well established. I didn't realize that I had been born into an alcoholic family, nor that these traits, which I would later identify as chief among my character defects, were the effects of alcoholism.

In fact, until I came to Al-Anon, I fervently denied that I had any problems. Denial made life possible. After a terrible, emotionally exhausting night of arguments and blame, promises, threats, and fear, my husband would leave for work, kissing me on the way out the door and saying, "Don't worry, everything is fine." And so it was. As long as I didn't think about the situation too hard, everything was fine. Denial was the pattern of a lifetime, and I practiced it without question.

So I believed there was nothing wrong with staying up 24 hours a day, waiting for my husband to come home, knowing that he would be drunk. Nonetheless, I called his place of employment daily to keep tabs on him. I also bailed him out of jail, covered up to the neighbors, and searched his truck every chance I got to see if he had been drinking. Of course he'd been drinking! My searches frequently unearthed evidence of his infidelity and, although I found it humiliating, I did nothing about it. In fact I actually had my mother cover his debts. I ranted and raved at everyone I came into contact with: bill collectors, bankers, utility company employees, Girl Scouts selling cookies, babysitters, policemen, and anyone who wasn't suitably sympathetic toward me and my tough life. But I didn't have a problem.

Finally, I reached the end of my rope. The utilities were cut off, my husband wrecked his truck, and my mother was on my back telling me what to do and when to do it. I was in a constant state of fear and rage, and thinking of ending a life but not sure whether it would be mine or his. Then my mother confronted my husband about his drinking, and all hell broke loose. How *dare* she say he had a drinking problem! But something snapped inside of me when I heard him say that he would drink if he wanted to and nobody was going to stop him.

His alcoholism progressed, and my "perfect" little world fell apart. Everybody knew. I could no longer pretend that everything was fine. My mother, long the wife of an alcoholic, suggested I try Al-Anon. Although it had been suggested to her many times, she herself had never attended a meeting, but she thought it might do me some good. Overcoming my pride and taking that advice was the best decision I ever made.

When I first came to Al-Anon I was asked what I wanted most. Without hesitation I answered, "Peace." I wanted to be rid of the disquieting residue from the alcoholic home of my childhood and the chaotic existence that my husband and I knew. I had become physically ill and emotionally distraught, and I couldn't take much more. I had to have serenity in my life.

Right away I got involved in service, although I didn't know it at the time. When I first started attending meetings, there were some "old timers" who handed me the coffeepot on a regular basis and told me to wash it. I did. I got to be real good at it. I washed that pot week in, week out, month after month. After a while I started noticing that some people in the group weren't pitching in, and I began to feel rather resentful. I shared these feelings with an Al-Anon friend, and he asked if I thought I was getting better. "Sure," I replied, "a lot better." He asked if I was any happier. You bet I was. "Well, then," he said, "why don't you just keep on washing that pot?" After that, I approached every opportunity for service with a sense of gratitude.

I still wanted to please other people, so when asked whether or not I believed in a Power greater than myself, I lied and said that I did. My soul ached for the calm of spirituality, but I had no idea where to find it. I bought every piece of Al-Anon literature. I focused on Steps Two and Three. I talked with countless members. I wanted what they seemed to have, but I just couldn't bring myself to believe in the God of my childhood.

I had been going to church faithfully, and I was in every auxiliary that there was to be in, but I never felt the presence of God. I did, however, feel a lot of fear and a lot of guilt. I had done many things in my life that I was not proud of, and I thought that if I turned my will and my life over to the care of a Being whom I perceived as angry and vengeful, I'd be zapped right then and there.

A wonderful Al-Anon friend suggested that I make a list of the qualities I wanted in a Higher Power. So I wrote, "Loving and caring, forgiving, understanding, fatherly, omnipotent, with a sense of humor, and permissive." (Permissive was important because I knew I had done a lot of things that even I couldn't forgive myself for, so He would have to be very permissive.) When I showed my list to my friend, she said, "There's your Higher Power."

I protested, "That's too simple!" But this is a simple program. I simply tried to be willing to believe that God was there for my betterment and not for my detriment. He was not waiting around the corner to get me—He could have done so many times in the past, but He had not. Meditation helped tremendously. Slowly I began to trust.

After several years of searching, I became comfortable with a God who is a higher dimension of my self. He is with me always, and I merely have to reach out to receive His help. Today this seems so simple, I wonder how it could have eluded me for so long. Once I found God, I knew that He had been with me all along.

He was certainly there when I wanted to get to my husband as he lay sick with alcohol poisoning in a motel room far from home. All flights were totally booked. I went to the airport anyway and by some miracle, a seat opened up, although I was told I would have to leave the plane at the first stop. When we got there, a young man unexpectedly volunteered to give up his seat and I stayed on the plane.

At the second stop, the attendant announced that the flight was again overbooked and that several passengers would have to get off. I shrunk down in my seat and held my breath. The attendant called out the names of three people with confirmed reservations, two seated to my right and the other to my left across the aisle. Again I was allowed to continue.

When I reached my husband, he was near death. Not knowing what to do in an unfamiliar town, I called A.A. Someone came within minutes and whisked us off to the hospital, where my husband's life was saved. Thus began a long and happy, though sometimes trying, life together with the help of our respective programs, Al-Anon and A.A. Upon reflection, I can see that my life has been filled with many miracles. I simply have not always recognized the look of God's grace.

Eventually I learned that, while God watches over me and gives me guidance, direction, and inspiration, He does not do for me what I can and should do for myself. I am expected to play an energetic role in living, and that's where the Al-Anon program comes in.

I explore spirituality in the Twelve Steps. The qualities I develop through the Steps, such as humility, acceptance, and self-discipline, lead me to make right choices in my life and allow me to feel good about myself. The Twelve Traditions give me a sense of fair play, the joy of participation, and the comfort of belonging. They allow me to feel good about myself and others. The ordinary act of sharing myself, of giving myself to the Al-Anon program, rewards me with a feeling of worth and the awareness that I am part of a greater whole.

It is the combination of these aspects of our program that sustains me today in what might otherwise be a dark period of my life. Several years ago the latent effects of the polio of my youth began to take their toll on my body. At first, I noticed that I tired easily and that daily tasks were more difficult than before. Soon I could no longer continue in my profession. Before long, I was unable to work in my beautiful garden and housework was too much for me. Later, after years of gourmet cooking classes and the delights of culinary excellence, I could not function in the kitchen. Finally, a medical crisis left me paralyzed.

Today I use a wheelchair. Someone else bathes and dresses me. Someone else cleans our house. Someone else prepares our meals, does our laundry, writes our monthly checks. I had to resign from my work with the polio organization that I founded. I cannot do any of these things that used to occupy my life and give me satisfaction. Thank God I learned from Al-Anon that who I am is much more than what I do. I no longer find my identity in producing spectacular flowers or having the cleanest house on the block or whipping up tantalizing gastronomic creations. I look inside, and there I am.

Of course there are days when I feel down, just as there are in anyone's life. These are times when I pick up my Al-Anon literature, telephone my Sponsor, and call a newcomer or someone who has been missing from meetings just to say I hope they are well and I'm thinking of them. I build personal contact into my life by serving on our Al-Anon Hot Line and arranging to meet with those I sponsor. I accept whatever small jobs I can do with my home group. Thus, although I am more limited than before, I can still participate in the Al-Anon fellowship.

I can also participate in maintaining a healthy relationship with my spouse. Now that I recognize the interactions involved in an alcoholic household, it has become much easier. Before I came to Al-Anon, I wanted to know *why* my husband drank as he did. The lesson of my childhood—that I was not adequate—left me wondering if I was responsible. But I learned in Al-Anon that he drank because he is an alcoholic.

This had never occurred to me. Strangely, after growing up surrounded by drinkers and their erratic bursts of temper, and after all the fury and turmoil in our marriage, I had never considered that alcohol might be the problem. As a child, I looked out our living room window and saw the man next door passed out, dead drunk, in the middle of the street. I had heard people whispering that he was an alcoholic. It was this image that shaped my understanding of the world. To me, alcoholism always happened on the other side of the window.

In a flash of clarity I understood. Alcoholism isn't simply drinking too much and lying drunk in the street. It can be eruptions of anger, attempts at intimidation and control, unaccountable moodiness and withdrawal. It can manifest itself through returning home at unexplainable hours, acting irresponsibly, and never saying "I love you." Through Al-Anon I identified the disease and its symptoms. Now I have a better idea of how to deal with it.

These are wonderful days for my husband and me. We often spend hours talking about our programs. Sometimes he reads a Step or Tradition from his A.A. literature to me, and I read the same Step or Tradition in my Al-Anon literature to him, and then we discuss it. We share our thoughts about a principle or an issue. Sometimes we pray with one another. After so many years in which alcoholism kept us apart, our programs bring us together and give us common ground. These are moments that I cherish.

With the help of a loving God as expressed through the Al-Anon program, I have finally found the peace that I have longed for all my life.

4

An Employer Overcomes the Patterns of an Alcoholic Home

Isolation characterized my childhood in an alcoholic family. As a boy, I was extremely studious and very involved in my school life. I kept quite busy but rarely let anyone get close to me. I never brought anyone home. I didn't know much about what was going on with my family, and I didn't want to know. And I certainly didn't want anyone else to raise any questions.

When my father went into treatment for alcoholism when I was 11 and again when I was 12, I was utterly shocked. Later, when he tried to tell me about his drinking problem, I didn't want to hear it. But when I reached young adulthood and wanted to participate more with my family, I was harshly confronted with reality. First, my father had a back operation on a tumor that turned out to be cancerous. Then, when my mother left him in my care while she went on vacation, my father went on a bender.

I discovered that I could confront my father about his drinking, but I could not handle the unexpected rage my mother flew into when she returned from her vacation and learned what had happened. I have often heard in Al-Anon that the insanity of the non-drinker can be more obvious than the insanity of the drinker, and this was certainly true in our home. I began to see how irrational my mother's behavior was, and how her days were spent in a rage or a panic over what the alcoholic might do next.

The pain of dealing with alcoholism and its effects overwhelmed me, and I withdrew again. It seemed so much easier to keep to myself, but without knowing it, I continued to carry the burdens of the family disease into everything I did. I was alone, not because I loved solitude, but because I was too terrified of the pain of involvement with others to dare to get close to anyone or to let anyone get close to me. Fear dominated my life. Denial clouded my perception. I ignored reality because it hurt when I thought about it. When painful thoughts emerged, as they inevitably did, I quickly and anxiously shoved them away. It was as if my thoughts were my enemies, and as they approached, I turned and ran as fast as possible in the opposite direction. Instead of expending my energy on living my life, I focused almost exclusively on avoiding pain, stuffing disturbing feelings, and keeping myself as numb as I could.

My father got sicker and died when I was not quite 21. I withdrew even further. By the time my mother revealed to me that my father had been not only an alcoholic but an addict as well, I had reached a point of devastation that I can feel even today, more than 20 years later. I felt completely alone. My emotions could no longer be contained. My grief was overwhelming. My rage knew no bounds.

My father's death brought to a head all the emotional immaturity I carried with me as a result of growing up with alcoholism. Through the intervention of many miracles, I managed to survive this difficult period, with a drug overdose, a couple of brutal fistfights, a broken nose, three cracked ribs, one misdemeanor arrest, and two potentially fatal car crashes. If I am ever tempted to believe that we who are affected by the drinking of another person have a less serious disease than the alcoholic, I need only look back to those days when my own life was in jeopardy.

Slowly, I began to realize that I was in a lot of pain and I tried to seek help. I got a number of quick fixes, all of which had some benefit. Still, I found dealing with my family extremely painful and frustrating, and I continued to feel like an outsider wherever I went. On the surface, I appeared to be fine. But I never let anyone get close enough to know about my problems with intimacy.

It was years before I found Al-Anon, and my attendance seemed to have nothing to do with my father. I came to Al-Anon because I couldn't control the people who worked for me. I had only recently become a manager when a crisis occurred in the office, resulting in a furious shouting match among my employees. I felt that, as the boss, I was responsible for correcting everyone's behavior, soothing everyone's feelings, and restoring peace. When I couldn't do so, I felt inadequate and frustrated. I took the failure very personally.

That old, familiar sense of isolation and despair took hold once more. Many people over the years had suggested I try Al-Anon, and on impulse, I did just that.

By the end of my first Al-Anon meeting, I had an inkling that the program could provide me with the framework for a satisfying life. Although my father had been dead for many years, what I discovered as I continued to attend was that the effects of his alcoholism still influenced every area of my life. My quick fixes had stamped out small brushfires burning at the fringes of my life, but they had not helped me quell the central inferno kindled by this disease.

With the help of many Al-Anon members and many meetings, I began to see that I had a problem—and that many others had this problem too. Though I didn't live with an alcoholic, alcoholism still raged out of control in my life. I had no idea how to have personal, or even professional, relationships. I had never gotten past the attitudes I had adopted as a child. And any potential unpleasantness still sent me scrambling for a quick way out, no matter what the cost. Fear continued to rule me. I began to talk about these problems in meetings, and as a result, I became more aware of the way I was being affected by alcoholism, so I wasn't caught by surprise as frequently. I still felt reluctant to talk about sensitive areas of my life, and I still spent time in isolation, but at least I began to feel the presence of a Higher Power even when I was alone.

The program helped me to concentrate on myself instead of other people. I learned to ask myself whether or not I was responsible in any way for the situations that caused the arguments at work. I studied the written requirements of my job and the goals of our organization. This helped me to sort the times when I was behaving intrusively from the occasions when I had an obligation to step in. For a change, I stopped trying to handle everything on my own. I prayed to the God of my understanding for help and started to find creative ways to solve our office's problems. I asked other people for suggestions. I talked about my feelings and my confusion.

I began to realize that my own behavior was part of our common problems. I imagined what it must be like for my employees to see my scowling, disapproving face every day and to hear the impatience, frustration, and anxiety in my voice. I thought about how often I criticized them and how infrequently I praised them. Then I considered how different it would be to work for me if I were light-hearted, cheerful, pleasant, and relaxed.

With the encouragement of my fellow Al-Anon members, and the clarity I was finding as a result of working the Steps, I began to put these thoughts into action. I learned to look for the positive things my employees were doing. I tried to cultivate a sense of humor, even in the middle of angry disputes. I thanked God whenever I was able to make small changes such as these.

I also stopped taking on everyone else's problems. Just because someone was upset didn't mean that I had to drop everything and try to "fix" them. I asked myself if my involvement was appropriate, and if it was not, I stayed out of it. I tried to remember that my employees had the right to feel their feelings, even if it made me uncomfortable.

I learned to listen to angry people as if I were at an Al-Anon meeting, even if the anger was directed at me. In other words, I listened without interrupting, didn't take it personally, and stopped reacting. By listening respectfully without making a single comment, I let them vent their anger harmlessly. I was amazed to discover that the longer I listened, the softer their voices became, until finally—and quietly—they would ask me what I thought. It was as if a thunderstorm had passed, followed by calm and even a ray of sunshine.

My employees were amazed whenever I refused to get upset. They saw a difference in my attitude and told me so.

Work was not the only area of my life that needed my attention. I realized that, except for my fiancée, I had no real friends and that, outside of work and meetings, I had very little social interaction with other people. I decided to take some action to overcome my social isolation and joined a martial arts class. Two weeks later I went to my first tournament. I won a spirit medal—which I thought of as a spiritual medal. I felt proud of having joined in an endeavor with other people and having dared to participate fully.

Such small victories deserve celebration, but real change often takes time. So much time has passed since then that I didn't realize how much progress I had made until recently, when I joined a gathering of men for an evening of entertainment that was almost comically stereotypical. We ate chips and salsa and some of the guys had a beer, while we sat in front of a large TV and watched a series of boxing matches. While commenting on the action, those who were truly dedicated to the spirit of the evening placed bets on the main event. When the final match ended we settled up, conducted a five-minute wrap-up analysis, and then went our separate ways.

As I drove home, I realized that I was experiencing an area of recovery in my life. Instead of leaving with a deep-seated feeling of isolation, exclusion, and disappointment reminiscent of so many childhood social events, I was leaving with a mild sense of amusement, perhaps even some satisfaction. Thanks to my experience in Al-Anon, I had managed to avoid placing unrealistic expectations on the event, and I enjoyed myself and felt that I belonged even though I neither drink nor gamble.

It was a long time before I was ready to look closely at my childhood, something I had spent a lifetime avoiding. Even after years of recovery, I cannot describe how excruciating an experience it was to reflect upon that time with open eyes. I had to take it one minute at a time because the urge to flee was almost overpowering. My Higher Power brought memories back to me in measured doses, so, despite my pain, I never truly had to face more than I could tolerate. I remembered scenes of public humiliation in which my drunken father shouted obscenities and called me names in front of my classmates. I recalled meals that ended up on the floor because they weren't cooked to my father's satisfaction. I remembered the day that a neighborhood cat had kittens and my father threw them into the fire he had kindled to burn the autumn leaves. I remembered the threats on my own life. Most of all, I remembered how sure I was that I was to blame. No wonder I was confused about my responsibility in relationships. No wonder I didn't want to get close. No wonder I had spent a lifetime trying to avoid the pain of those memories. But I couldn't ever truly be free from their domination until I looked them in the eye without running. Only then could

I take to heart all the valuable lessons I had learned in Al-Anon, such as the Three C's—I didn't cause alcoholism; I can't control it; and I can't cure it. I have been affected by a terrible disease. But because of my recovery in Al-Anon, I will not continue to let it rule my life. I am becoming free.

I once heard an Al-Anon member say that the will of God will never take me where the grace of God will not protect me. I believe God loves me always. I can now be alone without being lonely, and I can now spend time with strangers, casual acquaintances, employees, and friends without feeling such fear of close contact, or such disappointment if they don't happen to know the secrets of the universe. Through the simple experience of sitting and sharing with Al-Anon members I have come to realize that I have found a place where I belong. I find I can take this experience of community out into the world, bit by bit, and that, as I do, my sense of isolation from God and humanity falls away.

5

A Dual Member Copes with His Mother's Drinking

The day I first walked into Al-Anon, I felt as if I was in the enemy camp. As far as I could tell, I was nothing like these people. First of all, I was not and never had been married to an alcoholic, nor did I grow up around drinkers. For more than 55 years, I had no reason to suspect that I had alcoholic relatives. But after my dad died, my mother fell apart and "took to the bottle."

I know it is fashionable to say that, in retrospect, all the clues of some sort of alcoholic predisposition were there and I simply failed to see them, but I don't believe that was true in my case. My mother drank an occasional glass of wine with no apparent ill effect. She didn't seem compelled to follow one drink with another, nor did she display a change in personality or behavior. I cannot point to any abuse or neglect in my past, nor to serious distortions of reality. My mother was a kind, loving woman, and although she had faults and bad habits, as we all do, I do not believe she was any sicker than anyone else. She and my dad had a close and loving marriage for 61 years, and I have the utmost respect for that accomplishment.

The other reason I felt out of place at my first Al-Anon meeting is that, other than my mother, I am the alcoholic in my family. I have been sober for 30 years. But some years back I realized that I needed something in addition to A.A. or I would probably not continue to stay sober. I am fortunate to have found exactly what I needed in Al-Anon, although it took a while before I realized it. At first, every time an Al-Anon member referred to the alcoholic in his or her life, I felt that they were talking about me. Had I not been torn up inside worrying about my mother, I would have walked out and never come back. But I didn't know where else to turn, and my A.A. Sponsor suggested that I give Al-Anon a chance. Eventually I got past the feeling that I was the enemy. Since I was welcomed with warmth and treated with respect, it became clear that my own attitude was causing my discomfort.

In fact, by coming to Al-Anon, I learned that my thoughts and attitudes were the main source of my problems with my mother. Take, for example, my constant guilt and fear for her well-being. I didn't sleep at night for fear that she would fall down in a drunken stupor and break a hip, or hit her head on a table and knock herself out, or worse. If I did get a good night's sleep, I woke up feeling terribly guilty, as if, by dropping my vigil of worry and actually catching a few winks, I was failing to protect her. Somehow I had decided that worrying was helpful, and that if I stopped, something terrible would happen. Of course this was absurd, but alcoholism is not known for fostering rational thought. I first became aware of these feelings when meditating on the First Step. "Admitted we were powerless over alcohol—that our lives had become unmanageable." Even though I had taken the Steps with great dedication in A.A., I had to start from scratch when applying these same Steps to the effects of other people's alcoholism on *my* life. After 13 years of sobriety, 13 years of Twelve Step experience, I had to start all over. I was every bit a beginner. Just the thought that I might possibly be powerless to help my mother stop drinking sent me into a panic. If I didn't take care of her, who would? The answer came to me as I continued to take the Steps. Only a Power greater than myself, greater even than alcoholism, could help. If I was honest with myself, I had to admit that my fear and guilt hurt me—and didn't help her one bit. My Al-Anon Sponsor assured me that it was natural to feel fearful about the effects of a frightening and powerful illness on someone that I loved. Then he pointed out that I had allowed the fear to take control of my entire life.

Eventually I learned that I had choices about my thoughts and attitudes, and those choices largely determined the quality of life I would experience. My Sponsor said that, while I was apt to feel fearful or guilty from time to time, I didn't have to spend the entire day dissecting and replaying all the possible reasons for those feelings. He stressed that it was important to acknowledge my feelings rather than to deny them, but then to make a choice about where I wanted to expend my energy.

Whatever I choose to think about is the lesson I practice learning. If I choose to fret about all the potential dangers to which an alcoholic can subject herself, then I teach myself about fear, and I practice seeing a chaotic and dangerous world for which I feel somehow responsible and from which I am obliged to defend myself and others—but am unable to do so. If I choose instead to focus on the Serenity Prayer or an Al-Anon slogan such as "Let Go and Let God," I teach myself that I am in the hands of a loving God who knows better than I ever will what is best for all concerned. Thus, by making choices about my thoughts, I make choices about my attitudes. And when my attitudes are positive, the world looks a whole lot brighter, even when the situation hasn't changed.

I learned all this, but I still found it difficult to put it to work in my life. I was so obsessed with my mother's illness that I couldn't remember that I had options, until I was practically out of my mind with worry. My Sponsor assured me that God would help me to remember, if I asked for His assistance. In the meantime, my Sponsor helped me to become aware of what I could do when fear and guilt first popped into my head. When these thoughts first appeared in my mind and tempted me as seductively as a rich, chocolate dessert, beckoning me to indulge, this was my moment of opportunity. That was the time to say, "no." Just as a taste of a tantalizing dish makes it harder to resist, I found that a taste of the insanity that accompanies another's alcoholism is equally tempting. The best way to maintain sanity is to avoid that first indulgence. My Sponsor suggested that, when I noticed one of these thoughts, I could interrupt it by picturing an enormous stop sign. Then, before the thought could return and take hold, I could replace it with a healthier alternative. That's why the slogans were so useful. I found them easy to remember and always constructive to think about. I would put a stop to the obsessive thinking, replace it with an Al-Anon slogan, and feel some relief. Although I had my share of setbacks, my obsessive thinking ebbed, and I began to be restored to sanity.

Eventually I realized that I was not responsible for my mother's drinking or its consequences. I was responsible for myself—for behaving lovingly toward myself and making my own well-being my first priority. I was also responsible for behaving in a way that was supportive and loving to my mother, in spite of her disease. I discovered that a great deal of what went on around me was out of my control. So, in time, I stopped spending every waking moment trying to control everything.

Today I consider Al-Anon to be essential to my well-being. I have been accepted into the loving embrace of this fellowship and treated as an equal, and I have healed. I am grateful beyond measure.

A Sister Learns to Take Care of Herself

Unlike most others I have met in Al-Anon, the alcoholic in my life is neither parent nor lover. I am the oldest of seven children, and I came to Al-Anon to cope with my younger brother's drinking. I am eight years older than my brother, who was the baby for a long time. Then, unexpectedly, my mother had another child. I don't think my brother ever recovered from the change. He threw tantrums, demanded special meals, special treatment, and constant attention. It became a family joke: my brother wasn't the youngest, but he would always be the baby. My parents didn't seem to have time for him once the baby came, so I took on the responsibility for his care.

I suspect that this caretaking fulfilled a tremendous need for love and acceptance at a time when I felt unlovable. I was in the throes of adolescence, suffering from the effects of raging hormones and a desperate desire to fit in. And I was trying to ignore what was becoming all too clear—I wasn't like the other girls. I pretended to be interested in boys, but it was the girls, and especially the older women in my life—teachers, nuns, camp counselors—to whom I felt drawn. It took me many years to admit to myself that I was a lesbian, and many more before I felt anything other than shame about it.

So I took every opportunity to put my energy elsewhere, and my needy brother filled the bill. He became the center of my world. If he had a baseball game, I would be in the stands. I drove him to rehearsals for school plays and bought him his first guitar. If I was invited to a party on the same day he had a track meet, I always went to the track meet. Later, when he began writing songs, I was his biggest fan. I wasn't at all concerned about his drinking. Didn't all young people drink? Especially artists?

As my brother's band began to achieve some recognition, the drinking intensified. I didn't want to dampen his enthusiasm or spoil his success with my nagging, so I suffered in silence, worrying obsessively about his drinking, his wildness, his health. I had no boundaries when it came to my brother. He had always been my responsibility. Therefore, I felt responsible for his drinking. I spent most of my time scheming about what I could do to make him stop.

The band became quite successful and went on an international tour. When he came home, my brother was hospitalized, exhausted, addicted to alcohol and drugs. The doctor wanted to send him to a mental hospital, but another family member took him in. We all took shifts acting as his bodyguard. Everyone got caught up in his disease. Then, during his shift, another of our brothers took a large dose of a drug and was himself hospitalized. Who says it's not a family illness?

I was losing my sanity with worry and squandering my time trying to do everything to make my brother comfortable so he would recover. In the nick of time, a friend introduced me to Al-Anon. I began to hear that I could do nothing to solve my brother's problems or cure his illness, and that, although I could continue to love him fiercely, I had to stop protecting him from the consequences of his actions. The people in Al-Anon said that, just as the alcoholic wraps his arms around a bottle, those of us who love an alcoholic wrap our arms around him or her. I had to learn to "Let Go and Let God."

These ideas were totally foreign to me, but my sanity was teetering on the edge and I had to choose which way I would fall. I chose recovery.

One of the stumbling blocks I hit right away was my eagerness to fix all my problems at once. I read *One Day at a Time in Al-Anon (ODAT)*, *Al-Anon's Twelve Steps & Twelve Traditions*, *...In All Our Affairs*, *As We Understood...*, and half a dozen *Forum* magazines in the first four or five days. The phrase "work the Steps" kept coming up, so I jumped right in. In fact, I jumped right over to Steps Eight and Nine and started calling family members to apologize for times I had been critical or unkind. And, following the Al-Anon suggestion, I got a Sponsor right away.

My Sponsor seemed to be a very kind, calm, and intelligent woman. I told her about all the material I was reading and the actions I was taking to fix my problems. Then I told her I wanted her to help me get through them faster. She chuckled and said that she wholeheartedly believed in the Al-Anon slogans "Easy Does It" and "One Day at a Time." I thought I might have chosen the wrong Sponsor, but I liked her, so I continued the relationship.

While attending a different Al-Anon meeting, I heard an announcement that temporary Sponsors were available, so I got one of those too. To my disappointment, she told me essentially the same thing. I paid little attention to their wise words.

I almost quit going to Al-Anon altogether when I started trying to work Step Four "Made a searching and fearless moral inventory of ourselves" by myself. I sat down and wrote a list of all the things I saw wrong about me. It was a long list. I didn't know enough about the Steps to know that Step Four is meant to include positive as well as negative characteristics. At the same time, I continued my Al-Anon reading. Suddenly, everything I heard and read seemed to deal with how sick I was. It was overwhelming. I began to feel that there was too much to fix and I could never do it.

I was really depressed. Although I read the *ODAT* daily, it seemed to deal mostly with problems people had with the drinker they were living with. I was no longer living with my brother and felt more and more isolated. I didn't know any other lesbians in Al-Anon, so I really felt different. I had dug myself into a hole and didn't know how to climb out.

Fortunately, I kept in touch with my original Sponsor, and when I grew miserable enough, I finally became willing to hear what she had to say. She convinced me that I really wasn't a hopeless case. She explained that the Steps were numbered for a reason, and that many of the problems I was facing could be avoided if I took the Steps in order with the help of a Sponsor, starting with Step One. She told me that I deserved happiness in my life and that I would be able to find it if I kept going to Al-Anon. She also suggested that I take a break from the literature for a while.

Taking a break really helped. It made me slow down. As a result, I began to grasp the meaning of the slogan "Easy Does It." Sometimes, relaxing and letting go of my troubles can actually help me to solve them more effectively than all the struggle and attention I can muster. I found that life doesn't have to be a battle, even when circumstances prove difficult, as they did for my brother.

My brother continued to drink, and in a blackout, he attacked several people without apparent cause and wound up in court for assault and battery. His notoriety made it a very public case, and I feared the effect it might have on my life and my job as a schoolteacher. My Sponsor, whose brother was also an alcoholic, urged me to talk about my fears. She didn't "fix" me; she respected my feelings and helped me to accept them. And she helped me to set those feelings aside and take the actions I needed to take for myself. Her example taught me how to get through the bad days and enjoy the good ones.

But I still had trouble with the concept of detachment. I was convinced that to detach meant to stop caring. How could I do such a thing? We were talking about my brother, someone I adored, someone whose love and approval I had always sought. I read and reread the Al-Anon leaflet on detachment. Then one day, it suddenly became clear. I realized that detachment doesn't mean that one doesn't care, it means that one doesn't let something affect his or her daily life. I had always let my brother's actions influence my time, temperament, and serenity. I had covered up his violence and acting out, accepted his constant criticism, and taken responsibility for his actions. Detachment, once I understood it, allowed me to care about my brother while remaining unaffected by his criticism. While still loving him, I could refuse to make excuses for him. I could allow him to face the consequences of his actions and still be a good sister. Even when the publicity made him the subject of gossip wherever I went, I could know that his actions were a reflection of him, not a reflection of me. Detachment isn't a lack of caring. It's self-preservation for those of us who do care.

My brother still drinks when he can. He takes medication and mixes it with alcohol. Yet my life has blossomed since I came into Al-Anon. I have a well-paying job and a lot of supportive friends. My relationship with my Higher Power is strong and nurturing, and my Al-Anon program helps me to know how to go about finding answers to all of life's questions. I still love my brother dearly, and I know that love survives because of this program. Without it, I would have allowed myself to be dragged down the road my brother has chosen, and it probably would have destroyed me.

Little did I know that Al-Anon would become my life line when chaos unrelated to alcoholism posed a threat to all that I had worked to achieve in recovery. I moved from a major city to a small rural community to pursue a more peaceful lifestyle in a slower atmosphere. But I was unprepared for the rising wave of anti-homosexual sentiment that arose in the region shortly after I moved into my new home. At first, the antagonism was subtle. I was snubbed. Shopkeepers were suddenly out of stock when I inquired about a purchase. I received some dirty looks. I had lived through prejudice before and had learned to work my program and detach whenever I encountered it.

But then the situation took a more malignant turn. I began receiving death threats on my answering machine. My tires were slashed. A dead bird was left at my door. Naturally I was terrified. I couldn't think straight. I wanted to bolt, to flee the home into which I had poured my life savings. I wanted to revert to behavior that I had practiced so often when dealing with my alcoholic brother. I wanted to run from the problem and pretend it didn't exist. And if I couldn't do that, I wanted to blow everyone up. I had often entertained violent fantasies about retribution when people had treated my alcoholic brother unkindly or attempted to confront him with the reality of his alcoholic behavior, because I felt so personally threatened by his discomfort. Now those same violent fantasies returned, directed this time at those who threatened me directly.

But my recovery was too well established for such behavior. Because of Al-Anon, I knew I had alternatives. My program friends gave me tremendous support as I examined my options and tried to decide what to do. I took the situation and put it into the Steps, admitting my powerlessness over other people's prejudice and hostility. Step by Step, I sorted out my part in the situation and asked God for help with the rest.

Eventually I decided upon a course of action that seemed appropriate. I filed a police report and requested protection. And I decided to sell my house and relocate in a more hospitable climate. I had moved to enhance my quality of life. Since I had not achieved that goal, I felt my best option was to continue to pursue a more relaxed lifestyle. The only reason to stay was to take a stand, to prove that I would not be scared away, and I didn't see the point. I wasn't likely to change anyone's mind, and I wasn't interested in mounting a personal crusade. But I did commit to staying until I received fair market value for my home. In the meantime, I hired a bodyguard to ensure my protection.

By practicing the principles of Al-Anon in all my affairs, I was able to find and implement a solution to a very difficult situation. In retrospect, I feel that I made a very wise choice. My new home fits my needs beautifully. I found a much warmer community into which I have been welcomed, and I feel more confident about my ability to make decisions and to take care of myself in a crisis. Without Al-Anon and the Twelve Steps, this would not have been possible.

7

Learning to Live Single

Perhaps the most outstanding thing about my story is how far from outstanding it is. Although I have been acutely affected by another person's alcoholism, I never experienced the high drama, violence, conflicts with the law or the debt-collectors, suicide attempts, or physical illness that I often hear about in Al-Anon meetings and read about in Al-Anon literature. I suffered greatly at the hands of the family disease of alcoholism, but my suffering was relatively quiet and undramatic. And I was lucky enough to find and embrace Al-Anon before the situation got worse.

I did not grow up in an alcoholic family, nor a particularly dysfunctional one. We had our problems and our limitations, but we loved and supported each other as best we could. Since most of my Al-Anon friends grew up in relative turmoil, abuse, or neglect, I questioned my perceptions about my family for the first several years in Al-Anon. Surely I was in denial, I thought. People from "normal" families don't wind up in alcoholic relationships. But after much soul-searching, talking to family members, and praying for the truth, I have concluded that there are no hidden skeletons looming in the family closet, no lost generations of alcoholics in the family tree, no comparable physical or mental illnesses or compulsions inflicted upon my formative years that might have predisposed me to seek out alcoholic relationships in my adulthood. As far as I can tell, my family was as loving as they seemed, and to this day they remain a major source of strength and support in good times and in bad.

My teenage years were equally uneventful. I was something of a "brain," drawn to science and math at an early age, somewhat introverted and scholarly but not overly so. I did well in school and in the various clubs and activities in which I became involved over the years, and I always had one or two close friends. I was never much to look at and dated only occasionally in high school. This was a cause of some insecurity and sadness in my teenage years, but never a major catastrophe. In college I became more popular with men and, although I never had droves of men beating a path to my door, I didn't feel socially deprived. I was drawn to "exciting" men, full of bravado, living on the edge. They were different from me, different from most of the "boring" people I knew. Some were undoubtedly alcoholics. Others were probably just college kids experimenting with newfound independence. In any event, my relationships with these men were passionate, chaotic, and unpredictable. But they didn't dominate my life. I was very successful academically and very clear about my plans for the future.

It wasn't until I had earned a Ph.D. and was working as a biochemist that my life began to be adversely affected by the alcoholism of a man I was dating. I guess the signs had been there all along, but I hadn't been looking for them. We had met in a bar. I didn't spend much time in bars, and when I did it was only to spend time with friends, never to meet men. He felt that our meeting was therefore destined and, charmed by the romanticism of such a notion, I concurred. I ignored the fact that he had been drinking steadily for hours that first night, just as I dismissed his cancellation of our first formal date, a week later, because he was too hung over to meet me. He was a little wild, and that appealed to me.

Six weeks later we were living together, thrust into a whirlwind romance that was frequently interrupted by alcoholic episodes that were becoming more difficult to ignore. My lover was a binge drinker, never drinking on a daily basis or when it would interfere with his job. Mostly he restricted his alcohol consumption to one or two weekends per month. So his behavior bore no resemblance to alcoholism as I understood it. I thought he was simply irresponsible, inconsiderate, or lacking in common sense.

One night he failed to come home. I was hysterical, sure he had been killed. And then he returned. He had been at a party and lost track of the time. All night. He was sorry—he hadn't meant to worry me, and it wouldn't happen again. Two weeks later the same thing happened. Curiously, I found myself reacting in exactly the same way—hysterically. My mind was full of dire fantasies. I called all the hospitals. I was insane, obsessed. I couldn't read a book, watch a television show, do a load of laundry. I could only sit and worry. Already I had been so deeply affected by alcoholism that I had lost any semblance of control or rationality. My life was unmanageable. And it seemed to have happened in a flash. When my alcoholic lover finally got home and I ascertained that he was drunk but otherwise unharmed, I resolved to leave him. I was terrified about what was happening to me and feared that if I didn't leave immediately, I might lose the ability to make such a choice at all. But the next morning, perhaps sensing my resolve, he announced that he needed help and had called Alcoholics Anonymous. So I stayed.

From that day on he never took another drink. He told me that it had been recommended that I attend Al-Anon so that our relationship could grow along similar lines, and I was willing to do what I could to help. I felt uncertain, insecure about the relationship and the wisdom of continuing to pursue it, and self-conscious that so smart a woman could have found herself living with a drunk. But I can't say that I was in crisis as a result of alcoholism.

I stayed in Al-Anon because I felt completely at home there from the very first meeting I attended. I respected the courage and the honesty of the members who told their stories and shared both their problems and the solutions they had found. I identified with the feelings they expressed, although I rarely identified with the particulars of their stories. And I admired the commitment to personal growth.

At first, the greatest obstacle to my recovery in Al-Anon was the frequent mention of God. Like many scientists, I tend to be skeptical of anything I cannot experience empirically or subject to scientific scrutiny. Mine is a world of observable phenomena, and I hesitate to acknowledge, much less to trust, anything else. So I had a lot of trouble with the spiritual nature of the Al-Anon program. My Sponsor, who understood how alien I found spiritual and religious sources of information, suggested that I seek my Higher Power in a world I could understand, the world of quantum physics. I won't go into the details of my quest, except to say that as I probed this abstract, theoretical branch of science, my mind opened to the unknown and unseen. I believed in forces of nature that were beyond my control, and gradually I managed to evolve a personally meaningful understanding of a Power greater than myself. If I had received no other gift from Al-Anon, that would be more than enough, because my life has changed completely as I have pursued spiritual development and turned to a Higher Power for help.

But living with sobriety brought many challenges that would have been impossible to handle without the support of the Al-Anon fellowship and the practices I learned there. There was so much change, constant change. After his initial period of joy at being sober, my lover seemed to get worse. He wasn't drinking, but he was irritable, muddled, self-absorbed, unreliable, and often unavailable to me. All he seemed to do was go to work and go to meetings. I didn't understand what the problem was, and I resented his apparent unwillingness to participate in our relationship. My Al-Anon friends helped me to be patient and to learn about sobriety. One of them suggested that I had better change my expectations or I was in for years of disappointment. She said that a common assumption among her friends in A.A. was that it takes two years for an alcoholic to get his brains out of hock and three more years to learn how to use them. Expecting a newly sober alcoholic to function like a "normal" person or to be capable of a full-time, full-fledged intimate relationship right away was probably foolish. It would be much kinder to myself if I revised my expectations of us both. Otherwise I was only hurting myself.

This was only one of many situations in which I was forced to take responsibility for my part in creating my own misery. I had to examine my expectations and re-formulate them so that I was no longer setting myself up for failure. It would have been easier to simply continue feeling frustrated and resentful over my disappointment with the alcoholic, but it wouldn't have helped me to live a happier or more satisfying life. Although it was hard and sometimes embarrassing work, the self-honesty I learned in Al-Anon helped me to create a far better life than the one I'd been living.

As I worked the Steps with my Sponsor and tried to be honest with myself, I began to change. My expectations changed, and my lover changed as well. Slowly our relationship began to be more open, more comfortable, more interesting.

Yet as time passed, the relationship began to show signs of strain. We were both busy with our own lives, programs, and social circles. I was fairly comfortable with our relative independence because my life seemed so rich and varied, and I knew that one man couldn't meet all of my needs. Perhaps I went too far in revising my expectations of our relationship until I stopped expecting, or asking for, any significant signs of commitment or consistent intimacy. I probably gave just as little as I received. At any rate, my lover became involved with another woman, and before I knew what was happening, he had moved out.

I was devastated. I was full of self-recrimination for having been caught off guard, for "failing" to make the relationship work, for being too unattractive, selfish, dull, smart, independent, cold, caretaking—you name it, I accused myself of it. I also blamed the other woman. I pictured her in my mind and then attacked the picture. She had lured him away. She was a terrible person, a man-eater, a seductress. And I blamed him. I attacked his character, habits, attitudes, choices, and stewed over them for hours on end. I was the ultimate martyr. Hadn't I spent all this time working on myself for him? And this was how he paid me back?

But I couldn't keep this descent into hatred and self-pity going for too long. I knew better. I knew that, although I had played a role in the breakup of our relationship, I was not the sole cause. Neither was my lover, nor the other woman. I knew all this, but without Al-Anon's help during this difficult time, I don't think I would have been able to get past the blame.

One of the greatest sources of help during this time was Al-Anon service. My Sponsor advocated doing something for others whenever I felt the urge to feel sorry for myself, so I got busy volunteering for an assortment of small tasks and chores in my various Al-Anon groups. Service kept me busy and productive. It allowed me to do something worthwhile at a time when I felt worthless, and it gave me something to do other than obsess about my sad state. This involvement kept me out among the living when I wanted to isolate myself and wallow in my misery, and it kept my mind focused upon the principles of healing. Gradually I began to feel better.

Now that I am living more responsibly and consciously as a result of my years in Al-Anon, I find it much more difficult to adjust to life as a single woman. I can no longer be casual about sex, because I can no longer ignore my responsibility to protect myself in the age of AIDS. And now that I am so much more aware of my feelings, I find that I become terribly nervous before a date. When I feel attracted to someone new, I ask different questions than I did in my days of relative oblivion. Although I still find myself attracted to "exciting" men, the bravado, the excitement, the wildness that once attracted me now cause me to look more suspiciously at the person. I guess the difference is that today I don't always give them my phone number. I am trying to learn from my experiences and to make better choices. Sometimes that means that I look to myself for companionship and comfort, rather than to a man. My Al-Anon friends help me to work through my fears and confusions and let me know that my feelings, frustrations, and fears are perfectly accept-able under the circumstances. Whether or not I ever have another date, they will continue to love me.

I didn't come to Al-Anon to help me through a breakup or to get me back on my feet again as a single woman. I didn't expect to have to learn to let go of the love we had once had, or to find out in what new direction I wanted my life to aim. I came to make a particular relationship work. But I found that Al-Anon is a program that is helpful to me no matter what happens, no matter what changes I encounter, no matter what life brings. I no longer go through diffi-cult times alone. I have support from unconditionally loving people who hug me and treat me with kindness and compassion. I have principles that help me to straighten out my thinking, which leads me to take responsible and considered actions. I couldn't be more grateful for this wonderful program and for all the members who keep it vital, fresh, and consistent so that I can draw upon it when-ever I feel the need.

8

The Healing Power of Service

I recall very little of my childhood. Most of what I know was told to me by relatives. We lived above a saloon where my father worked part-time as a singing waiter to make extra money. Even when I was very young, my mother used to leave me alone in our apartment and spend her evenings in the saloon with my father. I remember many times when I woke up after a nightmare and found myself alone with no one to comfort me. I longed for someone who would take care of me.

I thought I had found such a person when I met a much older man who had the same first name as my father. I still felt like "Daddy's little girl," so this similarity seemed wonderfully poetic. The man had been married before and had three children to support. We married, but I rarely saw him because he had to work two jobs to pay all the bills. This was fine with me because it allowed me to enjoy the advantages of the single life and still have the security of a marriage. Since my role models had offered little guidance or consistency, I didn't know what to expect of marriage.

As my husband and I drifted apart, I began to enjoy the company of other men. I left the marriage when I became involved with a very charismatic aerospace engineer. Our relationship was like a never-ending party. We lived in the fast lane, traveled all the time in search of excitement, and decided to marry.

My new husband's drinking spiraled out of control, and we moved from city to city to escape the consequences of alcoholism. There was always new hope, a better chance, or a way out in the next town. Then the consequences of alcoholism began to catch up. My husband received several tickets for driving while intoxicated and spent more than a few nights in jail. He blamed everything on me, and I believed him. I no longer trusted my own perceptions, and because there had been mental illness on my mother's side of the family, I was sure I was losing my mind. The horror of an earthquake that occurred during one of our moves was nothing compared to the nightmare I found myself in as alcoholism progressed and its effects continued to beat me down.

Eventually, I did manage to get to meetings, and I was amazed to hear that I hadn't caused the alcoholism, couldn't control it, and couldn't cure it. I began to re-examine my belief that it was all my fault and to question my faith in the alcoholic's accusations. I was among people who really did understand my pain. They knew what I had been through in a way that no one else had ever known. They helped me to see that I had been affected by this family disease from the day I was born. I realized that both my parents had been alcoholics. My father had died of the disease, although the death certificate claimed he died of a heart attack. I started to fill in all kinds of gaps in my memory, and to explore who I really was and the kind of life I wanted to live.

After I had been in the program for about a year, my husband decided to go into a treatment center. I thought this would be the most glorious time of my life and that finally we would find true happiness. I had to learn the hard way that happiness is an inside job, a matter of personal choice. I can't pin my hopes for a good life on another person, situation, or outcome. But at the time, my happiness depended upon his sobriety. My bubble burst when, once again, he started drinking.

I had to find a way to detach from my husband's problems and to go on with my life. I made a much stronger commitment to my Higher Power and to working the Al-Anon program, and began to work the Steps in earnest.

But the real key to my recovery has been service. This was quite a surprise, since "giving" had always been one of my biggest problems. I had developed a terrible self-hatred in response to the alcoholic situations I had endured, and one way I dealt with this self-hatred was by running away. Often this involved throwing myself into other people's lives and distracting myself by trying to solve their problems. I felt that, by ignoring my obviously inferior and hateful self and by serving others instead, I could justify my presence on this earth and feel better about myself. But my efforts left me drained, resentful, and needy, and I ended up hating myself even more.

Much to my shock and relief, Al-Anon told me that it was my right and responsibility to take care of myself first and to attend to my needs before the needs of others. So I was confused about service. On one hand, Al-Anon was urging me to do things for myself and to be "selfish." On the other hand, it was telling me that service to others is an integral part of recovery and of taking care of *myself*. This made little sense to me, since my previous experience of service had had the opposite effect.

But I tried to "Keep an Open Mind" and found myself pitching in here and there without really understanding how or why it was supposed to help me. I set up meetings on occasion and picked up new meeting lists from the Literature Office when our supply got low. I chaired some meetings and occasionally volunteered for other small jobs.

Then came the opportunity for me to become an Alateen Sponsor. Because of the young ages of Alateen members, an Alateen group needs an adult Sponsor who oversees the meeting and is ultimately responsible for it. My Al-Anon Sponsor thought that this kind of service might help me to learn more about myself and to resolve some of the questions that remained about the effects alcoholism had had on me during my younger years, so when I heard about an Alateen group that needed a Sponsor, I decided to give it a try.

At the time, I kept hearing about how, when you serve others, you're really serving yourself. I continued to find this concept totally baffling. I reasoned that, when you do something for someone else, you know you're doing something "good," and that makes you feel better about yourself. Hence, serving others is serving yourself. But my heart knew that being "good" couldn't explain why being an Alateen Sponsor was helping me to love myself. I noticed something else about this service that was different from my past experiences—miraculously, sponsorship wasn't a drain on my strength or my energy!

That's when my lessons in service began in earnest. Sponsoring an Alateen group turned out to be (this phrase to be read through clenched teeth) a glorious opportunity to really get to know my character defects. One by one these defects—my need to control others, my arrogant assumption that I know what is best for everybody else, and so on—were paraded in front of me. "How am I going to develop any self-esteem if my faults are continually shoved in my face?" I complained. It wasn't easy, it wasn't comfortable, and I couldn't come up with an explanation of why it seemed to help, but as I continued to show up for the Alateen meetings, I continued to get better.

In time, I learned that when I'm giving within my limits, it is never draining. I learned to value what I have to give, such as love, courtesy, and respect, even though it does not magically remove the pain and strife from other people's lives or solve their problems. But I kept wondering why it was Alateen service and not some other that was so important for me.

I was about to speak at an Al-Anon conference one evening when I found myself remembering a night in my early Al-Anon recovery when I re-read some old high school report cards. During this reading, I had re-lived a lot of the self-hatred and loneliness that I felt in high school. That night at the conference, instead of condemning myself for my years of self-abandonment, I acknowledged that running away from myself was probably the most loving way I could find to survive the tremendous impact alcoholism was having on my life and on my self-image. I could have made much more damaging choices. Clearly I did the best I could at the time. I began to truly forgive myself and promised myself that with my Higher Power's help, I would never run away from myself again, no matter how bad the self-hatred got.

My thoughts then returned to the conference and the immediate goal of trying to describe what I do as an Alateen Sponsor. I heard myself say, "I go every week and listen to a bunch of teenagers talk about how much they hate themselves, *and I don't run away!* I stay and listen and am present, and I give them as much love and respect as I can." I had finally figured it out. By being an Alateen Sponsor I am making amends to myself for abandoning myself when I was growing up. I began to understand why service has been such a valuable experience. I can't go back to the past and change things, and I don't think I'd want to even if I could. I have accepted the past. Besides, changing the past isn't making amends, and sometimes mending things can make them stronger than before they were broken. I make amends to myself by changing how I treat myself now and by serving others, doing what I was unable to do for myself when I was in their situation.

By experiencing the healing that has taken place through my Alateen sponsorship, I see that my sense of isolation, separateness, and distance from the human race has been an illusion. We are all connected, all one. Therefore, when I do something for someone else, I'm doing it for myself by extension. Alateen sponsorship has not only provided me with the opportunity to make amends to myself, it has reunited me with my human family and put a huge hole in the wall of isolation I had built.

Through service and my commitment to working the program, I have gotten a lot better. So when my husband once again sought treatment, I was able to maintain some detachment. Although I wished him well, I was not so expectant this time, not willing to pin my hopes or my happiness on his choices. Instead, I decided to leave his recovery completely up to him. In the past, I had accompanied him to all of his meetings and aftercare because I wanted to offer support. I still supported his efforts, but I knew that he had to find his own way, and I had to attend to my own life.

I have found this period very difficult. My husband remains sober and has become quite involved in A.A., but there is little sharing or growth between us. A year of marriage counseling helped us to become more aware of our behavior toward one another, but it did not make us more intimate. Again, I have experienced that loneliness I always tried to escape, but this time I've refused to run away. As a result, I've discovered that loneliness won't kill me. Ironically, I don't have to go through it alone. My Al-Anon friends and my Sponsor give me tremendous support and encouragement, and service work continues to make my life shine more brightly.

When I came into Al-Anon years ago, I was told that I needed to surrender my self-will to a Power greater than myself and become willing to accept whatever that Higher Power offered me. At the same time, I was told never to give up hope. It was okay to want what I wanted, as long as I put my Higher Power's will above my own desires. So I kept hoping that my husband would find sobriety, and a Higher Power guided him along that path. Now I am hoping that, before we grow too old, we will have a life of intimacy and togetherness. But I will accept whatever my Higher Power gives me. I have been blessed with a wonderful life, and with my Higher Power and Al-Anon to support and guide me, I trust that I have a great deal to look forward to.

9

Surviving Personal Tragedy

I had a wonderful childhood. My father loved me unconditionally and treated me with respect. He was an officer in the United States Army and a true gentleman. My mother was the stereotypical sweet, domestic, loving homemaker you might see on TV shows from the 1950's. She baked, made dresses for me, and took gentle care of me when I was sick. My brother was five years younger than I, and I loved him. My childhood was wonderful until I turned ten years old.

My father became ill and was hospitalized practically overnight. My mother told us nothing about what was going on, and I was too frightened to ask. But after three weeks, I did ask, "Mommy, when is Daddy coming home?" She replied, "He's not." That was the end of the discussion. In time, I learned that he had had what they called a nervous breakdown. Today I know there were probably warning signs, problems that existed beforehand, but in my child's mind my perfect, happy world changed overnight.

We moved to a big city so my father could receive the care he needed. I thought I would be seeing him then. Not so. Instead, he was shuttled from one veterans' hospital to another for the next 25 years. During that time, I saw him only four times.

My mother quickly became a raging alcoholic. At first, I didn't know what was wrong with her—I thought that maybe she had the flu. She would just lie on the couch, and I would bring cold towels to place on her head. Unfortunately, alcohol brought out her rage. Life became terrifying. Physical and verbal abuse were frequent. I lost all confidence in myself. I began doing poorly in school. The boys teased me because of the hand-me-downs I wore so that my mother would have money for liquor. I felt I was truly ugly and stupid.

My teenage years were a nightmare. There was a parade of men coming and going from our home. My mother had sex right in front of my brother and me. She often accused me of the same kind of promiscuity, although I was doing nothing of the sort. But there was no reasoning with her.

I left home at 17. My last memory of "home" was being struck in the back of my head and neck with a bottle of bourbon that had been hurled at me across the room. Even after all I'd been through, I still couldn't believe that my own mother would do such a thing. It was too painful for me to fully feel the hurt that incident caused.

The following year I got married because I believed I could now have the happy family that I so desperately craved. We had two children right away. I was blissfully happy with the children, and I closed my eyes to the emotional and verbal abuse from my husband. I hear that many girls "marry their father," but I had married my mother.

After ten years of marriage, my husband left me. I was devastated, and the children were crushed. My childhood was being replayed.

I felt totally alone. My life began to unravel, and soon I felt there was nothing left. Although I continued to function at work, I developed an eating disorder and slid deeper and deeper into what I call "the black hole."

One day at work I felt as if I was going to explode. I was at the end of my rope. I called my minister, who referred me to a therapist. Finally I got out the words, "I need help." That was the beginning of the road back.

It was also the beginning of a lot of work and a lot of pain. I told my therapist that my mother was an alcoholic, but I failed to see what that had to do with my problems. Nevertheless, I committed myself to doing whatever he suggested, because I believed that if therapy didn't work I was going to die.

I began going to Al-Anon meetings. For the first time in my life I heard people say *out loud* the things that I was thinking.

As the old wounds were re-opened and actually felt for the first time, I grew more depressed. I continued in therapy, and at one point I entered a treatment center for 30 days. I learned to take it "One Day at a Time," and I got myself to as many Al-Anon meetings as I could find.

Eventually things began to get better, and I started having more good days than bad days. The people in Al-Anon became my life line. The more I shared secrets that I thought were so awful, the more people were drawn to me and I to them. I found some serenity. When I got out of the driver's seat, I found God working in my life and guiding my steps. I discovered that, although things didn't always turn out the way I liked, in the end all things work together for good if I just take the next right step.

I began to look at myself honestly. I had learned at an early age that it was much safer to think than it was to feel, so I had used my intellect to protect me from feeling any uncomfortable feelings. Maybe that's why I've been so attentive to the feelings of others. A typical example occurred when I was 12 years old and attended a funeral for my favorite aunt. When some of my close friends from school came to pay their respects, I spent the time in the ladies' room comforting *them* as they wept. This defense served me well when I had no other tools for survival, but one cannot live a productive, harmonious existence at war with one's deepest self. Therefore, if I had to name one of the greatest blessings I've gained from Al-Anon meetings, and especially Al-Anon's adult children meetings, I would say it was the encouragement, support, acceptance, and understanding I have received from others in Al-Anon as I've experimented with revealing my feelings in a safe place, with people I have come to love and trust.

I have learned that I do not have to be "up" to be loved. No matter what mood I happen to be in, I am accepted in Al-Anon, and that makes it safe to accept these moods myself. This opening-up process didn't happen all at once, but little by little, as I've watched and listened to the people around me speak of their hopes and fears and disappointments with painstaking honesty, without fear of rejection, judgment, or disapproval. Eventually I found the courage to do the same.

I used to wonder, "Isn't it more painful to dredge up these old memories than to just let them lie and get on with your life?" From experience, I know that it can be painful, sometimes excruciatingly so, to sit and listen and watch and feel again the darkest, most distressing memories of youth. But I truly believe that until I felt those feelings in my gut, not in my head, I couldn't learn to accept them or move beyond them. It has been my experience that they do not just quietly fade away if ignored. Today, when I find myself over-reacting to something, I realize that my reaction was triggered by something from my past. Now I recognize these "triggers" and understand why they still affect me.

But the process goes beyond mere understanding. The next step, for me, is to share my discoveries with other Al-Anon members, to talk about my feelings and reactions, and to know that I need not be ashamed or afraid. Somehow this has paved the road to my being able to accept and trust myself.

Today, Al-Anon is the sweet spice in my life. I go to my meetings and receive a free dose of mental health. I am now married to a wonderful man who treats me with love and respect. I am training to be an addictions counselor. I work part-time and do volunteer service work in an inner-city hospital. Al-Anon has helped me build a good life for myself and gotten me through the darkest of days.

I have not been condemned to lead a life of alcoholism like my mother, and I no longer blame her. She is not a "bad" person, only a sick one. She never had the opportunity to change and grow with which I have been blessed.

In Al-Anon I have found a new family, a family where there is no abuse, neglect, betrayal, harsh criticism, or chaos, a family in which we are all free to be exactly who we are. This family has taught me that I am worthy of love and goodness in my life. It has given me love, support, and compassion, and without it I don't think I would have survived the most devastating period of my life.

It happened on a warm, sunny day in early July. I remember looking forward to the upcoming holiday festivities—the picnics, the fireworks, the family gatherings. Then the phone call came informing me that my 17 year-old son had fallen from the back of a pick-up truck and was crushed by oncoming traffic. He was pronounced dead at the scene.

In an instant the world seemed to disappear. My heart froze. I felt as if all the oxygen had left my body. I was vacant, gasping for one last touch, one last moment, one last word.

I didn't want to believe it. Just that morning we had talked and laughed, and I had said, "Have fun and be careful." Now he was gone, and I felt empty.

I thought my tears were going to engulf me, and in a strange and comforting way, I hoped they would. I hoped that this thing called grief would consume me so that I, too, could die and escape the pain. I didn't think I could survive, and I was afraid that I would.

By this time I had spent about six years in Al-Anon listening to the personal experiences and new discoveries of others—and sharing my own. I knew it was my refuge. For me, Al-Anon was a place where sharing was sincere and where I could find support. But now I wondered if anyone could relate to my loss and suffering.

I had found, in the "outside world," that a room would quickly clear if I spoke about my son's death. People did not want to hear about it. I felt terribly alone. It was worse when well-meaning friends or acquaintances offered platitudes and theories about where my son was now and with whom. None of it really mattered to me, because all I wanted was to have my son back. I kept going to my Al-Anon meetings, but I did not share.

One afternoon the chairperson at my Al-Anon meeting chose the topic "loss." I wanted to bolt from the room. I panicked, but something, perhaps my Higher Power, kept me seated. As members shared, my panic grew. I was positive no one wanted to hear my story, and I didn't know if I could bear to tell it.

Then my turn came. Somehow, from deep inside, the truth poured forth. Sadness spilled out in tears, and I shared my anger, my despair, my hopelessness. Nobody ran out of the room, nobody tried to change the subject. They listened and they cared. I came face to face with my anguish but, surrounded by loving and supportive friends, I knew I could get through this. The loving interchange sustained me.

Members of our fellowship reminded me of God's unconditional love and that continuing to be aware of His presence would help me through this crisis. They encouraged me to be totally honest with God, sharing my innermost thoughts and feelings through prayer and meditation. I prayed for God's will and for the courage to go forward.

The miracles and gifts of Al-Anon can sustain, guide, and heal all kinds of wounds, and mine were no exception. It wasn't easy, especially at first, but when I became willing to acknowledge my feelings, my healing began.

Now, five years later, I have found peace and contentment. I no longer ask God why, nor do I blame myself. I now know that my son will live forever in my heart—and in the hearts of the wonderful Al-Anon members who have met him through my story.

I believe that our loved ones who are no longer on earth leave us a legacy, a gift. All I had to do was open my heart to see it. My son left me a treasure of compassion, love, empathy, mercy, and grace.

Yes, I am grateful. Not for the loss, which will always be with me, but for the faith, persistence, support, and miracles that are so freely given in the rooms of Al-Anon.

10

An Adult Child Uncovers Hidden Secrets

Al-Anon was my last hope. When I first walked through its doors I was terribly lonely, frightened, and confused. I brought with me 21 years of living with the family disease of alcoholism. During the first 19 of those years, I had no idea what I was dealing with. "Your mother is just a nervous person," my father had told me. "Your father has an awful temper," my mother would say. Everyone seemed to argue all the time. Whatever was wrong with our family, I was sure it must be my fault. And although I felt totally helpless, I was also certain that it was my responsibility to take care of my family.

When I was 19, my younger sister bluntly broke the news to me: "I think Mom has a drinking problem." It made perfect sense, because drinking had always been evident, but I didn't really want to hear those words. I had spent my life with blinders on, and I wasn't enthusiastic about removing them. But at last I understood why nothing I had done to help my family had ever worked—I hadn't been going after the real problem.

Armed with my new knowledge, I vowed to conquer this drinking business quickly! I approached the problem with great zeal, counting bottles, marking bottles, emptying bottles, hiding bottles, and rationing bottles. I begged, scolded, nagged, and pleaded. I redoubled my other efforts—I cleaned my room, washed the dishes, got home on time, and avoided or corrected all the things my mother had pointed to as the cause of the problem.

Yet I lay nauseated in bed each night, listening to the scrape of the bottle across her bedroom closet shelf. I heard the bottle cap unscrew, the liquor fill the glass, and the gurgle of fluid passing down my mother's throat. I was alone in my own room with a wall, a closed door, and 20 feet of space between us, but I might as well have been two inches from her face.

I never questioned whether or not it was my responsibility to take care of her. As far as I was concerned, that was a given. I was the only one in the family still living with my mother. Who else was there? I lived in a state of anxiety from which I saw no way out.

During those two desperate years, I heard of Al-Anon on television, and the seed was planted. Nonetheless, I didn't really believe that anyone could help. The TV show said that a loved one couldn't stop an alcoholic from drinking, but it went on to recommend that the family come to Al-Anon meetings. I thought that was the stupidest thing I had ever heard. "If it won't stop the drinking, why go?" I asked myself. So I didn't go. Instead, I wore my martyr face and silently suffered. I was unable to see how tense, depressed, and out of control *my* life was. All I could see was that my mother needed fixing.

But the Al-Anon seed began to take root. Although I thought it unnecessary, my younger sister promised to take me to Al-Anon as soon as she returned from college. Then, on a cold February day, I made the bravest decision of my life. I could no longer endure the family's situation. I couldn't wait for my sister. I told my mother I was going to Al-Anon. Secretly, I hoped my threat would stop her from drinking. Then I wouldn't have to go to Al-Anon after all. Instead, she called my bluff. "Go to Al-Anon," she urged. "You'll find out that alcohol is not a problem here and stop all this nonsense."

From the very first meeting I attended, I began learning about the family disease of alcoholism. I was told right away that Al-Anon is not a magical cure for someone else's drinking problems, but that it could offer a better way of life for me. I heard that, if I concentrated on getting to know myself and what made *me* happy and healthy, those around me might respond to the changes in me in a positive way. Health is attractive, and sometimes it inspires others to make changes. But there were no guarantees of any changes in anyone but myself. If I was willing to keep coming back, I would find that the Al-Anon principles could help me not only with my family problems, but in other areas of my life as well.

I had a lot of resistance. The members seemed to sense my fear and responded with warmth and reassurance. "I'm not even sure she's a 'problem drinker,' let alone an a... a... a...," I stammered, unable to say the word. The members of my group told me that I didn't have to have those answers. If someone else's drinking bothered me, I was in the right place.

I wasn't at all thrilled by their "way of life" talk. "I'm a young man," I protested. "I don't want to be going to these meetings for the next 90 years!" They suggested I live this program "One Day at a Time." If I felt better after the meeting than I had before I came, I might want to keep coming back.

Still I resisted. Almost all the members at this particular meeting were middle-aged wives of recovering alcoholics. What could they possible have in common with me? But something touched me. Their sharing came from a different place—from the heart—and I began to relate. Despite all our outward differences, we shared the same feelings. I didn't know such unspoken understanding was possible. Most importantly, they smiled and laughed. I'd never spent much time around happiness. I wanted to learn how these people managed to find anything to smile about, so I kept coming back, and my life slowly began to change.

I learned the Three C's—that I didn't cause; couldn't control; and couldn't cure my mother's drinking. It was a great relief to know this. My progress seemed painfully slow those first two years. Yet the problems which had initially brought me to Al-Anon ceased to feel so pressing. Although my mother was still drinking, I stopped reacting. As a result, we no longer fought all the time. In fact, it was hard to believe how well we were getting along. But as I took the focus off of my mother, I began to see how truly unmanageable my own life had become.

For the first time ever, I could see things about myself that needed changing. Despite a college degree, I had a dead-end job and was financially quite dependent upon my family. Although I had a driver's license, I was terrified of driving and went to great lengths to avoid it. There was considerable emotional distance between my father and me. My younger sister and I had a relationship that was overly dependent and unhealthy.

I was also in the fourth year of a relationship with my first girlfriend. Alcohol was not directly involved, but we both had other problems—attitude problems. I don't know about her, but I believe that I had developed these attitudes while growing up in an alcoholic family—problems with intimacy, honesty, insecurity, trust, blame, and guilt. Al-Anon taught acceptance, tolerance, and courtesy toward others, and I desperately tried to improve my behavior toward my girlfriend. But Al-Anon also helped me to learn that I didn't have to accept unacceptable behavior. I started to believe that I really did deserve to be treated with respect and dignity. The relationship was not good for either one of us, and before long, I was able to let it go.

By this time I was attending several Al-Anon meetings a week. I began volunteering at the local Al-Anon office, and I read my literature faithfully. I even made hesitant moves toward the *Blueprint for Progress*, Al-Anon's guide to the Fourth Step inventory.

Within a very few years, my life had changed dramatically. I had moved out on my own, was in love with a beautiful woman, and was working on a dream project. I was making friends easily and feeling better about myself and my interactions with my family. The program was working well in my life, so well that I didn't feel I had to work at it quite so hard.

Within two years, the dream project fell apart. The girlfriend left me for my best friend. My other friends dropped out of my life one by one. My younger sister, by then a recovering member of A.A., was no longer content to live under my thumb. To top it all off, my father was showing early signs of Alzheimer's Disease.

There was only one place where I didn't feel abandoned— Al-Anon. Despite the limited attention I had given it lately, the program and the fellowship were still there for me. With humility, I thought back to my first meeting. That night, the chairperson had been a member for six years, and this had sounded like an eternity. I expected one would know everything there was to know about this program in six years. By contrast, as my sixth Al-Anon anniversary approached, I felt I knew very little. I could see that I had made a great deal of progress in those six years, but in looking back, I noticed that my dragging feet had left skid marks all the way.

From that point on, I decided to pick up my feet and do some legwork. Someone had once said, "Stick with the winners," and for the first time I heeded this advice and surrounded myself with people who worked the Steps. I formed some very close Al-Anon friendships. I got a Sponsor. I began a steady diet of Al-Anon literature. I started to see the Traditions as useful guidelines for living instead of "boring rules." I got involved in service, sponsoring an Alateen group and attending conventions. I even made it through the entire *Blueprint for Progress*.

I had procrastinated for so long in taking my Fourth Step because I could only see the negative aspects of it. I had no idea of the tremendous improvement that was possible if I was willing to follow Al-Anon's simple suggestion to be honest with myself. Until I knew myself, I couldn't accept myself, and until I accepted myself, I couldn't even begin to love myself.

This self-honesty prepared me to become honest with my Higher Power and another human being (Step Five). I took the risk of sharing things I thought I could never tell anyone. Quite to my surprise, my carefully chosen confidante didn't bolt out the door. She just listened and accepted me, encouraging my fledgling self-acceptance. That experience opened a door within me. I slowly became more open and honest with all my friends. I was still afraid that they would run away, but they didn't. They just loved me more, for as I brought more of myself to my relationships, there was more to love.

Around this time, information about the effects of alcoholism on the grown children of alcoholic families began to proliferate. That information, along with my Alateen sponsorship, prompted further awareness. When Al-Anon's leaflet *Did You Grow up with a Problem Drinker?* came out, I read it with shock, shame, recognition, and hope. I had been in Al-Anon for eight years and yet I was answering "Yes" to all 20 questions. It was obviously time to apply my program on a deeper level. The leaflet did not take my inventory for me, but it gave me an opportunity to continue my growth. It also gave me the chance to change my answers as I grew.

My inventories became archeological digs. Every time I faced, dealt with, and accepted one layer of myself, I would uncover another. Repeating the Steps with each new layer was not regression, but progress. Yet I could not do it without constant reliance on the spiritual side of the program, which I sought through prayer and meditation. For a while, each new discovery seemed more painful and frightening than the last, but I trusted that all of this work was taking me to a place my Higher Power wanted me to be.

By digging deeper, I was able to see how compulsive overeating had become a way of hiding out. When I stopped hiding from myself by eating excessively, I discovered what I had been hiding from. Eventually I had to admit my homosexuality, something I had been denying to myself for years. Once I came to accept being gay, I was ready to face the terrifying realization that I had been sexually abused by trusted relatives as a young boy. Although I had entirely blocked these memories for 30 years, I must have felt enough support from the fellowship to allow the memories to return. I believe that my Higher Power knew I was finally strong enough to face the truth. Each of these revelations was achingly slow, tremendously painful, and took several years to fully accept. Yet most of my pain came, not from the truth, but from resisting the truth.

Al-Anon continually reminded me to be good to myself. I learned to find what made me happy and to follow that path. Through the program, I learned to do whatever was necessary to relieve myself of the burdens of my past because I deserved freedom, love, and happiness. As I uncovered each new layer of myself, I followed Al-Anon's suggestion to avail myself of as much help as I needed. I sought outside counseling, support, and information on more than one occasion. But through it all, the main source of strength and support came from the Al-Anon program and its members.

There were times when my feelings of "terminal uniqueness" resurfaced. At such times, I felt that there was no way that my fellow Al-Anon members could relate to me or I to them. But time and time again, I saw that, although we are all different, our common bond—having been affected by another's alcoholism—unites us. Our differences have helped me to "Keep an Open Mind," and in so doing, I have found myself. I am a strong, kind, and loving person who continues growing stronger, kinder, and more loving each day that I live this beautiful way of life.

Now I know that my Higher Power has a plan for me. It is not my plan. I am not where I once thought I should be or who I once thought I should become. As I improve my conscious contact with the God of my understanding, I let go of my old rigidity and prejudices. I am slowly becoming comfortable with myself and the world around me. I can now see my entire being as a beloved child of my Higher Power. I can accept my whole self, not just the parts I happen to like. I trust that I am being restored to the sanity and joy that were intended for me all along.

My growth through Al-Anon has yielded other dividends. My father died from Alzheimer's Disease, but before he died, I was able to make some strong, positive changes in our relationship and let him know of my love for him. My mother, who stopped drinking several years ago, has become an inspiration and a pleasure to be around, and I have healed enough to truly enjoy her presence in my life. My younger sister and I are no longer joined at the hip, yet in a much healthier way, we are closer than ever. My family has actually become a family that hugs, and we all do what we can for each other. My friends are a wonderful extension of my family, and after feeling abandoned and alone for so long, today I am surrounded by love.

I still go to meetings because I still feel better at the end of a meeting than before it started. I also want to give back a little of what was so generously given to me. The score never evens, though, for the more I give, the more I always receive.

Most of my days now are good ones because, for the most part, that is what I choose to make of them. My life is not free from problems, but thanks to Al-Anon, I have the tools to face whatever I encounter. I no longer have to live in fear and despair or hide out in denial. I am happier than I ever believed possible. I am nourished by the love of a caring partner, compassionate friends, a strong family, and a benevolent Higher Power. When I came to Al-Anon, it was my last hope. It has now become the sturdy root system from which all of my hopes spread out and reach for the sky.

11

Even a Therapist Can Be
Affected by Alcoholism

The first time I remember really feeling a part of my husband's family was when we were in a crisis. We were sitting in the hospital waiting room next to the Intensive Care Unit because my 19 year-old brother-in-law was in a coma after drinking and driving off a cliff. His head had hit a rock when he was catapulted from the car, and only the chill of the snow where he lay kept him from bleeding to death before he was found the next morning. Now, with a compound skull fracture and brain swelling, his life hung in the balance.

My husband and I had been married for five years when my brother-in-law's accident occurred. We were planning a move back to my home state. During my brother-in-law's recuperation, I found myself saying to him, "I wish you could go with us and get a fresh start." From deep within me a warning sounded, but the words were already out, and I wanted so much to help.

I made the move ahead of my husband, and had been at my new job for two weeks when he arrived with our furniture, bringing his brother to live with us. The ground rules were simple: his brother would work at a job or study to get his high school equivalency diploma, and there would be no illicit drugs in our home.

Licit drugs were another matter. The first night they got into town, we all went to the store. My brother-in-law asked for some beer, and my husband bought a six-pack. Inside me, something snapped. After we had put the groceries away, I invited my husband for a walk. As calmly as I could, I asked, "What are you doing, buying him beer when he was almost killed drinking and driving?"

"You're just afraid the people at work are going to find out," he said, smiling indulgently.

I knew this wasn't true. When a life was at stake, other people's opinions were the least of my concerns. As a chemical dependency counselor, I had seen the devastation alcohol can cause in families, and I had often thanked my Higher Power that I hadn't married the alcoholic I had been engaged to before I met my husband.

It was clear that I would get no understanding from my spouse about this problem. I needed help and turned to Al-Anon. Attendance at open Al-Anon meetings was already a requirement of my job—a requirement that I resented. In graduate school and in treatment centers where I had previously worked, it was never considered necessary for professionals to attend the self-help groups to which they referred their clients. Now, back in my own home community, attendance was a must. So I went with mixed hostility, nervousness, and desperation to solve what I saw as a life-and-death problem under my own roof.

At my first Al-Anon meeting, a plaque on the wall among the many slogans (such as "Easy Does It" and "First Things First") caught my attention. It said, "It's what you learn after you know it all that counts." That made me uneasy; I resented the implication that I had more to learn. Like so many others, I went to Al-Anon, not to help myself, but to straighten out the people around me. I don't remember anything I heard at that first meeting, but afterward I asked, "What do you do when someone's buying beer for someone who was almost killed drinking and driving?"

There were smiles and knowing glances, and I thought with chagrin that everyone in the room considered my question naïve, even irrelevant. No matter how much I burned for an answer, the only advice I received was to keep coming back. I did so, still hoping forlornly to find a way to make my husband see the light.

To make a long story short, my brother-in-law did not abide by our house rules. Although I felt we had failed in our efforts to give him a new start, I knew he had to leave. My common sense and new Al-Anon awareness told me that his failure was not our fault, but I still felt sad. That week in Al-Anon I said, "I'm not sure I need to keep coming now that I'm no longer living with an alcoholic."

More knowing glances and nods followed. I was assured by more than one longtime member that I was where I belonged, and that I had a lot to gain if I was willing to keep coming back. I was skeptical, but before long I had a revelation. For years, I had blamed myself for my former fiancé's refusal to go to A.A. I had shunned all Twelve Step programs because they accepted "God *as we understood Him*." My fiancé and I knew a very specific God who went by a very specific name, and we would have nothing "watered down!" We wanted nothing to do with any group that recognized any Higher Power other than the God of our religion. So we had no recovery. He had no sobriety, I had no sanity, and our engagement ended in sorrow. Now, seven years later, I realized that I was no more responsible for my fiancé's failure to get help than I was for my brother-in-law's eviction. Both of these men were responsible for their own choices.

As I continued attending Al-Anon meetings, the spotlight seemed to shift from one alcoholic in my family to another. An uneasy suspicion about my father led me to approach the woman I most respected in the group and ask her to be my Sponsor.

"Let's go to dinner," she said, "and you can tell me what you're looking for in a Sponsor."

I was speechless. Weren't Sponsors supposed to know what you needed? Soon after I arrived at the restaurant, I nervously blurted out how frightened I had been of her and how long I had put off asking her to sponsor me.

She laughed. "Why on earth were you afraid of me?" she asked, kindly.

"I was afraid you'd call me on my stuff," I admitted sheepishly. Yet to this day, I can never remember being confronted or forced by my Sponsor. Anyway, that night I managed to mutter the words, "I think my dad might be an alcoholic."

She never batted an eye. Instead, my new Sponsor leaned forward, smiled, and said something gentle—I can't even remember what—and she helped me to realize that it wasn't the end of the world even if my dad *were* an alcoholic. That was the beginning of my looking into a very painful and shadowy area of my past. My father never drank around our home while I was growing up, but as I began to hear about some current drinking problems he was having, I remembered things my mother had told me about his drinking before I was born. Other memories began to come floating back. I remembered a violent scene that happened when I was ten. My dad had come home drunk and taken out a shotgun, intending to kill my best friend and his parents. The crime was never committed, and the memory was pushed, with others, to a rear mental shelf where it secretly haunted and terrified me. As these memories came back, I felt as if they were ripping themselves out of me. It was painful, and it required a lot more courage and diligence than I thought I had. But all the work to remember and accept the reality of the past was worth it. I was experiencing increasing freedom in my life as I released myself from the enslavement of those dark secrets.

In one of my first Al-Anon meetings, I heard that recovery often begets recovery, and I have been blessed to see several members of my family receive this priceless gift. The first was my older sister, with whom I found the courage to share some Al-Anon literature about adult children of alcoholic parents. Not only did she realize that our father was alcoholic and become a wonderful help to me in evaluating what really happened, but she also sought help in A.A.

Our father never found sobriety. He committed suicide several years ago. I am very grateful to have had a program that helped us to cope with this tragedy, to grieve, to mourn, and to let go.

Meanwhile my husband's increasingly heavy drinking and surliness brought me to the most frightening realization of all. I had broken my engagement to one alcoholic only to marry another! Throughout the ensuing struggle to keep our marriage together, I used my Al-Anon program as never before. The daily meditations in Al-Anon's book, *Courage to Change* became a focus for my harried thoughts. I called my Sponsor every day and stepped up my meetings. At one of those meetings, I heard a statement that would change my life: "He doesn't have to be comfortable." When I stopped taking responsibility for my husband's feelings, I allowed him to experience the consequences of his behavior and feel his own discomfort.

I had hoped that this discomfort would lead my husband to seek sobriety. Instead he chose to leave our marriage. Throughout the incredibly painful process of separation and divorce, Al-Anon stood like a beacon, flashing the Serenity Prayer in the darkness of my pain, helping me to gain my balance as a single person.

Today I am amazed at the healing that has taken place in my life. Over the years, I have grown increasingly capable of letting go of denial and of accepting and recovering from the effects of alcoholism. I have created a new life for myself, one that is filled with joy and laughter, grief and sorrow, and all the other blessings of being more completely alive than ever before. I am so grateful that through it all, Al-Anon has been there to shed light and offer comfort, hope, and strength whenever I needed it—and especially when I didn't know I needed it.

12

A War Veteran Makes Life and Death Decisions

I lost my job and five days later found myself separated from my second wife. My three-year-old son was scared to death of me. I stood alone in my empty apartment and realized just how worthless and useless I felt. It seemed that all I had ever done was hurt people. The self-hatred, remorse, and guilt that I felt were so overwhelming that I knew I couldn't take much more. I had to do something about it. I didn't want to die, but I could no longer stand to live. I had hit bottom, but at the time, I had no idea that what I was experiencing was in any way related to alcoholism.

I decided to buy a gun and blow my head off in the parking lot outside of the store, as soon as the purchase was made. On the way to the gun shop, I noticed a Vietnam Veterans' Center on the right side of the street. I had driven down this street many times before and never noticed it. I didn't know anything about the center, but I had served with the Marines in Vietnam. I figured I didn't have anything to lose by stopping there.

I parked, walked to the door, tugged on the handle, and found that the door was locked. My heart sank. It seemed that everything I did pointed me toward suicide. I felt that nobody cared, not even God. I turned around to walk back to the car, when a voice said, "Can I help you?" One of the counselors inside the building had seen me drive up. "I don't know," I answered.

He invited me inside, and I broke down. No one had ever seen me cry like that. He listened to my despair and was convinced that I needed psychiatric help. He urged me to voluntarily check myself into the local veterans' hospital. I thought about it. I knew very well that I was crazy—just look at my life! Scenes from Vietnam endlessly played through my mind, keeping my memories sharp and painful. Having grown up in a home where feelings were neither acknowledged nor expressed, I had no resources for dealing with the feelings I experienced during the war. At the time, I had no idea that this was one of alcoholism's effects on my life. I just figured I was weak, incapable of coping. So when friends died right before my eyes, I stuffed my feelings of loss. When I myself was wounded in action, I suppressed my anger and fear. And when I witnessed the effects of bombs and booby traps on the bodies of young children, I kept my horror and my outrage at bay. I felt nothing. Over the course of years, this made me cold, angry, distant, and controlling. I pushed people away, while at the same time I longed to be loved. Depression became a way of life, and there was no energy left for living. So I went through the motions, trying to look normal, managing to fool many of the people who knew me. But I had two failed marriages, lots of people were afraid of me, and I was mad all the time, scared all the time, constantly on the defensive, and sometimes violent. Maybe the "nut ward" was the best place for me. Nevertheless, I didn't want to go to that hospital. Maybe I figured that, once I checked in, I would be locked away for life.

Instead, I relied upon the center to get me through the next couple of days, and soon afterward I was referred to a counselor who put me on the road to recovery. While talking to him, I mentioned that both of my parents drank a lot, but that it was no big deal because where I grew up, everyone drank a lot. He immediately suggested that I attend an Al-Anon meeting. I was shocked when he suggested that there might be a link between the way I felt, my behavior, and alcoholism. *"Alcoholism?!"* I protested. "That's something that affects skid row bums. My folks aren't like that! How could there be a connection between me and something that nobody in my family has?"

I didn't understand what he was getting at, but I was so desperate that I went to a meeting. I sat in that first meeting in shock. I couldn't believe that there were people who'd had similar experiences to mine. I don't remember any specifics, but I do remember their saying to me, "Keep Coming Back." So I did. I'd go to the meeting and then roll around in my apartment for a week, going nuts, surviving until the next meeting. The awarenesses came fast and furious, and I felt overwhelmed. I didn't think I could absorb so many new realizations about myself and my family. But I kept attending the meetings once a week.

After a couple of months, I heard about another Al-Anon meeting. I walked into a room full of women, and I was very uncomfortable, to say the least. I'd had a lot of problems with women in my life and here I was surrounded by them. I sat against the back wall and kept my mouth shut. These women were all spouses of alcoholics, and at first I didn't feel as if I belonged. I was convinced that they couldn't possibly understand what I was going through. I had never been married to an alcoholic, nor was I an alcoholic myself, so what could they possibly have to offer me? Again, they kept telling me to "Keep Coming Back," and again, I heeded their advice, although I don't know why I did.

Eventually, I began to really listen to these women and I noticed that many of them had been raised by alcoholic parents—just like me. Gradually my mind began to open a little. I spoke up occasionally. My distrust and suspicion loosened a bit. I identified with the feelings these people spoke of, both during the meetings and afterward, one-to-one. I began to look forward to the meetings because, by then, I felt that the people in the group were sharing the truth with me. They spoke of their deepest secrets; I had never heard people talk so openly and honestly about themselves. They shared about the tools they used and the simple things they did that seemed to work for them—they went to Al-Anon meetings, read the literature, and worked the Steps—and their lives got better and they felt better about themselves. I started to feel that maybe there was hope for me, too.

I had been attending meetings for about six months when my second wife divorced me. I was devastated. Couldn't she see how I was changing?! What was the matter with her? It was then that I realized that I hadn't come to Al-Anon for myself. I had come so that my wife would take me back after she saw how "good" I had become. Yet none of my Al-Anon friends had ever told me I would get back the things, or the people, that I had lost in the past. What they told me was that I could get well and be happy and content if

I was willing to be honest with myself and work the program. From that point on, I worked the program for myself because I believed that, once again, my Al-Anon friends were telling me the truth.

I got a Sponsor and started working the Steps. My focus shifted away from everybody else, and I concentrated on looking at *my* past, *my* behavior, and *my* thinking. As a result of the Steps, I came to recognize the attitudes and behavior patterns that hurt me as well as others. I finally began to see why I was so miserable most of the time. My natural human instincts had gone awry under the influence of other people's alcoholism, and I now had a long list of character defects.

I had reached a fork in the road. I could continue in the same self-destructive direction I had traveled before coming to Al-Anon, or, with God's help, I could choose to change. I had tried to will myself to change many times before. I would succeed for two or three days or even weeks, but then I would always slide right back into the old survival habits, which harmed me and those around me. My efforts to change had nearly cost me my life. It was clear that doing it my way didn't work. The Steps showed me that real change had to come from my Higher Power. I finally became willing to let go of the reins and humbly asked Him to take away those things about me that were unhealthy or undesirable.

As I continued to work the Steps, it became clear to me that I not only needed to make amends to individuals that I had harmed, but that I also owed amends for being a thief. I'd stolen money and goods throughout my life. I had gone from stealing two jars of olives out of a grocery store when I was a kid to padding expense account reports as an adult. Until I took the Fourth Step and made a searching and fearless moral inventory of myself, this behavior had never bothered me. I'd always justified it and then pushed it out of my mind. Even when I began to remember these incidents, I tried to push the memories aside. Again I justified the thefts, saying to myself, "Everybody does it!" But deep down, I knew that this wasn't true. Even if it had been true, I knew that stealing was wrong, at least for me. The longer I thought about it, the more I was able to challenge my denial. I realized that I had to make restitution.

How do you make amends for two jars of olives that had been stolen 30 years earlier? And what about the rest? Surely there is no column in an accountant's ledger for the return of money stolen by former employees! I consulted my Sponsor and others about this dilemma, and was encouraged to list the stolen articles and come up with a probable total dollar value. The grocer, who was quite elderly at the time of the theft, was most likely dead, and the companies I had stolen from had already accounted for the missing funds. What could I do to make amends? It was then suggested that I take the total amount to a charity, in cash. "Why cash?" I asked. "So you won't be tempted to use the cancelled check to write this off as a charitable donation on your income tax," my Sponsor responded.

I made an appointment with an officer of a major charity and set $1,760 on his desk. I told him who I was, that I had been a thief, that I was now in a Twelve Step program, and that I had to make restitution for all the things I had stolen. He paused for what seemed a long time and then asked if he could tell me something. I was uncomfortable, nervous about what he would say, but I nodded "yes."

He leaned back in his chair and said that he had been praying for some extra money. Seventeen youngsters had been scheduled to go on a weekend outing, but the funds had fallen through. He told me the trip would cost roughly $100 per child, and the money I'd delivered was just the right amount. At that moment, I knew God was in charge of everything. Talk about having a spiritual awakening as the direct result of working the Steps! And I was relieved of the secret guilt from years of stealing.

My life has changed, and I have changed. Today the strongest evidence I have is that my son is no longer afraid of me and no longer leaves just because I come into the room. Today we are able to play, kiss, laugh, and express our love for one another. This would never have been possible without the healing power of the program and the love of my Higher Power, and I am most grateful.

I have had to go back and relive many awful moments from the war in order to finally experience the feelings I held down for so long. Until I allowed myself to do so, I was an emotional prisoner of war. By holding tightly to my Higher Power and summoning the courage to feel what I had been unable to feel at the time, I was able to work through some of that horror, and then, for the most part, to let it go. A therapist, a Sponsor, and a loving God made it possible to survive this incredibly difficult challenge.

My mother continued to drink until her death a few years ago. My father joined Alcoholics Anonymous after I'd been in Al-Anon several years. I've discovered that I love him very much just because he is who he is, whether or not he continues to pursue sobriety.

By the grace of a loving God I knew nothing about, my life today has meaning and purpose. I continue to work the Steps, to attend meetings, and to keep in close touch with my Sponsor. Not all of my days are as I would have them be, but today I feel at peace with myself. I've learned that life can be a wondrous journey or a hopeless predicament. I've tried both, so I can say with certainty that I prefer to choose the former. Because of the new way of life I have learned in Al-Anon, that choice is now available to me with each new day.

13

Alateen Helps Calm a Teenager's Violent Temper

When I was 13, a judge charged my dad with driving under the influence of alcohol and sent him to A.A. I knew he drank a lot, but I didn't realize he was an alcoholic. All I knew was that we had a lot of money problems, and I only knew that because my mom complained about it all the time.

There had been incredible tension in our home for years. I couldn't stand being around either of my parents. My mom was nervous all the time, and I felt nervous in her presence. My dad and I barely spoke. I couldn't see much difference in him between the A.A. days and the drinking days. I just wanted out.

By the time my dad started attending A.A., I was already sneaking out my bedroom window at night to join my friends. It was fairly innocent; the mischief was in being out in the middle of the night without supervision. I loved the excitement of risking being caught.

When I was 14 I discovered a nearby pool hall. Looking back, I believe that God really looked out for me during that phase of my life. I knew some truly vicious men there, but my encounters with them were always harmless. Many of these guys used and sold drugs, many were drop-outs and crooks, and many had violent natures. I refused car rides with them, not out of fear or caution, but simply out of habit. I actually admired these people who seemed so "cool" and tough.

Toughness appealed to me because I felt that my life was full of hurt. It was as if I lived in a garbage can of emotional pain, and all I had to look forward to was other people lifting up the lid and dumping more garbage on me. I wanted out. I figured if I could just be tough enough, people would be too afraid to hurt me. And if I was "cool" enough, I wouldn't care even if they did.

I wanted no part of drugs, but I took up heavy drinking, and soon afterward I joined the "sexual revolution." I had no fears about anyone "using" me for sex. Instead, I planned to use *them*. I collected sexual conquests with a vengeance. Sex and drinking were the two ways I found to assert my independence and to be "cool." They were also the very best ways to thoroughly disgust my parents.

I got pregnant the summer I graduated from junior high school. My mother confronted me, forcing me to make a decision about the pregnancy rather than to simply ignore the problem. When I chose to have an abortion, she accompanied me. Although my dad supplied the money, he and I never discussed the situation at all.

I entered high school full of fear, remorse, and self-hatred. On one hand, I was disgusted with myself, but on the other, I still felt drawn to the wild lifestyle. The only alternative I had ever seen, the only example of moderation and "normalcy," was my parents' marriage, and it wasn't a very appealing example, since they didn't look all that happy to me.

My dad had been attending A.A. diligently for some time by then, and he often talked about a girl about my age who went to Al-Anon meetings. He said the kinds of nice things about her that I longed to have him say about me! I finally went to an Al-Anon meeting to meet this girl I'd grown so jealous of. Strangely enough, we hit it off. Her mom was going to A.A., and she had come to a few Al-Anon meetings, but had never worked up the nerve to try Alateen by herself. The following week, she and I attended our first Alateen meeting together.

The small room was full of people about my age—I was 16 by this time. They sat on the couch, on cabinets, in chairs, and on the floor. A particularly cute blonde guy behind a desk was chairing the meeting. After the meeting ended, a pretty, petite woman, who turned out to be the group's Sponsor, smiled at me, gave me a big hug, and said she really hoped I'd come back next week. She looked like someone my parents would want me to emulate, but unlike them, she looked happy.

That loving Sponsor and that cute blonde guy kept me coming back for the next six months, until I had recovered to the point where I could hear and learn from what was being said in the meetings. I do recall reading and evaluating the Steps early on. But I had decided that I was *never* going to do Step Nine and make amends to anyone! I wasn't going to shuffle up and grovel to a bunch of people who would never forgive me anyway—not that I blamed them. I knew all too well that I had caused more than my share of harm to others. I carried the guilt around to prove it.

I also remember seeing the word "sanity" in the Second Step, "Came to believe that a Power greater than ourselves could restore us to sanity." At the time, I thought, "Whoa, these people here have *serious* problems!" My next thought was, "Well, I guess that means I'm in the right place." I knew I was crazy. I had no control over myself. I cut classes that I knew I couldn't afford to miss. I hung out at the pool hall trying to hide from myself and the mess my life was becoming. At night I would find a party or a "date," even though I no longer felt so good about this lifestyle. When I wandered home at three-o'clock or four-o'clock in the morning, my dad was always asleep. Sometimes he was sober, sometimes not. Sobriety didn't "take" for him right away, and he had many slips. My mom always waited up, always ready with the inevitable questions about my antics, especially about my sex life. If I had slept with someone, I was angry about being confronted, and if I hadn't, I was indignant about being accused. I hated the nagging, and I reacted violently. I would push and shove her out of my way. Once I can remember trying with all my might to strangle my mom until, somehow, her pain penetrated my rage and I went limp with remorse and helplessness. Disgusted with myself, I wished that someone would just lock me up to protect both of us. At the time, I thought I was choosing to drink and sleep around, but I knew that my violence against my mom was never a voluntary act. I didn't want to hurt her, but I didn't know how to stop, how to break the pattern. That insanity was what got me to take Alateen seriously.

To break the pattern of violence, I had to take baby steps. Learning to live "One Day at a Time" meant that I didn't have to behave violently today; I could postpone the violence until tomorrow. At first, I would clench my fist and say under my breath, "Alateen, Alateen, Alateen. I will not hurt you tonight, but tomorrow I will kill you." I found that by living "One Day at a Time," that horrible tomorrow never came.

So "Just for Today," I began to choose not to hurt my mother. It didn't happen easily. More than anything, I wanted to go back to my Alateen group and say that we had not had a physical altercation all week. Eventually, it happened. The Serenity Prayer took the place of my "Alateen, Alateen, Alateen" utterances, and I learned to leave the room without yelling at my mother. Then I learned to leave without slamming the door. Eventually I could sit in the room and detach from anything I found irritating. The time even came when I learned to respond as an adult.

One afternoon, a few years after having moved on to Al-Anon, I was about to go home after visiting my mom. It had been the usual strained experience for me. I loved her, but she had never found Al-Anon and was still suffering from the effects of alcoholism. My dad was sober in A.A., but they had separated and she lived alone. My dad and I had long since mended our relationship and I was so grateful—but also sad that I still felt so uncomfortable with my mother after all this time. I remember telling God about this sadness and how I just couldn't seem to do any better. As I left her house, I prayed that, if this was as good as our relationship was going to get, would He please help me accept it?

Less than six months later, my mom and I were disagreeing about how we had suddenly come to be such close friends. Each of us thought it was because the other had somehow changed. I can only say that my prayers were answered. We spent many truly good days together after that, looking forward to our visits as if we had always been best friends. My mom stood by me through nine years of marriage, divorce, and a subsequent remarriage. She saw me finish a bachelor's and then a master's degree in night school. Because of Al-Anon, we became a mother and daughter who could appreciate and love one another, sharing in the joy and helping each other through the sorrows of our lives.

Today, thanks to Al-Anon, the old days are a dim memory. They have been replaced by much happier memories of a family that is proud of me after all.

14

A Wife Copes with Physical Abuse

My alcoholic father had often said that I needed to marry a man who would beat me, and I guess I took that advice to heart. My husband was physically abusive even before we were married. My life was a disaster, my dreams had fled, and I was filled with despair. Nevertheless, I put on such a great front that people at work called me "Suzy Homemaker" because they thought I had the perfect life—a beautiful home, wonderful children, a good job, and an ideal marriage to a handsome, successful husband.

My husband was drinking heavily, and nothing I said or did would stop him. I learned to keep my mouth shut because I didn't want to provoke a beating. Nevertheless, the beatings would come, regardless of how careful I was about my words, facial expressions, actions, and attitudes. He had affairs, and I said nothing. I didn't want to upset him. When he flaunted them in front of me, I willed myself not to care. It wasn't all that difficult. After years of abuse, I had stopped feeling anything. I became numb, a robot who went through the motions of living. Caring cost too much. I had long since given it up as a luxury I couldn't afford.

In the midst of an especially difficult period, a friend told me about Al-Anon. He helped me realize that some behavior was unacceptable, and I did not have to accept it. I began to feel there might be some hope for me and found a counselor who treated battered women. She also happened to be a member of Al-Anon. I began to attend meetings.

Things in my home were deteriorating rapidly. My husband's abuse of alcohol was worse, and his doctor was "helping" his depression with prescription tranquilizers. I prayed and prayed for a solution to this situation. One day a friend asked if I had ever considered taking my daughter and leaving. It sounded crazy at first, but as I discussed the idea with my Al-Anon friends and my counselor, I became convinced that it was the proper course of action for me. The support of my Al-Anon friends during this difficult time was priceless. I started taking small steps to prepare.

My husband was getting worse every day, and one night he took an overdose of tranquilizers. He had come into the bedroom, locked the door, disconnected the phone, and announced that he was going to commit suicide. I was afraid he would also kill me. It was then that he took a large handful of pills and washed them down with wine. I was terrified and didn't know what to do.

When he passed out, I let myself out of the bedroom. I was tempted to do nothing, just let him die. For a fleeting moment, I imagined that all my problems would then disappear, but I knew this wasn't true. I also knew I would never be able to live with myself if I made such a choice. I called the paramedics, and after several hours of treatment, my husband's condition was stabilized.

Despite my concern for him, I continued to make secret preparations for my move, which was scheduled for the next month. I could easily have set aside my intention to leave. Previous crises had often prompted me to change my plans and attend to my husband's needs. Wasn't that what love was all about, I'd thought—or at least marital duty?

But I was learning in Al-Anon that my needs were important, too. I had decided to move out, and I think my Higher Power was giving me an opportunity to prove to myself that I meant what I said. If I really wanted a better life, I had to stop making the same decisions I had made a hundred times before.

My husband was soon released from the hospital and placed on medication that made his depression even worse. Positive that I held his future in my hands, he accused me of not loving him enough. If only I would love him more, he argued, he would be fine. It took all of my detachment not to believe what he said. Even though I knew that he had a disease over which I had no control, and that I had a right to be free from abuse, I felt terribly guilty. I wanted to save him from his misery. But I knew that his well-being was his responsibility. When the nagging guilt rose, I would call an

Al-Anon friend who never failed to remind me that I was powerless over alcohol and that I, too, had a right to happiness.

Then things got even worse. My husband began threatening to shoot himself in front of our daughter. I didn't know what to do, so I went to Al-Anon meetings and talked about my fear and confusion. I prayed. I cried.

And I came to a decision to leave—now. I quit my job, contacted a mover, and arranged for my belongings to be picked up a few days later.

I called a few shelters for battered women in order to find my daughter and me a place to stay in the new town, but we had no luck. But the day before we left, a member of my church called and told me that some friends of hers would take us in. I was grateful for good friends—and even more grateful for a Higher Power who seemed to be taking care of us.

A group of friends and two movers helped pack our belongings and load them into the moving van. We were halfway along when my secretary called to say that my husband had just left me a message—he had been laid off from work. I knew my husband had an 11:30 appointment with his psychiatrist and would be home afterward. We speeded up the packing, throwing boxes into the van, said a quick goodbye, and departed.

I feared that my husband would come home, find us gone, and commit suicide, just as he so often had threatened to do. My feelings of guilt were overwhelming. While struggling with this, however, I had a sense of my Higher Power's presence, and a great serenity enveloped me.

I later learned that the combination of my leaving and my husband's job loss helped him to hit bottom and seek sobriety. I believe that only God could have arranged the timing to work out this way and to have this effect.

After a long and trying journey, my daughter and I finally reached our safe house. With help from the couple who had taken us in, I began trying to build a new life. But depression set in making each day a struggle just to get up. I took one step at a time, one day at a time, and the seemingly overwhelming task ahead of me became more manageable. I set what I thought was a goal I could achieve. I could make at least three calls about jobs or houses each day. After two weeks I found a very nice apartment. Although the rent was high and I still didn't have a job, I took it on faith, and we quickly settled in.

My money was running out. By the end of the week, I had less than 50 dollars, with no job in sight. That morning I received a call asking if I would like to work for a local company temporarily during a strike. I felt that God was again taking care of me, since I had not applied for this job but merely mentioned my interest to someone who had apparently passed on the information.

I found a soup kitchen at a nearby church and an Al-Anon meeting after lunch. All the members were married women, and I shuddered at the thought of hearing how happy they all were. I had just left my husband, and I wanted a divorce. Many of them did speak of their happiness, but what I remember most was their love and acceptance of me, a total stranger. I felt very much at home. When I got back to my apartment, two letters were waiting for me from friends and family, each containing a check for 50 dollars to tide us over. I had not asked for the money, yet again my needs were met in unexpected ways. Soon thereafter I found a very good job.

I attended as many Al-Anon meetings as possible, which helped me to survive my grief and to adjust to the tremendous changes in my life. Daily gratitude lists helped me to recognize that many wonderful gifts were being handed to me and kept my mind from dwelling on self-pity and "if onlys." My self-esteem was at rock bottom, but Al-Anon meetings and phone calls helped counteract my self-doubt.

The biggest help in changing my attitude was working the Steps. They gave me a foundation on which to build and grow. They helped me to shift my focus away from the alcoholic. I began learning about myself, my likes and dislikes, character assets and defects, and the trouble I had brought upon myself by refusing to recognize my powerlessness over alcoholism. I examined my part in the unhappiness of my marriage and stopped blaming all of my problems on my husband. I still loved him, and even though I had experienced a great deal of unhappiness in our marriage, I had to admit that I missed him. Nevertheless, I needed to acknowledge how deeply I had been affected by his alcoholism in order to recover from those effects. I faced the fact that his alcoholic behavior often involved physical abuse and that I couldn't change that. And most importantly, I needed to learn to turn to a Higher Power rather than my own self-will for help, for healing, and for direction.

As time passed, my husband worked his program and I worked mine. We began to talk and work on our problems over the phone. I went back for a visit at Christmas to see if we could work things out. The slogan, "Keep It Simple" was the motto of my trip. I made no elaborate plans and limited my activities to small gatherings with only the immediate family. Even though the visit went well, I kept in close touch with my Sponsor, just to anchor myself in reality. I knew how easily I could slip into denial or make self-destructive choices based on guilt or old habits.

I returned to my new home and my new life, but remained in frequent contact with my husband for the next six months. Although there were some rough moments when I reverted to old behavior, becoming overly concerned with my husband's thoughts and actions rather than my own, our relationship grew closer and more honest than it had ever been. We had both changed in many ways. Eventually we decided to reconcile.

Our respective recoveries have brought many wonderful changes into our lives. I no longer have to contend with suicide threats, guns, or beatings. We share more than ever. We go out. We celebrate special occasions without drunken brawls or fistfights. We both participate in raising our daughter, playing, hugging, laughing together. We try to live a spiritual life, and that gives us all a measure of serenity.

I wish I could say, "We lived happily ever after," but that is not real life, and today I am able to face reality, even when I don't like what I see. My husband has been a violent man all his life. Counseling and sobriety have helped him to cope with his rage, but it has been a very gradual process. Since my return, he has not struck me. But at times the violence is still there.

At first, instead of throwing me against the wall, he would

throw something else, a dish, my purse, whatever he could grab. Sometimes these objects were hurled in my direction, and although they missed me, I felt as terrorized as if they had struck. As time passed, this happened less often, and I believe that it has now stopped. Nonetheless, although his physical attacks seem to be gone, his rage continues. It will take me a long time before I truly feel safe, but I am learning to accept that this is a sickness that cannot be overcome very quickly. It is hard to acknowledge that a broken plate is an improvement over a broken arm, when I am so eager to have all the violence cease at once. But the fact is that I do see gradual improvements, and I can choose to acknowledge this progress instead of trying to demean him for not being further along.

However, I don't have to allow myself to be a target. Alcoholism has symptoms that can persist in sobriety, and arguing or trying to reason with someone who is acting irrationally is a waste of time. In the past, this was one of the ways in which I contributed to the sickness within our home. Now I don't even try. Rather, I acknowledge that I am dealing with insanity. If I feel that I am in danger, I take action to protect myself. I have several safe houses where I can go if necessary, and I have money and car keys hidden for quick access in an emergency. But I haven't felt the need to leave in quite a while. Today I know the difference between what I will and will not accept.

Now, if I am at all concerned for my safety, I simply need to step out of the line of fire for a few minutes. I have found that if I tell my husband that I love him (which I do) but that I need to excuse myself for a minute to use the bathroom, I often buy both of us enough time to calm down. In the meantime, I put a door between us, which offers me some security. This kind of detachment is hard work, and if I wasn't convinced that this marriage was right for me today, it probably wouldn't be worth the effort. My husband is increasingly able to handle this aspect of his disease, and I want to give us both a chance at a better and closer relationship. Seeing the changes over these past few years has helped me to grow more confident that it is right to stay, at least for today. But I would be lying if I said that he got sober and the violence came to a halt just because he hasn't hit me.

There have also been some wonderful times. My former employer took me back and even gave me a raise. He hadn't found anyone who did my job as well as I had, and he was grateful for my return. My Al-Anon friends welcomed me home with love and warmth, and I found another marvelous Sponsor. I continue to attend as many meetings as possible, read Al-Anon literature, and work in service. Al-Anon not only changed my marriage, it changed my life. It taught me to look inside and to work on my own life. I even went back to college at night in pursuit of my lifelong dream to get a degree.

I know that the journey I have begun in Al-Anon is an ongoing journey of recovery; there is no end to my story today. I am simply writing a new chapter as I live each day as fully as I can, "One Day at a Time."

15

A Son's Imprisonment Teaches a Mother About Herself

How was I going to get my son to stop drinking and using drugs? That was all I could think of when I first came to Al-Anon. I was completely obsessed with him. When he was out of the house, I worried about where he was, who he was with, what he was doing. The sound of an ambulance's siren sent me into hysteria, because I would imagine my son being rushed to the hospital after a terrible car accident. If it snowed, I would see him in my mind passed out on a snowbank, freezing to death. I couldn't function. I couldn't read a book, make myself a decent meal, or even think about sleeping until he returned, and sometimes he didn't get home until dawn. My job had flexible hours, but my work suffered terribly, and I'm lucky I didn't lose my job.

Things were no better when he was home, as I was constantly on the lookout for signs that he was drinking, thinking about drinking, saving or stealing money from me for drugs. Whenever he picked up the phone, I eavesdropped to determine whether he was talking to a drug dealer or making plans with his drinking buddies. I felt the need to distract him, to keep him entertained so that he wouldn't remember to drink. At the same time I was tearing myself apart with guilt because I wanted so badly to do whatever a "good" mother would do under the circumstances—but I didn't have any idea what that was. Should I be tougher, lay down the law, take away his privileges, lock him in his room, tie him to the bed and beat him up? Or should I be more understanding? Was this just a phase? Would he outgrow it? I had tried everything, from punishment to indulgence. Nothing I did made any difference, but I felt that there had to be an answer, and it was my obligation as a parent, and as someone who loved him so very much, to come up with it. He was so young, and I felt so guilty.

There were other problems as well. I suspected that he was stealing from local stores, but whenever I confronted him, he denied
it. His school attendance was poor, and his grades had fallen.
When he was home, he usually seemed depressed; indeed, he had
dropped the word "suicide" into conversation more than once. I was
terrified. Every day when I took my shower, I left the bathroom door
partly open in case he should call for help. Many nights I slept in
my clothes, ready to race to the emergency room if the need arose.
I had no life of my own. It never occurred to me that anything mattered except the well-being of my son. I had become insane as the
result of someone else's alcoholism, but I was completely unaware
that I had a problem. My son was the one who needed help.

I went to my first Al-Anon meeting to get someone to tell me
what to do to make him stop drinking. They passed around a note-
book where members were invited to write their first names and
telephone numbers if they were willing to be contacted by other
members between meetings. I wrote down my son's name and phone
number instead of my own, hoping that someone would call him and
do something to stop his self-destruction. No one did.

All I can remember about that meeting was that there was
another mother who spoke tearfully about her daughter's drinking
problem, and how wonderfully everyone responded to her, giving her hugs, nodding with understanding, talking to her after the
meeting. I couldn't bring myself to say anything to anyone or to talk
about my own situation, but I can't tell you how comforting it was
to see the program work for someone with similar problems. That's
why I kept coming back.

One of the early memories I have from Al-Anon was hearing that
the alcoholic has his or her arms wrapped around the bottle, and
we have our arms wrapped around the alcoholic. That image was
so clear to me that it broke through some of my denial and allowed
me to consider the possibility that I, too, had been affected by alcoholism. It was unbelievably painful to take the focus off of my son,
even for a moment, and look at myself and my own self-destructive
behavior. I began to notice that my life was unmanageable. But I
still couldn't quite believe that I was powerless.

I began to pray to a nameless, faceless Higher Power I didn't believe in because I was told that if I wanted to get better, I would have to develop some sort of relationship with a Power greater than myself. When I complained that I couldn't pray because I didn't know who God was, if indeed there was a God at all, people at the meetings strongly suggested that I pray anyway, if only to demonstrate to myself that I was wiling to try a new approach to my problems. I think I started praying with the intention of proving them wrong. I would do what they instructed, and when it didn't work, I would be proven right—and would feel smug. I have never been fond of being told what to do by anyone. I prefer to figure it out myself. If it hadn't been for my continual failure to fix my son, I don't think I would have made any effort to change. But I was desperate enough to try anything, even prayer. I prayed that God would do something to keep my son from killing himself.

Soon after, the police came to my house to arrest my son. He was charged with several counts of burglary and criminal trespass. My Al-Anon program was already working because, instead of simply falling apart, I called my Sponsor and got the support I needed to get through the crisis.

My son chose to cooperate, admitting his substance abuse problems for the first time as well as confessing to several burglaries. When the formalities of the arrest were completed, he was released into my custody pending the hearing sometime within the next month. Tearfully, he promised not to have another drink or pick up another drug.

That month I began to learn the meaning of the slogan "One Day at a Time." I knew that if I allowed myself to fantasize about all the terrible things that might happen to my son, I would have a difficult time waiting for his hearing. My Sponsor and other Al-Anon friends helped me to understand that I had a choice about how to spend each day: Just for that one day, I could wait, or I could live. My focus could be on myself, doing whatever came next, or I could let it wander onto my son's life and his future.

For the most part, I managed to keep my attention on myself and keep my thoughts on the moment or the day at hand. But in spite of my new clarity and fine intentions, I had some rough nights where I would awaken, imagining my son being subjected to atrocities while serving an endless prison term. Once these thoughts got started, they seemed to have a life of their own. The Higher Power that I had been so reluctant to turn to now became my best hope. Only a Power greater than myself could overcome my obsessive thoughts. With the help of that Higher Power, I began to find some relief. I had begun to work the Steps. I was powerless over the way alcoholism was affecting me, and my life was unmanageable. I was coming to believe that a Power greater than myself could restore me to sanity. And I made the decision to turn my will and my life over to His/Her/Its care.

For a while, the days passed calmly. But then another call came. My son was being held by the State Police on charges of breaking and entering with the intent to commit a crime. When I arrived at the station, I couldn't help noticing a picture on the wall that depicted a gun discharging at point blank range. All that was visible was the barrel with fire exploding from it. I felt a chill at the thought that some day my son might find himself at the end of that barrel. Before Al-Anon, I would either have banished the thoughts from my mind as if they had no bearing on my life or gotten hysterical right there in the middle of the room. This time, I simply acknowledged that I didn't know what tomorrow would bring, and that if my son continued his alcoholic and criminal behavior, I was powerless to stop him. I recognized that such behavior can have violent consequences, but I chose not to dwell on what might or might not happen.

The juvenile probation officer informed me of my rights and responsibilities and advised me about what he felt was in the best interest of my son. He asked if there was a history of drug or alcohol abuse. Because of the previous charges that were pending against my son, he was reluctant to release him into my custody again. When asked if I honestly felt that I was able to handle my son and assure the county that he would appear for a hearing, I said, "No." I could not honestly promise anything where his behavior was concerned, for I was powerless to control it. This was a heartbreaking admission to have to make, but I was proud of myself for being able to stay with the truth, even when I despised the picture it presented.

How does a mother prepare herself to see her son shackled on the floor? Since he was acting erratically, the police felt it was wise to restrain him for his own good. When I walked into the room, a sob caught in my throat, and I quickly turned away. But the moment passed. I managed to ask my son if he had anything he wanted to say. Although he tried to act nonchalant, he was visibly frightened and said he wanted to tell the police everything that had happened. They removed the shackles, and he made his confession. After that, he was remanded to the juvenile detention center until his trial date.

I continued to attend as many Al-Anon meetings as possible, sometimes driving long distances for my daily nugget of serenity. The program was my means of survival. Obsession was replaced with faith, living in the present, and replacing negative thoughts and fears with positive thoughts, slogans, and the Serenity Prayer. But this didn't happen overnight. Many days I had to make it through one minute at a time. Though I missed my son, the separation gave me an opportunity to focus on myself. I began to make a point of cooking real meals for myself, getting my work done with care, getting out of the house on my days off, if only to walk to the park down the street and see what the rest of the world was doing. I treated myself like someone who deserved kindness, even when I didn't believe it myself. In fact, I tried to treat myself as well and as generously as I would normally treat my son. And I began to heal.

The other Al-Anon members were unbelievably kind and supportive of my meager efforts at self-care. They had been through the pain and heartache that is such a part of the disease of alcoholism. They didn't give me advice or judge my parenting skills. They just shared a lot of helpful, positive tools and outlooks that they had already learned. Their love and support seemed limitless.

Because of their compassion, I learned to have compassion for myself. I realized that from the day my son was born, I had wanted the best for him. As a mother, it seemed only natural to do everything I could to help him as he grew up and to want to smooth his path and ease his pain. Maternal instincts are wonderful, natural, and loving. I was not bad for wanting the best for my son. But when alcoholism is present, what might normally be kind, loving, and helpful can often do more harm than good. Alcoholism distorts beauty and taints the most loving of gestures. I had to learn that enabling was not the same as helping. Bailing him out of jail or trouble was only perpetuating his pain. When he was a child, I had to force him to take bitter-tasting medicine to relieve his illness. Now I had to step back and allow him to face the bitter consequences of his actions. I hoped that this would be the best medicine I could provide, because I knew I couldn't control or cure his disease or his behavior. I was even beginning to acknowledge that I hadn't caused it.

When the court gave my son the choice of prison or rehabilitation, he chose rehabilitation. I was so thrilled, so relieved, so convinced that everything would now be fine. My son completed his treatment and was placed in a halfway house. For a while he seemed devoted to recovery. Time passed. Then the drinking began again. He was asked to leave the halfway house and chose to move in with a friend rather than return home. By this time he was old enough to be on his own, and I decided not to fight it. Under the circumstances, it seemed the best decision for both of us.

I am grateful that I have been able to accept the situation as it is, and I rarely get depressed over it. I still see my son fairly often. I love him dearly, maybe even more than ever, because today I am so much more truly myself and I can appreciate him for the sweet, bright young man that he is. I also accept the fact that he is sick, and that I am powerless over his sickness. He knows how to get help if he wants it. Meanwhile, I have had to let go of his sickness and his behavior, because I am unwilling to let it take over my life any longer. The Higher Power that saw me through these difficult years has become more of a friend and a comfort, although I am still unsure of how to define Him/Her/It. Nonetheless, I rely upon this Power to take care of my son and to know what is best for him.

The biggest trap for me today is feeling maudlin about my son's lost potential. I think back to happier times, how proud I was when he was reciting nursery rhymes at the age of two, how delighted I felt when he announced that he was going to be a "doggie doctor" when he grew up, the laughter and hugs that we shared. I have many fond memories, and I don't want to forget that there were good times. But I have to be careful not to dabble in "if onlys." His potential is his business, not mine. His life, present and future, is out of my hands. I also have to guard against searching for every mistake I ever made and blaming myself for his sickness. I made plenty of mistakes, but I did not cause alcoholism. I continue to struggle with guilt, and make many phone calls to Al-Anon friends who help me to find my way back to serenity.

I don't know how I survived all those years without a Higher Power and without the Al-Anon fellowship. Life doesn't always work out the way I would like, and I still have an occasional temper tantrum and slide into self-pity. But I know that I am well cared for, and today I am able to face whatever life brings, coping with the hard times and truly relishing the rest.

16

A Nun Finds Spiritual Peace

It was a troubling time, full of questions about my purpose in life, my vocation as a nun, the value of my very existence. Day after day I had been asking myself and my God, "What is wrong with me?" but no answer was forthcoming. Then, out of the clear blue, a staff member of an alcoholism and chemical dependency program came to talk to my religious community of sisters about the effects of alcoholism and drug addiction upon the lives of friends and family members. God had heard my prayers, and I felt that a door was being opened.

I related to much of what I heard that day, although, relieved as I was to find an explanation for the emptiness I had been feeling, I wasn't happy to be labeled as someone with a problem. But I came to realize that my problem was my way of coping—the only way I had been able to survive growing up as a teenager in an environment affected simultaneously by an older sister who drank and drugged to excess and a father dying of a brain tumor.

I had become a people-pleaser and had lost my own identity completely. I measured my worth by what others thought of me, how well I was liked, how perfectly I performed my duties. I thought that I was only of value if I made others happy, eliminated everyone's stress, and abandoned my own opinions to bow to those of others. What was left? A shriveled and weary young woman. I was surprised to see that I still used many of the coping skills developed as a child even though I was in the convent, far from my family and the alcoholic situation of my youth.

I decided to seek help, hoping to find some answers as well as some peace of mind and soul. The counselor recommended a short-term program for "co-dependency," and I found it very informative. But it was the required aftercare—attendance at Al-Anon meetings—that really made a difference. I found a meeting close to my convent and attended diligently. Slowly, the miracle began to unfold before my very eyes. I actually felt life entering my body and my spirit as I continued going to Al-Anon meetings.

I experienced unconditional love at these meetings, a respect for who I was—who I really was—in my brokenness and sorrow and in my joy and humor. For the first time in my life I could be *me* without performing, and people still liked me! I was listened to without interruption, and I felt a tremendous bonding with others as I gave full attention to what they had to say. Many times I heard stories similar to my own. I wasn't alone!

Gradually I realized that I had been searching for some tragic, irreparable flaw in myself that *didn't exist!* A missing or flawed piece had never been the source of my problem. There was just a lot about myself that I needed to discover and address, and Al-Anon was the place where I could do just that. One of the greatest joys in this process of discovery and recovery was that I found what it means to be truly alive! Instead of looking at life as a problem to be solved, I began seeing each day as a challenge to experience, embrace, and enjoy. My attitudes began to change as a result of the positive examples I found all around me in my Al-Anon group, and soon the whole world looked brighter to me.

But there were difficult times as well. I can remember dragging myself to an Al-Anon meeting one day, feeling terribly sorry for myself. I had been making great strides in my recovery after just a few months of attendance, and I was becoming pretty confident, perhaps excessively so. The alcoholism in my life was far removed, long past, and I was moving into a healthier world. Then, suddenly, I became aware that another sister in my spiritual community, someone I lived and worked with very closely, was an alcoholic, and I was duplicating childhood behavior in my interactions with her. I sat in that meeting, feeling dejected and lost, and then, as has so often happened, I heard exactly what I needed to hear. The meeting topic was "changed attitudes." The chairperson wrote the following sentences on a chalkboard:

Opportunity is nowhere.
Opportunity is now here.

It was a wonderful, graphic example of the fact that the way the world looks is all a matter of perspective. I began to realize that no matter what others in my life did or did not do, and no matter how "recovered" or "unrecovered" I felt, I had 24 hours ahead of me in which I had the opportunity to heal, to experience serenity, and to improve my conscious contact with my Higher Power. What I did with that opportunity was up to me. So whenever I feel as if opportunity is nowhere, I have the option to step back and detach for a moment—to create a little space—and I'm likely to find that opportunity is now here, and in fact has been here all along.

The Twelve Steps have become a new backbone for my life. The most startling result is that I have discovered a sense of profound intimacy with God that I never thought possible. One might expect a nun of ten years to have developed this kind of spiritual relationship long ago, but such was not the case with me. I believe that God's ways are not always my ways, nor are they restricted to my time frame. It is never too late to have a spiritual awakening, and as it says in Step Twelve, such an awakening is the result of working all Twelve Steps. Each step has its own importance, but for me, it is in the *whole* of the Steps, the total experience over time, that true freedom is found. I know that this process is only just beginning for me, since I am a relative newcomer to Al-Anon and I have a lot left to learn. Nevertheless, the changes have been profound.

My spiritual awakening finally took hold when I learned to surrender my desire for control and to simply flow with the tide of life. Since then I have redefined what spirituality means to me. Today I feel that something new can be discovered about God each day, each moment. In this process of discovery, so much is revealed about life and my own existence. I am more alive than ever before, able to participate fully and to be present for others in a deeper, more respectful, and more truly loving way than at any other time in my life. A new belief system is emerging in which I honestly feel that there is a God who cares, a God who can help me to have the courage to change the things I can and accept the rest. This helps me tremendously in dealing with others, especially the alcoholics in my past and present life. I have been reminded that the name of the family disease is alcoho*li*sm, not alcohol*was*m, and that recovery from its effects requires an ongoing commitment to the principles of this spiritual program.

I can remember feeling exhausted when I was trying to manage everything and everyone in my life. I stopped feeling exhausted when I learned to stop "playing God." Again, the Steps, especially Step Three, "Made a decision to turn our will and our lives over to the care of God *as we understood Him,*" were the key to my release. I became free when I finally turned the game of life over to my Higher Power. Everything is so much easier today because I am learning to let go of the things over which I have no power and to allow God to take control of them instead. I was amazed to find that letting go doesn't mean becoming an unidentifiable blob without strength, emotion, or desire. I have found just the opposite. In surrendering the things over which I am powerless, I am able to see where I do have power—over myself, my reactions, my attitudes, my choices. As a result, I have found a deeper sense of identity and self-worth. All that has been required of me is some willingness.

These insights have not suddenly purged me of my defects of character. Instead, I have had to view these defects with a certain acceptance. I know that with the help of my Higher Power, all of my shortcomings can eventually be transformed into something more loving, beautiful, and healthy. Al-Anon has taught me to pursue progress rather than perfection.

Now, when sadness, resentment of past hurts, unexpected and unpleasant memories, and new irritations crop up, I know that I have a choice about what to do about these feelings. Today I choose to acknowledge and feel my feelings and then let them slip gently away. This is not always an enjoyable experience. In fact, it can be downright agonizing at times, but it is gratifying to reclaim these long-lost parts of myself, even when it hurts. I am learning that my feelings are important and deserve my validation, but also that they are just feelings, not facts. I do not have to make decisions on the basis of those feelings. In fact, I must often detach from them in order to make choices that will be in my best interest.

As a result of my attendance at Al-Anon, I am opening up to others instead of closing in on myself. I'm smiling more. The questions that tormented me about my purpose in life, my vocation, and the value of my existence are finding priceless answers as a result of applying the program to my everyday world and turning my life over to God, not just in words but in actuality.

Al-Anon meetings have been a very important part of my life and sanity, and I'll always cherish the experience. But being a contemplative nun with a vow of enclosure, I cannot continue to avail myself of weekly meetings. There are many things about the meetings that I will miss, but I have no regrets. I don't think I would still be in religious life today if it were not for Al-Anon and my Sponsor, who has guided me so reliably and lovingly. The program gave me a new perspective on a life I once felt had to be endured, and now I greet each day with enthusiasm. But I don't have to leave all this behind just because I can no longer attend meetings. Al-Anon's strength and support continue to bless my life through correspondence. With the help of the Lone Member Service, I pursue my recovery from the effects of alcoholism and continue my personal growth through the principles of the Al-Anon program without ever stepping outside convent walls. Today I take each Step I need to take, reaching out for fellowship and reaching up for God, knowing that there will be someone to catch me if I need the support. Thus, this program lives on in my life, a life now filled with hope and a sense of adventure.

17

Facing the Physical Effects of Alcoholism

I was brought up in a strict but loving family where alcoholism did not exist. I was the middle child of five daughters, and our lives were filled with family activities—camping trips, birthday and holiday celebrations—all in a genuinely loving and caring atmosphere. I attended parochial grammar and high school and had a strong sense of God. The God of my understanding in those days was an Almighty Being sitting on a throne keeping track of one's mistakes and dealing out punishment to those who were not sufficiently good. He was a Being to be feared!

The first traumatic experience I can remember happened when I was 15 and learned that my mother was dying of cancer. I truly believed that I was being punished for being a bad person. My mother was being taken away because I hadn't been the loving daughter I was supposed to be! Even at that young age, I felt responsible for everything, and thought it was my job to control or fix whatever went wrong. I therefore had long conversations with God in which I made many promises about my future behavior, bargaining that if my mother lived I would always be a good person. When my bargaining didn't work, I was filled with rage and hurt. I decided that if I was going to be punished anyway, it didn't matter what I did.

After my mother's death, our family life disintegrated. We each grieved privately and could not share our anguish with one another. At that point I began to shut down emotionally. I was learning that feelings hurt, and I didn't ever want to experience that kind of pain again.

At 16 I met my future husband, and we dated for three years before marrying. At the time, drinking was thrilling since we were underage. Beyond the excitement of breaking the rules, I didn't think much about it.

I was 19 when we married. I believed that our marriage was going to be perfect and that my role was to take care of my husband. I began "mothering" him almost at once, disregarding my own feelings or needs. My husband was very active in sports, hunting, fishing, and snowmobiling at every opportunity, while I stayed home alone. I was unhappy about this, but didn't voice my feelings because I believed that my role was to make the house a spotless haven and cook elaborate meals so that we could have a happy marriage. It sounds a little silly now, but at the time my commitment to this way of life was quite sincere.

After we had been married for a year, my mother-in-law died, and my husband and I elected to move in with his father. Fearing that he would be terribly lonely, we wanted to take care of him. Again I was fulfilling my role as a caretaker for other people's lives and feelings at my own expense. I never considered whether or not the move would be good for me.

My father-in-law was a gentle and loving person—when he wasn't drinking! He was a binge drinker who became extremely violent during his periodic alcoholic episodes. He hollered a lot, which was distressing to me since I can scarcely remember any shouting in my family. But what was worse was that he abused his dog. I have always had a special feeling for animals, and this behavior terrified me. Since my husband had become involved with stock car racing and was gone most of the time, I was left alone to cope with the alcoholic. I didn't realize that I had choices and that I could have removed myself from the situation or refused to accept the unacceptable drunken behavior. Instead, I believed it was my duty to fix the situation. I believed that love and kindness could cure everything, so I tried to be as loving and kind as possible and to ignore the abusive behavior in hopes that it would go away. Denial was rampant in my life. And it was taking a heavy toll, not only emotionally but physically.

One morning I awoke with severe diarrhea. I figured it was something I ate and waited a few days for it to improve. Instead, my condition got worse every day. My weight dropped rapidly, and I was so exhausted I could barely stand. Yet I had learned to ignore my needs so thoroughly that I became critically ill before I finally addressed the problem. I ended up in the hospital weighing 79 pounds because of ulcerative colitis.

Today, because of Al-Anon, I understand that alcoholism is a threefold disease: physical, emotional, and spiritual. I also know that the effects of alcoholism on friends and family members can be threefold as well. In my case, it was the physical effects that eventually forced me to face the fact that I, myself, had become ill and needed Al-Anon's help. At the time of my hospitalization, however, I was not yet aware of this. I didn't recognize my part in the problem. I thought that if only I could get some distance from my father-in-law, everything would be fine. My husband was stunned when he saw me in that hospital bed and began to understand how devastating our living situation had been to me. A month later, when I was released, we moved into a small trailer. I was torn between relief at being removed from the violence and guilt at having failed to fulfill my role as a good wife and daughter-in-law.

Needless to say, moving out didn't cure me. The disease of alcoholism and its effects were flourishing in our lives and would continue to do so for some time. My husband's active lifestyle continued, as did my resentment of it. I felt abandoned, lonely, hurt, sad, and helpless. I still felt obligated to stay at home and to keep my mouth shut. I feared that if I acknowledged my feelings, they would become real and I would get even more badly hurt. So I kept quiet, stuffed my feelings, and ended up with nine hospitalizations in seven years. As a result of one of the surgeries, we were told we might never have children. So it was indeed a miracle when I became pregnant after nine years of marriage. This was what I had been hoping for—a baby to make our lives complete.

Naturally, this did not happen. Alcoholism had taken hold of my husband. His drinking progressed until he was obsessed with alcohol and I was obsessed with him. I couldn't understand what was happening, since we now had a wonderful baby and I was supposed to be happy. Instead, I became crazier and crazier. I counted bottles and dragged my 2 ½ -year-old son to the bars looking for his father. While I drove, my son searched the parking lots for Daddy's truck.

Then we would go inside and demand that my husband come home. He always promised to come right away, and he never did. I would go home and commence calling the bar every 15 minutes to see if he had left yet. Often I would be told that he was no longer there, but I could hear his buddies laughing in the background. I found this pattern humiliating, but I couldn't stop. I was obsessed.

Feeling that my life was spiraling out of control because of my husband, I tried to get a grip on it by seizing control of my husband's life. I became his social director, deciding what activities he could engage in and when. I became his spokesperson, answering for him when anyone spoke to him. Even if he replied, I would still answer for him, acting as though he hadn't given the correct answer. I scolded, wept, threatened, fantasized, and spent every waking hour planning and trying to control, but nothing worked. He still drank, still went to bars, still eluded my control. *I* got worse and worse.

My husband was involved in a car accident and charged with driving while intoxicated. I was grateful, sure that such a serious charge would "cure" him. It didn't.

During this period I decided to go to college. I had chosen to forego an education when I got married, but had always regretted it. Looking back, I think that this attempt was my last grasp at sanity. I wanted to prove to myself that I was still an intelligent being and that I could actually accomplish a task I set for myself. I secretly hoped that, if I was busy enough, I wouldn't have to look at my unhappy life and maybe it would somehow resolve itself! So on top of my illnesses and obsessions, I decided to become superwoman, juggling a job, school, home, and family. It was hell.

Like many people, I'm a slow learner. In spite of all I'd been through, I thought I could handle the turmoil in my life. It wasn't until my body signaled total distress one more time that I finally reached my bottom and reached out for help. Colitis is a stress-related condition. My doctor had often attempted to convince me that I needed help, but until this last physical crisis, I didn't listen. This time I called Al-Anon. And to my great surprise, three weeks later, my husband called A.A.

My life since then has been one miracle after another. I first learned that I was not responsible for the alcoholic's drinking or sobriety. I could not stop it, start it, cure it, destroy it, or fix it. I was not in control of his situation at all. I could only control my choices. It was as if a million pounds had been lifted from my shoulders!

Next I learned that my life was unmanageable and I needed to discover who I was and get my life in order. This has been a continuing adventure of discovery, and while it has often been startling and painful, the results and the growth have been wonderful! As a result of working the Al-Anon program, today I know that I am a real person with real feelings and real worth. I no longer shuffle through my days like a numb robot. I no longer wait for my husband to come home from his activities in order to have a life of my own. I live much more fully. I have discovered that it takes two to make a marriage work, and that my preconceived notions about the role of a wife were neither realistic nor healthy for me. So, with the help of my Al-Anon friends and the self-honesty I have developed by working the Steps, I am pursuing activities that interest me.

Today I have no illusions about being superwoman. A searching and fearless moral inventory and a Sponsor who insists upon rigorous honesty have helped me to recognize my limitations, physical and otherwise. It took me seven years to complete my college education, but I am no less proud of the achievement. I leaned heavily on my Higher Power during this time and prayed for courage when school and work felt overwhelming, which they often did, even at this more manageable pace. I graduated *cum laude* and was elected to an honor society. Graduation day was one of my happiest because I had achieved something I considered valuable—I had earned my diploma—and my family and friends were there to help celebrate my achievement.

Looking back, I am amazed that so many wonderful changes have come to pass. When I first came to Al-Anon and saw how much I had to learn and unlearn, I was overwhelmed and didn't think that I'd ever manage to change anything. But it was as if I had been handed a tool kit. Some of these Al-Anon tools were simple and easy to use, while I found others harder to grasp. Meetings were the first tool I used, and probably the most important one in the beginning. In meetings, I learned that I was not the only one suffering. Others shared every one of my problems, including the physical effects of coping with another's alcoholism, and many had endured far worse situations than I had. I learned that I had often played a part in my unhappiness by enabling the disease of alcoholism, and that if I wanted to, I could stop playing that role.

Another life-changing tool was the slogan "One Day at a Time." I was amazed to find out I only had to cope with the present moment. I could not change the past, and I did not have a note from God saying that I was going to get up the next morning. I only had this minute, or this hour, or this day to work with, and what I did with it was my choice. I could fritter it away with fear, resentment, and worry, or I could turn it to some more pleasant or productive purpose. Either way, no one was watching to chastise me for my choice. This was a great relief. I had always felt that my every move was being scrutinized, as if I was the center of the universe and on the verge of being found wanting. It was delightful to learn that I was free to make mistakes, to do more or less than I had planned, and even to squander time. That freedom has helped me to want to make good, healthy choices for myself.

So many of Al-Anon's tools involve a relationship with a Higher Power. Since I had given up on the God who didn't accept my bargaining for my mother's life so many years earlier, I hadn't given spirituality much thought. Now, in Al-Anon, it was time to re-examine that aspect of life. Today I realize that just because certain times in my life were extremely difficult, my Higher Power never used these events to punish me. Instead, I was punishing myself by refusing to accept reality. I now believe that my Higher Power has always been there for me and always will be. He doesn't mind if I seek His help and guidance 50 times a day—I never wear out my welcome.

Life has not suddenly become all sunshine and cheer. There are many difficult situations to handle, many challenges to face. But today I have a whole different way of dealing with whatever life brings. As a result of working the Twelve Steps, I have come to believe that everything happens for a reason. Even if I can't understand that reason, I can benefit and grow from it. As a result, I can find gifts in almost every situation, and my life is so much happier and more satisfying than ever before.

Even though I've now been in Al-Anon for many years, I keep coming back. I can't imagine my life without the program and the fellowship. For my sanity and survival, I still need to make it an important part of my life. I continue to attend meetings to find the hope and strength I need. I use the Serenity Prayer frequently to get me through the rough moments, and the slogans to remember to mind my own business.

My recovering husband and I now have a relationship based on choice, not neediness. We're together today because we want to be and not because we feel obligated. We have learned to be friends. We support each other, yet we give each other room to grow and change. Our greatest struggle has been in learning to communicate. Today, we know that communication is the only way out of the rut we were in before recovery. If I don't want to continue to be sick mentally, spiritually, or physically, I need to be in touch with my feelings and to express them. I try to do so with as much respect as possible. Sure, we argue—often. Sometimes loudly. But I see that as a huge step forward from the days when I kept silent, shutting down my feelings while my husband stormed out to the bars or the racetrack.

I've also learned that I don't have to express every feeling to my husband. Over the years I've built a wonderful network of Al-Anon friends and a great relationship with a Sponsor. I can turn to others to let some of the steam out of the pressure cooker rather than explode at my husband or myself. Thanks to Al-Anon, I am learning how to take care of myself.

18

Learning to Love in Alateen

My dad was an alcoholic. I grew up taking family trips to the liquor store and never knowing how my father would behave when he came home from work. My mother just sat in a chair in the corner of the living room, read books, and ate chocolate bars. When I was in the sixth grade, my dad's drinking became extremely bad. He showed up for parent-teacher conference drunk, ran over my bike with the car, kicked me out of the house twice because I was "ungrateful," and once, while my mom was out grocery shopping, he locked me in a crawl space and pushed a bookcase in front of the door.

Then, sometime during that year, everything changed. He stopped coming home at two in the morning, driving drunk, and reeking of alcohol. Suddenly, he was never home after dinner. My mom started going out too. One day, while I unloaded the groceries, my dad told me he was an alcoholic. I replied that it couldn't be true. I had never thought that my dad had a drinking problem. I thought all families were like mine and that all fathers acted like my dad.

My dad suggested that I attend an Alateen meeting, but I wouldn't go. He finally said that, if I didn't attend, he'd take away all the money I had made babysitting. So I went to two Alateen meetings and hated them both. I was 12 years old, younger than everybody else, and I told the group, "I love my dad. We don't have any problems." After that, I told my dad he could keep my money, but I wasn't going back.

During the next year, he practiced his A.A. program and my mom her Al-Anon program. I couldn't get away with my unacceptable behavior any more. Yelling and slamming doors were not allowed. When I had a bad attitude my parents pointed it out. They didn't let me manipulate them. I felt lonely, abandoned, angry, frustrated, and totally out of control. I thought I was going crazy. I finally swallowed my pride and asked my dad to take me back to Alateen.

In my first meeting after returning, I poured my insides out. I thought everyone would hate me, but they didn't. They gave me hugs and told me to keep coming back. Gradually I learned about love, about letting go of control, and about finding a Higher Power who could love me and be with me for the rest of my life. As my dad got involved in A.A. service work, I got involved in Alateen service work. We began to travel as a family to conferences throughout our region. Life improved at home until I finally felt like I had a real family.

Then my mom was diagnosed with cancer. The doctors said she had a good chance at survival, and amazingly, for the first time, my family survived a crisis relatively intact. But the next year my mom's cancer came back, and everything fell apart. I dumped my Higher Power in a trash can and slammed the lid. I went to read a Fourth Step to my Sponsor the next week and then avoided her for weeks. At school that year, I played three sports to use up all my anger, showed up for class only because I was afraid of my coaches, and developed ulcers that made me feel sick all the time. I still went to Alateen meetings and tried to listen, to comprehend, and to find that serenity that I had felt before, but it was gone. My Alateen friends didn't abandon me, though. They loved me and gave me more hugs, let me rage, and accepted me when I couldn't accept myself.

When it became evident that my mom would soon die, the Al-Anon member who sponsored our Alateen meeting suggested that I write her a letter to tell her that I loved her. I did so, but I was too frightened to hand it to her, so I mailed it. When she read it, she cried. I couldn't hug her yet, but when she said, "Thank you," I knew she understood. Soon after that, because I had set this sort of communication in motion, I learned to hug her, to tell her that I loved her, and to talk to her about her death. She said that she wasn't scared to die, that she was more afraid for us than for herself. She apologized for not being able to attend future events like my high school graduation. She wanted me to know that she was proud of me and said that maybe she could be my guardian angel, looking out for me when things got tough.

She died three weeks after we moved halfway across the country, but we returned for a week to our old home for a memorial service. The church was filled with members of A.A., Al-Anon, and Alateen, and my mom's Sponsor spoke about her. I will never forget what these programs did for our family.

When we returned to our new home, my father quit going to his A.A. meetings and started using large quantities of prescription drugs. I found Alateen right away and began working on putting my life back together. I started the 11th grade in a kind of daze that gradually passed. Life became clearer. It took me a long time to trust my new Alateen friends, but their help and their love were there for me whether I trusted them or not. A year passed before I reached out and called someone, found a close friend, and started going to conferences. I had a lot of work to do on the first three Steps, admitting I was not only out of control of much of my own life, but powerless to help my alcoholic dad. I found God again. This God doesn't always give me what I want, but I do get what I need to become a stronger, more beautiful person. I also found a wonderful Sponsor whom I am not afraid to call, or to tell all the horrible—or maybe not really so horrible—things I've done.

The Steps have provided the guidance I need in my life. They are the one area in which I always know what comes next, and although it is sometimes hard, if I take them honestly, I always feel better in the end.

I almost quit high school many times, but I finally made it through. And although my dad tried to stop me, I attend an out-of-state college. I now go to Al-Anon. I am starting to get used to being the youngest one again and I have begun to find my place. But when I go home for vacations, I return to my Alateen meetings and my best friends. I am one of the lucky people in the world who can count on my fingers and toes the people who love me unconditionally.

What Alateen has taught me is love. I have learned how to love myself and others. Today I know that I am lovable. I have learned to trust my Higher Power to take care of what happens in my life. The program is my home, and whenever I am at an Al-Anon or an Alateen meeting, I know I am safely where I belong.

19

A Husband Learns to Detach with Love

If I could point to the single most useful notion I have learned since coming to Al-Anon, it would have to be the concept of detachment. Of course, when the alcoholic in my life and I were both in the throes of her active, unarrested alcoholism and I with its effects, I would never have considered detachment a viable approach to my personal life. At the time, I did gradually separate myself from family, friends, and even reality. All became less and less important, less a part of me. This gave me more time to obsess about that mysterious, ill-defined "something" that made our lives so uncomfortable. This may have been a kind of detachment, but it wasn't detachment with sanity or with love.

As for the alcoholic, I could not separate from her, leave her, or even leave her alone. Wasn't it my right, my duty, my obligation to stay by her, direct her, and guide her (otherwise known as trying to control her)? Certainly "society" not only condoned such efforts, I was sure "they" expected them of me. After all, a husband must do everything possible to help his spouse, mustn't he?

I can recall thinking that the more I was able to "protect" the alcoholic from the adversities of life, the better she would be able to cope (and therefore not drink so much). Since, as far as I could tell, most anything was capable of causing her to drink, I was thus trying to throw a shield around her and keep the whole world out. I remember actually envisioning her with a cocoon wrapped around her. I might as well have wanted her to assume a vegetative state with no need for words, action, or productive thought. Yet somehow I had convinced myself that this would actually be helpful.

At the urging of a very wise therapist, my wife and I entered recovery at the same time, she in A.A., I in Al-Anon. During her first days home from the rehab, I was so determined not to say or do *anything* that might upset her for fear of making her drink that I did very little and said practically nothing. My thinking was, "If I say such and such, she will think thus and so, and then she'll drink." This was uncomfortable for both of us. It was controlling and unproductive, and I'm not sure that it was all too well-intentioned, since my main goal was to keep her from drinking rather than to allow her to work on her problems while I worked on my own. But, looking back, I suspect it was my first attempt to detach, or at least to keep myself from actively managing her life. Those were difficult days for both of us, but despite my slipping and sliding, I did gradually start to learn some of the Al-Anon principles and even put some of them into practice.

Still, detachment eluded me. It was so hard to let go, so hard to give up old ways, so hard to admit that I did not know what was best for someone else. The fact that I had tried for years to manage my wife's life and had failed miserably never discouraged me from thinking that this time would be different, if only I could have another crack at it. The word "surrender," if not alien to me, certainly had a negative ring to it.

I doubt if it ever occurred to me at the time that I was completely depriving my wife of her dignity. It is often said in Al-Anon that people must be allowed the dignity to fail. I think that they must also be given the dignity to succeed. As long as I failed to detach— as long as I was always there trying to pick up the pieces, doing for her what she could do for herself, eliminating anything unpleasant from her path to help her avoid drinking—I stood in the way of her self-esteem. I didn't give her the opportunity to do anything she might feel good about. I continued in this self-righteous, martyr-like fashion, imagining myself quite the hero. I don't mean to be overly harsh about this. I didn't know any better, and I was doing the best I could. My intentions may have been impeccable at times, but my misplaced sense of responsibility was monumental.

Even now, a compulsive need to control is one of my most nagging character defects, one that I mention frequently at my meetings because I know that sharing about a defect often releases me from the need to act it out. I also recognize that I have come a very long way over the years. I remember how upset I felt the first time my wife decided not to go to her A.A. meeting when I went to my Al-Anon meeting. I was so consumed by her decision that I failed to get anything out of at least the first half of my own meeting. I just *knew* that she *should* be at an A.A. meeting that night. Of course I was afraid that, although she probably would not actually drink while I was out, this night would be the beginning of her downfall. Once again, I was obsessed and forgot to focus on my own recovery. Any time she chose not to attend one of her usual meetings, I became acutely uncomfortable, often pleading or even demanding that she go. I became skilled at dropping broad hints about her attendance, even a day or two before the meeting. But I continued to attend my meetings and to work the Al-Anon program to the best of my ability. Eventually I was able to cease dropping even those little hints and congratulated myself that at least there was one area that I no longer tried to control. I had at last begun to detach.

As they say in A.A., alcoholism is cunning, baffling, and insidious, and to me, its effects on my thinking are equally sneaky. Almost immediately after congratulating myself on my ability to detach, I heard myself remark, ever so casually, "What are you wearing to the meeting tonight?" (Translation: "You *are* going, aren't you?")

It takes time, lots of time, to change old habits and replace them with more appropriate behavior. Meanwhile, I am learning to put progress into perspective. I tend to exaggerate my errors and ignore my achievements. If I am 20% wrong, I tend to feel that the effort was a complete failure. It has taken a good bit of time and a lot of encouragement to reflect that, if I am 20% wrong, I must be 80% right, and partial success does have value. My Sponsor inadvertently helped me with this during a casual conversation about baseball, a mutual passion. He was talking about a favorite player who was having a fantastic year at bat and hitting almost .400 during a particular series of games. My Sponsor happened to comment on the ironic fact that to hit .400 means that you get four hits out of every ten times at bat. In other words, the very best batters fail to get a hit more times than they succeed! So when I make a mistake, or mess up a portion of a project, I try to think about baseball, and I wind up feeling a lot better about myself. I know that I will never be perfect. But perhaps, warts and all, I'm doing better than I think.

I must acknowledge that, although I am not yet an expert on detachment with love, I have made progress. To do so, I had to learn that there is a difference between meddling and offering bona fide help. Really valuable help sometimes requires only a sympathetic ear for someone who needs to share. The other person may not need any feedback at all, much less a parcel of advice that I expect them to heed. I do believe that it is appropriate to help when asked, and sometimes my experience, strength, and hope can be of use to others. I may even have a good idea that will make someone's situation more manageable. But because I have the tendency to lose my own boundaries and to lose myself in the process of trying to help, I have to be very careful about what I offer and why. Close contact with my Al-Anon support system is vital whenever I do get involved in trying to help, if I want to remain reasonably sane and honest with myself.

In my long struggle to achieve detachment with love, I must have often said and done things that were confusing to the alcoholic. We were so enmeshed with each other that my early, feeble attempts at detachment probably were dismaying to her. At times, I was cold and distant because it was the only way I could find to separate myself from my own desire to interfere. At other times, I was more intrusive than ever. As time passed, I had to make amends for many errors even though I had been doing my best at the time. Growth is messy, but unbelievably worthwhile. I feel that our relationship today is much stronger because I am better able to detach with love and focus on myself.

With the help of a loving Higher Power, I have gotten to the point where it is no longer acceptable for me to simply distance myself from my wife's problems or ignore her needs. I believe that marriage is a partnership. It is meant to be a sharing of life together, and it requires a certain flexibility, a certain give and take. At times, her feelings and needs come first, and at other times, mine take precedence. When I begin to lose myself, I know I need to detach. Today, detachment with love is a tool, not a lifestyle.

20

A Wife Leaves Fantasy Behind

My earliest memories revolve around feelings of self-pity. My brothers liked to play with the girl next door more than with me, and I felt very sorry for myself. They wouldn't let me join their club unless I swallowed a minnow, something I couldn't bring myself to do, and I felt sorry for myself. Still, I tried to look and act cheerful even though I was constantly wallowing in self-imposed misery.

When I met my husband, I thought he was just another guy, nothing special. Our dates seemed to revolve around drinking, which didn't bother me much, but didn't excite me either. One day, however, he asked me what my father did for a living. "He's dead," I replied, feeling very sorry for myself, and my soon-to-be husband felt badly for me as well. I asked him about his father and he told me, "My father has tuberculosis. He's in a sanitarium and will probably be there the rest of his life. So I'm responsible for my four brothers and sisters still at home." I felt sorry for him, and he felt sorry for himself. Suddenly our relationship blossomed on the basis of our mutual self-pity.

Eventually we married. But alcoholism and our respective character defects dominated our lives, and our relationship soon showed signs of wear and tear.

I began to feel inadequate as a wife, just as I had felt inadequate as a child and responsible when there was trouble in our home. I felt that something was wrong with me because my husband didn't want to go to bed with me at 11:00 o'clock each night. I thought that newlyweds were supposed to go to bed together, but my husband insisted upon staying up to watch the late, late show. Drinking. In order to help relieve my feelings of guilt and inadequacy, my husband suggested that he might be an alcoholic. I told him that, as an educated woman, I was well acquainted with the definition of an alcoholic and that he certainly wasn't one. I wanted to relieve him of his feelings of guilt.

After several moves and job changes and the birth of two children, the effects of this disease began to take a heavy toll. My compulsive thinking was making it impossible to keep up the act of cheerfulness, and my sunny disposition was replaced by anger and depression. I hated what was happening in my life, but I didn't see any way to change it. I began living in a fantasy world which, in time, consumed every waking hour.

There were two major fantasies. In the first, I lived with a prince and we spent every day in total harmony, romance, and togetherness. In the second fantasy, my husband died a violent death. I envisioned him dying in a variety of ways, although he never suffered. I imagined the wake and the funeral, but the fantasy couldn't end until the life insurance man came to the door with the check that would allow the children and me to live happily ever after. For years, while these imaginary soap operas kept my mind too busy to be bothered with their needs, I neglected my children.

I can remember spooning baby food into our son's mouth while thinking about my husband's death. I didn't talk to my children or play with them or interact with them emotionally in any way. I looked forward to ironing because I insisted that the children stay away from me and the hot iron. Ironing gave me uninterrupted fantasy time.

One day during the children's nap time, I heard a noise in the bedroom and discovered my daughter playing with the shoes in the closet. I was furious, not because of what she was doing, but because my fantasy had been interrupted. I started throwing the shoes into the closet, but missed and smashed the mirror next to where my daughter was sitting. I threw her onto the bed and picked up the broken glass from the floor, leaving what remained of the broken mirror on the closet door to show my husband what *he* had made me do!

This incident took place about six months before my first Al-Anon meeting. At the time, I was unaware that there was a problem with my behavior, and I had no idea that it was in any way related to the disease of alcoholism. It wasn't until a year later that I realized I had caused that mirror to be broken, and I finally removed the remaining shards from the door. But I left the tape residue to let my husband know that he had just a little responsibility for that event. It was another year in Al-Anon before I could admit that I was the *only* one responsible for that broken mirror, and I cleaned up the tape—but I left the scratches on the door. Recovery comes slowly to some of us.

I learned of Al-Anon in August of that year through an advice column. A woman had written to say thanks for recommending Al-Anon several years earlier. She and her two children were attending meetings and having a decent life in spite of her husband's drinking. I clipped out the article, which included the address of the Al-Anon Family Group Headquarters, and put it away—in case I might ever need it.

A few months later, I wrote to that address and asked for information about the program. In the letter, I made it very clear that our only real problem was financial. I received a few pamphlets and the address of the local contact person, Natalie. I read the pamphlets, found nothing to answer my questions about finances, and put them away—in case I might ever need them.

A few weeks after Christmas, I found myself in Natalie's neighborhood and decided to look for her address. I found her house and drove by, making a mental note of it—in case I ever needed it.

The following week, I drove to Natalie's house again intending to stop. As I pulled up in front of the house, I noticed that the ground was covered with snow, yet my daughter didn't have any boots on. I was very embarrassed, but I assumed that Natalie was watching out the window, as I usually did, so I couldn't turn back without her knowledge. (I later found out that she had 11 children, which did not leave much time for looking out of windows, and I'm sure that there were times when one or two of those children went out without boots.)

Natalie acted as if I had made her day very special, and as if there was nothing she wanted to do more than talk to me about the Al-Anon program. Before I left, she told me that there would be a meeting the next night at 8:30 and that she would ask her husband to look out for me, since the meeting was in an upstairs room that might be hard to find. He could easily spot me from the A.A. meeting downstairs.

My husband agreed to be home by 6:00 P.M. so that I could go to a meeting. I drove up to the building at 8:25, but I didn't want to arrive too early. To avoid having to talk to anyone, I drove around the block. But by the time I parked and went inside, I was late. I started to turn around and leave, when Natalie's husband saw me and motioned for me to follow him up to the Al-Anon room. I was very embarrassed.

Nevertheless, I immediately felt welcome at my first Al-Anon meeting. I barely remember what was said at that meeting, but I vividly remember the warmth in that room. I felt accepted and loved, regardless of my appearance or what I said or didn't say. Whenever I spoke up at a meeting, no matter how foolish I felt, heads would nod and faces would smile. No one criticized me. No one treated me like the doormat I felt I had become. For the first time in my life, I felt as though I was an important person in my own right.

After so many years in a fantasy world, I had no idea of who I was or what I could become if I practiced the principles of the Al-Anon program. The members of the group gave me a glimpse of what might be possible by the kindness and consistency they showed me. I especially remember arriving early for a meeting where some of the members were confused about the meaning of a word in the book ...*In All Our Affairs*. As I walked in the door, one of the members exclaimed, "Here's Marcia. She'll know what that word means!" I had never before realized that other people might think that I knew anything of value or that I might be able to help them.

The Fourth Step, "Made a searching and fearless moral inventory of ourselves," was the topic at my sixth meeting. Although I didn't really understand that the purpose of the Step was to take *my own* inventory, I dutifully filled out the Fourth Step Inventory form that was passed out at the end of the meeting. I checked the boxes to show my husband's shortcomings and my own strengths! I proudly showed my homework to the other members at the next meeting. No one laughed or corrected me. No one told me that I was wrong. I was allowed to make my own mistakes and to find my own answers when I was ready.

The members of this group were very loving toward me, and I tried to follow their example in relating to my own family. I learned more by example than from any lecture I ever heard, learning how to love by experiencing their love for me. I became capable of allowing my children to be themselves and to make mistakes because these wonderful people allowed me to make my own mistakes and learn from the experience. I learned how to get organized and to focus on one task at a time by applying the slogans and by observing the organization of the Al-Anon meetings. I learned how to handle responsibility by taking on service opportunities in my group—chairing meetings, helping to set up and clean up, serving as literature assistant and eventually as Group Representative. Although I made quite a few mistakes along the way, I learned that I could change my behavior and my attitudes if I wanted to.

Accepting my powerlessness over the alcoholic was terribly difficult. After so many years of communicating with him only in my fantasies, I had forgotten how to actually express my needs, ideas, and feelings. I was also afraid of how he might react. Instead, I tried to communicate in a more subtle, more manipulative way. When he bounced checks to buy liquor, I bounced checks to buy groceries, hoping to show him what he was doing. The result of this round-about message was that the sheriff confronted me about my bounced checks!

Another way that I tried to communicate was with the silent treatment. I remember being so proud of the fact that I had refused to talk to my husband for 13 days! He begged me to tell him what was wrong, and I finally explained that the neighbor always took out the garbage for his wife, but that I was always the one at our house who had to take out our garbage. My husband very sweetly took out the garbage that night. I was certain that everything had changed. The next night and every night thereafter, when the time came to take the garbage out, my husband was nowhere to be seen. But I still hadn't really gotten the message of the First Step, that I was powerless over alcohol (and the alcoholic), and that refusing to acknowledge this was making my life unmanageable.

Nevertheless, I was getting better. I had been able to modify my fantasy life by replacing it with thoughts of what I might say in an Al-Anon meeting. I was learning how to detach, to distinguish between the disease of alcoholism and the loving and lovable person who was afflicted with it. I was learning to live "One Day at a Time." My concept of a Higher Power had changed from a God who had stuck me in a life from which I could not escape, to a God who loved and guided me every day of my life.

But alcoholism progressed, and problems mounted. Money was more of a problem than ever, and the mortgage, taxes, and other bills often went unpaid. My husband had a good job, but his money went toward beer before it ever bought groceries. I felt it was best to stay home and take care of my son, accepting babysitting jobs and growing vegetables in order to help out. My husband was often angry when I refused to lend him my babysitting money to pay his debts or buy his beer, but I was learning that I had choices, and that it was acceptable for me to say "No."

When my son was old enough, I went back to school in an effort to become more self-sufficient.

One night my husband was in a serious automobile accident. He admitted that his drinking had caused the accident and vowed to go to A.A. as soon as he got out of the hospital. On the day he was discharged, my hopes were high that our troubles were coming to an end, but that ended abruptly when he asked me to drive him to the local bar on the way home. By the time we got to the house, I had taken him to five different bars "so that he could let his friends know he was all right." I promised myself that this would be the last time I would allow myself to indulge in fantasies about how life could be.

By this time, I had been attending meetings for a number of years and felt that I was doing quite well practicing the Al-Anon principles. However, one day as I was making the bed, I noticed that I intentionally placed the covers so that the cigarette burns, scars from my husband's drunken carelessness, were all on his side of the bed. Although I had been making the bed this way for years, I had never thought about this before. It had been my subtle way of trying to force him to take note of the results of his drinking. It was then that it occurred to me that perhaps I was not practicing the program as well as I could and that maybe I needed to put renewed energy into the Twelve Steps.

I got stuck on Step Three, "Made a decision to turn our will and our lives over to the care of God *as we understood Him*". I found that I could easily turn my life over to God's care, but I willed my husband to quit drinking. I wanted to believe that my love for him would conquer his addiction to alcohol; with my help, he would see those cigarette burns and exclaim, "Look at what I am doing! I must quit drinking!"

Even after all these years of trying, my will hadn't made my situation any better. In fact it was making me sick. It was high time to let go of my will and trust my Higher Power. I had to accept that my husband might continue to drink and that, no matter what I did, I was powerless to change that fact. I made a promise to myself that I would "Let Go and Let God." I would let go of my self-will, and I would let God take care of my husband. Together, and without my help or my signals, they would determine whether or not the drinking would end. Within an instant, I felt more at peace than I had ever felt before. And that peace has remained. Within six months from that moment of surrender, my husband took his last drink, and with A.A.'s help, he has now been sober for many years.

I continue to attend Al-Anon meetings to help me deal with day-to-day problems. They aren't as big or as earth-shattering now as they once were, but Al-Anon is my insurance that I will never again revert to being that sick girl who found the real world so horrifying that she had to live in a fantasy night and day. There have been problems related to losing a job, adjusting to life with a sober alcoholic, children growing up and making their own choices about drugs and alcohol, physical illness, and aging parents. I find that Al-Anon provides techniques that help me to deal with all of these problems in a healthy way.

I also continue to come to Al-Anon because I want to give newcomers a little of the love and support that was given to me when I came to my first meetings. I cannot imagine what might have happened if those wonderful Al-Anon members had not been there for me when I so desperately needed their help. I cannot begin to express my gratitude for the renewed enthusiasm for life that I have found, so I will have to let my actions speak for me by giving service, by coming back, and by continuing to learn and to grow.

21

A Parent Sets Boundaries

I believe that my oldest son has a drinking problem. He doesn't consider himself an alcoholic, but after four DUI's, numerous fines and court costs, repeated loss of his driver's license, fist fights and trips to the emergency room, inability to keep a job, and brief imprisonments on alcohol-related charges, I know that his drinking and its consequences bother me.

Until recently, my son was single, living at home with me. In an effort to be a good parent and stand by him, I did everything I could to bail him out of trouble—and jail. I paid his fines, helped him find work, and provided transportation for several years when his license was revoked. During those years, our house seemed to be in constant chaos as we ricocheted from one crisis to another.

When I first came to Al-Anon, my smothering attention to my son's problems grew even worse than before. I wanted so badly for my son to realize that the real problem was alcoholism and to find recovery in A.A. I lectured him repeatedly about Twelve Step programs, invited him to meetings, and besieged him with literature that I "knew" he needed to read. He did try one or two A.A. meetings and then decided he did not have a drinking problem.

After attending Al-Anon for almost a year, listening, reading, and absorbing the wisdom that the other members shared with me, it began to sink in that my son's life was his own responsibility. I had heard the slogans "Let Go and Let God" and "Live and Let Live," but suddenly I seemed to understand them in a deeper and more personal way. It was very hard to use these slogans with my "child," but what I had been doing all along seemed only to make things worse. I cared about him, and about myself, enough to try a different approach.

My Al-Anon program has taught me to keep the focus on myself and to set boundaries I can live with. I never knew about boundaries before finding Al-Anon. What freedom it gives me to know that

I do not have to accept everything that others say or do. I believe that I have always had boundaries on a subconscious level; I always had a sense of what was and was not acceptable to me, but I didn't feel entitled to act on those feelings. Instead I grew resentful, frustrated, and angry whenever those hidden boundaries were crossed. I felt like a helpless victim and spent many long hours with the "poor me's." Today I have the option to set limits, to draw a line that I will not allow to be crossed. I may not please everyone when I do so, but in the long run, I think that this is a more open and honest approach.

The last time my son was locked up for drinking and driving, he had to spend seven days in jail, pay a large fine, and lose his driver's license for another year. While he was in jail, I decided that it was time for me to stop taking responsibility for his life and the consequences of his choices. This time I wouldn't "help." When I visited him in jail, I told him that I would not pay his fines and that when he got out of jail he would have to find another place to live. At first he didn't believe me. Who can blame him? He had heard it all before. But in Al-Anon I had learned not to make threats unless I intended to carry them out. I repeated my position several times in the next few days and set what I felt was a reasonable time limit within which he was to remove his belongings from my home. Finally, he realized that I was serious. Soon after that, he made his own living arrangements and moved out.

The hardest part of setting and sticking to my boundaries has been to do it with love. It is so easy for me to justify my decisions by blaming him and making him the villain so that I won't feel so guilty. But there is no villain. Alcoholism is a disease. Nobody wants to be afflicted by it—not the alcoholic, not the family, not anybody. Blaming and judging and justifying only harm an already fragile relationship. I don't ever want to forget that I love my son. I am acting out of love just as much today as I did when I was "helping" him to avoid the consequences of his actions. I have learned that that kind of help doesn't help at all. It only allows the alcoholic to avoid the painful consequences of his actions. Why should he consider changing the way he lives if I continue to make it comfortable for him to drink and act out? In Al-Anon, we sometimes call this "enabling," because we enable the progression of alcoholism by protecting the alcoholic from the difficulties he has created for himself. Today I believe that it is far more loving to allow my son the dignity of facing the consequences of his actions without interference from me.

This was not an easy decision for me to make, and I have paid a price. I have had to let go of my self-will and give up my tremendous need to control what happens to my son. Instead, I have been forced to place my faith in a Higher Power, trusting that He has a plan for my son.

Since that time, my son has gotten a job. He recently married a beautiful woman who will fit right into the Al-Anon program—if and when she decides she needs it. This, too, is none of my concern.

Today I have a life of my own. I have work that I love, hobbies, good friends, and even a growing relationship with my very lovable, alcoholic son. His drinking still bothers me, but thanks to Al-Anon, it is no longer the single most important issue in my life.

22

A Husband Changes His Attitudes

Once upon a time, my wife had a problem, my life was unmanageable, and I didn't even know it.

Instead, I thought that she was the crazy person and I had all the answers. Was I sane? Not for a minute. Was it sane to kick down the bathroom door in order to talk to my wife? Was it sane to break all the dishes when my wife disagreed with me? Was it sane to believe that, if I abstained from drinking, she would get better?

With the help of her Higher Power and meetings and Sponsors, my wife regained her sanity. She worked her program through the death of both her parents, three miscarriages, and a successful pregnancy. She felt good about herself. She exercised. She had fun. Her life became manageable.

And I was still insane.

I read all her recovery books. I read the "Big Book." I analyzed the Twelve Steps to be sure they were acceptable. I was compulsively involved in someone else's life, and *my* life was unmanageable. I couldn't decide whether it was better to kill myself, kill my wife, or run away. When I didn't do any of those things, I hated myself for being weak. At night I imagined that I would put the whole world in a line and shoot everyone down one by one. I found this very calming.

Then came the transformation.

Two and a half years after my wife began her recovery, I crawled in desperation into an Al-Anon meeting and started my own recovery. Four or five times a week I sit with spouses, children, parents, and friends of alcoholics and listen to their words of experience, strength, and hope so that I can gain some sanity and start to manage my own life. It works. The magic of the fellowship and the Twelve Steps works for me as well as it does for my wife.

I can best describe my Al-Anon recovery by echoing some rabbinical writings from 2,000 years ago. One scholar's prescription for sanity is as follows:

1. Get yourself a rabbi.
2. Acquire a friend.
3. Judge everyone favorably.

How does this apply to my recovery in Al-Anon? Here is the way I interpret these small nuggets of ancient wisdom.

GET YOURSELF A RABBI.

The word "rabbi" means teacher. My teacher is the Al-Anon program. I attend meetings several times each week and, as a result, I have noticed a miraculous change in myself. Even my wife finds me easier to get along with. The most important message that I hear in these meetings is that I am powerless to change my wife. I would be wise to stop trying to force her to be the way I would like. Instead, *I* can start living the kind of life I want to live.

My task is to look at my own behavior and change what I can about myself. The Al-Anon slogans have been very helpful in this regard. For instance, I am a recovering perfectionist. Al-Anon reminds me that "Easy Does It," and teaches me to value "Progress Not Perfection." I am recovering from judgmentalism and self-righteousness. The antidote I hear about in meetings is the slogan, "Live and Let Live." And I am recovering from my own fears and my own shame by learning to "Let Go and Let God." These slogans and phrases, these small, simple clichés, help me to cut through years of automatic reactions, self-destructive habits, and lousy attitudes with clarity and precision that I find very restorative.

ACQUIRE A FRIEND.

When my wife was my only friend, we were not very friendly. I was so neurotically needy that I couldn't be much of a friend myself. I was empty and had nothing to give. And when she tried to give to me, I was insatiable, a bottomless pit. Nothing she did was ever enough. In my desperation to fill myself up with the love and companionship that every human needs, I demanded more than any one person was capable of giving.

Today I have the Al-Anon fellowship upon which I can draw. I supplement the interactions that I have at meetings by joining members for coffee and conversation at the "meeting after the meeting" at a nearby restaurant. I am learning to share myself and to listen compassionately without criticism. I have a Sponsor who listens and guides me. I am acquiring friends inside and outside of Al-Anon, becoming more and more a fellow member of the human race.

Today my wife is not my only friend; therefore, we are better friends. The changes we have made are substantial. At one point, we were calling lawyers and contemplating divorce. But with the help of our respective programs, we have found a better life together.

JUDGE EVERYONE FAVORABLY.

When I first came to Al-Anon I heard that "changed attitudes aid recovery." At the time, my attitudes toward other people tended toward the paranoid. They were out to get me; they interfered with my plans, they robbed me of the privileges, opportunities, and rewards to which I was entitled; and the world—my world would be a better place without them. It was much easier to excuse my behavior and my failures by pointing to the limitations I so readily found in others than to admit my own shortcomings, take responsibility for myself, and change my attitudes about others. This kept me stuck in the same old miserable rut I had wallowed in for years. Finally I was ready for change. I was ready to consider the possibility that we might all be in this together, all doing the best we can at any one moment. I was ready to give others a break. Instead of assuming the worst, I learned to give people the benefit of the doubt. Sure, sickness and insanity abound, and nobody in Al-Anon has ever suggested that I close my eyes to it or volunteer for abuse. Instead, they suggest that I accept what I can't change and change what I can. So I try to accept people the way they are without condemning them for it. And I strive to change what I can, which is mainly my attitude. Changing my attitude to look favorably on others gives me great peace of mind. When I do this, I can truly detach with love.

The best thing I can do for my wife is to accept her as she is. I realize that she has a lifelong disease that has no cure. Recovery is possible and so is relapse. A Power greater than either of us will take care of us both. I can love my wife unconditionally and respect her enough to stay out of the way of her recovery. We share many jobs around the house, but her program is 100% her job and 0% my job.

Step One says that I am powerless over alcohol. I am also powerless over other people. There is no graduate school where those who have worked all Twelve Steps now get to have power over others. Instead, working all the Steps has convinced me that I am and always will be powerless over other people. Thinking otherwise made my life unmanageable. I need a Higher Power to restore me to sanity. I need Al-Anon to help me make healthy choices. And I need to carry this message to others, because the only things I get to keep are those I give away.

23

Lessons in Faith

After living with my alcoholic husband for 25 years, I was a very angry, unhappy person. I could see no way of escaping the horrible situation in my home. My energy, when I had any, was fueled by rage. The rest of the time I was like a robot. Each day seemed worse than the day before. But we had four children, and I felt I had to keep trying for their sakes.

When my husband bought a go-go bar, I was horrified. My religion didn't approve of such places. Besides, owning a bar was the perfect excuse for my husband to stay out until four or five in the morning, and I didn't approve of that either.

I turned to my minister for help. He introduced me to a happy, calm woman whose husband was an alcoholic. I was shocked by this news. She was so serene, so capable of functioning! She told me how much Al-Anon had helped her and invited me to a meeting. I couldn't bring myself to go, for I didn't want anyone to find out that my husband owned a go-go bar. I also worried about his professional reputation, since he was a lawyer.

Instead I depended upon this woman from my church. I tried to get her to tell me how to stop my husband's drinking. She never did. I called her at 3:00 A.M. when anger, fear, and frustration were eating away at me. She was wonderfully available. But after a while, she got tired of the late night crisis calls and told me in no uncertain terms that she was going to take me to an Al-Anon meeting. Though I resisted, eventually I went.

I was even angrier after the meeting. No one would tell me how to get him sober! So I wasn't about to return.

One morning, one of the children asked a simple question and I screamed the answer. I hadn't intended to scream, but I was no longer capable of just talking. This terrified me. I went into the bedroom to try to calm down, but when I tried to talk just to see if I still could, a scream came out. I was out of control. I was sure I was ready to be committed to our local mental hospital.

Then, for the first time in my life, I prayed to God *for myself.* All I said was, "God help me!" And He did. I found that I was once again able to speak normally.

This incident marked an important spiritual awakening for me. It also convinced me that I needed help more desperately than I wanted to believe and propelled me back to Al-Anon.

I was still angry at what I heard. I didn't like the idea that alcoholism was a disease and that I had been affected, too. To make matters worse, every time I sat down in a meeting, I cried. I remember little of what was said in those early meetings. I do remember the smiles and the laughter. They made me even angrier. "How could any of these people be living with a drunk?" I asked myself. "If that were the case, they'd be miserable, too." But I stayed because I knew how badly I needed help and I didn't know where else to go.

The idea that alcoholism is a disease was the first to sink in, but I didn't know what to do with the information. Since I couldn't get my spouse to go to a doctor for treatment, I did what I thought was the next best thing. When he was asleep, I would put both hands smack in the middle of his back and pray for a healing. This "laying on of hands" didn't work any better than my other attempts to cure him. The next day he got up and drank again.

Slowly, I learned about the disease of alcoholism and its effects. So when my husband parked the car in the middle of our well-manicured lawn, I left it there. It took all of my resolve not to put it into the garage, but I knew that he would never believe me if I moved it and then told him about the incident. Later, when he asked how the car got there, I told him I had no idea. I knew I couldn't keep the recriminations out of my voice, so I decided to break my old pattern of finger-pointing and let him figure out what had happened for himself.

My faith has always been very important to me. I believed "Seek and ye shall find," and "Knock and it will be opened unto you." Faith was a great comfort. But my prayers were always for others. I thought that since I had faith, I should be able to take care of myself.

Until I came back to Al-Anon, I had fervently believed that prayer was the answer to my husband's alcoholism. I practically wore out a spot on the floor from spending so much time on my knees praying for his sobriety. When the drinking continued, I assumed that I wasn't a good enough person and God was punishing me. I was unworthy to have my prayers answered. It never occurred to me that God might be giving me a very clear answer to my prayers: "No!"

Morning, noon, and night, I would pray, "God, bring him home safe and sober tonight." Even though my husband always came home safely, I could never get past the fact that he was drunk once again. Somehow God didn't seem to be getting my request straight. So I vowed to be a better person. I offered up some tremendous deals to God. I promised to give up, take up, and fix up all sorts of things about myself and my life if God would only do what I requested and strike my husband sober. I'd be an even greater paragon of virtue than I already was.

Then, as the desire for sobriety continued to elude my husband, I played the martyr. How ungrateful he was, after all I was doing to ensure his salvation! I was sure he couldn't possibly love me or he wouldn't continue to drink someone who loves you doesn't force you to make such sacrifices. The fact that he had never asked me to make any sacrifices was irrelevant. I felt that I knew what had to be done. There was no choice in the matter. And I blamed him—except when I blamed myself.

This continued until I came to Al-Anon and one of the women asked me if I thought I was God.

I was thunderstruck. "Of course not," I replied.

"Then why do you continue to give God orders? Don't you think anyone besides you knows what is best? Not even God?"

It came as a great awakening to me to discover that I did indeed tell Him exactly what I wanted and then felt discouraged when He did not carry out the plans that I had so carefully spelled out. I can't describe the relief I found when I finally began to "Let Go and Let God." I learned to do this by turning over each and every person I could think of, by name, each day. It was wonderful to be freed from all that planning, scheming, outsmarting, and manipulating, and small miracles began to occur. People treated me better. I was less obsessed with the alcoholic. We even had some relatively pleasant moments. And when I added my own name to the list of people I turned over to God, the rewards were even greater. I finally began to know what the longtime Al-Anon members were talking about when they spoke of serenity.

It was a little disconcerting at first to have so much time on my hands. Free from all that obsessive mental activity, I didn't know what to think about. I often found myself reverting back to my "stinking thinking" just to fill in the gap. Or I'd take a minor irritation and blow it up in my mind until it was a crisis. But I was recovering. It didn't take long before I *caught myself* creating a drama where none existed. Then I really had to pray. I found that the prayer written on the back of the *Just for Today* bookmark was a wonderful replacement for my old insane thoughts. And if I was too far gone for anything so lengthy, just repeating one of the slogans usually turned my thinking around and restored some measure of serenity.

As I recovered, my life got busier. Eventually I decided that I knew enough and stopped going to meetings. After all, I had the literature, and I still had the friend who had brought me to Al-Anon in the first place.

About a year later, I learned that my husband was having an affair with a much younger woman. The feelings of betrayal were overwhelming. All the old thoughts flooded back. God, I decided, had turned His back on me. So I turned my back on him. I was once again a victim, a martyr, obsessed with the behavior of others. And I was consumed with jealousy. Secretly, I blamed myself. If only I had been a better wife, a better lover, a better human being, he wouldn't have had to turn to another woman. I was frantic.

I picked up the phone to call my Al-Anon friend, but the person on the other end broke the news that she had just died in an automobile accident. I couldn't believe what I heard. My dear friend and the person I considered to be my only link with sanity was gone. I hit bottom.

The days and nights passed, and eventually I returned to Al-Anon. I didn't return willingly. By that time I was in the midst of a divorce. I felt I didn't need Al-Anon since I was ridding my life of the alcoholic. But I was miserable and it showed. My friend's widower, a good friend, dragged me back to a meeting. And from then on, I knew I was where I needed to be. I felt better almost immediately as I embraced the Al-Anon way of life once more, and I became willing to make a new commitment to recovery.

Over the years, I have spent much of my time trying to bend life and other people to my will, only to fail miserably. I have also tried to change myself, eliminate my character defects, and force myself to feel differently. Again I have always failed. So why did change happen so much more readily after I returned to the program? The most important difference I can see is that by the time I returned, I was willing to be helped. It was the same old lesson God didn't need my instructions about how to heal me. My job was not to identify all of the changes that should be made so that God would know what to do. My job was to be willing to accept His will for me, willing to heal.

Since that time, I have done a great deal of thinking about willingness, which seems to be the key to any changes I want to make. I keep remembering a vacation I took with my children. Equipped with 18-wheeler inner tubes, helmets, and leather gloves, we "tubed" the Yakima River for three days. We chose a four-mile stretch of river near a dam. The more water released from the dam, the faster the river flowed and the greater the rush of water over the rocks. After each run, we were exhilarated, a little scared, and ready to go again.

The picture of this trip kept nagging at me whenever I thought about willingness, but I couldn't see how it related until I looked up the word in my thesaurus. "Agreeable, open, responsive, pliable, yielding, bending, shapeable, teachable, compliant, obedient" were some of the synonyms I found. I thought about pushing the inner tube away from the bank into the rush of the stream. It was important to relax and not fight the rapids, to bend and steer away from the rocks, to be responsive to sudden changes, to be pliable and yielding. In order to experience the thrill of the ride, we had to be willing to go with the flow.

Then I thought about my attitudes. I often sit with my arms crossed in front of me. I sleep curled up in a ball. I hold my mouth tightly closed. I am frequently inflexible about changing my attitudes or plans. I tend to be brittle and reluctant to do things unless they are done my way.

When I'm not willing to let go, I'm trying to control. When I'm not willing to listen, I'm self-righteous. When I'm not willing to accept reality, I'm in denial. But my life can be as exhilarating as tubing the river if I develop the habit of meeting each situation with openness, ready to "go with the flow" and see what happens. I can just show up at the river willing to push off into the stream, knowing that I have my inner tube under me (God) and my helmet and gloves (the tools of recovery in Al-Anon, especially the Twelve Steps). I haven't mastered this approach to living, although I am excited about it. My progress may be slow, but I inch forward a bit every day.

Today, after many years in Al-Anon, I have the same Higher Power that I came in with, but we have a much better, much more realistic relationship. I may not always understand God's will, especially when I see a loved one's suffering or lose someone who is dear to me, but I trust that He is a loving God who does have a plan. I no longer expect to be convinced that this plan is a good one before I relinquish my hold on life.

By working the Al-Anon program, I have come to believe that I'm really not in charge of anyone or anything. I'm just here to do the best I can with what God gives me. If I truly put my life and the lives of my loved ones into God's hands through daily prayer, He will be good to me beyond my wildest desire.

24

A Pueblo Indian Learns to Feel Alive

When I first joined Al-Anon, I doubted that the program could ever work for me, a Pueblo Indian woman. (For reasons of my own, I prefer not to be addressed as a Native American.) My culture was unlike that with which others at the meeting were familiar. Unlike the typical Anglo family, with a father, mother, and children, I was raised in an extended family. I was subject to the whims and under the authority of many different adults, some of whom were alcoholic. There was no privacy; there were no boundaries, no rules that couldn't be changed depending upon who was in the room at the time. I was regularly physically abused and publicly humiliated by a raging alcoholic mother, and everyone was free to criticize, scold, or punish me whenever they chose.

Also, I was brought up to play a well-defined role. As an Indian woman, I was to perform rigid tribal rituals, to be a care-giver, to please others, to be unendingly courteous and subservient, and to hide my anger. I was rarely given an opportunity to express my opinion. The men and the older women of the tribe were more important than I. My function was to serve them.

Perhaps this way of life still works for some tribal women. It did not work for me. I had no self-esteem. I didn't know how to take care of myself or value anything about myself. I had stuffed my feelings to the point that I forgot I had any. Most of my energy went into trying to be invisible. Moving away from the reservation didn't help. These effects of alcoholism, these attitudes, were too deeply ingrained.

After leaving the reservation, I worked on an assembly line in a factory that made airplane parts. The work was tedious, and the working conditions were awful. Blaring noise, stifling heat, and tedious repetition with no breaks made it very difficult for me to do my job. But I didn't know that I deserved better working conditions or a more stimulating position. I only knew that I could be invisible on the assembly line. As long as I was merely one of many faceless, nameless employees, as long as I did nothing to call attention to myself, I could feel safe. The price I paid for that sense of safety was unbearably high. I became one of the living dead.

Then things got worse. I began to get terrible migraine headaches. I never knew when one would occur, how long it would last, or how severe it would be. Because I had to miss work whenever a migraine flared up, this condition threatened to attract my supervisor's attention and ruin my invisibility. I feared I would lose my job. Several doctors, a chiropractor, and a neurologist all told me the same thing: my migraines were the result of stress-induced muscular tension. There was nothing they could do to offer me relief.

I never intended to go to Al-Anon. I had never even heard of Al-Anon. I had planned to attend a Bible study group at my church and must have wandered into the wrong room. The meeting was well under way before I realized that the Bible was not on this group's agenda. I stayed because I didn't want to call attention to myself by getting up in the middle of the meeting. I take that as evidence that God can use anything for the purpose of healing even my compulsive need to blend into the background.

By the time the meeting ended, I knew I had found a home. I had never connected my migraines with alcoholism. I never knew the source of the continuing stress in my life. But that night I began to learn how powerfully I had been affected by alcoholism.

One of my earliest discoveries was that I did not know how to breathe correctly. At first this seemed ridiculous, and I was embarrassed to admit it. But when I looked back, I realized that when I had tried to be invisible as a child, I had held my breath and tried to take up as little room on this planet as possible. Without consciously meaning to, I would tense the muscles in my upper back, shoulders, arms, neck, and head. It's a wonder any oxygen ever reached my brain at all. This was how I girded myself against the dangerous and unpredictable outside world.

So the first step I took toward recovery involved changing my breathing habits. I had to increase my awareness of breathing. I learned various forms of meditation, took up swimming, and even got an occasional massage to loosen up some of the tension I still carried.

I got a Sponsor quickly and without much forethought. I had never heard of "obedience to the unenforceable." I thought that I had to get a Sponsor or I would be asked to leave. Again, I thank my Higher Power for this "error." If I had known that there was a choice, I would never have felt worthy enough to even consider asking anyone to sponsor me. As things worked out, God found me a wonderful Sponsor.

One of the first things she told me was that I deserved to be happy. She suggested that I try to do something kind for myself every day for a week. At first I found this task impossible. I squirmed just thinking about it. I almost stopped going to meetings because I didn't want to face my Sponsor and tell her that I had "disobeyed" her instructions.

Then one day I found myself buying a small, pink azalea plant for my kitchen. That plant has been one of my most wonderful teachers. At first it was covered with tightly folded pink buds. I have watered it daily and exposed it to light, and those flowers have unfolded in beauty, following their own timetable and the gentle prompting of the sun. Even when the flowers fade, the plant will keep growing. New leaves and branches will appear. Roots will grow stronger. And each day this plant will be alive and changing and growing. If it stopped changing, it would be dead.

Like that azalea, my recovery in Al-Anon is alive. I have learned along the way that I am a beautiful flower, no matter in what state of unfolding I am. I cannot rush my own blossoming. I see newcomers to Al-Anon who verbally lash themselves because they "should have" gotten to Al-Anon years ago, or because they cannot detach the way they want to, or because they do not have the wisdom of someone who has been in the program for many years. I, too, used to scold myself regularly for all the "stupid" things I had said or done in meetings and at work. Even now, many years later, I still catch myself on occasion, telling myself, "You must not work a very good Al-Anon program because you're not handling this situation very well." But I cannot force myself to grow faster. Neither can I stop my petals from opening, even when I say fearfully, "Not now, God, I am not ready for this!" God sets the timetable for my growth. And when I look back along the road I have traveled, my unfolding has always been perfectly timed. I have been given exactly what I needed at each stage.

My Higher Power will be calling me forward into change every day for the rest of my life, so I have learned to try to take each day as it comes and to be grateful for whatever it brings.

When I think about my Al-Anon recovery, I visualize myself going through an open door. Beyond that door is another door and another, and another, and another. Never in my life have I felt so much freedom. Never have I been so aware that I am *alive*. And never have I felt such wonder. Wonder and gratitude, because I know that down the road are more and more doors to open, more insights into myself and others, more things to do that I never felt capable of doing before, more acceptance of myself, more growing. I have a Higher Power who walks through those sometimes frightening doorways with me and people with whom to share my spiritual odyssey, good people who have chosen a similar path.

It has taken a long time for my low self-esteem to be replaced with a healthy sense of self-worth. Although the process of recovery is steady, it is sometimes slower than I would wish. But when I question whether I should be further along, my Sponsor reminds me that the only "should" in the program is that I "should" be exactly where I am.

I no longer endure a dead-end, unstimulating, self-destructive job. Today I make a living doing something I love writing promotional articles for a large corporation and also writing original fiction.

There is a famous writer whom I have admired all my life. Until recently, I was too shy ever to attempt to meet her, feeling that she is so wonderful and that I am nothing beside her. I recently admitted feeling this way to my Al-Anon group. In this way, I did what I could, and God did the rest.

Last night I dreamed about meeting this woman. In my dream, she praised my writing. Then I heard God saying quietly, "Why must you compare? You are like two different colors, each of them beautiful. She is she and you are you, and both of you are lovely.

The beauty of your writing extends beyond the written word. It is expressed in the loving words you speak to your children, in the words you speak at meetings, in the way you look gently at a friend, in the whispers of your heart, and in your prayers." I felt healing in that dream. The sense of inadequacy that I have carried all my life was diminished. Someday, I believe, it will be gone forever.

It has taken a long time to believe that it is okay for me to claim my rightful place on this planet, to breathe deeply, to sight loudly, and to feel that I have the right to exist happily. I've learned to be proud of my Pueblo heritage, and to take what I like from my culture, and leave the rest. I still get migraines, but they don't come as often, and they don't last as long. I am grateful for this, for I have learned to value progress, not perfection.

I have experienced many miracles in my life since coming to Al-Anon, but I can't tell my story of recovery by pinning down the past, by pretending that I am all healed, or always serene, or that I've received the answers to all the questions that bother me.

What I do have is a wonderful way of life that challenges me greatly while satisfying me deeply. It's called Al-Anon. It's the best thing that ever happened to me. It's a gift, straight from the gracious hand of God.

25

On the Road...to Recovery

Before I found Al-Anon, one day I experienced a strong urge to crank the steering wheel across the center line and ram my car into the opposing traffic. It wasn't something that I planned to do. I was just following my usual routine of driving a car without thinking about what I was doing.

Although I didn't drink alcohol, I had the uncanny ability to duplicate an alcoholic state of mind. My own version of "feeling no pain" was something I trained myself to do when I was a kid. If I thought it was too dangerous to let my parents know what I thought or how I was feeling, I tuned out. I have since learned a great deal about myself and my family, including why I came to Al-Anon in the first place.

My father worked a physically demanding job Monday through Friday. During evenings and on weekends he volunteered to do charity work for our church. I always thought his absence meant everyone else was far more important than we were. Not until Al-Anon did I consider the possibility that he was minimizing the time he spent with my mother. His absence didn't have anything to do with me or my four younger brothers. During those rare times when our father was home, I had to act as though I needed him to do everything. But when he was gone, which meant the vast majority of every week, either I figured out what to do or we went without.

My mother neglected to do a lot of the things around the house, so my brothers and I had to fend for ourselves when our father was gone. As the oldest child, it fell on me to do quite a few things that no one ever showed me how to do. The worst time of the day was the last half hour before Dad came home. Mom went crazy with fear. She screamed and yelled at us to clean and straighten everything, or she would tell Dad. Then she felt even more terrified that Dad would discover that she didn't do the work herself. In her child-like fear of being found out, Mom wanted to hide the evidence–which turned out to be me. Because of my adaptive personality, my natural reaction was to disappear, just as she wanted.

I studied hard in school because I wanted to earn a scholarship to college, but the real result was a migraine that lasted for months. It became impossible for me to study. Eventually I ended up in the hospital because my father wanted an explanation for my pain. An event occurred in the hospital that meant much more to me, years later, after I attended Al-Anon. At the conclusion of the tests, my doctor told me to sit on the edge of the bed. He started to push me, so I pushed back. With a smile on his face, he put one hand on each of my shoulders. Looking me straight in the eyes, he said, "Son, when you leave home, everything's going to be fine." That was all he said. He didn't explain what he meant or why he said it.

Before graduating from high school, I decided to join the military. Actually, I begged the recruiter to let me sign up early so I could leave right after graduation. I was a year young for my class, so I needed parental permission to enlist. My father took my decision pretty hard because it seemed to him that I was abandoning our family. When I explained that I could go without his permission on my next birthday, he decided to sign the permission form. Rather than limit my term to the usual enlistment, he said I might as well sign up for ten years—because he never wanted to see me again. The morning I left for boot camp, he went to work several hours early so he wouldn't have to say good-bye. He called me from his job, but I don't remember anything he said except that he was crying.

The doctor was right. Compared to what I was used to, everything seemed easy. I was one of the lucky ones in military life. I enjoyed wearing clean clothes and having orderly living quarters. Work went quicker and the food tasted better than what I was used to at home. I grew a little taller and added a few pounds. I even had dental and medical work done when I needed it. And I qualified for a college education. It took a little longer that way, but it was worth it.

College was where I met my wife. I have no idea what might have happened if I had found Alateen and then Al-Anon when my wise doctor first diagnosed my family's condition. Maybe I would have missed out on having four of the best children anyone could imagine, but I might also have become a much better husband and father. I also wish I could have been more supportive of my wife's recovery from alcoholism. More than anything in the world, I wish I had not treated my children some of the ways that my parents treated me.

My daily habits included staying up until three o'clock in the morning, drinking strong coffee, and smoking cigarettes. Abject loneliness was my main complaint. I always felt tired, even when I first woke up. I wasn't in touch with any anger, but I blamed myself for everything. I completely denied my wife's drinking, because she could get up in the morning, have a cup of coffee, and go off to work. If anyone had a problem, I knew it was me.

That day when I considered cranking the steering wheel across that center line, my knees began to shake. The shaking turned into leg spasms that caused me to veer toward the side of the road instead of toward the middle. If my knees had remained steady, I probably would have let an accident happen. Someone could have died on the highway that day without anyone knowing that alcoholism played a role. Tests wouldn't have detected any alcohol in my body, because there wasn't any.

In the middle of this self-induced numb state on the highway, the notion crossed my mind that it didn't really matter whether I lived or died. It wasn't that I wanted to die, although it occurred to me that my wife and kids would probably be better off if I wasn't around. What I realized was a vague sense of guilt, as though I was taking up space or breathing someone else's air. I felt embarrassed about being unemployed. I felt humiliated about my family, especially my kids, seeing me so discouraged and without a sense of purpose. I saw myself as desperately lost, but somehow making a public spectacle of myself.

I believe my Higher Power used this drastic situation to get my attention. It worked, but somewhere in the back of my mind was an awareness that it had happened before. The shock from my close call put me in touch with two forms of gratitude. As I sat on the side of the road waiting for my legs to calm down, I felt a dribble of tears because I knew what could have happened. Next, I promised in my heart that if I arrived home safely, I would make enough phone calls to find out what was happening to me.

Our health maintenance organization referred me to its family counseling department. The therapist who interviewed me asked among other things if I would describe the use of alcohol in my home. I said I might have a cold beer in the summer if the weather was hot, but my wife was more of a normal drinker. She might have a glass or two of wine at dinner, plus a bottle or two on the weekend. Apparently, my description of what happened on the highway, the way I answered the interview questions, and probably the way I looked while I was in her office, led the therapist to send me to Al-Anon right away.

My first Al-Anon meeting took place in a church kitchen. On my way to the beginners' session, a very attractive woman asked me if I would like a hug. Although I must have looked surprised, I managed to accept her offer. When she stepped back to see if I was smiling, I could tell from her face that I wasn't. Later, I wondered why, because I know how good it felt when she hugged me.

When it was my turn to speak in the beginners' meeting, I said I didn't know if I belonged there. I described what happened on the highway and shared what the counselor had told me. The leader invited me to "Keep Coming Back" until I knew for sure whether Al-Anon could help.

When I realized no one at the meeting was going to tell me what to do, I nearly lapsed into one of my stupors, but a couple of messages broke through, anyway. I heard it was very important to take good care of myself. Although I readily agreed, I didn't know what that meant or how to do it. A man offered the acronym HALT. I heard if I found myself feeling too hungry, angry, lonely, or tired, it would be a good idea to drop everything else and take care of that primary need right away. Of course, I felt overwhelmed in at least three of the four categories. The only category that didn't fit me was the angry one. I stayed too depressed to feel angry at anyone but myself.

My first real breakthrough occurred one afternoon before the kids came home from school. I found myself feeling the same way I had on the highway. It seemed as though I didn't deserve to take my next breath, and that everyone would be better off if I was gone. I went from a feeling of deep despair to a sense of well-being in about one hour. I took a nap. I couldn't believe something that simple could make me feel so much better. All my life I thought naps were what adults did to kids when they grew tired of having them around. Instead of a nap being a form of punishment, I started looking forward to it as a way to calm my troubled spirit and bring some new energy into my day.

A few members suggested that, if I wanted the full impact of the Al-Anon program, I attend many meetings. They also mentioned taking names and phone numbers so I could contact people between meetings. The most important thing they said was to spend time with the winners—those who had already succeeded with the kind of dilemmas that I faced. They commented that if I found myself looking forward to a certain person speaking at the meetings, it might be a good idea to ask that person to be my Sponsor.

I went to numerous meetings. I was desperate to straighten out my life and to learn how to drive on the right side of the road. The person I asked to be my Sponsor had eight or nine years in the program. Even though he was only half my age, he and his family dealt with hopelessness, depression, bill collectors, embarrassment, fear, and loneliness. It was as though we were made for each other.

The first time we met for coffee, my new Sponsor said, "You know the way you usually drive home from here?" In a flash, I knew exactly which way I would go. "Try taking a different way home to see how it feels." Little suggestions like that did me the most good because they helped me focus on the present.

Another idea he gave me had to do with the telephone. "You know how you feel when the phone rings?" he said. "Why don't you pick it up right away, instead of giving yourself so much time to feel afraid of who's calling?" His ideas saved me a lot of grief. If it was a bill collector who called to set up a meeting, he suggested that I spruce myself up and arrive early for the appointment. After being honest and brief in the meeting, I was to shake hands with the person and say, "Thank you for talking with me." These simple suggestions were priceless. He helped me accept the truth about my circumstances, while showing me how to keep my dignity intact, so I could hold my head up. I will always be grateful.

My situation in Al-Anon was a little unusual in that I had yet to learn how alcoholism affected my family. I simply scared myself behind the wheel of a car. I was in a hurry to learn how to drive safely before someone told me I had to leave. I worried about whether I belonged, but I wanted my kids to try Alateen. I guess I wondered out loud, because one day my wife interrupted my thoughts by saying, "Well, you know, I *am* an alcoholic."

After getting herself into recovery, my wife explained that the one or two glasses of wine she drank at dinner, and the bottle or two that she consumed on weekends, were only the quantities that she let me see her drink. The reason she didn't want me to do laundry or certain kinds of housework was because her main stash of alcohol was in the utility room. She could function enough to drive and work, but she felt no pain, or anything else. The main impact that her drinking had on me was the feeling that nothing mattered. We didn't talk about anything more personal than what I discussed with co-workers, when I worked. It was as though my wife and I were strangers who cared about each other, but we were still strangers.

Little by little, I heard Al-Anon members say things about their families that helped me understand how alcoholism affected mine. For example, I never knew at school or in books why women, especially mothers, received credit for providing warmth, nurturing, and affection in the home. I thought it sounded like so much wishful thinking, or some kind of cruel joke that everyone knew was false. In Al-Anon I found that many women actually do have tender feelings toward their families.

When I say most of what I understand about my family came from listening to Al-Anon and Alateen members talk about theirs, it's not that I don't remember what happened. It's just that I wouldn't have any reason to think about those events if I didn't hear other people sharing their stories. Thinking about what really happened and sharing my memories with people in the program has made a big difference. Instead of reliving my embarrassment and shame, what I've received from Al-Anons and Alateens is acceptance, compassion, and love.

For example, I used to associate certain unpleasant memories with various angry expressions on my father's face. Now, as I think about the same events, I picture the nods, smiles, and tears from Al-Anon members who helped heal my injured spirit. The more I express what really happened in my life, the more I can relax and be myself. This "loving interchange of help among members" also gives me opportunities to forgive my loved ones and friends for the ugly side-effects that came from the disease.

After I had been in the program for a few years, a couple of my children complained to me about the treatment I was giving their youngest brother. They said I was too easy on him, that I was failing to prepare him for the real world, and that he was spoiled. This was my first real opportunity to do a Ninth Step with my children. I said when they were their younger brother's age, they deserved to be treated exactly the same way I was treating him, but at that time I didn't know how. I think it meant something for them to hear me say that. I know it meant a lot to me.

Several program friends and I decided to quit smoking at about the same time. Part of our incentive was to put the money we normally spent on cigarettes into a jar to use for something personal. Eventually I used mine to buy a set of golf clubs. My oldest son confronted me about it. He explained that where he went to school a lot of his friends received new cars for their birthday. It was hard for him to feel as though he fit in with that kind of crowd. He said the least I could have done was to use my cigarette money to buy some new school clothes for him.

Of course, I felt terrible about what he said. I knew how he felt because I attended a high school like that. I told him it was important for me not only to buy the golf clubs for myself, but also to use them. All the time I was talking with my son, I acted as if I believed what I was saying was right. Although I did not completely believe it, I trusted the people who encouraged me to take good care of myself.

Within a day or so, my son asked me if I would come to his room to see something. He was so proud of what he showed me. He had bought beautiful clothes with paychecks from the two part-time jobs he had as a stock boy and a lifeguard. He had been saving his paychecks because, until I bought my golf clubs, he didn't feel he had permission to spend any of his own money on himself.

I would never have guessed that by taking good care of myself, things can also work out well for the people I love.

As I look back on the significant events in my life, I see how Al-Anon has helped me put them into perspective. As an adult, I repeated the same patterns that I experienced as a child. I went from having four younger brothers and an unavailable mother to being the father of four children, married to an unavailable wife. Major changes came as the result of working a recovery program and hanging around the winners in Al-Anon. My biggest problem became the easiest thing to overcome in Al-Anon. Abject loneliness started to leave me as soon as I began sharing my feelings with people who shared their feelings with me. Since I attended my first meeting, I have had the confidence and faith of all Al-Anon to support my efforts.

In Al-Anon during my forties I learned the basics of self-care that people learn in healthy families when they are about four. My second Sponsor, a woman who was the big sister I never had, encouraged me to find safe ways to express my anger. If there was no one I felt particularly angry with at the moment, she suggested that I pretend I was angry. One technique was to write people's names on the bottom of my shoe and spend the entire day walking on them. By the third or fourth step, I always started laughing.

I went through a separation and divorce after 23 years of marriage and five years in recovery. It would have devastated me if it happened any earlier. I asked my wife to leave at least half a dozen times, but she said she couldn't do it. I believe her motives were similar to my mother's. She was terrified that someone would find out I had been doing her job. I understand how both of these women felt, because although I did their jobs, I failed to do my own.

All through the drinking and recovering, my ex-wife performed well on her job. She always brought home a good income. If she spent the night drinking, I was the one who woke up with a hangover. While she made steady progress at work, I lost my concentration, all my confidence, and my income. My humiliation nearly drove me across the center line.

If there was going to be a significant change in my life, I knew I was the one who had to make it. My most painful experience was telling my children, especially my seven-year-old son. Today, as I look at pictures of the way he was then, I don't see how I could possibly have left. All of my children are beautiful—one daughter, followed by three sons—but my youngest is the one who came with me to my early Al-Anon meetings. He is the one who had the best father, because my recovery started when he was two years old.

It was also difficult for me to tell some other special people about my decision to leave my family. The women in my Thursday morning Al-Anon meeting listened as I shared my embarrassment and shame for failing to take care of my responsibilities as a father and a husband. They responded by taking me in their arms and assuring me that I had done my best. Instead of shunning me and kicking me out of the fellowship, they told me to "Keep Coming Back" and to start living my own life.

Of the millions of people all over the world who qualify for membership, support, acceptance, and the unconditional love found in Al-Anon, I don't know why I am one of the lucky few to receive it. One of my pure pleasures today is driving down the highway, listening to music, enjoying the view, and trusting myself behind the wheel of a car. I can concentrate on my job and make use of the skills my Higher Power gave me. Today I have more things to be grateful for than most people are willing to let me list.

When I finally overcame my tendency to blame either myself or women for the hurts that came from alcoholism, I allowed love to re-enter my life. An Al-Anon friend became my loving partner. Although each of us has twice as many alcoholic relatives as we used to have, neither of us has to do anything alone. We have the confidence and faith of all Al-Anon to support our efforts as individuals and as a couple. My life is not perfect today, but I have so much support that even on my bad days I feel that I am a valuable person. I'm glad my Higher Power finally got my attention.

26

A Mother Lets Go and Lets God

As a teenager, our daughter was quiet and withdrawn. We knew she smoked pot, but thought it merely an occasional social choice. She never missed school or work and was always home by our curfew. As far as we knew, she obeyed the rules and never smoked pot in our house. One day my husband came home for lunch and found our daughter and a friend drinking and getting stoned. I confronted her, demanding that this behavior cease at once. She replied that she couldn't stop using drugs or alcohol and would move out if we forced the issue.

At first, I didn't believe her. Then I panicked. I couldn't allow her to move out! What would happen to her? Where would she live? I decided to get her some help.

The counselor at our local youth center asked our daughter some questions and quickly concluded that she was a drug addict and alcoholic who needed immediate treatment. I figured he meant a few counseling sessions. I could handle that. But when he started talking about cities that were hours away, I got upset. Then he mentioned treatment programs that required our daughter to spend six weeks away from home! I became very defensive. I hated the idea. After much talk, I finally consented, with the condition that treatment would be delayed for at least a week—we were scheduled to go camping to celebrate our daughter's 17th birthday, and I wasn't about to give up the trip. But the counselor was insistent. If our daughter was willing to go now, it had to be now.

I had terrible trouble accepting that my daughter was an alcoholic. As far as I knew, I had never been acquainted with an alcoholic before. I didn't even think about the fact that my dad had often stolen money from my sisters and had taken the welfare check from the mailbox before my mother could get it, spending it at the local bar. My brother had been a daily beer drinker since he was 13. I had memories of a sister who left me in the car for hours while she and her boyfriend went drinking. This was normal, everyday life for me. I never thought to question it. So I was honestly sure I had never known any alcoholics.

The next day we drove to the treatment facility. I didn't know how to act or what to say. It was probably the most uncomfortable drive I've ever taken, and I spent most of it silently torturing myself. I knew nothing about alcoholism or addiction, yet I was convinced that somehow I was to blame. I had been told that it was a disease and that our daughter would have to consider herself an alcoholic for the rest of her life.

I was horrified to learn that part of my daughter's recovery included abstention from alcohol for the rest of her life. Why, she wouldn't be able to have champagne at her own wedding! I couldn't imagine anything worse that that! Like all of my friends, I had always been a social drinker, with occasional bouts of excess in my younger days. During family week at the treatment center, I decided that my own drinking, while not alcoholic, had probably gotten me into more trouble than it was worth. I decided it would be best if I stuck to soft drinks and only an occasional glass of wine. I worried about the reactions I might get from friends, but for the most part, they didn't much care whether I drank or not.

My husband and I did all the things we were asked to do during treatment, including attending Al-Anon meetings twice a week. I remember spending that first meeting trying to get the courage to tell all those poor, troubled souls how they could help their loved ones. I truly believed that we, the friends and family members, had all the answers to our loved ones' problems and it was our job and our duty to keep everyone functioning well. Now that I realize how foolish and inappropriate my words would have been, I am grateful that I did not speak.

At our first meeting, we heard an Al-Anon member tell her story. I only remember that she said she had learned to stop asking questions about where her daughter was going, when she would return, or who she would be with. I wondered how on earth this woman managed to refrain from asking! How did she ever know what was going on with her daughter? She wasn't even sure whether or not her daughter was drinking! How could she possibly go about her day without this information? Didn't she love her daughter? With the knowledge that most alcoholics who continue to drink will eventually end up insane, imprisoned, or dead from this disease, how could she possibly have a moment's peace without being sure that her daughter was not active in her disease?

What convinced me to take Al-Anon seriously was the realization that my behavior, my denial, my enabling, had the potential to make a bad situation worse. I couldn't stop my daughter from drinking or using drugs, but I could stop contributing to the problem by changing my behavior and my attitude. So I became willing to find out how that other mother had achieved such gargantuan feats, and I began to learn about detachment. I learned that alcoholism is a disease, and that in my mind I could separate the person I loved from the disease. This allowed me to make choices about how to express my love for my daughter so that I was supporting *her* rather than her illness.

When her time at the treatment center was completed, she moved into a halfway house from which she could work and attend school. Within a few weeks, we were notified that our daughter had violated the rules. She had entered the halfway house with the understanding that she could not drink or use drugs there, nor could she come home if she used them. Until another halfway house had room for her, she was on her own. I was extremely upset and went to an Al-Anon meeting at the first opportunity. The topic turned out to be "Let Go and Let God," and it couldn't have been more timely. I saw that I had not begun to let go of what was happening with my daughter. And I had resisted the notion of a Higher Power because all of my images of God were authoritative male figures to whom I could not relate. Now I saw how very much I needed to find some sort of Power greater than myself who could help me to find serenity even if my daughter chose to drink. I decided that, because I found so much solace in my Al-Anon group, I would use the group as a Higher Power, at least for the time being. My commitment to the group deepened.

Of course, I was not cured. When the group needed a new Group Representative (GR), I nominated my husband. I was sure that he needed to become more involved. I was proud when he was elected, but my plans for him didn't work out, and he resigned from the position shortly thereafter. Until then it hadn't occurred to me to take my own advice, but when the opportunity arose, I volunteered to take over the position myself. To my surprise, I found it a wonderful way to learn about distinguishing between my responsibilities and the responsibilities of others.

As time passed, my personal concept of a Higher Power evolved. Since I couldn't relate to a fatherly God, my Sponsor suggested exploring female images. This led me to find a feminine Higher Power with whom I could feel comfortable enough to open my heart and soul. A spiritual awakening happened soon thereafter. While traveling to a nearby town to take a graduate school admissions test, I suddenly realized that I did not have to be scared because my Higher Power was right there in the car with me. Later that day, I accidentally locked my keys in the car, delaying a series of plans that involved other people. Yet I was amazingly free of impatience and anxiety over something I couldn't control!

I had a similar experience a few weeks later when unexpected delays caused my family and me to miss a special luncheon for the new graduates, something I had looked forward to attending. I actually laughed about it! My sister could not believe it was me! Al-Anon and my Higher Power were helping to transform me into a much happier, well-adjusted person right before everyone's eyes. This was not the kind of spiritual awakening that I had imagined. There was no sudden flash of light, no deep insight into the mysteries of the universe or the depths of the human soul. Instead there was a quiet change. I had been granted serenity.

Serenity came and went a lot during that first year of recovery. My Al-Anon literature, especially the daily readings in the *ODAT* (*One Day at a Time in Al-Anon*), made it possible to recapture a little serenity each day. I learned that what I feel is not the fault of other people. I have choices about how I react to what happens in my life, and no one else can determine how I feel. I stopped making excuses for my self-pity and inertia, and began to consider what I could do about changing my attitudes in order to make my day more pleasant and more constructive.

I began to recognize evidence of alcoholism in my family of origin. I suspect that my father, who died when I was only five, was an alcoholic, and that my mother suffered from the effects of his disease. Although I hadn't realized it, alcoholism had affected my life from the beginning. I found both comfort and insight by reading the Alateen daily reader, *Alateen—a day at a time* because it dealt very directly with the effects of alcoholism on youth.

I continue to use the literature on a daily basis and am grateful that Al-Anon continues to produce new publications. I need to hear the Al-Anon message again and again, in different words, forms, and voices. A thought, phrase, or principle that had no particular meaning for me yesterday may be extremely significant today. And now that I have some recovery, I find it important to contribute to the creation of our literature by writing and submitting my own story. I am also learning to take my ego out of this process. The first essay I sent to *The Forum* was not published. I had been so proud of that piece, so certain that it contained the great wisdom of the ages that would enlighten Al-Anon members all over the world. I took the rejection personally and vowed never to write again. But then recovery took over, and I had to admit that I hadn't acted in the spirit of love or service when I sent the sharing. I had acted in the spirit of arrogance and self-aggrandizement.

So I tried again. I sent in a personal story for one of Al-Anon's new books. I really tried to take the action and let go of the results. Whether my story was used or not, I was prepared. When the book was eventually published, I tried not to allow my ego to take over as I leafed through. When I stumbled across some familiar words, I was delighted, but as I read further, I discovered that only portions of my sharing had been used. The rest of the piece had come from someone else—it was a composite. And although I admired what was said, I felt rejected.

My Sponsor helped me to remember that I had written my story because I wanted to be of service and to give something back to the body of Al-Anon literature that had helped me so much for so many years. I had benefited greatly just from writing the story. I had grown by learning to let go of the results. And now I had received a wonderful compliment. My experience, strength, and hope had been recognized as valuable enough to share with other members of our fellowship. Instead of focusing on the negative, I could choose gratitude for the gift I had received. In other words, rather than lamenting over the portions of my story that had been omitted or edited, I could choose to respond to the acknowledgement I had received through this opportunity to serve.

Despite her rocky start at the halfway house, my daughter eventually chose recovery. I did my best to let her know that I love and support her, and to help her only when she wanted it. For example, my husband and I agreed to support our daughter through college—but only if she wanted to go. She chose to attend a local junior college and then spent a year away at a university. We had to work hard at detaching during that year for we had reason to doubt that she was attending her A.A. meetings, and her grades were beginning to drop. We knew that we were powerless over the drinking, but once again the elusive question of enabling came up. Was it enabling to support her through school if she wasn't living up to her end of the deal? We realized that we hadn't really agreed upon what her responsibility was. So the three of us sat down and discussed it, and when we reached an agreement, we drew up a contract. She agreed to keep her grades above a certain level, and we agreed to support her financially as long as she did. Whether or not she drank was her business and did not enter into the discussion.

By the end of the year, our daughter's grades had dropped below the point we had agreed upon. So we ended our financial support of her education. I was extremely upset. How could she earn a decent living with just a high school diploma? That night my husband and I went to a movie. I sat in the darkened theater and cried for her lost opportunity.

When I look back, I realize that I still had a finger on her life. Higher education was my dream, not hers. Even today, now that she's been sober for several years and also qualifies for financial aid, she hasn't returned to school. Yet she has a good job with benefits and supports herself quite well.

When she reached her first A.A. birthday, our daughter thanked Al-Anon for her sobriety. The things we learned about enabling and about detachment with love really did make a difference in her life. By that time it was obvious how much of a difference they had made in ours.

In fact, I took the advice I had wanted to thrust upon my daughter—I pursued my dream of furthering my education. Without Al-Anon I would never have been able to stick out the five difficult years it took to get my M.B.A. degree, but with lots of help I stayed with it, worked hard, worked my program, and graduated.

My life today is better than I ever dreamed it could be. I work in a field I enjoy, I feel good about myself, and I have a good marriage. My relationship with my daughter is one I especially cherish because it has taught me so much about love. I don't regret the tough times I've passed through along the way, nor do I fear the difficulties to come. I have too much to be grateful for today to waste my time moaning about the past or dreading the uncertainty of the future. Instead, I thank my lucky stars to have found this wonderful way of life, and I try to give each day my full and undivided attention.

27

Finding Reasons to Live

For many years, death seemed an attractive alternative to my life. I read many books on the subject, always searching for an author who painted death beautifully enough to overcome any hesitation I had about ending my life. I simply hated living.

I had married at seventeen, and had four children within ten years. My husband was a heavy drinker who spent most of his time at the local gin mills. After 20 years of battling his drinking, I divorced him, hoping to find peace of mind and to recover what was left of my life.

Instead, a year after the divorce, I found myself yearning to die. The pain was worse than any pain I had felt while still married. This confused me since I had been so sure that the solution to all my problems was getting rid of my husband! But I was still attached to him, and my insane reactions to his antics while we lived apart frightened me more and more. I didn't know that I had been and continued to be affected by alcoholism. I only knew that my days were spent fighting an invisible monster that slept only when I slept. My obsession with the past engulfed my personality, and my mind was so far out of control that I was afraid of my thoughts. Soon I had lost 40 pounds. My eyes were sunken and surrounded by dark circles. I looked as if I was dying. I *was* dying.

I sentenced myself to death, believing that I caused nothing but pain to others and that my children would be relieved to be rid of me. I told my doctor that I had been unable to sleep since my divorce and that my nerves were so shattered that I felt I needed a sedative to function normally. Much to my surprise he wrote the prescription before I had finished explaining the problem. It was too easy.

The doctor prescribed tranquilizers and gave me three refills. That meant that I would have 120 pills. I felt satisfied that this amount would be foolproof.

Ironically, that same week my children persuaded me to see a counselor at an alcoholism treatment center. I didn't believe she could help, for I was not sure that my ex-husband was an alcoholic, although I was quite sure I had caused his drinking. There could be no remedy for my severely damaged heart and mind. I kept the weekly appointments with the counselor, but I kept the pills as well, tucked into the pillow of the Queen Anne chair in the corner of my bedroom.

My former husband's actions continued to control me. He was as bitter and angry with me now as he had been during our marriage, and although I could not please him no matter what I did, I continued to try and to fail. He acted; I reacted. My living room floor was decorated with piles of self-help books, but I absorbed little of them. I didn't bother to pray, because I felt I had prayed more than anyone in the world for God to help me and He never did. I would not look in the mirror in the morning when I dressed for work because I did not like what I saw there. I kept losing weight until I got down to a size three. I had always been known for my strength both physically and mentally. I was the person people turned to for comfort. What had happened to me? Where had that person gone?

The moment finally came when I reacted so badly to an encounter with my ex-husband that I felt I could not go on any more. I went to the Queen Anne chair, thinking that the time was right. My children were asleep for the night. I ate those pills with the passion of a hungry child with a big piece of chocolate cake. Death was to be my gift to the world. I was exterminating a malignant disease.

My 18-year-old son, who was supposed to have spent the night out, came home unexpectedly and found me unconscious on the kitchen floor. I spent the next week in a mental institution. After two days in a coma, I opened my eyes in utter disbelief, tremendous anger, and disappointment. My oldest daughter held my hand and chanted, "Why Ma, why?" My boys tried to convince me to live for their sake. My youngest daughter was stone silent and was clutching me in the way that one might hold a favorite doll. They tried to persuade me that I had a reason to live, but I felt inhuman, invaded by demons. I wanted to explain how I felt, but I could not. I wanted help, but did not believe there was any.

Bewildered and sick, I was led to a group therapy session, where a counselor assured us patients that recovery from our various problems was possible. I felt a bit fearful of recovery. To me, it only meant a return to my miserable life. When asked to share our experiences, I sat blankly until a man spoke. He said, "I guess I'm an alcoholic. I stopped drinking and tried to make amends to my family for all I had done to hurt them. Then my wife ran off with some nitwit, and my children used up all my money and never appreciated my efforts to love them. I got angry and hurt, and I started drinking again."

Boiling inside, as if I were the wife this man described, I felt compelled to speak. I talked about my husband—how he acted when he drank and how I felt about it. "He has no feelings," I said.

The man retorted angrily, "What makes you think that alcoholics have no feelings? Why do you think we drink? You are not over your divorce, lady, and you never will be."

I was stunned. He was right. I was nowhere near being over my divorce. That day, for the first time, I was able to acknowledge my anger toward my husband. I felt vengeful and hateful and grateful that I could still feel at all.

This man in group therapy taught me about alcoholism. He explained that my ex-husband was not cruel, indifferent, evil, or impossible to please, nor was I a failure. We were victims of a disease called alcoholism. I listened intently and began to see how fruitless my efforts to control the drinking had been.

My new friend spoke of the time when he had been a member of Alcoholics Anonymous and said that those had been the best years of his life. He talked about the Twelve Steps and what they had meant to him. The work that had to be done in order for him to stay sober sounded too easy, and I was perplexed by his agony. All he had to do, after all, was stop drinking. How simple, I thought. I feared that he had a far better chance at happiness than I did, for I was insane *without* the drink.

Upon my release, my psychiatrist gave me a prescription for an anti-depressant. She promised relief for my suffocating depression and advised me to take one at a time. I wanted a personality transplant. I wanted to be free from my thoughts. The pills only made matters worse. I looked dead and moved slowly, but the obsessive thoughts and severe pain in my soul remained. I was trapped again, but in a new way. I had found a new terror—guilt for trying to kill myself.

The psychiatrist told me to ingest large doses of vitamins along with the anti-depressant, again promising full recovery from my sad condition. Part of me questioned the logic of adding more chemicals to my already saturated blood stream, but I obeyed anyway. I did not trust myself to think logically.

I kept in touch by phone with my friend from the hospital, and soon I began to accompany him to A.A. meetings. I felt a spark of life each time I heard A.A. members speak about their sorrow and pain. It eased the guilt I felt about causing my husband to drink. After about 16 weeks of struggling to think clearly, I stopped taking the anti-depressant.

My friend began to look and speak more tenderly. I was exhilarated to find myself regarding him fondly but terrified as well. I was afraid to love. Yet together we laughed, listened, learned, shared, and cried. Love grew.

On our way to an A.A. meeting one night he suggested that I try Al-Anon. He claimed that I could get more help there because I was not addicted to alcohol but affected by someone else's drinking. He said it was important to our relationship that I get involved with people who were like me. He promised I would feel good there and said he loved me and wanted me to feel good. I argued that A.A. helped me. I loved to hear alcoholics confess their shortcomings! But he kept after me until it became difficult for me to resist any longer.

I felt like a defeated child being dropped off at kindergarten for the first time when I stood at the door of my first Al-Anon meeting, but I managed to go inside. A group of people were sitting around a conference table. Some of them smiled at me and when I sat down, a small blue book was handed to me. It was *One Day at a Time in Al-Anon (ODAT)*. I nodded a silent "thank you" but wanted to leave. The meeting began with the reading of the Twelve Steps. They were almost exactly the same as A.A.'s Twelve Steps, and I wondered why. I was miserable for much of the meeting, so I can't explain why I knew that I had to keep coming back.

After three months of almost nightly Al-Anon meetings, I began to change. I resisted, giving myself every excuse to quit, from "I hate Al-Anon" to "This is a cult and they are reprogramming me!" But I kept coming back because it was working.

I felt as if the Steps, especially the First Step, were written just for me. My life had become unmanageable because I had failed to admit that I was powerless over alcohol. Fellow members spoke of their vain attempts to stop their loved ones from drinking. I heard about attempted rescues and attempted murders. I recalled my own futile rescue missions and a horrible night when I, too, plotted the murder of the alcoholic. Al-Anon was not a cult. It was a gift.

I changed dramatically, but so slowly that I did not see the changes happening. It was like watching a pot of water and waiting for it to boil. My depression began to lift, and the yearning for death disappeared with it because I had begun to have hope. I smiled more and laughed more, and my appearance improved. I gained back the weight I had lost. My memory returned. The deep, icy fear that had been my companion for most of my life was lessening. I was able to understand the simple words of the Serenity Prayer and learned how to apply it to my life.

My friend and I became engaged. Soon after, he suddenly slacked off on his A.A. meetings. He convinced me that he could stay sober on his own. I saw how strong I had become as a result of my Al-Anon recovery and decided that I, too, was cured. In all too short a time, our relationship resembled the marriage I had left. He relapsed, and I relapsed with him. The recurrence of old behavior began to devour the joy we had found in recovery. My depression returned. My obsession with the alcoholic's every move returned. And suicidal thoughts began to creep in once more.

But by now I knew too much to go down without a fight. Al-Anon slogans and phrases came back to me in my suffering. I remembered that I could "Let Go and Let God" and that I was powerless over alcohol. With the Serenity Prayer on my lips each day, I began to take painful steps to separate from the alcoholic. But without the support of Al-Anon meetings and fellow members, I reacted to his drinking in the same old familiar ways. I remember seeing the exit light flashing incessantly one night as I approached my alcoholic friend in his favorite bar and slapped him in the face—my usual way of reacting to drunkenness in the past. The exit light told me to "Go home!" And so did the alcoholic.

I felt doomed and unteachable, hating him, hating life, and hating myself for leaving Al-Anon, but too ashamed to return to meetings. I watched the alcoholic deteriorate. He lost his job and moved out of our apartment and into a dilapidated rooming house. His pants began to loosen, and his walk lost its sureness. I found myself unable to detach. I was completely obsessed with him, consumed by anxiety about where he was and what he was doing. I felt the same old despair, the same yearning to put a permanent end to my suffering. An occasional week of sobriety would pump up my illusion that he would return to A.A. and be well again. But finally I couldn't deny what I was seeing. My beloved friend was going insane. He was dying. And I was spiraling down with him.

Suddenly I felt the impact of what I had allowed to happen to my life. I felt stupid. God had spared my life, and judging by my actions, I had wasted my second chance. I knew that if I continued to go on this way, I would take my own life. I decided to sever my relationship with the alcoholic and return to Al-Anon.

Then the phone rang. After a month's absence, my alcoholic friend was calling to ask for help. He said he wanted to stop drinking. I didn't want to go to him. I remembered all the other times he had wanted my help—and all the disappointments. I still knew, at least intellectually, that I was powerless to stop his drinking. And I was determined to stop abusing myself. Still, although I couldn't have explained why, I went.

When I arrived at his house, I found my friend stumbling up the stairs with a bottle in his hand. I knew at that moment—not just in my mind, but in every cell of my body—that I needed help. The next day, embarrassed but desperate, I returned to Al-Anon. My flirtation with death came to an end, and my life began anew.

Now, as I apply the Steps to my life on a daily basis, I grow closer and closer to the God of my understanding. This is amazing, because I had previously avoided all the Steps that mentioned God. But enough pain convinced me to work all the Steps and find a Higher Power who would be available to me. Since I didn't know how to do this, I simply said a prayer asking for help and then sat back and waited. I felt foolish, embarrassed, and self-conscious praying to some unknown Being in whom I didn't believe, but I did it anyway. My Higher Power soon made Herself known to me in a very clear and very personal way, and the relationship has sustained me ever since.

But the real turning point in my recovery came when I took Step Four and made a searching and fearless moral inventory of myself. I bought myself a red leather diary, the kind teenagers like to keep under lock and key. Every chance I got, I'd write about my shortcomings. After a few months, I reread my words and was stunned to see the rationalizations and outright lies I had written about myself. Much of what I read wasn't about me at all. It was a searching and fear*ful* inventory of the people in my life, especially the alcoholic.

That was when I became ready to get honest. This time I asked God to help me write what needed to be written. I wrote of lies, deceptions, and violence toward my children. I described self-righteous behavior toward those I professed to love. I admitted the conditional nature of the love I gave and the problems it engendered. Memories of terrible abuse from my past came flooding back, situations long since repressed and forgotten that now spilled out of my pen. I told those clean white pages of my hatred for myself, the suicidal wishes I had entertained, and the desire for an easy way out of every uncomfortable situation. I detailed my poor behavior toward the alcoholic and admitted to harboring a seething hatred for him.

When I finished, I put the diary under my mattress and cried. I prayed for the courage to tell another human being the exact nature of the wrongs I had confessed (Step Five), and then I waited. Eight days later, I shared what I had written with a clergyman from a church I hadn't attended since childhood. I had dreaded the experience and almost backed out at the last minute, but by the time I finished, I felt free. The clergyman acknowledged my courage and bid me go in peace, and for the first time, I was able to do just that.

Since that day, I have noticed a tremendous difference in myself. I am much more calm and accepting. Most of my shortcomings remain, but I know with absolute certainty that as I continue to work the Steps, I will be freed from anything that stands between me and the will of my Higher Power.

The alcoholic eventually returned to A.A., and our relationship since then has blossomed into something quite beautiful. My life-long ambition to be a writer has been realized, and to my astonishment, one of my manuscripts has been accepted for review by a publisher. I attend three Al-Anon meetings each week and hold a service position in my home group. Service is important because sometimes I love so intensely that I can feel it verging on obsession. Service work heals the emptiness within me by replacing my dark obsession for another with my own loving light.

Best of all, I am incredibly grateful to be alive. I know that my days are filled with blessings, and I cherish each one. When I first heard about finding contentment and even happiness through the Al-Anon program, I scoffed. I never thought it could possibly happen to me. Now I know first-hand how miraculous this program can be.

28

Transformation of a Military Man

Growing up in a military home was a full-time adventure. We moved every year or two. Fourteen school transfers in my 12 years of school provided me with a very unusual perspective on learning and social interaction. At each new post, I had to figure out how to get along with my new playmates. Chameleon-like, I learned what to do to fit in.

Just as instability was a central fact of life, so was alcohol. Drinking was the daily lubricant that promoted civility among the adults in my young life, or so it seemed. The first two or three drinks brought forth relaxation and laughter. Only after supper and the apéritifs did the mood become ugly. There was no physical abuse, but the verbal combat left deep wounds. The words were abrasive and biting, leaving fearsome scars.

I don't think my mom was an alcoholic. She just tried to keep up with my father, and later, after they divorced, my stepfather. My dad was mellow and quiet when he drank, but mom was someone to avoid when she was drinking, because she became mean and demanding. The opposite was true with my stepfather. He and I only got along when he drank. He was a sailor who spent a lot of time away from home, and while he was gone, my mother and I were very close. She called me her "little man." It did not occur to me until much later that that probably was not a very healthy relationship. When my stepfather was home, I had asthma attacks, some severe enough to hospitalize me.

Socially, alcohol was always present. Abundant beverages and mounds of food promoted a lively atmosphere with singing, laughing, and bawdiness. Later in the evening, someone would signal the end of the festivities by vomiting on the porch or refusing to leave the "head." I grew up thinking this was normal social behavior.

It was very clear that, just as the Division Officer was entirely responsible for the welfare, work, and conduct of his men, so was the military dad entirely responsible for his family. Misbehavior of children or non-participation by the wife were just as likely to initiate a reprimand as an officer's own failure to perform. So I learned nothing about personal boundaries or privacy or minding my own business. My life was an open book, and I grew up feeling responsible for everybody, just like my dad.

Thirteen days after graduation, I escaped to the waiting arms of the Navy. Soon thereafter, I was re-introduced to a girl I had dated in high school. In an Autumn whirlwind, I courted and won her, and we eloped in January. November brought our first child, a year later came our second, and two years later we had our third. I had a military identity, a military family, and my ship was very much on course.

Through a rapid succession of military schools, high marks, and exceptional work, I advanced professionally. I was ever mindful of my responsibilities and saw to it that my work and family life "looked good." My wife and I participated in a more refined social life than I had grown up with. My daughters dressed appropriately and were reminded of their responsibilities.

My responsibilities, as I saw them at the time, even extended to my wife's makeup, conversation, eating, and of course, drinking. In the latter area, I was repeatedly met with resistance and outright rebellion. When she drank too much, she became loud, giddy, and just plain inappropriate. We went out less, and at home she drank more. I took this personally. I thought that the fact that I could not convince, persuade, cajole, or browbeat my wife into not drinking made me a failure.

One of my collateral duties as a Naval officer had been to serve as Drug Control/Drug Education Officer. My job was to educate people about the evils of illegal drugs. Alcohol, however, was quite all right. Drinking was an acceptable Naval tradition.

But this was in the 1970's, and the Navy was in the process of change and had instituted an alcohol rehabilitation center. As Drug Control Officer, it was a simple matter to handle people with alcoholism problems. I got their problem documented, and with the approval of the Commanding Officer, sat them down and told hem, "You're going to the Alcohol Rehab Center." They went away for 30 or 60 days and came back changed. It was a wonderful program with a high rate of success.

The same options were not available to my spouse. Ordering her to go to rehab didn't work. Instead I tried reasoning, talking about her health, our relationship, her weight, and anything else I could think of. It was our custom at the time to read in bed before going to sleep, and I would read book after book about alcoholism, feigning casual interest as I commented, "Oh, this is fascinating. Did you know that…" In other words, I tried to trick and manipulate her. I really thought that I could make a difference. I couldn't.

At the time when I walked into my first Al-Anon meeting, I had cut back significantly on social contacts, professional activities, even teaching. I worked late. You know how it is when you call home and say, "How's everything?" and you hear *that voice*? That drunken voice? I'd stay at work because I couldn't bring myself to face what I was going to find at home.

By this time the girls had grown and flown. I had retired from the Navy, attended graduate school, and had launched a successful second career. My wife's social skills, native intelligence, and sheer hard work were responsible for at least half of the success of our new enterprise. At home, though, she drank more and more, working less and less. I became even more obsessed with her drinking.

My first Al-Anon meeting was in the basement of a church where I had worked as a janitor while in graduate school. I knew something went on there that had to do with alcoholism. In my desperation I turned to that basement, hoping that I would find something that would help our situation. But I didn't want to be recognized. If I were recognized, that would prove that I was a failure—I wasn't taking care of and controlling the family. So I sneaked down the stairs and listened to people tell their stories.

Now I can see that, by walking in that door, I had done the most important thing I could do. I had begun my First Step. I had physically, palpably admitted that I was powerless over alcohol and my life was unmanageable.

Nonetheless, I didn't want to change me, I wanted to change her. I didn't want to know how to get better, I wanted to know how to get her better. I played at Al-Anon for a few months, going sporadically to one meeting here and another there. Meanwhile I searched the entire house, trying to find the bottles. I never found one. To this day, I have no idea where she hid them, but it was one more piece of evidence that I couldn't control her or her drinking. Then I found my Al-Anon home group and made a commitment to myself and my life that made all the difference.

Although I am a very visual person, I benefited most in the beginning from hearing. Listening to tapes, attending speaker's meetings, and hearing people share their stories at meetings struck me at an emotional level I had never previously experienced. Maybe it penetrated my defenses because it *wasn't* visual. I couldn't read it, so I couldn't intellectualize it. Listening to these stories helped me to see that I was 39 years old and needed to grow up. I heard that a Sponsor could help me do it.

So I went in search of someone who was wise, older than me, better looking than me, a whole lot smarter—Moses would have been perfect—but I didn't find him in any of the meetings. Instead, I found a wonderful man who spoke of Al-Anon as a gentle program, a program that taught us to be gentle with ourselves and others. That was so very far from my orientation that I knew he had to be my Sponsor. There was nothing gentle in my life. Thank God, he accepted when I asked him to sponsor me, and as a result, I had my first honest, vulnerable relationship with a man. And by becoming intimate with another man, I learned to be intimate with, and accepting of, myself.

During those early meetings, there were two men who talked frequently about childhood incest and molestation. I thought, "Why the hell are they bringing that up? This is Al-Anon. We're here to talk about problem drinking and how it affects families." I got very angry every time that topic came up. One night, I heard one of those men tell his story in detail—and I got it. He was talking about me. That had happened to me. Until that moment I had denied it, but I suddenly realized that I had been sexually abused as a child. It was an earth-shattering discovery.

Over the next several months, a lot of secrets from my past came to the surface where I could deal with them. I'm very grateful that we have Al-Anon meetings that focus on particular relationships and situations. We have Al-Anon adult children meetings, and for a while, that was exactly what I needed. We have meetings attended primarily by spouses of alcoholics, and for a while, that was exactly what I needed. We even have meetings that deal with childhood molestation, and for a while, that was exactly what I needed. We shared our stories, we shared our experience, and as time passed I was able to drop layers of this garbage from the past.

I came into this program because I was married to "the problem." I came to realize that I was the problem. From that point on, the Twelve Steps became the key to changing my life.

My Sponsor helped me with the first Three Steps. In pursuing a relationship with a Higher Power, I found that I was hampered by an Old Testament image I had of God, a very judgmental man with a flowing beard. So I renamed my Higher Power. I called Him Eli. And my life became a whole lot easier.

Eventually my Sponsor encouraged me to take a Fourth Step inventory. What I found underneath a lot of resentments was that I was completely dedicated to winning other people's approval. I wanted you to love me. I wanted everyone to love me. And I didn't know how to love myself. I thought if you could do it for me, it might make me whole.

My Fifth Step, when I admitted to God, to myself, and to my Sponsor the exact nature of my wrongs, was the most cathartic, the most cleansing experience I had ever had in my life. It was the first time I had ever been really honest about myself, even though I had grown up in a religious tradition of which confession was a part. What I learned from the Fifth Step is that the shame and judgment that had hampered me for so many years were not necessarily part of life, but acceptance and accountability were. What a liberation!

This experience taught me that my defects are the same as my assets, except that they have been exaggerated to the point of obsession. The perfectionism that I had all my life was simply an obsessive desire for excellence. Excellence is wonderful—perfectionism, not so good. Distrustfulness and cynicism were obsessive forms of self-protection. For a long time, it was appropriate to protect myself. Although I wasn't consciously aware of it, I was very fearful about what had happened to me in the past and what might happen again. But once the past abuse was uncovered and I was able to share what had happened, it lost the power to control me. And I lost the need to keep people at such a great distance.

After the Fifth Step, I thought I was entirely ready to have God remove all these defects of character, but I had no idea how accustomed I was to having these protections. I was afraid of change. I didn't know how to converse with someone without lying or trying to "one-up" the other person. I had no idea how to be truly vulnerable in relationships, or how to truly let go of others. I asked God to remove all my defects, but I wasn't yet ready. I didn't understand that change was a long-term process. So I charged ahead.

I have often heard in a meeting, "When in doubt, don't!" or "Don't just *do* something, sit there!" Ignoring this wise council, I forged ahead, made a quick list of those I felt I had harmed, and proceeded to go to my alcoholic spouse to make amends. I didn't know enough about the Ninth Step, "Made direct amends to such people wherever possible, except when to do so would injure them or others," at the time. I didn't understand its spirit. Instead, I tried to use my amends as a way to get her to stop drinking. And in the process, I hurt her badly.

From that experience, I learned that Sponsors can be very helpful—but only if you use them. And I learned to go back and accept the Steps, and my recovery from the effects of alcoholism, as a miraculous, but gradual process.

Later, when I got back to the Eighth Step, "Made a list of all persons we had harmed, and became willing to make amends to them all," my Sponsor told me to put my name at the top of the list. This has allowed me to do many things. For instance, in making amends to myself, I have given myself permission to feel things passionately. Skiing! It's a new thing for me, and at my age! I love it passionately! I started with cross-country skis, then I got back-country skis, and then I got telemark skis. Three sets in three years! Wow! That's passion!

I've learned to climb mountains. Somewhere inside me, I've always felt that God lives on mountaintops. Whenever I've been close to a mountaintop a sense of spiritual serenity has settled around me. Mountaineering does that for me. I may not make it to the top every time, but the journey is what matters.

The Steps, especially Step Ten, "Continued to take personal inventory and when we were wrong promptly admitted it," have helped me come to grips with the knowledge that being right is not good enough. Right facts with a wrong attitude is *wrong*. It's not really so much an issue of wrong vs. right as it is fear vs. love. When I'm acting out of love, you can say anything, and it's okay with me. When I'm acting out of fear, I argue. I have to prove I'm right. I have to get the book out and show you. When I'm acting out of fear in a classroom or business setting, I feel challenged if people ask questions, and I come down hard on them to put them in their place. When I'm acting out of love, I understand that they want affirmation, or confirmation, or maybe just information. Quite a difference in attitude. Quite a difference in perspective.

My Sponsor told me initially to make no major changes in my life for at least six months, preferably a year. After 18 months of working this program, I determined that living with active alcoholism was not possible for me anymore. My spouse and I separated. I continued to work my program, and my wife of 27 years continued to seek her own path. She filed for divorce, and it was a very upsetting time for both of us, with a lot of anger between us.

Just before the divorce became final, some internal guidance urged me to call her. It certainly didn't come from me. I told her that after the divorce she would no longer be covered by my medical insurance, so if she had any plans to enter a treatment center, it might be a good time to do so.

There was a long silence, and then she told me she had been thinking about doing just that. She asked if I knew of any programs. I said no. Now I could have given her the phone numbers of 20 programs, but I had learned that she had to take those steps for herself. And she did. She went into a treatment center, expecting a quick assessment, and instead, they put her in for 30 days. When she came out of treatment, she had been relieved of the need to use alcohol. Her life changed.

My life is changing. Sobriety did not bring us back together. My spouse—my dear friend—and I went through a divorce after 30 years and four months of marriage. We are good friends through the grace of this and other Twelve Step programs.

The emotional containment of my past has been breaking down as a result of this program. I know that, when I have felt my feelings, the answers I seek have come directly from my Higher Power. This process has caused a transformation, not the kind of transformation I sought when I was doing encounter groups and self-help seminars, but a kind of transformation that has been gentle. It has not been of my making. When I came here, I was a "human doing," not a human being. Today, my Higher Power has made me a spiritual being who fully embraces his humanity.

29

Living with a "Dry Drunk"

I came to Al-Anon many years ago. It's hard to believe that so many days have gone by and I'm still here, since Al-Anon has fixed neither my marriage nor my husband. Instead, it worked its miracle on me. I never expected that, because when I came I knew there was nothing wrong with me. I only came out of spite toward my sober husband.

I'm an adult child of an alcoholic: my father. And I married a man who drank—it was familiar to me. The drinking progressed over the years, and eventually, by the grace of God, my husband found A.A. and sobriety. It was wonderful. For the next three years we were extremely happy. Everything changed in our home. He spent time with our children and me, and it was obvious from his behavior that we were important to him. I wouldn't have believed that this was the same man I married had I not lived through the transformation.

Later, however, things began to change. He reverted to his old self, though he never drank. He no longer spent time with us. Instead he withdrew, and again I felt the old loneliness and fear. In the heat of an argument, he shouted, "Why don't you go to Al-Anon if you don't like it?" So I did. I came out of spite, and ten years later you can't tear me away.

The program has offered me many experiences, some of which felt good and some of which were unfamiliar and scary. For instance, in Al-Anon I learned that I had choices. I didn't automatically have to do what I was expected to do. I could say "no" as readily as "yes" if that was how I felt. I could change my mind. I could put my own needs first. I could change my attitudes. The possibilities seemed unlimited.

While this may be a really exciting discovery for some, I wasn't so sure that having choices was good news. If I avoided choosing, I could always complain. What if I made a decision and it didn't work out? Who would I blame? I'm not being facetious. I was very reluctant to accept this responsibility. But my Al-Anon friends cared about me and kept encouraging me, so I made my first choice. Unfortunately, I made it for someone other than myself.

I decided my husband could help out at home. Don't get me wrong, it would have been quite all right if I had decided to ask for his help, recognizing that he was an adult who had the right to say either "yes" or "no" to my request. I certainly would have benefited from some assistance. I worked full-time and seemed to have endless jobs around the house. The children, too, had jobs. So I felt justified in asking him to alternate with me in doing the dishes and making supper. When I brought up the subject, he was reluctant, but he didn't exactly say "no."

Whether he drinks or not, I know that my husband is an alcoholic, and I know that he has difficulty saying "no" to me if he thinks I will be angry or disappointed. As a result, he often agrees to do something and then neglects to do it. My experience has taught me not to depend upon him when he agrees to do something, especially if he isn't enthusiastic about the prospect. So when I interpreted his response—or—non-response—as a "yes" and expected his help, the choice I really made was to set myself up for disappointment.

I offered to do the cooking the first week while he did the dishes. The children were very excited, since doing the dishes had been one of their jobs. But as soon as dinner was finished, my husband got up and went outside. When he didn't return, I went out after him and discovered that he was gone. I was furious. Who was going to do the dishes?

In my frustration, I called an Al-Anon friend and told her that my husband and I had this agreement and that he wasn't fulfilling his end of the deal. She suggested that I leave the dishes for him. I told her I couldn't live in a house with dirty dishes all over the kitchen!

"Then do the dishes," she said.

"Me! Why should I do them? It's his job," I shouted.

"Then leave the dishes," she repeated.

More frustrated than ever, I got off the phone and did the dishes in a rage. By the time he came home I was livid, but I never said a word about the dishes.

The next evening I watched my husband get up from the table after dinner and leave the house. Still I never said a word. I called my Al-Anon friend and we went through essentially the same conversation—do the dishes, leave the dishes, do the dishes, etc. By now I was just as frustrated with her as I was with my husband. Again I hung up and washed the dishes.

You'd think I would have confronted my husband by the time the third night rolled around, but that never entered my mind. After all, I had decided that he was going to help! Why should I have to risk the discomfort of an argument, or worse, face the possibility that he might refuse to help? So I continued to keep my part of the bargain and cooked dinner. Again he left the house as soon as we had finished. This time, the children volunteered to take back the responsibility for the dishes. Tears came to my eyes at their offer, and I said, "No, we're going to leave the dishes for Dad to do when he comes home."

This time, when I called my friend, she asked if I was calling about the dishes. I replied that I was, but that I had decided to leave them for my husband. I added that I just could not stay in my house and not do those dishes, so I would appreciate it if I could come to her house for a few hours, and she welcomed me to do so. Later that night, after I was in bed, I heard my husband downstairs. He was washing the dishes.

Nothing was said about this by either of us. After that night, even if I left the dishes, they usually went unwashed. I soon decided that I couldn't continue to live that way, and the children and I went back to doing the dishes ourselves. It took me a while to realize that, while I have the right to make choices, so do other people, and our choices may not coincide.

Meanwhile, my husband's behavior looked more and more as it had during the drinking days. My Al-Anon friends told me that this is typical of a "dry drunk," where the old attitudes and behavior return, even though the alcoholic is not drinking. I had come to expect sobriety to fix lots of our old problems, and now those problems were all coming back. I began to go to more Al-Anon meetings and put a lot more energy into working the Steps with the help of my friend, whom I asked to become my Sponsor.

All the same, I still had a lot to learn about my powerlessness over other people's choices, and the situation at home was getting worse. My children began to realize that they could get away with not cleaning up, for they knew that I couldn't stand to have a messy house. More and more they ignored their responsibilities, and I silently and resentfully took them on. I was angry and frustrated, but I couldn't see my own part in it.

My husband and I entered counseling. I complained about having to do everything around the house in addition to my full-time job, and my husband argued that housework was "women's work" and he shouldn't have to do it. This went on and on. Suddenly I realized that he was angry. I saw that look, the one that told me I would pay for causing all this trouble. Instantly I recoiled in fear. I apologized, offered to do all the housework, and said that I had made too much of a small issue. I dodged the counselor's questions, and when she turned to my husband, he acted as if he didn't know what was going on. I told the counselor that it wasn't going to be necessary for us to return, and then I left.

On the way home, when my husband offered to help me dust, I responded in absolute defeat, "No, it's okay, I can do it, it's no big deal." I felt only dark despair. I had hit bottom. I knew in my gut that, even if he did help, it would be only temporary. There was no sense in getting back on that merry-go-round.

I was back at Step One, powerless. I finally understood what that meant. I could not make him change. Trying to do so would be like running full-speed into a brick wall and then backing up and doing it again. But this revelation did not make me feel any better. I felt dreadfully ashamed of my inability to confront my husband and children on this issue. I knew that I was allowing myself to be treated poorly, yet I couldn't bring myself to speak up for myself. Although I continued to attend Al-Anon meetings, I was very depressed and negative. I began to blame the program for not fixing my marriage.

But the program worked in spite of me. All I had to do was show up. There was enough of me that was willing to feel better that, even with my hopelessness and anger, I began to heal. My Sponsor urged me to work through the Steps again, capitalizing on my new understanding of Step One. As a result, I realized that I was still acting like a child under the authority of my powerful alcoholic father. My dad was dead now, but I had transferred that authority to my husband. Finally I understood why confrontation felt like such an insurmountable obstacle.

Step Six helped me to become an adult. It says, "Were entirely ready to have God remove all these defects of character." For years, I had waited for somebody else to make everything better for me. In this Step, I was being asked if I really wanted to get better. If so, I had to stop blaming others and take responsibility for myself, my happiness, my sadness, my actions—all of my choices.

I must admit that my response to this prospect was not an enthusiastic "yes!" I had to think about being entirely ready. But I knew too much to back out now. I believe that when God helps us to see the right path, He sticks around to lead the way. I felt that I had no choice but to follow. It was time to grow up. I took the Seventh Step and humbly asked God to remove *my* shortcomings.

The Serenity Prayer helped me to sort things out. I needed to accept the things I could not change. I could not make my husband want to help. And I could not make him answer my questions clearly and honestly. But I did have the power to change the things I could. I could choose to stop expecting a non-answer to mean "yes." I could stop expecting him to do what I wanted just because I wanted it. And I could learn that just waiting in silence rarely initiates change or encourages other people to meet my needs. It only feeds my martyrdom. I felt foolish about being unable to discuss the situation further with my husband, but I simply was not able to do so at the time. Here was something I could work on, something I could change.

As I said before, Al-Anon worked its miracles on me, but it fixed neither my husband nor my marriage. I am still married to the same man, and for the most part, I am quite happy to be here. I care for him and choose to stay. In Al-Anon I have learned how to enjoy the good times and how to take care of myself in the hard times. My attitude is a lot more positive, and I have discovered that I have a sense of humor.

I will always be grateful that my husband never went back to drinking. He now admits to being a "dry drunk" but is unwilling to do anything about it. I think our relationship is much better now that I've changed and stopped expecting him to change.

One of my reasons for putting this on paper is that I believe that the "dry-drunk" story deserves a place in our literature. I always felt so alienated when I read those happy stories in the literature where one spouse goes to Al-Anon, the other spouse goes to A.A., and they live happily ever after. Well, that wasn't the way things worked out for me, but I still found contentment, and even happiness, in Al-Anon.

30

Learning in Al-Anon What Books Never Taught

To employ a cliché, I have had a million dollar experience that I wouldn't pay a nickel to repeat. Yet, as a professional in the field of alcoholism, it is the type of lesson that I could ill afford to forget if I am to maintain my serenity while working with alcoholics who continue to drink actively.

Two weeks before defending my dissertation, a dissertation on providing treatment to lesbian and gay alcoholics, a former lover of mine walked back into my life. I first met this man many years ago. At the time, he was an active alcoholic expressing a desire to get sober. When he returned to my life, he was still an active alcoholic expressing a desire to get sober.

We first met in a bar. I thought he was the most gorgeous and exciting man I had ever met. He was also quite drunk. I moved in with him not long after our first date, and we lived together for several years. Most of our socializing (no, *all* of our socializing) revolved around drinking and bars. All of our friends drank. Many of the evenings ended in violence; others ended with his going home with someone else. I could never count on him, yet I could not manage to do anything about the situation. Leaving seemed inconceivable. So I stayed, tolerated the intolerable, and tried to force him to change. I began to resent and then to hate him.

Eventually, I'm ashamed to say, I became physically abusive to him. He would say something derogatory about me or threaten not to pay his share of the bills. I'd become enraged and slap him, even pound and kick him, all the time seeing him as the monster. I was out of control, insane.

After my lover had lost several jobs because of his drinking, I refused to continue to support him financially and he reacted by becoming extremely abusive to me. He said hurtful things to me, calling me "old," "fat," and "ugly." He brought home groups of friends after the bars closed, turned up the volume of the stereo as loud as it would go, and then came into the bedroom to ensure that he was keeping me awake. Whatever love had once existed between us was nowhere to be seen.

I ran away. I packed what I needed and left town, asking a friend to put the rest of my things in storage. Then I traveled, took jobs in cities where I knew no one, and moved on whenever I began to get restless. Years later, when I finally returned, I found a house on the opposite side of town and refused to give that portion of my life another moment's thought. I was continuing my education and had retreated into a distant, safe, and comfortable world of scholarship, philosophy, and intellectual activity. Even though my studies centered around the treatment of alcoholism, I never truly related what I read or heard to what I had experienced except in the most distant, clinical way. It was as if I were now someone else. And then this man re-appeared, and in an instant our love for one another was rekindled.

In the course of writing my dissertation and doing other research, I have read literally thousands of articles that deal with substance abuse and recovery. As part of my job, I have familiarized myself with most of the materials concerning alcoholics in a number of special populations. My book knowledge has served me well in preparing articles, conference papers, and a forthcoming book. Yet none of this reading adequately prepared me for the trauma of becoming involved with an alcoholic who was still drinking. So, in spite of a head full of knowledge about alcoholism, I finally turned to Al-Anon. I knew I couldn't cope with our relationship without help.

The week before I defended my dissertation, I spent a night in the emergency room watching my lover go through delirium tremens (the DT's), an acute delusional reaction to alcohol poisoning—and a horrifying thing to witness. At three o'clock in the morning, when I was feeling lonely and afraid, I did not try to call the nearest library to help me get through the night. Instead, I dialed a friend I had met in Al-Anon.

During the next several weeks, when my alcoholic friend was in and out of a detox center, a long-term treatment program, and

A.A., I was able to maintain a surprising amount of serenity. But again, this serenity was not the result of reading the latest book on alcoholism and its treatment. Instead, it came about as a result of regular attendance at my Al-Anon meetings and regular contact with friends who worked the Al-Anon program in their day-to-day affairs. These friends were able to show me very practical ways by which I could maintain my serenity regardless of what the alcoholic chose to do with his life.

A marvelous Sponsor helped me to learn that it was okay to take the First Step and admit that I was powerless over my lover's alcoholism. He assured me that by working the other eleven Steps, I would find the power that truly belonged in my life. This Sponsor, and other wise members of the fellowship, helped me to cope when the alcoholic cut himself while breaking into my apartment, smearing blood all over my bedroom wall. Hearing their experience, strength, and hope helped me to find appropriate ways to experience and express my anger instead of falling into old patterns of abuse. When I wanted to beat on the alcoholic, I learned to beat on a pillow. When I wanted to call and berate him, I learned to call an Al-Anon friend and reason things out. When I worried about the repetition of such an episode in the future, I learned to take only "One Day at a Time" and to concentrate on what could be achieved "Just for Today." And when I wanted to blame him for my distress, I learned to "Let It Begin with Me."

Later, when the alcoholic was unable to distinguish fantasy from reality, it was by talking to friends in Al-Anon that I was able to stay grounded. When I felt as if I, too, were going crazy, they were able to assure me that my feelings were natural, and that I had choices about how I would act on those feelings. When I felt so emotionally drained that I did not want to get out of bed, my friends responded with great compassion. They helped me to determine for myself that it was perfectly acceptable for me to take naps in the afternoon *after* I had finished teaching my classes. Furthermore, they helped me understand that I did not have to feel guilty because I did not feel like teaching on a particular day, as long as I followed through on my responsibilities. With their support, I learned to accept my feelings without judgment, but I also learned that sometimes those feelings have to be set aside so I can act on my own behalf. The choice is mine.

Intellectually, I already knew about the information I was given by the people in Al-Anon. I had read it all before in books. The problem was that I did not know how to put all this information to work in my life. Intellectually, I knew that I had to detach. I knew that I could not save an alcoholic who didn't want to get sober. But if the people in Al-Anon had not shared their experiences with me, I would never have learned *how* to detach, or how to work the Third Step and turn the alcoholic over to the care of God. Intellectually, I knew that I needed to acknowledge my feelings and deal with them in an appropriate fashion. But had the people in Al-Anon not shared their experiences with me, I still would have no idea what process to use to deal with my feelings.

I put great stock in my education and all that my studies have helped me to understand about alcoholism. The knowledge I receive from my research is extremely valuable to me, and with it, I will be able to advance in my chosen career. Nonetheless, if I want to maintain my sanity, I need to seek a more tangible kind of knowledge, the kind that goes far beyond the intellect and depends upon personal experience.

Alcoholism has far-reaching and often subtle effects, and it is easy to underestimate how vulnerable to it I continue to be. Today I know that I am powerless over this disease, not only as it is manifested in my lover but also in my clients. In order to maintain my health and serenity and to function effectively in my profession, I must recognize how susceptible I am to other people's alcoholism and I must act accordingly. For me, this means attending Al-Anon and doing my best to put its principles into practice in my life.

31

Letting Go of a Loved One's Alcohol, Drug, and Money Problems

The alcoholic in my life wasn't an alcoholic as far as I was concerned.

He was an insomniac who liked to have deep philosophical discussions on the meaning of life and the fate of the universe, preferably between two and four o'clock in the morning. Every morning. For several years, I never got more than two or three consecutive hours of sleep. I started falling asleep at my desk at work. I had a reputation in the office for being extraordinarily good at what I did but not easy to deal with. You may recognize the syndrome; it's mentioned in the Suggested Welcome that is read at the beginning of most Al-Anon meetings. I became "irritable and unreasonable without knowing it."

He was often angry in the morning when I left for work, angry when he called me during the day to tell me what I'd done to make him angry, angry and depressed when I got home. I thought that if I just tried harder to please him, he wouldn't get angry and everything would be all right. I didn't understand why the things I did made him so angry, but I kept trying harder and harder to please him, hoping to clear up what was obviously a relationship problem. And I cried at my desk at work. I knew perfectly well that he drank and used drugs. I did not realize that his behavior was classically alcoholic.

Fortunately, other people did. Two women who knew me only from work recognized the problem from *my* behavior and, independently of each other, suggested I try Al-Anon. After months of waffling, I finally gathered enough nerve—or became sufficiently hopeless and despairing—to go to a meeting. I didn't say anything at that meeting, and I didn't understand anything either. In addition to the other words they used in ways that made no sense to me, the members used words like "joy" and "comfort," so I knew they were crazy. There was no comfort in my life—and certainly no joy. I went away and didn't come back for six months.

Alcoholism is a progressive disease, a medical description which means that it only gets worse. I had loved this man for over 20 years. His health was terrible, and I worried endlessly about it, except in those moments of rage when I wished he'd die. I had found brandy bottles stashed behind the books in the library. Drug deals were made using *my* car. Sometimes the deals fell through, and I found myself driving around with neatly folded little packets of cocaine tucked in the door pocket on the driver's side. I let him drive drunk with an open beer bottle between his legs, because I didn't want to get into a fight by suggesting that I drive. His business partners began calling me to get him to pay his debts or to pay them myself. Because my credit was excellent, I had no problem securing a $60,000 loan that I in turn loaned to him so he could finish a huge remodeling project on a house he owned. I knew he loved me and I believed he'd never do anything bad to me, no matter what he might do to his partners and friends.

One day a book came across my desk about women and alcoholism. It had a list of 20 questions you could answer to determine if you were an alcoholic. I read the list, answering for him. When I read, "Do you have more than two drinks a day?" I thought it was a misprint. How about two six-packs before noon? Not to mention the fifth of brandy in the evening, the drugs, the "social" drinks with friends. I went back to Al-Anon and found a Step study meeting held at a nearby church. I still didn't understand most of what was said, but it didn't matter. For one hour a week in that room, nothing bad was going to happen to me. The choir practiced in the room next door. When I couldn't grasp what was being discussed at the meeting, I listened to the choir and it comforted me.

Come hell or high water, I went to that meeting. I went when I was tired, when the house was dirty, when dinner wasn't cooked, when I had a deadline to meet. I went when the alcoholic was angry and resentful and convinced that "you" were telling me to leave him, or worse, that I was telling "you" all about him. I told him Al-Anon was about me, not him. And I meant it.

Being naturally inclined to manage other people's lives, I came to Al-Anon already knowing that the only way I can push people is away from me. I had never poured out his liquor or tried to control his drinking, as I heard others say they had. I saw people who came to meetings and cried, week after week, and I heard about members who were beaten, who lost their homes, who feared for their children, and I gained a sense of perspective and a deep gratitude that my troubles were no worse than they were. I already believed in God, so the concept of a Higher Power did not trouble me as I heard it trouble some people.

Steps One and Two were not too difficult. Even Step Three wasn't too much for me. Step Four was another matter entirely. First of all, I had no idea what a "searching and fearless moral inventory" might be. I heard other people talking about their faults, but while I knew I shared some of those faults, I couldn't for the life of me see what that had to do with *his* alcoholism. Things at home had gotten much worse financially. The payments on the loan were late or not paid at all, and I was struggling to make the payments on time for my own house, my bills, and his house. My feeling was, "Hey, I'm the one who's keeping this damned ship afloat!" When I said that, after months and months and months of wondering what the Fourth Step was all about, I listened to the tone of my own voice and said to myself, "Hmm, do we have a little resentment going on here?" And I answered, "No, we have a whole lot of resentment!" And a whole lot of fear and rage and martyrdom and sarcasm and impatience. That was the beginning of a sometimes intimidating but always exciting adventure of self-discovery.

One of the most productive aspects of my growth in Al-Anon has been in the area of communication. Today I try never to use sentences that start with "you" to other people. No sentence that starts out, "Well, you started…" or "You're the one who…" is going to come to a good end. I try to talk about me. Instead of saying, "That's ridiculous, you're wrong," I've learned to say, "I don't see it that way." With the alcoholic, I've learned to say, "I can't tell when it's you speaking and when it's the brandy, so I'd prefer to discuss this when we both know it's only you."

I am learning to deal with my overwhelming fear and worry by asking myself, "What is the most productive thing I can do at this moment?" In other words, I try to put "First Things First." Sometimes this means I take a deep breath, or go for a walk, or do my work. Whatever the answer, it is never fret or worry. I can't change the past, I can't know the future, so I work to keep my attention firmly pinned on right now, and deal with it as best I can.

I try to give priority to taking care of myself. I eat good, nutritious food at sensible hours, whether he joins me or not. I make a serious effort to exercise every day, either walking or swimming. I read my *Courage to Change* book first thing every morning. I also make a daily gratitude list, a mental list of everything wonderful in my life, from the sunrise to a project that is going well or a funny joke told by a friend. It's amazing how much I have to be grateful for, when I look for it.

My situation did not get better the instant I returned to Al-Anon. In fact, it got worse. I never knew what illicit activities he was involved in, and I lived in constant terror of the local police and the Drug Enforcement Agency. I tried harder and harder to appear perfect so that no one would associate me with anything the alcoholic was doing. I sold a rental property we owned jointly and generated another $30,000 that was supposed to finish remodeling his house. The $60,000 loan had disappeared in two months, and still the house was nowhere near finished. He insisted that his share came out short, so I gave him another $2,000 in exchange for the promise that he would never mention that house again. All told, I contributed close to $100,000 in less than six months. And the house still wasn't finished. Every penny was gone, however, and he was in financial trouble again. My credit was ruined and I was liable for $20,000 in taxes because his house was in my name.

I even ended up the prime suspect in an attempted murder. The alcoholic had been having some trouble with his car, so he took it in to be fixed. The mechanic found that the car had been rigged with a device that was supposed to explode when the car was started.

When the police questioned the alcoholic about who might do such a thing, asking for a list of people they could check out, he insisted that he couldn't think of a single soul who would want him dead. So they asked who was closest to him and he mentioned me. Since there were no known enemies as far as the police were concerned, I became the prime suspect. They followed me around for months and asked all of my neighbors about me.

Al-Anon helped me enormously, and I was coping better than I'd ever dreamed possible because I realized that I was powerless over alcohol and the whole mess in which I had become entangled. I couldn't change the actions or choices other people made, but there were steps I could take to change my own life. When I was ready, the opportunities began to appear.

I had been freelancing as a writer for a number of years, specializing in travel writing. I would rather travel than breathe, so when I was offered a chance to spend two months in Africa, I went. In the past, fear would have held me back, fear about my job, about my future, about my finances. All my life I had abandoned my dreams because of my fears, but in Al-Anon I was learning that fear didn't have to dominate my life. So I turned the whole situation over to my Higher Power. Then I went to my employer and announced that I would be gone for two months. I said that he could handle my absence as he thought best, as a leave of absence, an advance vacation, or a resignation. He said he'd let me know.

When I truly "Let Go and Let God," miracles started to happen. I suddenly realized that I was proposing to leave six weeks before I became fully vested in my retirement program, a choice that could potentially cost me thousands of dollars. I had no savings to speak of, but I simply refused to abandon myself to fear any longer. Even though I fretted and worried and obsessed, I stuck with my plan. I had learned in Al-Anon that I deserved to have happiness in my life. I spent a lot of time communing with my Higher Power, trying to replace my fear with faith. Two days later, the personnel director told me that I would receive the full retirement package, despite my absence. Not only that, but I had been put on a list of employees slated for temporary layoff, which meant that I would receive my full salary and benefits for six months!

I went to Africa to go on safari, but I met some friends along the way who offered to recommend me as the writer for a television show that was planning to do six segments on Africa. Not long after that I met a marvelous woman who recommended me to her publisher. I am now under contract to write four books for them.

When I left for Africa, I had pretty well decided not to return. I had given up all hope of the alcoholic ever achieving sobriety or giving up drugs. I figured the six months' pay would cover my expenses until I found a job there. A month after I left, the alcoholic called me in Capetown and told me he was going to A.A. and had given up drinking, smoking, and drugs. He has remained clean and sober ever since.

I spent almost nine months traveling all over the world. Today, I write books out of my home in addition to working on the Africa project for the television show. But the most important achievement is that I sleep soundly at night, even though the alcoholic is still in my life. His sobriety helps the situation, but I have redefined my priorities so that my needs are no longer shoved aside. He's happier than I've ever known him to be and we're working out the financial problems little by little, "One Day at a Time." Al-Anon has given me the tools to work on every aspect of my life, not just my life in relation to the alcoholic. I don't know the words to properly express how grateful I am.

I once worried that working the program would only make me more functional in my crazy, terror-stricken, perpetually exhausted life. Instead, I have been given a life more wonderful than anything I'd ever dared to imagine. The most important words I ever heard were the last words I hear at every meeting: "Keep Coming Back."

I certainly will. And I thank you with all my heart.

32

Making Major Decisions

"Living with an alcoholic is like two crabs in a bucket," a friend in Al-Anon used to say. "One crab alone can always haul itself out. To keep it in there, you have to cover the bucket. But with two crabs, you don't need a lid. If one tries to crawl out, the other will reach up and yank its companion back down." I'd never heard a better description of my alcoholic marriage.

Every day of my first year in Al-Anon, this friend and I agonized on the phone. Should we end our alcoholic marriages? At the end of each conversation, we'd agree to turn the decision over to our Higher Power, just for that day.

I couldn't decide whether to buy artichokes or broccoli for dinner, much less what to do about my marriage. As the book *One Day at a Time in Al-Anon* (*ODAT*) puts it, "Our own thinking is so confused that we are in no condition to make decisions." I knew that was me. So I was grateful for the suggestion I heard in meetings to avoid making major changes in my life for the first six to nine months of coming to Al-Anon. I was in no shape to do so. All the same, I agonized over my options on a daily basis.

An ongoing mental struggle was nothing new to me. As a child, I worried about what other people thought of me. I used to feel ashamed when teachers wrote on my report cards that I lacked maturity, or when other children called me a baby. Their words bothered me, I think, because they rang true. Yet in other ways, I was old beyond my years. As a child of alcoholic parents, I grew up too fast.

My parents couldn't nurture me emotionally. I suspect they badly needed nurturing themselves. I was insecure, fearful, and passive, traits I carried into adulthood. I was terrified of abandonment. I have always felt like a child among adults, convinced that everyone knows what they are doing except me.

As I got older, I buried my insecurity deep down inside. I acted sure of myself, took on more responsibility than most people can handle, pushed myself to do things perfectly, and told everyone, "No thanks, I can do it myself." Inside, of course, I was scared.

During my teens I discovered that alcohol and drugs made me feel more confident. I was hooked. At 26 I hit bottom and joined Alcoholics Anonymous.

I stayed sober for four years and struggled to make sense of my chaotic emotions. Then I met a man at an A.A. meeting who was recovering from a recent binge. He had a spiritual quality that attracted me. He was 20 years older than I and had no money, no place to live, and no car. This was the person I selected to help me straighten out my life.

A week after I met him, he moved into my place. He disapproved of my A.A. friends and family, and I, eager to please, turned my back on them. He complained about the town we were living in, so we moved 2,000 miles away. He started drinking again, and I soon joined him.

After what I'd experienced with alcohol, I knew this was crazy, but I couldn't help myself. I was obsessed by his drinking. People in A.A. say that, when an alcoholic drinks again after a period of sobriety, the disease quickly worsens. My own drinking, however, was mild. I now believe I had switched addictions, from alcohol to my lover!

I tried to get him to quit, but he ignored me. I tried to counsel him. I nagged, badgered, and sulked. I didn't know what to do about this man, so I married him.

Whenever we fought, which was often, he would say, "This isn't working. We should go our separate ways." I was terrified of losing him. I even got on my knees and begged him to stay. Those old feelings of fear and abandonment overpowered me.

I couldn't believe my life was in such a shambles. I'd been with this man for only two years. We lived on food stamps and public assistance. Our mobile home had no furniture. We had no friends. Charitable organizations supplied our clothes. We often stood in line at the food bank. I had handed over my life to this man, and I didn't understand how it had happened. Devastated, I dragged myself to Al-Anon.

As a newcomer, I was a know-it-all. Because of my A.A. experience, I figured I knew all about alcoholism. But I had never understood this disease as one that affects the whole family. Life with an active alcoholic had made me so sick that I'd gone back to drinking, which was about as wise as slitting my own throat. I sobbed when I finally admitted to my Al-Anon friends how bad things really were at home—the emotional abuse, the fear of my husband, the poverty, the shame. That admission, plus a return to A.A., was the beginning of my recovery.

Several months later, my husband told me to pick up some beer at the local market. I steeled myself.

"You'll have to go yourself," I said, as calmly as I could manage. I expected a nuclear explosion.

While I held my breath, he considered this. He finally said, "Okay," and drove off to get it. My jaw dropped. Somewhere I'd picked up courage without even trying.

During my first year in Al-Anon, my husband drank more and more. I knew that, to survive the situation, I had to retrain myself to quit thinking about his problems and concentrate on my own. My new friends encouraged me to detach with love. I spent weeks rereading the passages on detachment in the Al-Anon literature.

I realized that I was making progress one morning as I got ready for a job interview. I put on my make-up and best clothes. I bustled around the kitchen to prepare breakfast and wasn't even fazed by my husband's sitting at the table, slumped over his beer. As I got into the car, I realized that I was actually humming!

Still, I debated whether to stay in the marriage. All my talks with my Al-Anon friend hadn't given me the answer. I prayed for guidance.

Finally the drinking took its toll, and my husband checked into the hospital. That first week alone, I was surprised to find myself calmer and happier than I'd been in years.

When he returned, we began to argue as usual. He uttered those familiar words, "This isn't working. I think we should call it quits."

Again I felt the terror those words always triggered. I was being abandoned. This time I knew better than to beg him to stay, but I couldn't turn off those feelings.

I called my Al-Anon friend. "What am I going to do? He wants to leave."

"What if you let him?" she said. "You've been praying about this marriage for over a year. Maybe God's trying to tell you something."

That sounded right to me, really right. I took a little time to be sure. Then I quit fighting. I agreed to a separation.

Eight years of Al-Anon and eight years of sobriety haven't given me a perfect life. But I am healthier. I have close friends in three different states. I have a profession. I'm now married to a non-alcoholic man who has a job—and a car, too.

I have a new relationship with myself and a new compassion for the part of me that grew up too fast. Al-Anon is helping me to explore both my childhood and adulthood. I've discovered a long buried part of myself that is imaginative and creative. Today, for the first time ever, when I get an occasional urge to quit being so very responsible and do something just for fun, like going to the zoo, I do it. I still feel like a child among adults, but I've shared that feeling with others, and they tell me they feel the same way!

33

A Survivor of Family Alcoholism
Deals with Fear

Almost five years ago, in telling me about himself, a friend showed me a list of characteristics of adult children of alcoholics. I read it, expecting to recognize my friend. Instead I was shocked to see myself.

I grew up unaware that alcoholism was a problem in my family. I never saw any alcoholic beverages at home. I never saw either of my parents drink. The message in my nuclear family and the extended families of both parents was clear: "In this family, we don't drink." The alcoholics in my life have always kept their drinking away from me, so this was easy to believe.

Shortly after the experience with my friend, Al-Anon was suggested to me by a couple of longtime members. I knew that there was illness in my family—my sister had an eating disorder. But when she went into treatment, I began to sense that her bulimia was not the secret our family structure was designed to protect. I didn't have any hard evidence, just a vague sense that somehow some other illness was involved in my family situation.

At the time, I knew I needed help too. Despite many blessings in my life, I felt stuck and out of control. Though I was in my late twenties, I still lived with my parents. I also worked for my father. In fact, after graduating from college, I had increasingly centered my life around my family, devoting my energy in turn to whoever seemed to have the most serious problems at the time. I had become more and more withdrawn from friends outside my family and hadn't dated since college.

From early childhood, my purpose was to please my parents and, later, other authority figures. As the oldest, I felt responsible for taking care of and protecting my sisters. I also felt responsible for my parents' emotional needs. For a long time, taking care of those around me made me feel strong and important. I enjoyed the praise and attention I received for my non-demanding, "mature" behavior.

I'm not sure I ever knew what to do with my own problems, feelings, wants, and needs. I definitely didn't feel comfortable asking for help. It was never easy for me to admit, even to myself, that I wanted nurturing experiences such as being hugged, or soothed when I was upset.

Others had always seemed more comfortable when I acted strong and happy, so I learned to mask the frightened child who wanted to be comforted and guided. Even in my youth, many of the adults in my life came to me for comfort and guidance. It was easier to focus on them, and I was rewarded for appearing strong and in control. I guess I didn't want to give that up by allowing my vulnerability to surface. When it came to my problems, feelings, wants, and needs, if I recognized them at all, I tried to control or bury them as quickly as possible.

I knew I could find help in Al-Anon for the self-neglect I had carried into adulthood, but I was just too scared to go. I hid from Al-Anon for three and a half years and tried to fix myself with my own do-it-yourself program of recovery.

Beginning with those least closely related to me, I gradually recognized the presence of alcoholism in my family. It was hard to accept that there were alcoholics in both of my parents' families of "non-drinkers." Both of my sisters married alcoholics, and my father's secret drinking bothered me too. Many of my friends throughout my life have been children of alcoholics. I have also tended to date men from alcoholic families. Now, I can see that I've reacted to the alcoholics in my life in basically the same way I reacted to my bulimic sister. I "knew" that if I just did the right things and stopped doing the wrong things, they would be fine. I thought it was my job to fix them.

I wasn't ready for Al-Anon until my sister had been in her own recovery from bulimia for three years and I had found another person's disease to be crazy over. I now became more and more afraid for the safety of my other sister and her children as her husband's alcoholism progressed. I continually found myself racing in a panic to their house to rescue them from crises that often existed only in my imagination.

My own life hadn't been working well for years. I had accepted other people's responsibilities and had postponed or ignored my own. When I put off taking care of my interests for too long, I ended up feeling unappreciated, angry, and helpless. Then I avoided others. I didn't know how to set boundaries, so I hid. It frustrated me to know that I was doing this to myself. I was the one who was running around trying to please and help and save everyone. Why couldn't I say "no" and mean it? Why couldn't I just stop?

Despite my "I'm okay" façade, I didn't really believe I was good enough. I found that I couldn't fix myself on my own but didn't see any alternatives. My life was a mess when my sisters finally took me to my first Al-Anon meeting.

From the beginning, I was overwhelmed by the unconditional love and acceptance in Al-Anon. Being treated that way by strangers confused me. I just didn't know what to do with it. For months I raced out of meetings as soon as we finished the closing prayer. I had been living in an emotional vacuum for a long time and could only take so much good stuff at one time. Someone might hug me. I liked it and was afraid of getting used to it.

Do you know what these loving Al-Anon members did? They let me run away as long as I needed. They let me run until I could accept their acceptance and affection in larger doses. They were always warm and welcoming, but they let me be where I was, as if that was okay (as if *I* was okay).

Throughout my first year in the program, every Step seemed to shout to me, "This is not a do-it-yourself program!" And I know now that I don't have to recover alone. In Al-Anon I have found other resources. I have the help and guidance of my Higher Power. I also have the support and encouragement of others who understand my problems. Today I have hope that I can make the necessary changes in my life with the help and support of my God and my Al-Anon family.

I have learned in meetings that tiny steps are perfectly acceptable and that they add up. That's good news for me because my fear has been so great that it has nearly paralyzed me, so microscopic steps are the only form of progress available to me. These baby steps have included driving by and sitting in the parking lot of new Al-Anon meetings when I was too scared to go inside. This may not seem like much, but for me it was one step closer to actually going to a new meeting than sitting at home. I've learned that every effort counts. My Sponsor's gentle reminder of "Progress Not Perfection" encourages me to give myself credit. In time, I actually began to believe that I don't have to be perfect to be good enough. Now I am able to go to three to six meetings a week, and I'm spending more time in meetings than in parking lots.

I didn't realize how emotionally shut down I was when I first came to meetings. It has been a long time since I let anyone be close to me. It took all the faith and courage I could muster to ask someone to be my Sponsor. Part of me has never believed it was all right for me to need help or support. The idea of opening up to others filled me simultaneously with hope and fear.

Making and receiving Al-Anon phone calls has been one of the most difficult challenges I've had to face. Dialing is the hardest part for me because I feel so vulnerable and full of doubt. As a newcomer, I was sure I wasn't worth listening to, and I was equally sure that the person on the other end of the phone would know that instinctively. Who was I to take his or her time? And what if they rejected me, brushed me off, judged me, preached at me, or put me down? I thought I would shrivel up and die right there, for I had no idea how to handle such a situation.

So I would pick up my home meeting's phone list, run my trembling finger down the column of names and numbers searching for a "safe" name, struggle with the fear of calling, and give up. Again, my Sponsor helped me to see that I could take one step at a time. She suggested I practice by making three Al-Anon calls each week. But I didn't know how to begin. So I just dialed one of the numbers and said, "Hi, do you have five or ten minutes for a 'program call?'" If the answer was "yes," I continued, "My Sponsor suggested that I make three calls this week. You're my second. Phone calls are really hard for me. How do *you* manage them?" That broke the ice for me.

Ironically, telephone sharing has become one of my favorite tools because it allows me to begin acting like a real person without those old feelings of uniqueness and terminal unworthiness. It's how I give myself opportunities to be vulnerable and just as imperfect as I am. But sometimes I still have to pray for the courage to dial.

I still don't know much about healthy friendships. I don't know what is "normal" or appropriate in many everyday situations. What do people talk about? How often do they call each other? If I'm willing to take a risk, my Sponsor is a safe person for me to learn with. She patiently accepts me no matter how awkward or backward I am. She gently encourages me to try new behavior, such as talking about my problems and feelings.

My fear of being close has really become evident in this special relationship. Opening up to her has been an extremely slow and often frustrating process. Just learning to call her consistently has been a struggle. I get impatient and angry with myself for so frequently shutting down and running away. Sometimes I get so scared that everything I intend to tell her flies out of my head and I go blank.

I don't begin to understand why, but talking and spending time with my Sponsor is incredibly healing. When I call, she talks to me as if she's glad to hear from me. When I'm tired and discouraged and want to give up, just thinking about her kindness and gentleness makes all the difference.

I think the love and acceptance of Al-Anon members have been the basis for any progress I've made. There is something so healing about being treated as if I matter. Little by little, this support is allowing me to let go of some of my defenses, my denial and isolation, the thick walls I've built around myself. I'm beginning to believe it might be safe to love again and to let myself be loved.

I no longer run around in a panic trying to rescue people. (I still tend to rescue; I just don't race in a panic to do it.) I'm more patient with my nieces and nephews. I'm kinder to myself. And I've actually said "no" without subsequently backing down and doing the task I had refused to do. What a miracle!

I am so grateful for Al-Anon. I can't imagine a life without it. I truly believe that God is using the program to save my life.

34

An Abused Husband Gains Self-Esteem

For most of my life I had felt like the proverbial square peg forcing itself into a round hole. The round hole was the person I "should" be, and the square peg was the real me. I never felt at home in the world of people. There was enormous stress in all of my relationships, with family and women and taxi drivers and everyone else. Other people's opinions of me, from the grocery clerk's, in a one minute, never-to-be-repeated encounter, to those of family members and business colleagues, were of critical importance and would largely determine the level of my self-esteem for that day.

The "shoulds" extended to my feelings as well, which most often ranged from fear to insecurity to fear to jealousy to fear to panic. I constantly strove to hide behind the more acceptable expressions of love and acceptance—the things I "should" feel.

As an adult, my life was controlled by the dark rage of my alcoholic wife. I have Multiple Sclerosis (M.S.), which primarily affects my legs, right arm, bladder, and bowels. Although the alcoholic knew that by late evening I became severely fatigued as a result of my illness, she generally chose this time to go into her tirades. Often she would torment me by refusing to let me go to sleep—not allowing me to lie down or turning on the light after I had turned it off. I wondered what the neighbors thought when they heard her shouting and throwing things around. Sometimes she pushed me into the wall or out the bedroom door while I prepared for bed. When she flailed at me with her fists, I was physically incapable of defending myself. At best I could protect my face from her blows.

Twice I escaped to spend the night in a local motel. This angered her even more. After a few months of this constant battle, I was growing desperately weak and did not know where to turn. A friend suggested I try Al-Anon. I had never heard of it.

My wife's brother, a recovering alcoholic, also urged me to go to Al-Anon. He wanted to try a family intervention as well, a formal confrontation during which we would present evidence of the amount and the destructiveness of my wife's drinking. I agreed to both. When the intervention failed to produce the desired results, I steeled myself for yet another horrible, draining ordeal and attended my first Al-Anon meeting. Instead, I found a place where I could belong and a group of people who understood what I was going through.

I was too humiliated about the abuse I was enduring to admit it at first. Men aren't supposed to be abused by women in our society. Not that anyone is supposed to be abused at all. But I felt emasculated by it, and I didn't dare let anyone know.

I was lucky. There weren't many men in Al-Anon at the time, at least not in my home town. But I did have the good fortune to meet one man who spoke very openly and very bravely about being attacked by his alcoholic wife, who once came at him with a pair of scissors while he slept. It was a relief to hear that another man, a perfectly normal individual, was also dealing with domestic violence. It was even more of a relief to see that no one seemed to think less of him for it. In fact, he received a great deal of support and encouragement. That meeting changed my attitudes about my situation, and as a result, it changed my life. Not my wife's life—my life.

Al-Anon has helped me learn that the way I choose to perceive my circumstances has a tremendous impact upon my enjoyment or lack of enjoyment of life. I now believe that everything that happens is for my betterment, and that it is I who place the labels "good" and "bad" upon the events of my life. These labels, these reflections of my very limited human vision, are what led me to view life as a system of punishments and rewards meted out in seemingly random fashion. But my unhappy childhood, my illness, my abusive marriage, and the other events in my life can also be looked upon as positive opportunities if I can break the habit of viewing them as punishments.

Not long after I came into this program, I had an opportunity to put my newfound perspective to the test. I met a very attractive woman who worked at the library. I remember feeling an immediate affinity with her, and she seemed interested in me as well. After that day, I found excuses to go to the library. She began to call and leave messages on my answering machine at work about material I had requested, usually adding a personal comment that grew more intimate and suggestive as time passed. Then she asked me if I was married. When I told her I was, she apologized for calling and hung up.

The next day I stopped by the library and told her I was flattered by her interest. I was aware that my feelings for her were intense, and the mutual attraction was powerful. It was tremendously exciting to feel this way after my long and passionless marriage, and I was consumed with fantasies about her.

We began sending notes to one another, exploring in writing what neither of us had the nerve to express aloud. But as time passed, I became increasingly uncomfortable. I know myself well enough to realize that I am incapable of a casual sexual relationship. I didn't know what to do. One minute I was convincing myself that I should pursue the relationship with this woman, and the next I was trying to pull away. I was unhappy in my marriage, but I couldn't casually brush aside the commitment I had made to it. Besides, my wife was dabbling with sobriety and I wanted to give us the chance to rediscover what our marriage could be without the cloud of active alcoholism. On the other hand, I felt that this woman was very special, and I didn't want to let her go. I felt a spiritual conflict as well. God had finally brought a warm, loving woman into my life at a time when I was too far into recovery to blithely disregard the consequences. I felt that God was setting me up, dangling a carrot just to torment me. Again it felt like a punishment, or at least a trap.

This conflict was the catalyst I needed to get a Sponsor.

I was driving myself crazy trying to decide what to do and getting no closer to a solution. There were two Al-Anon members I considered asking. One had many years of recovery and always seemed to share with great insight, but I found him intimidating. The other had been a member for only a year longer than I, but I felt so comfortable with him that I decided to ask him to sponsor me. After all, if I couldn't feel comfortable enough to be honest, a Sponsor wouldn't do me much good, regardless of how experienced or enlightened he might be. In retrospect, I think I made a wonderful decision because I wound up with a truly great Sponsor.

As I talked about my yet unconsummated affair, I began to realize that the real power of our encounter was its secrecy. I was afraid that, once I had aired my conflicting feelings, my embarrassment, and my shame, my Sponsor would judge and humiliate me for putting myself in this position. I feared that I had failed Al-Anon—and that he would tell me so in no uncertain terms. Most of all, I feared that he would order me to give up the other woman. Instead he said that, regardless of what I decided, I would have his unconditional, positive regard and support. He shared with me that what was crucial for him when he faced moral dilemmas was how he felt about what he was doing, and whether or not he could live with the long-term consequences of his actions.

I realized that I had to make a decision without self-righteous or misguided concern for what others might think or feel. If I did not make the decision for myself, it would be meaningless, and I would be unlikely to stick with it. Still, I didn't know what to do.

My Sponsor helped me to turn the problem over to God. He told me that this problem was really a gift in disguise, and I would learn a lot about myself and about the life I wanted to live by working through it. Thus he helped me to gain some perspective on the situation, and to at least open my mind to the possibility that God was on my side, presenting me with an opportunity rather than a set-up. He encouraged me to be honest with God, and honest with myself. So I prayed. I told God about my marriage, my feelings for the other woman, and my confusion. I admitted that I was powerless over my feelings, and that I felt very resistant to letting either woman go. I also told God I was angry about being in this position at all.

The clarity I received about what to do came at an Al-Anon meeting where the topic was self-esteem. I have learned that self-esteem is just that—*self*-esteem. Not wife-esteem or lover-esteem or even Sponsor-esteem. It has to come from *me*, not from other's opinions of me. And the way to gain self-esteem is by performing estimable acts, acts that I would feel comfortable performing before a Higher Power, the only authority to whom I need answer for my innermost convictions. The discussion at the meeting focused on making choices that would help us to feel good about ourselves.

Suddenly it seemed obvious to me that I would never feel good about an affair. I had to face it. Since I was not willing to end my marriage, the other relationship had to end. I was tempted to take the passive route and do nothing, hoping she would simply forget about me, hoping to avoid a confrontation altogether, but again, I wanted to be able to feel good about myself. I cared for this woman and she had been very patient with me while I struggled to come to a decision. I had to be honest with her.

I may always feel a little wistful about what might have been, but I think I made a good decision, one that I will be able to live with. More importantly, I learned that God is always there for me when I need Him. He brought a wonderful person into my life for a brief but memorable encounter. Instead of disregarding this gift because the relationship was temporary and limited, I feel grateful. I learned a great deal from the experience. I discovered that I have a strong moral code that I have to uphold in order to feel good about myself. I cannot passively slide into decisions anymore. I must take responsible actions or deal with the consequences, the first of which is tremendous discomfort with myself.

Al-Anon has taught me many lessons, but more importantly, Al-Anon has given me the tools to negotiate the lessons ahead. I've found that there is a Step, a Tradition, or a slogan that applies to every situation that arises, if I am willing to quiet down and hear the guidance they offer.

What I've learned, then, is that life is eternally renewable, and begins afresh each day at every age with infinite potential. I now know that the "round hole" into which this square peg really does fit has nothing to do with pleasing or imitating other people; the "round hole" is emotional sobriety. And for this, I am willing and eager to soften my fear-hardened edges. The way is through Al-Anon, the Twelve Steps, and a never-ending deepening of my faith in a Power greater than myself.

35

Alcoholism Crosses Racial Lines

I was an only child for about five years when my parents decided to have another child, my brother. As the only male child in our large family, he was considered extra special because he was to carry on the family name. Although he got extra attention, I loved him from the very beginning.

My brother was always afraid to sleep by himself, so he would climb out of his crib and toddle into my room to sleep with me. I let him because I needed to be needed and to have someone accept me. One night a cousin spent the night with me. My brother jumped out of his crib as usual and came in and whispered, "Can I sleep with you?" I was getting ready to let him into the bed, when my cousin got up and told my mother that my brother was out of his crib. My mother came into the room, spanked his little legs, and sent him off to his room. I was crushed.

But instead of allowing myself to accept my own feelings, instead of listening to my own truths inside, I listened to someone else. My cousin sat on the bed and laughed because my brother had gotten in trouble. She thought it was really funny. That's not the way I felt, but because I had such a deep desire to be liked by whoever I was with, I assumed those feelings. I laughed with her. That was the beginning of one of my earliest patterns—allowing others to dictate my feelings and my beliefs.

My parents, to my knowledge, were not alcoholics. They were social drinkers. They went to parties and entertained a lot, but I never saw them drunk or discourteous to one another. In fact, my parents didn't fight in front of us at all, and later that became a problem because I had never learned to deal with other people's anger, or even my own.

Somewhere down the line I developed a real insecurity about myself—who I was, what I was, and how I was going to fit in. My parents never told me that I was anything less than the best. They always said I was pretty and smart and that I could be anything I wanted to be. They couldn't have been more supportive, but somehow the signals got mixed up in my head. I thought they were just saying those things because they were my parents and they had to, so I didn't listen. I felt I had to do more than the next person, be more than the next person, put out more than the next person in order to fit in.

My parents were not wealthy, but we were a little bit better off than some of the other blacks in our area and, unlike some of the other children, we got allowances—$1.25 a week. I didn't spend that money on myself. There was a dime store down the street from where I lived, and once a week I would stop in to buy $1.25 worth of candy and toys to take to school. I was always met by an entourage of my classmates who knew I was going to dole it out. I didn't think I could have friends just because of who I was. I felt I had to buy them.

I met my husband in high school. We both happened to be in the guidance counselor's office, and he grabbed the tie belt from my dress and said, "If you want this back, follow me." We laugh today because, had we known then what we know now, he wouldn't have taken the belt and I wouldn't have let him have it. But as my Higher Power would have it, we did meet and we did date and we did get married.

I fell in love with him because he made me feel special. At home, I was never special. My brother was the special one, the one all the cousins and aunts and uncles came to see, the one who got all the attention. Now, to my delight, I was the center of my boyfriend's world. When I talked, he listened. He walked to my house, and I lived a long way from where he lived. Even as a high school student, he brought me flowers and candy and took me to nice restaurants for dinner. He drank, but it didn't bother me. I thought, "Oh, boy, have I got a good one!" So when we got married, I just knew that this was the answer to all my prayers.

Our honeymoon night was unique. Having just gotten out of high school, we were living with his mom and his six brothers and sisters. We had gone to sleep in his single bed, and sometime during the night my husband rolled over and I rolled out. Normal people would get up, scoot their partner over and get back into bed, or at least wake him and ask him to move. I, on the other hand, sat there on the floor waiting for this man to realize that his wife was missing from his bed. I mean, I was the center of his world! He was supposed to know that there was something wrong! He never even stirred. I got so frustrated that I woke him up—in a very lady-like manner—by beating the tar out of him with a pillow, screaming at the top of my lungs that he didn't love me and I wanted a divorce. Nobody else in the house came to see what was wrong, and that should have told me something. But that's how our marriage started off, and that's how it continued until we found recovery in Al-Anon and A.A.

We had a lot of problems. Our kids were born right away, so we never had time to adjust to one another as a couple. I knew nothing about alcoholism. I knew that he drank, but everybody drank. It didn't seem relevant to the difficulties we had.

I tried everything I could to make this man happy. I wanted him to feel pampered, so he was served breakfast, lunch, and dinner in bed! I tried to be as sexy as I could be. I read a lot of books on how to please a man and was willing to try almost everything. But something wasn't working. We couldn't seem to get along. I thought it was my fault. I wasn't sexy enough. Or perhaps it was my cooking. If I cooked a big meal, he wasn't hungry. If I didn't cook, he was starving to death. I couldn't please him.

Other things also made me think I was the problem. We entertained and went to parties and my husband, the life of the party, always had a wonderful time. But the minute the party was over he fell into a deep depression, so I assumed that he was happy with everyone but me. It never dawned on me that the real source of his unhappiness was alcoholism.

We'd get into major fights in which I'd leave the house in a hurry and he'd follow me, and we'd have high-speed chases down the highway. There was physical abuse. There were incidents with guns. Bless our children's hearts, I'm surprised they survived. Clearly my Higher Power loved me even when I didn't know to call on Him.

Eventually I decided I was crazy, and my husband agreed. I was at my wits' end and I had tried suicide several times. When we spoke with a counselor at the local psychiatric hospital, my husband told her all about me. He didn't leave out a thing, and I didn't open my mouth because he was telling the truth. I sat with my head down and waited for the verdict. When he finished, the counselor looked at him, and then she looked at me. She looked back at him, then at me, and then she turned to my husband and said, "Mr. _____, I think we need to put you in the hospital."

We laugh about that today, but at the time, it wasn't a bit funny. I was hurting with every fiber in me. I knew there was something wrong with me and I was crying out for help, but I couldn't even get myself committed. Do you know what that does to a person's self-esteem?

My husband didn't like the outcome of that session one bit, but he decided to give the hospital a try. Now let me get something straight here—he didn't go into the hospital for alcoholism. He went into the hospital because he was "stressed out." I figured it was my fault.

I thought I knew what mental hospitals were like. I've seen them in the movies. They always seem to have a large room in which people wander around in a daze, thinking they're God or Hitler or Santa Claus or Napoleon. This institution was like a hotel. They had swimming pools, tennis courts, a game room with a pool table, and nice dormitory rooms, not to mention three square meals plus snacks. I couldn't believe I was being left to take care of myself and my five children while my husband went on vacation! I tried to talk them out of keeping him there, but they didn't listen. So he stayed and I felt resentful.

I was about to be outdone by the alcoholic, so I soon got myself committed to the psychiatric hospital. That was only one of many hospital stays for both of us.

I went to my first open A.A. meeting at that hospital during one of my husband's stays. I was scared, sure that he had told all of those people how badly I had treated him. But the A.A. members came up to me and put their arms around me and welcomed me with so much warmth and affection. I didn't have to pay anything, I didn't have to be anybody, I didn't have to do anything. So I went to a lot of A.A. meetings. My husband and I decided that I, too, belonged in A.A., since the only requirement for membership in A.A. is a desire to stop drinking. Half a beer made me severely ill. After trying it twice, I didn't want to drink anymore, so I figured I qualified. I went to 90 meetings in 90 days, I studied A.A. literature, and I got my three-month chip. Finally someone had the good sense to direct me to Al-Anon, where I really belonged.

When my husband and I attended our first Al-Anon meeting, the room was full, and every face in it was warm, kind, accepting—and white. My husband leaned over to me and asked, "Honey, do you think I've caught something our people don't get?!"

But I kept coming to Al-Anon, where I was greeted with a lot of love, understanding, and caring. I wanted and needed the people in those rooms so badly that I was willing to do whatever it took to stay. I bought all the books, I got all the free literature, I went home and studied, and I sat in meetings and watched people share. I wasn't really listening because I wanted what they had. I was listening because I wanted the approval I saw in the room for those who shared. For example, somebody would say, "So I 'Let Go and Let God,'" and everybody in the room would murmur, "Yeah," and nod and smile. I picked up on that. I wanted those "Yeahs" and pats on the back. So I started parroting what I heard. I tried to impress everyone in the group with my knowledge and never admitted to any problems. I memorized the Twelve Steps and Traditions, and when I shared at meetings, a lot of people thought I had been in Al-Anon for many years.

The sad part was that I was still the same old me, still hurting. I only felt good in meetings. As soon as the meeting was over, I became depressed and felt alone. I couldn't understand it. I was doing all the things I had been told to do. I was attending lots of meetings and sharing and reading, yet I felt no better.

I looked good on the outside, but I was dying on the inside. Somebody saw that one day in a meeting. I was sitting there thinking about the wonderful pearls of wisdom I was about to spout, not listening to anyone else because what they said didn't seem important, and I was just about to share, when this lady turned to me and said, "Honey, I say this with love: take the cotton out of your ears and stuff it in your mouth."

I thought, "How dare she! She doesn't know who she's talking to! Everyone in this room thinks I'm wonderful—they tell me so every week. I know this literature backwards and forwards. Who does she think she is?" Now I didn't say this out loud because I was still a coward. But I decided that I would show her. I would not open my mouth at another meeting she attended—and everybody would be angry with her because I wasn't saying anything!

Again God did for me what I could not do for myself. When I finally shut my mouth, I started to hear people share and to understand what they were saying. I heard how others applied the tools of the program to their lives. I heard their courage and their hope. And I learned from what I heard.

After that, I found a Sponsor who was very active in Al-Anon service, and she motivated me to become active as well. She took me to assemblies, round-ups, and conventions, talked with me one-to-one, and helped me to understand myself.

My story is like anyone else's story because when alcoholism strikes, the feelings are the same; the fear, the anger, the hopelessness and helplessness are all the same. But there was something a little different about my experience. I was the only black person attending Al-Anon in my area. I don't know why this was so. Personally, I feel that when you hurt badly enough, when you hit a bottom deep enough and it dawns on you that you are dying, it doesn't matter who throws out the life line as long as it is thrown. That's how desperate I was. I knew that there was something wrong with me. I knew that if I didn't get help, I was going to die, and I feared dying more than I feared anything else. So I attended meetings and was treated with warmth and acceptance in neighborhoods where no one would have associated with me ordinarily. Because the principles of Al-Anon were held in high regard by my groups, I was not treated any differently from anyone else, so I didn't feel different.

My upbringing may have made it easier for me to attend Al-Anon than it has been for others. My parents taught us that all men and women were created equal, no matter what color their skin, no matter what their religious beliefs, and that there were good and bad people in all races. Maybe that helped to soften the blows, because for the most part I did not feel the pressures of racism when I grew up. I know others who literally had to fight for their lives and their rights, who sometimes died for those rights, and I can see how they might think that members of another race could not possibly understand what they were going through. But I feel that, if we truly share what we've lived through and how we've made it through, and if we truly extend our hands and allow others to feel welcome no matter how different they may appear, the barriers can be overcome. I try to share from the heart what's going on in my life, what has gone on in the past, and how this fellowship has helped. And I try not to see color but to see people.

In my first six or seven years in Al-Anon, I never heard anyone talk about physical abuse, and in that respect I felt different as well and wondered if this might be a racial difference. But I finally heard a lady share about the physical abuse in her home, and for the first time I could totally identify. Although it took a long time to find them, it has been important for me to share with others in Al-Anon who have had similar experiences with violence.

I feel that the God of my understanding has allowed me to go through everything I went through in order to be able to share with others, especially others of my race, that there is hope in this fellowship. Mostly though, I just do what I can do—share when it seems appropriate and be there with love.

It took me several years in this program to realize that pain is pain, because when I first walked through those doors there was no way you could tell me that being slapped around was anything like being yelled at, or that being called a bad name could feel just as awful as a punch in the ribs or the stomach. Since then I've learned that, although our lives are not identical, the feelings are the same—anger is anger and fear is fear, no matter who's feeling it. Al-Anon can help anyone to change any time we make the effort to practice the principles, to share with one another, to love, and, above all, to keep an open mind.

36

A Gay Man Copes with Sexual Intimacy

Even though my earliest memories involve living with an alcoholic parent, I didn't believe that my problems were related to alcoholism, for my parents were divorced and my alcoholic parent had died. I thought my relationship problems existed because I was a gay man.

I live in a fairly conservative part of the country. Growing up, I was taught that being gay was bad. Later, my choice to live as an openly gay man was not considered appropriate by the majority of society. I consistently got involved with people who needed me. The fact that he or she had nothing to offer me was unimportant—I felt I deserved no better. That was just what happened to gay people.

Eventually I met a wonderful man, another adult child of an alcoholic. We got involved, but before long the relationship began to deteriorate. I often complained about my problems to a close woman friend who happened to be a member of Al-Anon. "If only..." started most of my sentences. She suggested Al-Anon, but I declined. After all, alcoholism hadn't affected my life. It was because I was gay that my friend and I were having problems. I complained for the next three and a half years.

Even the most patient Al-Anon members have a limit on listening to pain and complaints. My Al-Anon friend told me that I could either go to Al-Anon and deal with my problems or I could continue to be miserable. Either way, she refused to listen to my sad tales if I failed to get help. I can't tell you how much I hated her for that response. For the next month, I used her rejection as one more excuse to feel like a victim. Once again someone had abandoned me.

The problems in my relationship were getting worse. Finally I announced to my lover that the next week I would go to Al-Anon. It was really more of a threat than a statement. He responded as many children of alcoholic parents would—he went first and attended the meeting I intended to visit. I was furious, victimized again. My Al-Anon friend responded with loving understanding and offered to take me to a different Al-Anon meeting later that week. I agreed. After all, this had become a challenge.

On the night of the meeting, my Al-Anon friend was sick and couldn't go. I went to that first meeting anyway, to show both of them that Al-Anon was not necessary for me to be happy. I just needed to find the right man.

When I walked through the door that first night, I was terrified. What if you knew me? What if you found out that I was gay? What if you rejected me? So I used the wrong pronouns. Instead of "he," I would say "they" when referring to my significant other. "They" didn't call, "they" showed up late, "they" were drinking again. This went on for years. It was hard enough to admit my behavior to you. I couldn't expect you to accept my sexual orientation too.

I continued to suffer from a feeling of uniqueness in Al-Anon. It wasn't just that I was gay. You all had an alcoholic to work your program on. I had no one. Poor me.

Then, sometime during my first year of recovery, several members spoke very enthusiastically about a workshop on sexual intimacy which had been held at the Al-Anon State Convention. My home group decided to have a meeting on this topic. I was anxious and apprehensive. I decided that what these heterosexuals had to say about their relationships would be irrelevant to me, and I almost didn't go.

But the topic stuck in my mind. When I first got to know my friend, sex had meant enjoyment for us. It was a part of our being in love and an expression of our bond. But after only a few months, sex had degenerated into a repulsive experience. As he drank, his desire increased while his ability diminished. We both became very frustrated. His personal hygiene became an even greater problem for me. I don't know how often he bathed or cleaned his teeth. I only know that he smelled when he was undressed.

I decided that I might benefit from a meeting on sexual intimacy, even if I kept quiet about my own sexuality. It was at that meeting, when male members discussed the loneliness and frustration of trying to make love to a passive, motionless drunk, that I began to relate. The women talked about how hurt and unloved they felt when their partners were unfaithful, treated them abusively, or were too drunk to complete the sexual act. Again I knew what they were talking about. I shared my need to be wanted, to be held, to be the only person desired by my partner, and both men and women expressed similar feelings. I truly recognized at this meeting that being gay was simply a part of me. The problems I had in having healthy relationships were a result of living with alcoholism. I was in the right place, and Al-Anon was there for me.

After that, I started sharing more honestly and openly about my situation. Whether other members were comfortable or not with my homosexuality, they certainly identified with the heartache of an alcoholic situation. The respect, dignity, and healing of Al-Anon was extended to me without reservation. We were all just human beings struggling for serenity in the face of a difficult situation. We were not that different after all.

None of this would have been possible without the anonymity that is the spiritual foundation of our program. I believe that the freedom we gain from anonymity lets us shed our outer differences and superficial identities, revealing our true nature as God's children. In Al-Anon, no matter what our external differences, gay or straight, rich or poor, black or white, we are all equals, and all one.

I continued to examine my feelings about sex. While taking the Fourth Step, I came across a question regarding whether I let my body be misused. This completely threw me. How often had I had sex in order to avoid quarrels or abuse? I know that for a while I tried to count the flowers on the wallpaper when we slept together in order to maintain distance. I feigned headaches and tiredness. I put my own needs and feelings well below his.

After I shared all this with my Sponsor, my situation became increasingly intolerable to me. Finally I worked up the courage to tell my lover that I would not have sex with him anymore if he was drunk. I expected an explosion, but there was none. He didn't take me seriously at first, but I stuck to my decision as calmly and politely as I could, and eventually he respected it. As a result, we began to put some of the intimacy back into our sex life, and I stopped feeling so resentful.

My lover chooses not to involve himself with any Twelve Step program. With God's help, I am better able to love him unconditionally and leave his choices up to him. He has tested HIV positive, and while I choose not to discuss this in my Al-Anon meetings, I confide my various feelings to my Sponsor. I know that, like alcoholism, AIDS is a disease over which I have no control. I use the program to help me deal with those affected by this disease, including my lover and myself, in a more loving way. This, to me, is the magic of our program. We can put it to work in our lives in any situation.

Al-Anon restored me to sanity. It gave me back my self-respect as a gay man and helped me to join the community of humankind as an equal citizen. I am blessed with a Sponsor and a group of friends who accept me unconditionally, even when I have problems accepting myself.

37

Coming to Terms with Another's Disease

My husband had finally entered a treatment center. I was supposed to be happy. Instead I was furious. I resented the fact that he had gone to strangers for help. After all, he had me to help him! Why did he feel the need to go elsewhere?

I especially resented the fact that he went for treatment in the middle of winter, leaving me home to care for our children and the house, keep the two wood fires burning for heat, feed the cows, chickens, dogs, cats, pigs, and goats, shovel snow, and hold down a part-time job taking in mending. I later realized that it would have seemed no better had it been the middle of summer, when there would have been a whole different set of chores to complain about. What bothered me was that I had been left behind while he went off to get help for himself.

One day while he was still in treatment, the stovepipe broke on the cellar stove. I had no idea how to fix it. I called my husband and told him I was coming to pick him up. He *had* to come home and fix that stove. And I did—I went to the hospital and picked him up. We got about ten minutes from the hospital, when he asked me to stop the car, turn around, and take him back. He realized that he needed the help he had been receiving there and that he wasn't yet ready to leave. I was angry and hurt. I felt he was being ruthlessly inconsiderate of his family. Didn't he care that we could freeze to death?! I cried all the way back to the hospital and all the way home again, even though he had promised to arrange to have the stove repaired.

He kept his word, and a few hours later a friend had fixed the stovepipe. The house was warm, we were taken care of, and I was still angry and resentful. I clung to that resentment even after my husband returned home.

Sobriety didn't last long. On the morning of his first hangover since treatment, I took the opportunity to remind him of how he had abandoned us in our hour of need—and for nothing. He couldn't even stay sober—after all I'd been through!

Soon everything was back to normal, if anything about life in an alcoholic household can be called normal. One warm, rainy night stands out in my mind, although it wasn't much different from hundreds of other nights. Just as I had a hundred times before, I jumped off the couch and looked out the window. I glanced back at the clock. It was 4:00 A.M. and my husband still wasn't home. Where was he?

I thought, "Something's happened. Is he hurt? I'll kill him! What if he had an accident?" Then a strange voice added, "There's nothing I can do, so why am I still awake at this hour? Why can't I just leave it alone?" Wearily, I lay back down on the couch and finally drifted off to sleep.

My husband walked into the living room, woke me, and sat down on the chair across from me. He told me that he had spent the night in jail for drunk driving. He claimed he had gone to a party for someone at work and someone had slipped corn alcohol into his beer. He said he had tried to call, but the line was busy.

So it was my fault. I wondered if he had tried to call when I was calling around to find out where he was? If only I'd….

Then the anger returned. With a voice that could freeze water, I said, "Was it worth it?" I turned and lay back down on the couch. He stormed out.

We had to go to court, which led to ten weeks of outpatient group therapy for us both. I just *knew* that things would surely change. He'd quit drinking again, this time for good, and everyone would find out what I had been through. With tears streaming down my face, I related how I felt like a post out in the middle of a field. All the members of my family leaned on me, I said, draining all my strength and leaving me limp. If you listened closely enough, you might have heard violins playing.

The counselor listened patiently, and then said, "Ah, a martyr!"

Now that wasn't exactly the response I expected. In fact, I was so angry that I fumed all the way home. I was furious at the counselor for even suggesting that I had a problem, at my husband for causing this mess, at my family for not pitying me, and at all our friends for ignoring us.

When we first married, I had no idea life would turn out this way. It was love at first sight for us. My husband-to-be set me on a pedestal, put up with my constantly changing moods, went along with most anything I wanted, listened endlessly to my every concern, and promised to love me, unconditionally, for the rest of my life. At my request, we moved to the family farm. I imagined a *Little House on the Prairie* life, and at first, it was everything I had hoped for. For about seven years, my husband and I farmed side by side. We visited friends, sharing coffee and cards, and our friends visited us. We attended church and joined in many community activities.

Somewhere along the line our lifestyle began to change. We were now attending parties and often frequented a local bar, although I didn't drink. My husband was now working at a manufacturing company in town. He'd begun stopping after work for a drink with the fellows. I felt totally justified in calling around to try to get him to come home. As far as I was concerned, he was spoiling dinner, so I had no choice.

When he began working weekends and longer hours, I took on more chores at home, caring for the animals, cutting wood, and taking almost full responsibility for the children and our church, community, and school activities. The drinking increased. He often blamed his drinking bouts on something I had said or done. I took him at his word, for I had become angry and frustrated and often took it out on him.

I had not yet grasped the concept that alcoholism was an illness. I simply believed that my husband had become a selfish, hateful person who was ruining our family life. He was earning a good salary, but we never seemed able to afford anything and our checking account was often overdrawn. All that had been wonderful about our pastoral life was vanishing. We stopped visiting others, and the only people who visited us were those who drank. I decided it was all my husband's fault, and it was my job to cover up and lie for him so that we could still have some dignity, some social life. I even took the blame for things he did. I felt I had every right to yell at him for "making me" do such things.

The counseling sessions were soon over and things had not changed. My husband was very proud that no one had been able to get anything out of him. I was angry that they had zeroed in on me. Why me? I was the one who held things together, the one who sacrificed! My husband was the drinker!

Then the strangest thing happened. A little voice that had begun chanting, "You can only work on yourself" led me to an open Al-Anon meeting, something I had heard about from another member of our counseling group. I walked cautiously into the room. People were milling around, talking, laughing, and drinking coffee. My first instinct screamed "Run!" but I couldn't seem to get the message to my feet. Someone walked over to me and introduced herself. She looked so happy that I was sure I was in the wrong place. Soon I was being led to a chair and someone put a cup of coffee in my hands.

The meeting began. The speakers related stories of anger, fear, and sorrow, but the amazing thing was that they also found humor in their pain. I remember thinking how I wanted so much to be a happy, loving person again, and I wanted to learn to share a good life once more with my husband, who I still loved but didn't always like very much. (I'm sure he often felt the same about me.) And I wanted to share this with my children, who had become strangers to me.

So I attended Al-Anon meetings regularly, and soon I enrolled in classes at the community college. On my way to becoming a new me, I began to realize how sick we had all become. I hoped to learn to forgive and forget all the awful words and actions that had damaged our relationships so that we could begin again. I saw that I, too, had done much for which I needed forgiveness. I even came to a better understanding about my feelings for my family and friends. My negative attitudes had distorted my view of everyone and everything in my life. The next several years of my Al-Anon recovery were focused on sorting through the real and the imagined. In time, I came to like the new me.

Of course, all this took time. At first I was impatient and lonely, and I felt like an outsider among longtime Al-Anon members who had formed close friendships. At the same time, I was becoming increasingly uncomfortable around our old friends. I no longer wanted to spend time in bars or around people who preferred to be intoxicated when socializing. I found their behavior irritating and superficial, yet I felt guilty and snobbish for rejecting people who had been in my life for many years. Some of these people had stood by me in the worst of times, and I had some fond memories. But I had changed, and for me, change often involves some loss. I realized that I didn't do anybody a favor by pretending to enjoy their company while secretly criticizing or disliking them. They deserved better treatment than that. So I declined invitations I didn't want to accept and gradually let certain relationships slip away. This wasn't completely a one-sided change. My old friends seemed as uncomfortable around the new me as I was around them, and they, too, let the relationships come to an end. Then I really felt alone. I had outgrown my former friendships, but was not quite ready to form new ones.

Close friendships grow slowly. It took time, but I eventually grew quite close to several Al-Anon members and a couple of my classmates at school. It was so comforting to be surrounded by people who really seemed to care about me, people with whom I had something in common.

My husband's manufacturing plant closed down, and he had to get a new job. I tried to find work, so I decided to pursue a college degree that would help me to find employment. I returned home only on weekends for the next three years. My husband was supportive, but I didn't realize just how deep was his pain, guilt, and disrespect for himself. His drinking continued. He feared that I would soon leave and he would be alone, but he behaved as if nothing was wrong.

Ironically, I began to recognize what I'd been reading and attempting to practice in Al-Anon coming out of my active alcoholic husband's mouth and in his actions. He began treating me with great courtesy, and his attitude toward life in general improved. On

Fridays I would come home, often to find flowers and a candlelight dinner. Once he surprised me with a small typewriter. He threw himself into gardening, cooking, and canning. He was very good at these and many other things.

But I was unable to appreciate his efforts. I was still caught up in the drinking. I thought I had learned to "Let Go and Let God," but in fact I had merely let go. I had made no room for God in my plans. My life was busy, and I had begun neglecting my meetings and my Al-Anon readings. I was slipping fast. I once again became angry, frustrated, and irrational. He had taken over *my* home, *my* gardens, even *my* program. How dare he!

Then my children got into the act. My oldest son confronted me. Me! Not the sick one! He spoke of things *I* had done and said! He had the audacity to remind me of the Al-Anon slogan "Live and Let Live!" I felt furious and betrayed—and then humiliated by the truth I heard in his words. I wasn't letting anyone live without blame or criticism. Resentment had overtaken me once again. So I swallowed my pride and renewed my commitment to myself and my family. I took my body, mind, and soul back to Al-Anon.

Only a year later we were sitting in a cold examining room awaiting the results of tests taken on a lump found on my husband's larynx. Cancer. We both just stared at the doctors, dumbstruck. Surgery seemed the best option, but we were told that the cancer was advanced, and the odds were against survival. Yet the nine-hour operation had positive results.

When we returned home, I went to work to try to repair the damage to our finances. The bills were staggering, and the paperwork was mountainous. I was caught up in my own problems that it took a while to realize that my husband was dealing with the fight of his life, and he was understandably scared. He had been laid off from work, and he had to learn to talk all over again. But this was only the beginning. By May another lump had appeared. My husband underwent six weeks of daily radiation and another surgery. His face swelled with fluid from the radiation, the incision in his neck wouldn't heal, and arteries often bled. We both needed to face the fact that this could be the end. We truly learned the meaning of living "One Day at a Time," because one day was all we could really count on.

I had always disliked the idea that one of Al-Anon's Traditions included encouraging and understanding the alcoholic because I had never truly comprehended that alcoholism was a disease. Cancer taught me about alcoholism, and I finally learned the meaning of compassion. I had gained enough self-esteem to know that my problems were important. My financial difficulties were quite real, and my fear and sense of loss were staggering. The stress was terrible. I was again affected by the disease of another, and I owed it to myself to pay attention to my needs and take extra special care of myself. But for the first time, I was able to recognize that my husband was suffering as well and needed my support and my strength. I finally understood what I had so often heard in Al-Anon meetings—that I didn't have to neglect myself in order to care about him. Love was not in short supply to be doled out in tiny, miserly portions which left less of me; love was abundant, and it grew and multiplied with use. The more I loved, the more loved I felt. The more compassion I had for my husband, the more I was able to validate my own feelings and appreciate the way all of our lives were being affected. I also developed a profound appreciation of how many wonderful gifts were crammed into each day that we were able to share.

We began watching each other, touching hands and shedding tears in silence. We discovered a wonderfully effective way to communicate, something that had become difficult for us over the years. We began writing to each other. We could finally share and understand one another's feelings and show our love.

Our children were wonderful through all of this. They were an unfailing source of support. My Al-Anon friends kept me going when I wanted to run away and pretend that none of this was happening. They reminded me that I could wrap my mind around a single, simple concept such as "First Things First," or "Easy Does It," and the panic would eventually pass.

When the seizures began, we returned to the hospital and spent the last month and a half in a hospital room. There was a lot of time to think back and to make amends. Although I had always been afraid of making amends, especially after so many years as a martyr, the "wronged" one, I knew that I had done a great deal of harm, and it was a cleansing experience that I am so grateful to have had. I was able to admit my wrongs and to ask for forgiveness. And in the process, I found that I no longer harbored resentment for the things I felt had been done to me. It was no longer personal. Every one of us had done the best we could under the circumstances.

My husband was beautiful. He faced his illness with great courage. And it taught all of us about the disease of alcoholism. After he died, I thought that alcoholism had died with him, but the effects of alcoholism lingered in our home. There's a good chance that alcoholism will spread from generation to generation in our family, but each of us is working to change that. That's why I keep coming back to Al-Anon.

I have a wonderful, imperfect family, and I'm proud of them. For years I couldn't seem to grasp the importance of letting go and letting God. Now I'm convinced that this is what I must do. I take those I care for from my mind and place them in my heart, where the God of my understanding can take over. And I pray for the wisdom to build a better tomorrow on the mistakes and experiences of yesterday.

38

Loving Alcoholics and Still Finding Joy

I grew up in an alcoholic family. My father died when I was four years old, and my mother married my "pop" when I was six. Pop was, and is, a good, kind man, but I soon learned that the way he drank wasn't normal. I remember watching my mother get ready for an evening out—doing her nails, putting on her prettiest dress—and knowing full well that before the night was over, chaos would strike. From the moment they left the house, I sat by the window and waited. I remember the knot I always felt in my stomach and the desperate need to watch for the headlights of their car coming back up the hill. Although I never made the situation any better, I needed to know when the madness would begin. Eventually they would arrive home. My mother would limp inside, her dress torn, her makeup smudged with tears. Sometimes Pop would storm off; otherwise, the battle came home with them. I always wondered how two such good-looking people could leave together so happy and return so angry. And today I wonder why the four of us children never, ever talked about it.

I often feel that I did my apprenticeship for Al-Anon at my mother's knee because, as an adult, I found myself in the very same role she had assumed in her marriage to Pop. Alcoholism is truly a family disease that, if left untreated, continues to be passed from one generation to the next. My own first marriage was one of late night violence, shouted insults, incredible fear, and increasing desperation. I watched my love for my husband turn to fear, hate, and then to numbness, a void. I felt nothing. The only joy in my life was my child, and I felt that my love for her was the ransom I paid to remain my husband's hostage. He wouldn't let me leave and take her with me.

I felt trapped, unable to stay, unable to leave my child behind. The violence was escalating along with my husband's drinking. I came to learn that yesterday's indignities paled beside the indignities yet to come. I dreaded the dawn of each new day.

And then, late one evening, my husband was killed in a car wreck, the indirect result of alcoholism.

For a while, I thought his death was the answer I had been waiting for, yet I did not feel any better. I was still desperate, still hurting, still sick. So I did what many others have done before: I got involved with another alcoholic.

This man had been around A.A., and I thought he was "safe." I didn't realize that he was a periodic binge drinker who rarely attended A.A. meetings and never let anyone know he was still struggling to attain sobriety. Nor did I realize that I would soon feel the same anger, confusion, shame, and desperation I felt before.

This was the baggage I brought with me when I walked into my first Al-Anon meeting full of false bravado. It was big bad me who swore, "Just fix this drunk and I'll be fine." That might have been true, if fine stood for *F*rantic, *I*nsecure, *N*eurotic, and *E*motionally unstable. Thank God for the wise, longtime member who saw through my tough façade. She *gently* told me to "Keep Coming Back." Well, no one had said anything gently to me for years and that was enough to pique my curiosity. I left the Al-Anon meeting that first night with every intention of returning, but only to come back and "rattle that longtimer's cage!"

I did come back. I tried my best to blow her cool, but it never worked. What happened instead was that, in spite of myself, I absorbed enough of what I heard at the Al-Anon meetings to get a glimmer of hope. As I listened, I began to feel a sense of belonging. These people understood. They cared, and they loved me long before I felt lovable. It was amazing!

I didn't feel I was getting better right away. In fact, in some ways I felt I was getting worse. I hadn't yet found the willingness to turn my will and life over to my Higher Power. I needed more convincing. A part of me still believed that the alcoholics were the only ones with problems. Sure, I had been affected, but I was getting over it. I didn't have any idea of how serious a disease alcoholism is, nor did I see how deeply affected I continued to be. But in reality my life was completely unmanageable.

Over the next three years, I experienced two horrible examples of my own blind rage. The first time, I attacked the alcoholic with my fist, and the second, I tried to run over him with my car. It took something that obvious to make me realize that I was out of control. I had run out of excuses. I could no longer rationalize my own atrocious behavior. I finally got scared, really scared. So I did what perhaps others have done: I got involved with yet another alcoholic.

I must admit that I find something quite thrilling about living with an alcoholic. But by now I might have known better than to expect a new man to solve my problems. My friends in Al-Anon did. They also knew that there was nothing they could do but let me fall once more and to be ready to help me up again when the time came.

I fell hard. I had been attending Al-Anon meetings for nearly four years, yet I had never tried to put into practice what I had learned, and I continued to live in ever-worsening insanity. I felt unique. I was sure that no one else had felt the sense of total worthlessness and absolute defeat that haunted me. One night I was traveling down a dark and twisting road toward my house. It was late, and I was tired. With each curve in the road I felt like I was going down more deeply into despair. I had failed. Even Al-Anon couldn't help the likes of me. I went into my house that night with every intention of ending my life.

I believe that God did for that night what I couldn't do for myself. At the moment of greatest despair, He brought into my mind a verse I dimly remembered from childhood: "You were not born of a spirit of fear, but of power and love and of a sound of mind." At that moment, I realized that the problem was not my situation, my husband, my latest boyfriend, or a bottle of alcohol. The problem was me. I was not of sound mind. I was not sane. But I had learned in Al-Anon that my Higher Power could restore me to sanity. I realized that the only thing that separated me from the "winners" in the program was the sincerity with which they had taken their Third Step, making the decision to turn their will and their lives over to the care of a Power greater than themselves.

I made that decision that night, truly and wholly turning my will and my life, my mind and my heart over to my Higher Power. From the moment the decision was truly made, evidence of my God's love for me replaced the defeat and incredible remorse that had been haunting me. Thus I experienced my first spiritual awakening, and I have never been the same since.

I credit my continuing recovery, first and foremost, to this God of my understanding. Long before I even acknowledged Him, He loved me. He picked me up whenever I fell. For a long time, I'd stay near Him only until things got better, then go off on my merry way again, taking back the control, only to fall once more. He never failed to pick me up, no matter how willfully I behaved. As I grow in my understanding of this Higher Power, I am learning to stay close to Him and let Him run the show.

I think of putting Al-Anon to work in my life in terms of what I call the "Four S's"—Slogans, Sponsorship, Steps, and Service. I think of them as a set.

The slogans offer us some common sense directions that got misplaced while living with active drinking. "Let Go and Let God" is my favorite, because I learned the hard way that if I try to force my own solutions, I easily become obsessed with things that are none of my business, and my whole world turns upside down.

Sponsorship may be the single most wonderful blessing the program has given me. A Sponsor is someone who loves me, someone I can love and learn to trust, someone who will share with me the path to spiritual progress. My Sponsor is wise beyond her 20 years of Al-Anon recovery. She has shown me, by her example, how to make this program my own. We share laughter and tears, good times and bad. All she requires of me is honesty, but what she gives to me is immeasurable.

The Twelve Steps are a way out of the darkness. These simple guidelines show me how to walk through the tough times and offer a path to serenity in everyday life as well. I especially like Step Two, "Came to believe that a Power greater than ourselves could restore us to sanity." This Step reminds me that only things of value get restored—Victorian homes, antique cars, and me! By working this—and all the other Steps—I have learned that I do have something to offer. I am worthwhile.

Service is my opportunity both to give back and to keep that which has been so freely given to me. Whether it's setting up chairs, answering the phone in our local Al-Anon office, or just listening when someone else is in need, service works for me. I get better when I give freely of myself. I don't do this out of a heavy sense of obligation. I suspect I would be resentful if I felt I had to serve out of guilt, and no one would benefit from such a hostile gift. Instead, I think of service as a privilege which allows me to grow while I do something that's worth doing, something that will help others as well as myself.

I am remarried today to a delightful recovering member of Alcoholics Anonymous. My husband is truly the great love of my life. Again, God did for me what I could not do for myself. He gave me another alcoholic to love. He allowed me the opportunity to learn how sincerely thrilling it can be to live with an alcoholic in a home filled with joy and recovery. The gifts of this program are evident today in every aspect of my life, thanks to all of you. Although it has taken many years to say it, my life is a miracle.

39

A Father Takes
Responsibility for Himself

The first thing I learned in Al-Anon was to face facts. I had spent years doing the opposite, hoping my situation would magically change and repeatedly being surprised when alcoholic chaos and confusion persisted.

I got into the habit of preparing myself to go home after work by imagining the worse-case scenario. Otherwise the disorder always caught me off guard. The kitchen tablecloth would be half off the table, and the countertop would be littered with empty beer cans, candy wrappers, and half-eaten sandwiches. Big high-topped basketball shoes were everywhere. The floor was often sticky with spilled orange juice. My sons, high school students with part-time jobs, kept juice in the house to mix with their vodka. When they weren't in the kitchen, my sons and their friends spent their spare time in the attic above the garage, where giggles and murmurs and whiffs of marijuana smoke wafted out despite the locked door. My wife, herself the daughter of an alcoholic, simply stayed away. As far as I know, she spent most of the day shopping or driving around, and at night she locked herself in the bedroom. If I neglected to prepare myself, I would explode when I got home. I had done so many times, and nothing ever seemed to change. The only one that got hurt by my reactions was me.

In Al-Anon I discovered that reacting was one of my most finely honed skills. It was my way of ventilating a lot of feelings I was unable to identify at the time—frustration, anger, resentment, and fear about living with limited resources, never having the money to get anything repaired, and trying to help the oldest three of our seven children with their college expenses. It was the youngest two sons who were testing me, and I was failing.

So when drug dealers knocked at the back door at 4:00 A.M., even on weekdays, I reacted. I stormed outside to take down the license numbers on their shiny, new, expensive cars and cursed them as they sped away. I reacted when I found drug-dealing paraphernalia in my living room. The biggest shock to me was finding a handgun, a "Saturday night special," on my coffee table. I screamed and yelled, but nothing changed. I didn't realize that, instead of waiting until something unacceptable happened and then reacting to it, I could initiate action on my own when I was calm and reasonable and had thought about my options. At the time, I didn't see any options at all.

I regularly attended an Al-Anon meeting especially for parents of alcoholics, but as my marriage became more and more troubled and my home life grew more unmanageable, I found that attending several other Al-Anon meetings was necessary to my sanity. My wife ridiculed me for attending, and if I returned later than expected, she locked me out. I'm not the type to break down the door, so I spent more than a few nights sleeping in the garage. Had Al-Anon not been so terribly helpful, anxiety about the consequences of attending might have kept me at home. But I was willing to tolerate almost anything because the program became the source of my strength and confidence.

Until I went to Al-Anon, I didn't think I could cope with my situation unless it changed. After being in the program for a while, I knew that I couldn't count on anyone changing except me. But it took some time before I figured out how to make changes in myself. Meanwhile, my two sons had a habit of stealing my credit cards and running up charges all over town. Since these were debit cards, the bank automatically deducted the charges from my bank account. As a result, my account was frequently overdrawn, and I felt obligated to scurry around covering the charges, even when I had nothing to do with them. I felt unspeakably resentful about this because money was so tight, but I didn't recognize that I had any choice.

When I complained about this problem to my Sponsor, he handed me an Al-Anon leaflet called *Detachment*. There, in print, were the solutions to this mess in which I felt so trapped. It suggested that I could choose not to do for others what they could do for themselves. It said I didn't have to cover up for another's mistakes or misdeeds, and that in Al-Anon we learn not to suffer because of other people's actions.

I interpreted all this to mean that it was high time I stopped paying for items I hadn't purchased and could not afford. So when I got the next phone call from the bank, I told them that the card had been used without authorization, and unless my signature was on the charge, I would not pay it. I directed them to my sons and told them to take whatever actions they felt was appropriate. I felt embarrassed, guilty, and sure that I was ruining the lives of my children. But I knew that these feelings were not reliable gauges of reality. I stuck to my guns. Then I confronted the boys myself. I told them that the next time they stole from me, I would report the theft to the police. I meant it. I never had another problem with the credit cards.

My Al-Anon attendance taught me that this habit of taking care of my sons in inappropriate ways permeated my life. My wife would come home from work at the end of the day and say, "Didn't I tell you to make sure those boys cut the grass?" I was working out of the house at the time, and I had taken on the role of message carrier. I would respond, "I told them this morning, but I'll tell them again." Then I'd go find the boys and tell them, "Mom wants you to cut the grass." I often added, "You know your mother is going through a hard time right now, so if you'd do this for her, she'd feel a lot better," or some such manipulative nonsense. The boys would have some excuse why they couldn't do it now, and I'd go back and report to my wife, and so on. Meanwhile, I got nothing done—and felt resentful toward the bunch of them.

Finally I called an Al-Anon friend, and she said, "Who do you think you are? Why don't you let your wife and your sons talk to each other?" That was all it took. Suddenly an option was available that hadn't been there before. When my wife told me to tell something to one of the boys, I simply said, "Don't tell me, tell him." I was consistent. I wouldn't have believed the benefit I got out of that small stand. Just by removing myself from that one situation, I became better able to set other limits for myself, and soon I was able to say, "I will not discuss it unless you are sober." My self-esteem began to grow, and I believe that everyone in the family was touched by it.

My wife died suddenly, and although things had been strained between us, I felt the loss very deeply. I had once had so much hope for our marriage, and as I recovered in Al-Anon, some of that hope had been rekindled. Now I was filled with regret for what would never be. The love and caring I received in my Al-Anon group kept me going from one day to the next. Our children also went through the crisis of loss at the time, but alcoholism doesn't take vacations. At our weakest moments as individuals and as a family, alcoholic behavior always seemed to flare up. Without my meetings and all that I had learned about detachment, I don't know what I would have done. The ongoing support of my Al-Anon friends gave me the hope that sanity would be restored in my life.

It took me another year before I had built up enough self-confidence to realize that I did not have to tolerate drug abuse in my home, but finally made my stand. I told my sons that they could not use drugs if they wanted to continue living with me. They chose to move into a house with some of their friends, and I feared that they would not survive. Then, after three attempts at sobriety, one of their new housemates committed suicide. The shock forced my sons to take this disease seriously and led both of them to seek help. Today, by the grace of God, they are both sober.

There are still alcoholics in my life. Before Al-Anon, it was as if they were standing at the bottom of a ladder and I was right behind, urging, begging, and pleading for them to climb it. As they began their ascent, I propped myself behind them, pushing all them up with all my might. With each unsteady step they took, I pushed all the harder. Eventually, when they lost their grip and fell, I fell too, cushioning their blow. As they got up and climbed again, I was right underneath, all the more concerned that they hold on tight. Each time they slipped and tumbled, I fell beneath them and took the brunt once more.

Injured and sore, I came to Al-Anon. I began to notice that some of the alcoholics weren't even holding on tightly or being careful with their footing. Why should they? They had fallen several times without sustaining injury. We fell once again.

Then I noticed that next to this ladder was another one—a ladder with my name on it. I picked myself up off the ground, walked over, and began to climb it. Although I was concerned about the alcoholics, I realized that they must climb their own ladder by themselves. My attempts to help had only hindered.

As I climb my own ladder, I discover that it requires a great deal of concentration and strength to move up. I can't effectively climb while keeping an eye on the other ladder. So I focus on my own climb up the rungs, and let the alcoholics focus on their climb. If they fall I will empathize, but I will not be injured. Their own injuries may help convince them to hold on tighter. Their success, or failure, in climbing out of the pit of alcoholism is their responsibility. Whether or not I climb out is up to me.

40

A Minister Works through Childhood Pain

I remember how my dad changed after he first discovered Al-Anon. My three sisters, and I, the only son, were all unhappy because he had stopped trying to control Mom's drinking. Dad had always been our savior. He was the one who had gotten Mom into the hospital, resulting in days of relief in our house. He was the one who had fought back on our behalf in the face of her criticism and unfair demands. He was the one who always knew what to do with Mom when her drunken behavior got out of control. Then Dad went to Al-Anon, and all of this "help" we depended on came to a stop. Instead of intervening, Dad now said, "It's beyond my control." How we hated Al-Anon!

I could only see the worst in our future. Dad tried to explain that Mom had a disease and that none of us had the power to cure it, but I didn't understand. As far as I was concerned, he was asking us to stop trying to help Mom. If it hadn't been for us, I thought, she would have been dead by now. How could Dad ask us to leave her to her own devices?

Dad tried again and again to help us understand all that he was learning from Al-Anon, but it fell on deaf ears until he discovered that there was a program for us as well—Alateen. Well, we wanted nothing to do with it, but we were driving him crazy, begging him to disregard all he was learning in Al-Anon and jump back into his old ways. So he insisted that we try one Alateen meeting.

I'll never forget how scared I felt at that first meeting. I didn't move or utter a word. I just listened to the kids who told their stories, which were all my story! I remember realizing that I was not alone—this was happening in other families, too. That very first night, I knew I belonged there. The next week could not pass quickly enough. I was hungry to learn about the problems our family had had all these years. Where did I fit in? What could I do about all my fears and frustrations? So I kept coming back. My sisters did not share my feelings. After that first night, they never went back.

I learned enough in Alateen to make it through my last year of high school alive and in one piece. I, too, stopped rescuing my mother from crises of her own making. I began to have a sense of serenity in my life that I had never felt before. But confronting the harsh reality of how greatly I had been affected by alcoholism was hard and painful work. I jumped at the chance to go away to school, and, once out of the house and away from the alcoholic, I stopped attending meetings and tried to forget all about alcoholism. I had come a long way, and I managed fairly well on my own for a while.

I was a mess when I again reached Al-Anon years later, after an insane, alcoholic marriage. It's easy to underestimate how potent alcoholism can be. I have found that recovery from the effects of this disease is possible, but conquering the disease is not. I will always be powerless over alcohol, and when I forget that and try to combat it in yet another situation or relationship, I get myself in a heap of trouble.

There were very few other men in attendance when I came into Al-Anon. Coming from a family with three sisters and many aunts, I was accustomed to being around women, but I yearned for the fellowship of other men, others to whom I could relate more directly. In truth, I was afraid of women. There had been so many hurtful experiences, not only with my mother and my ex-wife, but with two abusive women bosses. Because of past experience, I expected women to tell me that I didn't measure up, that I wasn't good enough. And I expected to be abandoned. Even my first wife, the one woman with whom I had enjoyed a happy relationship, had died of cancer at a very young age, leaving me alone with a young daughter. Having taken some pretty hard knocks from women, I was wary of getting clobbered again. I didn't realize that one of the effects of alcoholism is feeling all alone, isolated in an unsafe world in which intimacy leads to pain.

I also felt isolated because I am a minister. I believe that, like Job, I had been singled out for a life of hardship in which my faith would be tested again and again. I didn't realize that another of the effects of alcoholism is perceiving oneself as a victim and a martyr. I needed a lot of help. Fortunately, Al-Anon was there when I needed it.

By this time, my father was no longer living. My mother was still drinking, and my sisters were either drinking heavily or involved with alcoholics. Nobody in my family was pleased to hear that I was going to Al-Anon. Nobody wanted to talk about alcoholism at all. After a while, I decided that I needed some time away from my family. I decided that I wouldn't see them or speak with them on the phone, even during the holidays. I wasn't strong enough to be my true self in their presence. Because I was so vulnerable at the time, I feared that their efforts to undermine my commitment to my Al-Anon recovery would succeed. I needed time to grow and mature and accept myself first. So I wrote to each one, explaining that I was going through some changes that I had to make alone. I said that this was only temporary, and I hoped they wouldn't take it personally because I didn't mean to hurt anyone. They didn't under-stand what I was doing, nor did they like it. They tried to change my mind, to get me to feel guilty, to find excuses to maintain the status quo. But I held my ground and gave myself the time I needed.

The separation didn't last forever; I was trying to heal my rela-tionships, not sever them. But it took quite a while before I could be at ease in the presence of my family. I still get pulled into some of the family's crazy, alcoholic thinking, but it doesn't last long. Taking time out from the insanity allowed me to learn to detach from my family in a loving manner.

At first I had a lot of unlearning to do. Many of my beliefs were faulty. This became clear to me when I heard someone at a meet-ing say, "People from alcoholic homes are so curious. We're always asking, 'Why? Why? Why? Most of our questions boil down to this single lament: 'Why am I such a jerk?'" Much of my Al-Anon experience has revolved around coming to the repeated realization that I don't have to spend time answering this question, because it's the wrong question. I am not a bad person trying to become a good person or a stupid person trying to get smart, but a hurt person trying to heal. Taking my Fifth Step, in which I admitted to God, to myself, and to another human being the exact nature of my wrongs, was a big help to me in establishing the realization that I didn't feel unhappy because I was bad or worthless, or even because God had destined me for a life of trials and tribulations, but that I felt unhappy because I was hurt. I do not behave in a morally reprehensible or unethical manner, but I do carry with me the hurt of growing up and subsequently living with alcoholism.

At some intellectual level, of course, I "understood" that growing up with alcoholism had been painful, but it took a while in the program before I began to feel just how painful. As time passed, I felt less and less isolated, less and less different from others, for I often heard my feelings or experiences coming out of other people's mouths. More and more men found their way to Al-Anon, and I even discovered another member of the clergy who was recovering. Indeed, I found that my story, once the most tragic of all in my opinion, was considerably more fortunate than many I heard in my meetings. But understanding that my circumstances had been relatively fortunate didn't take the pain away.

Taking my Fifth Step didn't solve my problems or miraculously lift a great burden of care from my shoulders. What it did, on the contrary, was to confirm that I had unfinished business in my life, that I still felt a degree of isolation and fear that I hadn't resolved, and that I wanted some help in sorting out my painful feelings, especially my feelings about women.

While my Sponsor supported me in accepting my feelings as natural, he also encouraged me to follow my inclinations to seek professional help. My version of admitting the exact nature of my wrongs was admitting that I had not been honest with myself about the extent to which I still experienced the hurt of growing up with alcoholism. I still carried a burden of feelings that made it difficult for me to find pleasure and fulfillment in my life. I would probably continue to feel like a victim until I found some relief from that burden.

What I began to learn when I took my Fifth Step was that, for me, doing the "right" things in life meant not only treating others with respect and compassion, but also learning to extend fully that same respect and compassion to myself. Or as the Al-Anon slogan puts it, I had to learn to "*Live* and Let Live." I was not unhappy because

I was a jerk; I was unhappy because I was in pain. I needed assistance to learn how to care for my own feelings, and by taking the Fifth Step, my willingness to get that help began to increase.

I can honestly say that, at least in this area of my life, I have made progress. Now, when I begin to get close to a woman, my first impulse is no longer to run for cover. Not only is this important to me as a human being who hopes to live a balanced life, but it is also important to me as a minister and as the father of a wonderful young daughter.

41

A Grown Daughter Gains Freedom

I'll never forget the way my minister stared at me. I'd gone to see him because I felt spiritually and emotionally dead. He wanted to hear about my childhood and about what was going on in my life today. After listening to all the gory details, he stared at me in utter amazement and said, "Why aren't you in Al-Anon?!"

Why wasn't I in Al-Anon? I'd heard about Al-Anon at the treatment center where my father had made one of about a thousand attempts to get his act together, but the idea of a support group didn't appeal to me. I imagined a collection of sad, worn-out, old fogies talking about all the mean things their alcoholic relatives did. They would listen to each other's sob stories, shake their heads, and say, "Tsk, tsk, tsk." Besides I'd spent years talking about my father in therapy and, frankly, it was getting a little boring. Still, I respected my minister's opinion, and since his reaction was so strong, I figured I'd better give Al-Anon a try. After all, I could use some advice on how to make my dad sober up.

So I went to a meeting. I was terrified. Twenty men and women, mostly my age, sat in a Sunday School classroom, and I could tell that they all hated me. Well, not *hated*, but they were all so confident-looking. Just the sort of people I'd felt inferior to all my life. What was I doing here? A minor crisis ensued when they passed around a sheet on which people wrote their names and phone numbers, indicating that they were willing to receive Al-Anon phone calls. At the time, I thought I had very stupid-looking handwriting. I just knew that when I signed my name, everyone would notice my handwriting and think, "Look at the stupid handwriting! Boy, is she an idiot!" So I totally changed the way I sign my name, trying to make it look more intelligent.

There was a second crisis. I noticed people were being called on to speak, and I was scared to death they would call on me and I'd say something stupid. I started listening carefully in order to get a grasp on what sort of thing I was supposed to say. What I heard was so amazing, I almost forgot to worry.

The topic was Step Seven (Humbly asked Him to remove our shortcomings) and everyone was talking about his or her own shortcomings. Amazingly, no one talked about the alcoholic at all! I felt as if I had discovered America: *I could do nothing to make my dad sober up, but I could make myself into a better person!* It was as if the gates to a beautiful garden had swung open. I instantly fell in love with Al-Anon. When a woman spoke of her feelings of fear and inadequacy, I said to myself, "I'm home."

In spite of having discovered this new world, I still felt inferior to everyone there—until another woman came in late. She seemed just a bit off-balance, and I immediately thought, "Hmpf! Drunk!" Now here was somebody I could really feel superior to! I spent the rest of the meeting alternating between envisioning my new world and sneering at this woman.

Then, before I knew it, the meeting was over. I'd introduced myself as a newcomer during the meeting, so I waited eagerly for someone to greet me. I waited. And waited. Nobody came over. The members stood around in little groups, chatting and laughing, while I stood there feeling more and more stupid, wondering if there was anybody at this meeting with enough compassion to notice that I was a lonely newcomer.

Then, from across the room, I saw someone coming toward me with a big smile on her face. Oh no! It was the drunk lady! The one person I felt superior to! I desperately wanted to run away, but it was too late! Here she was!

Actually, upon closer inspection, she didn't seem drunk after all. She was very pleasant and friendly, gave me a hug, introduced herself, and told me to "Keep Coming Back." (Today I think this is one of the funniest jokes my Higher Power has ever played on me.)

After my new friend left, I hung around the fringes of one of the little clusters and was quickly invited to join them. As I listened, tears filled my eyes. Here were people exactly like me, only happy. I felt like a drowning person clutching a life preserver (which is exactly what Al-Anon has turned out to be!). I never wanted to leave that room.

Then I didn't go back for two weeks. (Well, I was busy!) At the end of my second meeting, the group again broke into little conversation groups, but this time I did something I'd never done before. I went up to two women who were having an animated conversation and stood next to them. They totally ignored me. After about five minutes of this, I left in a huff, thinking, "I'm never coming back!" But two weeks later, I returned. That was the beginning of learning not to take everything personally.

Despite having attended three whole meetings, I still didn't feel any better, so I went back to my minister and said, "I went to Al-Anon, but it doesn't help." He asked, "How often do you go?" I said, "Oh, once every two weeks." He said, "I think you're supposed to go more often than that."

So I started going to one meeting a week and began to feel significant relief. Toward the end of my first 90 days in Al-Anon, I noticed that a friend who'd entered the program after I did had a lot more serenity. I found out she'd been going to an Al-Anon meeting every day. So I started going twice a week, and found a direct correlation between the number of meetings I attended and how good I felt.

My life is unbelievably better today, thanks to Al-Anon, but I'm not totally free from the effects of alcoholism even though I gain more and more freedom all the time. I can still become a four-year-old girl in the presence of my father's disapproval, can still feel panicky when he is drunk and out of control. But I don't become totally debilitated any more. I have learned to detach with love, and although I do not claim to be a master at this art, I am a bright and eager student who improves with practice.

I also know more about myself today, and when I feel especially vulnerable and have an urge to reach out for support, I know better than to reach out to my dad. There was a time when I seemed compelled to turn to him at my most difficult moments, only to have him kick me when I was down. Then I would be hurt or angry or both. Al-Anon taught me that I was a victim in that situation only because I volunteered to be victimized. I hadn't accepted my father for who he was. It was as if I kept trying to stop a speeding train by stepping directly in its path. I wound up flattened every time.

Today I realize and accept that my father isn't capable of giving me the support I sometimes crave, and because I accept that reality, I no longer insist that he give it to me. Instead, I turn to a wonderful group of Al-Anon friends who have plenty of love and support to give, and I attend a lot of Al-Anon meetings because they provide me with nourishment I often don't even know I need.

I liken attendance at meetings to dialysis for a kidney patient. If I had a potentially fatal, debilitating kidney disease that required me to receive frequent treatment, you can bet I'd find a way to get there. It's the same with Al-Anon. I would probably have killed myself long ago if it weren't for this program. With it, I'm not only alive, but I'm living sanely. In fact, I'm living the life I'd only dreamed of—taking risks, avoiding abuse, feeling confident, getting along with friends and family, growing. And my handwriting keeps getting lovelier and lovelier!

42

Learning to Live in the Present

It should not surprise anyone to hear that I was born into a dysfunctional family. I once read that over 80% of families are dysfunctional in one way or another. Neither of my parents drank—at least not alcoholically—but most, if not all, of my uncles and great uncles drank excessively.

When I was growing up, these uncles were some of the nicest people I knew. They were always merry, and always reaching for the stars though they never quite touched them. They also were extremely generous. I was assured of coming away with a quarter or two just walking up and talking to them. That was something you could get your hands around and relate to.

So I was confused to discover my parent's attitude toward all these fun-loving alcoholics in our lives. No one in our grim family ever talked about alcoholism or any such problems. Their attitude seemed to be, "Don't hate them, just stay angry." Note that I did not say, "Just stay angry with them." My parents' anger seemed constant, although the drunken relatives were only around occasionally.

I didn't understand this anger, because I could not see what my uncles were doing wrong. I do recall one holiday when the family met next door at my grandparent's house. After the meal, word got around that someone had gone into our house (they never locked the doors) and had broken into our piggy banks. No one said so directly, but today I suspect that one of my uncles took the pounds of pennies the piggy bank contained. I was too young to even imagine that my sweet old uncle might be a thief, but I knew that something was wrong and that nobody wanted to talk about it.

Much later in my life, I remember walking down Main Street in my hometown with my wife-to-be. My uncle was walking toward us from the opposite direction but did not appear to see us. As he got close, I raised my hand, waived, and said, "Hi, Uncle Carl," He did not even pause as he staggered past, totally unaware of our presence. I felt a tidal wave of shame rise up inside me because I recognized that, once again, Uncle Carl had been drinking. But I had learned well from my parents. I did not talk about it.

These and other such moments from my past left me feeling very ashamed, inadequate, and unlovable. I felt I had to win the approval of anyone from whom I wanted love. After all, the drunks in the family consumed everyone's attention while I felt abandoned and neglected. I was also very angry and confused. The mixed messages from my youth were at the heart of my confusion. The anger was deeply ingrained.

Both of my parents had been affected by other people's drinking, and really could have benefited from Al-Anon had it been readily available to them. Unfortunately, it wasn't and they didn't. So my role models taught me survival tactics for dealing with drunks. They warned me about what drinking would do to our lives, and their actions spoke louder than words. Nonetheless, I developed the idea that I probably could find my own solutions to whatever drinking problem I might encounter in others who were in my life. Diligence was the key; I *must* be diligent. I don't blame my parents for the attitudes I developed; they were doing the best they could.

Alcoholism aside, diligence was a part of how I approached life. When I began thinking about getting married someday, I made an unconscious commitment to myself that whoever I married would become my partner for life. I had no intentions of even considering divorce as a possibility. I did not find out until my first marriage was nearly at its end that the girl I had chosen did not share my convictions. She was 14 when we first met and I was 18. She loved to party, with no limits on drinking and drug use, and to me, drinking seemed to be a way to have fun. I did not label this girl as an alcoholic, even after all my parent's warnings. At the time, I couldn't have done so without pointing the finger back at my own drinking habits.

I had very little self-esteem. I believed that the only way I could keep a wife was to do something that would make her eternally beholden to me. The "magical event" turned out to be rescuing her from her father. Frequently, in a drunken rage, he would chase her around the house with a butcher knife, threatening to kill her. Thus my "savior" pattern was born.

We married when I was 20 and she had just turned 17. The effects of someone else's drinking were already taking a toll on me. Whenever I was not with her, I worried about what she was doing and who she was with. But I had made a commitment to our marriage, and no matter how miserable I was, I was in it "till death do us part." Even after catching my wife committing adultery with my best friend two years later, I did not want our marriage to end. That was when I began to learn how unhappy she had been right from the start. In a marriage counseling session, she told me that she had entered the marriage believing that if things did not work out, we would simply divorce. This devastated me. Eventually we did end the marriage.

My second marriage got off to a much better start. I met this woman at a Bible study at a new church. She had used alcohol and drugs in her past, but the church did not allow the use of any such substances, so I was unconcerned. One more time, I had no awareness that alcohol had anything to do with the problems she and I were having.

Our first years together were difficult but, based on my previous experience, I believed that was to be expected in the first year of marriage. I spent a lot of time pointing out my wife's many faults. I would ridicule her and tell her how surprised I was at her lack of willingness to work on her flaws. What I was unwilling and unable to see was the adverse effects the disease of alcoholism was having on me.

After about five years of this "marital bliss," her drinking began again. At first, I did not notice, because my education and my career preoccupied me. Once I became aware that she was having a problem with alcohol, I was very angry and demanded that she stop and resume her more responsible role as wife and mother. When I discovered that I could not intimidate her with my anger, I tried reasoning with her. When these tactics failed, I quickly turned to pleading and giving in to her every demand.

I developed a severe case of tunnel vision, focusing almost exclusively on what she was doing and not doing. All I could see was that she was ruining my life. What I could not see was how, by my actions, I was voluntarily turning control of my life over to her.

Monitoring became my favorite pastime. I marked her bottles and searched the house for hiding spots. I was so sick that I marked the bottles in pencil, then wondered if she had moved the marks. Convinced that drinking was not her only problem, I jealously monitored her phone conversations with a small device I picked up at a local electronics store. I also monitored her auto mileage. The only thing all this monitoring did was destroy my emotional and physical health. The anxiety and panic attacks were continual. I often felt I was being consumed from the inside.

Our children were also being affected by this disease. We were told that our seven-year-old son was suicidal. Today I realize that my actions toward my wife and my inaction toward my son had just as much to do with his mental and emotional state as my wife's drinking. Alcoholism is definitely a family disease.

I came to Al-Anon. I don't even remember who had suggested it, or how or when I got here. The room was full of women, and I wondered if I was in the right place. I do recall the love I felt in the room. Here were people who seemed to genuinely care about who I was and what I was going through. I didn't understand this, because I was sure none of them had any idea what was going on in my life, but there was something indescribable at the meetings that kept me coming back. At first I only went to meetings when things were bad. I still believed that I was self-sufficient. At the same time, I was sure that I was sicker than anyone and dubious that any program could help me.

But I was beginning to identify what was wrong with my life. First: unmanageability. I did not understand how I was powerless over alcohol, but there was no doubt that my life was unmanageable. It was not until I heard the Three C's (I didn't cause alcoholism; I can't control it; and I can't cure it), week after week, that the concept of powerlessness sank in. Slowly my illusion of self-sufficiency melted away. Later I found the courage to rely upon my group for strength and support. At the end of my first year, I began to rely upon a Power greater than myself and today I depend upon God as I understand Him.

Step One taught me that I had to *admit* that I was powerless over alcohol and that my life was unmanageable. The Serenity Prayer helped me to *accept* this powerlessness. But this meant giving up my control. To me, giving up control meant I was inadequate and too stupid to solve the problem myself. I had learned from my parents that I *should* be able to control alcoholism, and I had great difficulty believing that they were wrong. This kind of thinking kept me sick for a very long time.

Alcoholism is not only a drinking disease. It is also a "thinking" disease—and my thinking was wrong. When I finally admitted and accepted my powerlessness over alcohol, I got my first real glimpse of serenity.

The *Detachment* flyer became my favorite piece of literature. My two favorite lines were the "crisis" lines: "In Al-Anon we learn not to create a crisis; [and] not to prevent a crisis if it is in the natural course of events." Until then, I would smooth over a potential crisis, responding to the accusations of others, "She's not *that* bad," although I knew deep in my heart she was even worse off than they were suggesting.

On the other side of the crisis coin, I would create crisis after crisis with her. One favorite threat of mine was "taking the children and leaving if you don't do something about your problem!" At least when I said this, I got a reaction. Of course, I never left. My empty threats merely demonstrated that I had become insane.

That brought me to Step Two, "Came to believe that a Power greater than ourselves could restore us to sanity." When I first read this Step, I remember saying to myself, "I already have a relationship with God, so I can skip right over this." What I had not yet learned was that believing in God but acted like I didn't. It took a long time to believe in a Power greater than myself, even after He had begun to restore me to sanity, but eventually I did come to believe.

Working these and the subsequent Steps would have been impossible for me without the guidance I received from my Sponsors. They quickly helped me to see when and where I was getting off track. They seldom gave me advice but frequently offered suggestions. It was up to me to decide which of the suggestions I was willing to try. Invariably, the more I followed their suggestions instead of relying upon my own devices, the better my life became.

In time my wife found her way into A.A. recovery. One mistake I made early in her recovery was to act as if I were her Sponsor. Sometimes this was my idea; other times, it was hers. Either way, it was not healthy for either of us. I had to turn over to a Higher Power for the sake of my own sanity as well as hers.

One way I was able to do this was by getting involved in service work. Service work got me to lots of meetings that I would not have otherwise attended. I didn't know it at the time, but service proved to be an essential part of the process of rebuilding my sense of self-worth.

There were many things I did not want to hear when my wife first got sober. The worst was "No guarantees!" Although we were both involved with recovery, there was no guarantee that our marriage would survive. It was risky at best, and the odds were against us. Today, more than five years later, we are still together. But there are still no guarantees that we will be together for the rest of our lives. All we have is *now*. So I try to live "One Day at a Time" and make the most of the time we have together.

I believe that recovery is a process, not an event. The further I go into recovery, the less I know. To me, this is a positive sign. I have come to believe that healthy people continue to grow through out their lives. Thus, I no longer have to pretend to be Mr. Know-It-All. I can openly admit that I don't have all the answers. I want to remain teachable for the rest of my life, daily applying new ideas and letting life be a real adventure.

43

Never Too Old to Change for the Better

I'll be 75 this fall, which makes me the second oldest Al-Anon member in my country. But don't let my age fool you—my memory is plenty good. I can remember when the word "dysfunctional" was used to describe a coal-burning furnace that wasn't working. In those days, few people recognized alcoholism as a worldwide problem or considered that it might affect anyone other than the drinker.

Those were also the days of good old family values, like love, respect, and faith. Parents were supposed to be solid role models, and mine did that job very well. Supper was our daily family gathering with plenty of fine, Jewish chicken soup that cured whatever ailed you, and roasted chicken with stuffing that would outdo the masters of the culinary arts. I am what I am today because of that chicken.

To my knowledge, there was no alcoholism in our family. In fact, I was brought up believing that there are no Jewish alcoholics—though I would later come to discover that this is far from the truth. I inherited many things from my family, but I didn't inherit alcoholism or the love of alcoholics. Instead, from my mother's side I inherited business savvy—my uncle was the cofounder of a large chain of auto parts stores. From my father's side, I inherited my artistic flair. I had a good voice, a voice full of potential, and I had bold dreams of becoming the next great crooner to hit the stage. But those dreams served only to taunt and frustrate me as they went unfulfilled. Instead I wound up in the family business, disappointed and low, although I became very successful.

In 1935 I met, dated, and married a beautiful redhead. We had one son. He was something else, handsome, with flaming red hair like his mother. His charm he got from old Dad, of course.

In time, my wife miscarried and later gave birth to a stillborn son. She also developed a liking for martinis, and that liking soon became an obsession. Her father had died of alcoholism, and she seemed determined to follow in his footsteps. Her brother and sisters were recovering in A.A., and eventually she chose A.A. as well. By the time I felt relief over her sobriety, my son had grown up and fallen in love with alcohol and marijuana. I was miserable, embarrassed. My mother-in-law suggested I look into an organization called Al-Anon.

I didn't know what Al-Anon was, but I soon checked it out. My first impression was that it seemed to be a bunch of female neurotics—hand-wringers—who met in church basements or cafeterias or hospitals, drank coffee, cried a lot, recited a litany of excerpts from their literature, and complained about their awful marriages. Men were as scarce in Al-Anon in those days as the hair on my head is today. The literature was all geared toward women and didn't even include words like "him" except to refer to the alcoholic.

When I came into the program, I hated everything and everybody. I hated my wife, my son, Al-Anon, me, and you—you *ODAT*-clutching devouts who uttered slogans and hackneyed clichés, at the drop of a kleenex box.

But within six months of attending meetings, there was a big change in me. I had fallen in love—with Al-Anon, with you, you beautiful people, and to a certain extent, with my family. With every day, I became more accepting of everyone around me.

This acceptance didn't come easily, however. I had two problems. First, in order to achieve acceptance, I had to feel the discomfort of knowing that I was fighting reality, refusing to accept life and other people as they really were. It was hardest to experience this discomfort when it came to my son. I didn't look fondly upon the idea that my attitude, and not his substance abuse, was causing me all kinds of trouble. It was easier just to hate him. It took a long time to be able to be honest enough with myself to admit that I was refusing to accept him as he was and to feel discomfort of the fruitless battle I was waging.

Second, for a long time after coming to Al-Anon, my mind continued to automatically snap shut whenever I heard any reference to a Higher Power or God. This was a real obstacle for me. Although

I was brought up in a moderately religious family, I never felt a personal connection to God. Too many atrocities had been committed in that God's name for me to accept Him as my Higher Power. Besides, I liked the idea of being an atheist. I suspect that I overlooked some of the more useful teachings from my youth in an effort to maintain my position as a religious rebel.

This position caused me to have a lot of trouble with the Steps in the days of my early Al-Anon recovery. I knew that the Steps were the basis of the program, and if I wanted to find the serenity that the longtime members seemed to have, I would have to come to believe in a Power greater than myself (Step Two). But I couldn't seem to talk myself into any real personal faith.

I now believe that the Steps are written in order. I don't have to tackle them in order, but any deep knowledge of a Step seems to depend upon an understanding of the Step that precedes it. I couldn't fully take Step Two because I had not fully taken Step One, "We admitted we were powerless over alcohol—that our lives had become unmanageable." At the time, I was still scheming about what I could do about the alcoholics. I finally took the First Step when I realized that all of my considerable energies had never changed the alcoholics in my life or made the situation appreciably better. No matter what I had done, what plans I had made, how hard I had tried, how loudly I had hollered, nothing about the situations had improved. Obviously, I was not the answer. If there was any answer, it had to lie outside of me.

By admitting that I was powerless over alcohol and the alcoholics, I found it necessary to turn to a Power greater than myself. If there was hope for any of us, there had to be something greater than me—and greater than alcoholism—to rely on. I still had a lot of trouble defining exactly Who or What that Power was. Unlike many others, I could not accept the group as a Higher Power. The groups were composed of individuals just as fallible as me. I didn't have all the answers, but the important thing was that I was "coming to believe." I took it on faith that clarity would come later.

My faith was well-founded. Gradually I established a good relationship with a Higher Power who I can accept. My Sponsor was a great help with this. I chose her (as I said, there were no men around at the time) specifically because of the way she seemed to incorporate her strong spiritual life into her program.

She also taught me how to set up chairs, to make coffee, to serve my group in all kinds of ways, and I grew and healed beyond measure as a direct result. If there is any one tool that helped me to overcome my obsession with other people, it was service work. I will always be grateful.

But with all that terrific experience, after several wonderful years, I still managed to say to myself, "Who needs Al-Anon any more?" I left abruptly, without any explanation. My wife left A.A. at about the same time.

An eight-year period of sheer hell followed. If you heard a loud "BANG!" it was probably me, crashing to my bottom. It took a lot of suffering before I was ready for help. I have often heard that alcoholism is a progressive disease that can be arrested but not cured, and that it continues to get worse unless it is treated. I always believed that this was true for the alcoholic, but now I am convinced that this applies to me as well. A nervous breakdown forced me to retire from work on disability. I subsequently endured six confinements in psychiatric hospitals, with endless medication and even shock treatment. I attempted suicide three times. My wife had several slips and did three tours in an alcoholism rehab. Physically, we were little better. I had triple bypass heart surgery, and my wife had surgery for ovarian cancer. And then the ultimate tragedy struck when our son, our only child, put a shotgun to his head and committed suicide.

We were devastated. His death almost broke our hearts and spirits. I believe we made it through the terrible anguish and loss only because we each believed a Higher Power was taking care of us. The unfathomable agony that I experienced ripped open my closed heart and made it possible for my Higher Power to take over. I can't describe the spiritual awakening that came at that time. Words aren't adequate. But the result was that, after eight years of suffering, I finally was able to climb out of depression and lethargy and to get myself into action. I returned to Al-Anon.

To be so warmly greeted by familiar faces, even after all these years, was overwhelming. Some things hadn't changed a bit. Others had changed a great deal. I found that there was now an Al-Anon meeting attended exclusively by men—75 of them! These wonderful men and women at my various Al-Anon meetings urged me on, shared with me, called, cared for me, laughed a lot, teased me, and eased me back to life and to reality. The eight years of nightmares and unrelenting suffering were finally over, and I had survived.

I am experiencing the wonderful knowledge that it is never too late for a fresh start—even at my ever-ripening age. I owe my life to Al-Anon, and with its help, I can be proud of the person I am becoming.

44

A Very Special Way

We all have unique stories to tell—but because we've been affected by another's alcoholism, our stories have much in common. Although a variety of circumstances may have led us to Al-Anon, we discovered that in time, with the help of our program and fellowship, we can recover. We can even become a source of strength and inspiration to others.

The following words, which are read at the close of Al-Anon meetings around the world, remind us that love, hope, and healing are available to us. All we have to do is keep coming back.

SUGGESTED AL-ANON/ALATEEN CLOSING

In closing, I would like to say that the opinions expressed here were strictly those of the person who gave them. Take what you liked and leave the rest.

The things you heard were spoken in confidence and should be treated as confidential. Keep them within the walls of this room and the confines of your mind.

A few special words to those of you who haven't been with us long: Whatever your problems, there are those among us who have had them, too. If you try to keep an open mind you will find help. You will come to realize that there is no situation too difficult to be bettered and no unhappiness too great to be lessened.

We aren't perfect. The welcome we give you may not show the warmth we have in our hearts for you. After a while, you'll discover that though you may not like all of us, you'll love us in a very special way—the same way we already love you.

Talk to each other, reason things out with someone else, but let there be no gossip or criticism of one another. Instead, let the understanding, love, and peace of the program grow in you one day at a time.

Will all who care to, join me in closing with the _____ prayer?

It is suggested that groups close in a manner that is agreeable to the group conscience.

Twelve Steps

1. We admitted we were powerless over alcohol—that our lives had become unmanageable.

2. Came to believe that a Power greater than ourselves could restore us to sanity.

3. Made a decision to turn our will and our lives to the care of God *as we understood Him.*

4. Made a searching and fearless moral inventory of ourselves.

5. Admitted to God, to ourselves, and to another human being the exact nature of our wrongs.

6. Were entirely ready to have God remove all these defects of character.

7. Humbly asked Him to remove our shortcomings.

8. Made a list of all persons we had harmed, and became willing to make amends to them all.

9. Made direct amends to such people wherever possible, except when to do so would injure them or others.

10. Continued to take personal inventory and when we were wrong promptly admitted it.

11. Sought through prayer and meditation to improve our conscious contact with God, *as we understood Him,* praying only for knowledge of His will for us and the power to carry that out.

12. Having had a spiritual awakening as the result of these steps, we tried to carry this message to others, and to practice these principles in all our affairs.

Twelve Traditions

1. Our common welfare should come first; personal progress for the greatest number depends upon unity.

2. For our group purpose there is but one authority—a loving God as He may express Himself in our group conscience. Our leaders are but trusted servants—they do not govern.

3. The relatives of alcoholics, when gathered together for mutual aid, may call themselves an Al-Anon Family Group, provided that, as a group, they have no other affiliation. The only requirement for membership is that there be a problem of alcoholism in a relative or friend.

4. Each group should be autonomous, except in matters affecting another group or Al-Anon or AA as a whole.

5. Each Al-Anon Family Group has but one purpose: to help families of alcoholics. We do this by practicing the Twelve Steps of AA *ourselves*, by encouraging and understanding our alcoholic relatives, and by welcoming and giving comfort to families of alcoholics.

6. Our Family Groups ought never endorse, finance or lend our name to any outside enterprise, lest problems of money, property and prestige divert us from our primary spiritual aim. Although a separate entity, we should always co-operate with Alcoholics Anonymous.

7. Every group ought to be fully self-supporting, declining outside contributions.

8. Al-Anon Twelfth Step work should remain forever non-professional, but our service centers may employ special workers.

9. Our groups, as such, ought never be organized; but we may create service boards or committees directly responsible to those they serve.

10. The Al-Anon Family Group have no opinion on outside issues; hence our name ought never be drawn into public controversy.

11. Our public relations policy is based on attraction rather than promotion; we need always maintain personal anonymity at the level of press, radio, films, and TV. We need guard with special care the anonymity of all AA members.

12. Anonymity is the spiritual foundation of all our Traditions, ever reminding us to place principles above personalities.

Twelve Concepts of Service

The Twelve Steps and Traditions are guides for personal growth and group unity. The Twelve Concepts are guides for service. They show how Twelfth Step work can be done on a broad scale and how members of a World Service Office can relate to each other and to the groups, through a World Service Conference, to spread Al-Anon's message worldwide.

1. The ultimate responsibility and authority for Al-Anon world services belongs to the Al-Anon groups.

2. The Al-Anon Family Groups have delegated complete administrative and operational authority to their Conference and its service arms.

3. The right of decision makes effective leadership possible.

4. Participation is the key to harmony.

5. The rights of appeal and petition protect minorities and insure that they be heard.

6. The Conference acknowledges the primary administrative responsibility of the Trustees.

7. The Trustees have legal rights while the rights of the Conference are traditional.

8. The Board of Trustees delegates full authority for routine management of Al-Anon Headquarters to its executive committees.

9. Good personal leadership at all service levels is a necessity. In the field of world service, the Board of Trustees assumes the primary leadership.

10. Service responsibility is balanced by carefully defined service authority and double-headed management is avoided.

11. The World Service Office is composed of selected committees, executives and staff members.

12. The spiritual foundation for Al-Anon's world services is contained in the General Warranties of the Conference, Article 12 of the Charter.

General Warranties of the Conference

In all proceedings the World Service Conference of Al-Anon shall observe the spirit of the Traditions:

1. that only sufficient operating funds, including an ample reserve, be its prudent financial principle;

2. that no Conference member shall be placed in unqualified authority over other members;

3. that all decisions be reached by discussion vote and whenever possible by unanimity;

4. that no Conference action ever be personally punitive or an incitement to public controversy;

5. that though the Conference serves Al-Anon it shall never perform any act of government; and that like the fellowship of Al-Anon Family Groups which it serves, it shall always remain democratic in thought and action.

Index

402